PROCEEDINGS OF THE SHORT PARLIAMENT OF 1640

edited for the Royal Historical Society

by

ESTHER S. COPE, Ph.D., F.R.Hist.S.

in collaboration with

WILLSON H. COATES, Ph.D.

CAMDEN FOURTH SERIES

Volume 19

LONDON

OFFICES OF THE ROYAL HISTORICAL SOCIETY

UNIVERSITY COLLEGE LONDON, GOWER STREET

LONDON WC1E 6BT

1977

ISBN 901050 37 7

Printed in Great Britain by Butler & Tanner Ltd
Frome and London

CONTENTS

ACKNOWLEDGEMENTS

WE began our study of the Short Parliament independently, Willson Coates in the 1940s and Esther Cope in 1969 when she found Lord Montagu's Journal. Through mutual friends we became aware of each other's work. Since neither of us wished to give up what we regarded as an important project, we agreed to collaborate. The division of labour has been informal. Although distance has kept us apart, we have exchanged ideas and material through correspondence and some *viva voce* consultations. Grants in aid of research by the Council of Learned Societies in 1949 and 1971 and a Folger Library Fellowship in 1951 made it possible for Willson Coates in those years to devote considerable time to the Short Parliament as well as to his Long Parliament projects. Grants from the American Philosophical Society in 1972 and 1974 and from the American Council of Learned Societies in 1974 enabled Esther Cope to take full advantage of the limited time she had available for work on the project while Willson Coates was occupied with other research.

Our volume has been made possible by those who have graciously allowed us to publish manuscripts in their possession or care: his grace the Duke of Manchester; his grace the Duke of Buccleuch and Queensberry; the Trustees of the British Library; the Clerk of the Records, House of Lords; the Provost and Fellows of Worcester College, Oxford; the Trustees of the Winchelsea Estates; the Chief Archivist, Northamptonshire Record Office; the County Archivist, Somerset Record Office; Norfolk Record Office and Norfolk Genealogical Society; Yale University Library; the Bodleian Library; the Trustees of the National Library of Scotland; the Board of Trinity College Dublin; the Huntington Library, San Marino, California; Harvard College Library; the Controller of H.M. Stationery Office. The staffs of these and many other libraries and record offices have assisted us in the discovery and identification of manuscripts. Those at the Institute of Historical Research, the University of Rochester, Bryn Mawr College, and Ursinus College have repeatedly made our work easier.

In the course of this project we have each incurred many additional scholarly debts. The footnotes acknowledge some of these. We owe particular thanks to the late Wallace Notestein; the late Hartley Simpson; David Willson; Maurice F. Bond, Clerk of the Records, House of Lords; P. I. King, Chief Archivist Northamptonshire Record Office; P. J. Locke, Archivist, Huntingdonshire Record Office; W. W. S. Breem, Librarian, Inner Temple; Jean Preston and Ann Caiger, Huntington Library; Robert E. Brooks,

Yale Law Library; Stephen Parks and Elizabeth Riehly, Osborn Collection, Yale. Maija Cole at the Yale Center for Parliamentary History has made resources there available to us and answered many questions by mail.

Discussions with Conrad Russell, Charles Carlton, and others in Britain and in the U.S. challenged our thinking. Christopher Thompson and Gerald Aylmer read a draft of the manuscript. John Wickersham of Ursinus College helped with the classical references, and Anne Cope went beyond the obligations of typing and indexing to point out inconsistencies and illogicalities in form and content. Valerie Pearl's term as visiting professor at Bryn Mawr gave Esther Cope a special opportunity to exchange ideas with her. As our Literary Director she has given us invaluable support. If Elizabeth Foster had not decreed that her name should be mentioned only once, the footnotes would be far longer. At informal 'parliamentary luncheons' during the period of most intense work on this project, she shared the fruits of her experience with Esther Cope. She read the entire manuscript, and through her questions, she has saved us from errors and omissions. Most of all her enthusiastic interest provided inspiration for us. Any remaining errors are, of course, our responsibility.

Postscript. Professor Willson H. Coates died on 22 September 1976 after a brief illness. Professor Cope informs us that he read the final version of this manuscript shortly before his death.

Royal Historical Society   VALERIE PEARL
                                                         Literary Director

ABBREVIATIONS

Add. MSS.	Additional Manuscripts, British Library London.
App.	Appendix (this volume).
B.I.H.R.	*Bulletin of the Institute of Historical Research.*
Bills	Bills (this volume).
B.L.	British Library, London.
Bodl.	Bodleian Library, Oxford.
Bond, *Records*	Maurice F. Bond, *Guide to the Records of Parliament.* (London, 1971).
Braye	Manuscript formerly in the collection of Lord Braye, now scattered.
Clarendon, *History*	Edward Hyde, earl of Clarendon, *History of the Rebellion,* ed. D. W. Macray (Oxford, 1888).
Clarendon, *Life*	Edward Hyde, earl of Clarendon, *Life of Edward Earl of Clarendon,* 3rd ed. (Oxford, 1761), i.
C.J.	*Journals of the House of Commons* (London, 1803–).
Commons Debates, 1621	W. Notestein, F. H. Relf, and H. Simpson, eds., *Commons Debates, 1621,* 7 vols. (New Haven, 1935).
Commons Debates, 1629	W. Notestein and F. H. Relf, eds., *Commons Debates, 1629* (Minneapolis, 1921).
CSP	*Calendar of State Papers, Domestic Series.* Charles I. 23 vols. (London, 1858–97).
CSP Ven.	*Calendar of State Papers and Manuscripts Relating to English Affairs Existing in the Archives and Collections of Venice and Other Libraries of Northern Italy,* 38 vols. (London, 1864–1947).
Declaration	*His Majesties Declaration to All His Loving Subjects of the Causes Which Moved Him to Dissolve the Last Parliament.* Published by his Majesties speciall command. Printed by Robert Barker and the assignees of John Bill (London, 1640).
D.J.	Draft Journal, House of Lords (1640), House of Lords Record Office, London.
D.N.B.	*Dictionary of National Biography.*

Eng. Hist.

English History Manuscript, Bodleian Library, Oxford.

Finch-Hatton MS.

Manuscript from the Finch-Hatton Collection, Northamptonshire Record Office, Delapre Abbey.

Folger

Folger Shakespeare Library, Washington, D.C.

Foster

E. R. Foster, ed., *Proceedings in Parliament, 1610*, 2 vols. (New Haven, 1966).

Glanville MS.

Uncatalogued Manuscript, Law Library, Yale University (see above, p. 31).

Harley Letters

Letters of Lady Brilliana Harley, ed. Thos. T. Lewis. Camden Society, lviii, 1853.

Harl. MS.

Harleian Manuscript, British Museum, London.

Harvard MS.

Manuscript, Houghton Library, Harvard University.

Hist. MSS Comm.

Historical Manuscripts Commission, London.

H.L.R.O.

House of Lords Record Office, London.

HM

Manuscript, Huntington Library, San Marino, California.

H.R.O., M36/1

Manuscript in the Collection of the Duke of Manchester, Huntingdonshire Record Office, Huntingdon.

Hunt. Cal.

Henry E. Huntington Library and Art Gallery, San Marino, California.

Inner Temple

Inner Temple Library, London.

Intro.

Introduction to the Sources (this volume).

Lambeth, Conv.

Records of the Convocation of the Clergy of Canterbury, Lambeth Palace Library, London.

Lee Warner

Diary of John Warner, bishop of Rochester, Lee Warner Manuscripts, Norfolk Record Office.

L.J.

Journals of the House of Lords (London, 1846).

L.K.

Lord Keeper.

M.C.J.

Manuscript Journal, House of Commons (1640), House of Lords Record Office, London.

M.L.J.

Manuscript Journal, House of Lords (1640), House of Lords Record Office, London.

Montagu Papers	Manuscripts belonging to his grace the Duke of Buccleuch and Queensberry.
Nalson	John Nalson, *Impartial Collection of the Great Affairs of State*, 2 vols (London, 1682–3).
Neilson MS.	Neilson Manuscript, National Library of Scotland.
Notestein, *D'Ewes*	*The Journal of Sir Simonds D'Ewes*, ed. W. Notestein. (New Haven, 1923).
O.E.D.	*Oxford English Dictionary.*
Official Return	*A Return of the Names of Every Member returned to serve in each Parliament*, (London, 1878). Parts i, iii.
Oxinden Letters	*The Oxinden Letters, 1607–1642*, ed. Dorothy Gardiner, (London, 1933).
A Perfect Diurnall	*A Perfect Diurnall of Passages in the late memorable Parliament begun the 13. of April 1640.* (London, 1649).
Petitions	Petitions (this volume).
Petyt MS.	Petyt Manuscript, Inner Temple Library, London.
Precedents	List of Precedents (this volume).
P.R.O.	Public Record Office, London.
Rawl.	Rawlinson Manuscript, Bodleian Library, Oxford.
Rot. Parl.	*Rotuli Parliamentorum ut et Petitiones et Placita in Parliamento*, 6 vols (London, n.d.).
Rushworth	John Rushworth, *Historical Collections*, 8 vols (London, 1721).
S.P.	State Papers, Public Record Office, London.
Speeches	Speeches (this volume).
S.R.O., DD/Mi	Mildmay Manuscript, Somerset Record Office, Taunton, Somerset.
Stanford MS.	Braye Manuscript, now in the Beinecke Library, Yale University.
State Trials	*Cobbett's Complete Collection of State Trials*, 34 vols (London, 1809–28).
STC	*A Short-Title Catalogue of Books printed in England and Ireland and of English Books printed abroad, 1475–1640*, ed. A. W. Pollard and G. R. Redgrave. (London, 1926).

STC	*A Short-Title Catalogue of Books printed in England, Scotland, Ireland, Wales, and British America, and of English Books printed in Other Countries, 1641–1700*, ed. D. Wing (New York, 1945–51). Citations are by number.
Trinity, Dubl.	Manuscript, Trinity College, Dublin.
Worc. Coll.	Manuscript, Worcester College, Oxford.
Yale	Beinecke Rare Book and Manuscript Library, Yale University.

I. GENERAL INTRODUCTION

THE Parliament which assembled in April 1640 was the first to meet in eleven years. Summoned to uphold the king's honour and provide means of reducing the Scots to obedience, it sat for three weeks, from 13 April until 5 May, and produced neither subsidies nor statutes. The Lords and Commons quarrelled; the king and Commons failed to agree about the granting of aid and redress of grievances. In both Houses there were serious differences of opinion about the proper solution to the controversies. Claiming that prolonging the session would endanger the kingdom, King Charles ordered the Parliament dissolved on 5 May. Crowds in the City of London demonstrated their unhappiness with his Majesty's decision. They threatened the Archbishop of Canterbury and the earl of Strafford, who, they thought, had advised the king. The king and Council took steps to quell the disturbances and to prevent other difficulties from arising as a result of the Parliament.

For contemporaries the Short Parliament was important. Lady Brilliana Harley wrote, 'The effect of this Parliament will not be indifferent, neather good nor evell, but eather very good or ells the contrary'[1] The Parliament is likewise important for historians. Members faced unprecedented pressures of time and business. They and their countrymen had grievances and concerns which had accumulated over the years when there had been no Parliament. The king urged them to act quickly to supply his needs. Both his Majesty's statements and memories of previous Parliaments aroused fears of imminent adjournment or dissolution. The circumstances required development of more efficient procedures for receiving petitions, for separating matters requiring immediate consideration from those which could wait, and for preparing arguments and motions for resolutions. Though the Parliament ended before significant reform could occur, during its brief session members debated basic questions about the nature of Parliament and the relations among king, Lords, and Commons. The men who would lead in the institution of change during the next Parliament were those who were prominent in the assembly of 1640. John Pym achieved general recognition with his speech of 17 April in the Lower House and his address to the Upper House at the conference of 28 April.

Without the Short Parliament Englishmen in the fall of 1640 would probably not have been so conscious of or informed about

[1] *Harley Letters*, p. 94.

public affairs. John Gruenfelder[1] has shown that issues such as shipmoney and religion had affected the outcome of the elections in the spring, and candidates found that support from the court was not a guarantee of success. The Parliament stimulated discussion even more. Writing the day after dissolution, Thomas Peyton declared, 'Some say wee are where wee were, but I thinke wee are worse; for what greivances so ever the subjects thought themselves molested with, and therefore would resist 'em this striving with the King could bee thought butt the Act of private men, till now it is in Parliament made the Act of the third Estate.' The dissolution thus contributed to a sense of frustration for Englishmen. Since the Parliament, Peyton said, 'I cannott meete with any man butt knowes what will become of these things; soe inspird are the more zealous, soe ready to execute mischeife are the souldiers, soe provident are worldly successes, and generally soe wise are become the Commons having received a diffusive knowledge from the dispersed house.'[2]

In the Short Parliament were a number of men who had not sat before. According to Mary Keeler[3] the Parliament of the spring of 1640 was the first for 167 of 332 M.P.s who were elected to Parliament again in the autumn of that year. Their lack of experience was the cause of comment on 16 April. Sir Henry Vane suggested that the explanation for the humming which had occurred during the Lord Keeper's speech the day before might be 'soe many young men' in the House who were 'ignorant of the indecencye of it'.[4] Since no work comparable to Mary Keeler's has been done for the earlier part of the century, the information for a more complete estimate of previous parliamentary experience of members of the Short Parliament is not readily available. Although Oliver St. John, John Hampden, and Robert Holborne, who had become famous through the Shipmoney case, were newcomers to Parliament in 1640, many of those who spoke frequently were veterans of parliament. John Pym, Sir Benjamin Rudyerd, Sir Walter Erle, and Sir Francis Seymour had all served in the 1620s. Continuity with previous sessions is evident in the proceedings of the Commons. A body dominated by new men would hardly have devoted so much attention to investigating the dissolution of 1629.

The membership of the Upper House also included both new and experienced parliamentarians. Among the latter were the earls of Warwick and Dorset, Lord Montagu, and his brother, the earl of

[1] 'The Elections to the Short Parliament' in *Early Stuart Studies*, ed. H. Reinmuth (Minneapolis, 1970).
[2] *Oxinden Letters*, p. 173.
[3] *The Long Parliament* (Philadelphia, 1954), p. 16.
[4] Harvard MS., fo 29.

Manchester. All had been in the Lords for at least one session and had sat in the Lower House prior to obtaining their titles. During his years in the Commons, the newly-created earl of Strafford had played an important part in the proceedings concerning the Petition of Right. In 1640 he was one of eleven temporal lords introduced to the House. The Lords Spiritual likewise had differing backgrounds. The most active prelate in the Parliament was probably Laud, Archbishop of Canterbury, who had to divide his attention between that assembly and the Convocation of the Clergy. The business of king and Church prevented some lords and bishops from attending the Parliament at all. Age and health interfered with the presence of others. Many of these had not even filed proxies when the Parliament was dissolved.

The varied experiences and philosophies of the men who collectively composed the Short Parliament of 1640 make it difficult to determine how they would have proceeded if they had been permitted to sit longer. In retrospect the Parliament seems more royalist in temper than was its successor. Telling of the dissolution, Clarendon wrote, 'It could never be hoped that more sober and dispassioned men could ever meet together in that place, or fewer who brought ill purposes with them; nor could any man imagine what offence they had given which put the king to that resolution'.[1] The suspicion of the crown and fears for subjects' liberties stirred by the dissolution were expressed in the elections for the Long Parliament and in the proceedings of that assembly. They weakened the royalist group, which might otherwise have been slightly stronger than that of Pym when parties emerged in the summer and autumn of 1641. The Grand Remonstrance, which passed in the House of Commons on 22 November 1641 by a majority of eleven votes, might have been defeated in a parliament elected in the spring of 1640. Although further speculation about such a parliament cannot confidently be undertaken, it can certainly be said that, brief as it was, the Short Parliament was far from inconsequential. Both through its proceedings and its dissolution, it played a critical role in British history.

We fully recognize the achievement by the great S. R. Gardiner when he deals with the Short Parliament in his monumental work on the period from 1603 to 1642. We also have not overlooked what Veronica Wedgwood accomplished in her briefer account in *The King's Peace*. That the time has come, however, for a new extended appraisal of the Short Parliament and its historical sources should, we hope, be made sufficiently apparent by what we have done in this book.

[1] Clarendon, *History*, II, 77.

EDITORIAL NOTE

THIS volume includes journals, speeches, and petitions from the Short Parliament of 1640. More indirect accounts of proceedings, such as those in newsletters or diplomatic dispatches, are cited in footnotes or introductions. Speeches and petitions apparently not delivered are treated in a similar fashion. A list of the manuscripts printed in this volume appears in pages 14–15.

The sources for the Short Parliament are discussed in Part I. Both sources in this volume and others are examined. The introduction concludes with a calendar for the Parliament.

Part II contains the accounts of proceedings, those for the House of Lords, then those for the House of Commons, and finally those which deal with both Lords and Commons. Each is presented as an individual unit. Braye MS. 16 and Finch-Hatton MS. 50/Harvard MS. Eng. 982 provide the basic accounts for the Lords and Commons respectively and are printed in full. Neither is without blemish. Both vary in the depth of their coverage. The text of the Braye manuscript is much revised and sometimes almost impossible to follow. Even though not all of its additions and deletions are shown here, readers may find that Lord Montagu's brief journal can guide them through the complexities of the Braye manuscript. The latter is placed first because it is a far more comprehensive record of proceedings. The Finch-Hatton manuscript lacks pages 5–36 and 71–80, which were apparently torn from the volume at some time in the past. Because it avoids some of the omissions and copyist's errors evident in the Harvard manuscript, it is used for the periods when it is available. The Harvard manuscript serves as the basic account for the remainder of the Parliament.

Both the Braye and Finch-Hatton/Harvard manuscripts include material which also appears in the Journals of the Lords and Commons. The differences between the Manuscript and printed Journals of either House (or between the Draft and printed Journals of the Lords) are too slight to justify their use as the basic accounts. They lack the notes of debate which Braye and Finch-Hatton/Harvard provide. Only those parts of the Draft Journal which supplement Braye MS. 16 or illustrate changes in text between Braye and the Lords' *Journal* are printed here. At the beginning of each day's proceedings in the basic accounts are references to the appropriate pages in the Lords and Commons' *Journals*. Material is quoted from the *Journals* only when necessary for the understanding of the manuscripts. A similar policy governs quotation from Rushworth's *Historical Collections* and the *Calendar of State Papers, Domestic*.

For the convenience of the reader, references are made, where possible to the *Calendar of State Papers*, rather than to the State Papers themselves.

Notes clarify the text and refer the reader from the basic accounts to other diaries. Explanations and clarifications given to points in the basic accounts are not repeated in notes to supplementary diaries. Where these diaries repeat in a similar version speeches or reports in the basic accounts, the repetitious sections are omitted and a note indicates where the material appears. Special procedures show the close and complex relationships among the diaries in Worc. Coll. MS. 5.20, *A Perfect Diurnall*, HM 1554, and the Glanville MS. *A Perfect Diurnall's* variations from Worc. Coll. MS. 5.20 are given in the footnotes to Worc. Coll., and the Glanville manuscript's variations from HM 1554 are handled similarly. At the beginning of each day's entry in the Worcester College manuscripts are references to the relevant parts of HM 1554. Only where it adds to or differs from Worc. Coll. MS. 5.20 is HM 1554 printed; daily headings and notes to the appropriate passages in Worc. Coll. MS. 5.20 are shown.

Part III includes speeches, bills, petitions, and other notes directly concerning proceedings but not incorporated in any of the diaries. These are arranged by *genre* and within each type by date. If there are several from the same day, alphabetical order by title or speaker is followed. Endorsements are shown in the notes. Revisions, cross-references, and editorial comment follow the same general pattern as elsewhere in the volume. References are to the basic accounts for each house, where full annotation appears, even when the version of a speech in Part III may be better. Specific Commons' *Journal* and Lords' *Journal* references are kept to a miminum. These can be established by date or from the basic accounts.

The Appendix provides lists of copies and versions of the major speeches and of the grievances voted in the Commons on 24 April. Although the proliferation of copies makes it virtually impossible for the lists to be complete, they cite some of the important collections of speeches from the Parliament and serve as an index to those printed here. Accompanying many of the lists are additional notes about the speeches. An annotated list of bills read during the Parliament and a list of precedents also appear in the Appendix.

The spelling of the texts has not been modernized, although a few changes have been introduced, *e.g.*, *j* is substituted for *i*. Contractions, including those for *with* and *which*, are extended even when the copyist has neglected to indicate that he has omitted letters. The list below includes some of the forms which appear frequently in the manuscripts and are retained. Other abbreviated words are completed. *His Majesty* and *Parliament* are always written out. Names of places, *e.g.*, *Exon*, *Sarum*, are left as they are except when they seem obscure. Speakers are identified the first time they appear. Their names are given as they are in the diaries with necessary clarification in the footnotes and variant spellings and additional identification in the Index. Where definite identification cannot be made, possibilities are shown. The names of speakers are capitalized when the House was formally sitting; they are in lower case letters when the House was in committee or conference. The capitalization and punctuation of the original have not been reproduced exactly. Some very long sentences have been divided and some commas added. Where the author's meaning seems doubtful, the original punctuation is retained.

Both a general and a chronological index are provided at the end of the book, the latter index arranged as a calendar of the Parliament bringing together all references to proceedings on specific days.

EDITORIAL PRACTICES

In the text:

Words struck out in MS. are in italics.

Words added in MS. are in brackets.

Editorial insertions are italicized and placed in brackets.

In the notes:

The spelling of variations normally follows that of the first of the sources listed.

Quotation marks are used for phrases of more than three words.

Variations preceded and followed by ellipses should be inserted into the existing text.

Where ellipses only precede, the variation should follow the existing text.

Where no ellipses appear, the variation should be substituted for the last word of the existing text.

Forms and abbreviations appearing as in MS.:

yt	that
ye	they; the; you
yn	then
yr	their; your
y	they
ym	them
wr	were
or	our
K	king
Q	queen; question
L Keep; Lo Keep	Lord Keeper
L; Lo; Lop	lord; lordship
Lds; Ls; Lopps; Lods; Lls; Lps; Llps	lords; lordships
Arc; Archb; Archbpp	Archbishop
B; Bps; Bpps; Bopps	bishop(s)
HC; HCo; HCom	House of Commons
H; Ho	House
Sr	Sir
Kt; Knt	knight

LIST OF MANUSCRIPTS IN THIS VOLUME

DIARIES:

H.L.R.O., Braye MS. 16, fos 3^r–47^r.

Montagu Diary, pp. 1, 1b–d, 2, 2b–d, 3a–d.

Lee Warner 1/2 (441 × 1), pp. 1–5.

Finch-Hatton MS. 50/Harvard MS. Eng. 982: Finch-Hatton, pp. 1–4, 37–70, 81–83; missing sections supplied from Harvard, fos 1^r–84^v.

H.R.O., M36/1, pp. 1–28 (selections).

Worc. Coll. MS. 5.20, fos 1^r–30^v and selections (unnumbered).

Hunt. Cal., HM 1554 pp. 252–62 (selections).

B.L., Harl. MS. 4931, fos 47^r–49^r.

S.P. 16/451/16 and S.P. 16/451/57.

MISCELLANEOUS

Speeches: Rudyerd, 16 April (Bodl., MS. Clarendon 18, fos 147^r–49^r).

Seymour, 16 April (S.R.O., DD/M1, Box 18, 96 (selections)).

Pym, 17 April (B.L., Harl. MS. 6801, fos 58^r–69^r); note (Dublin, Trinity College, MS. 623, unnumbered).

Hyde, 18 April (Bodl., MS. Clarendon 18, fos 155^r–55^v).

Holland, ?20 April (Bodl., MS. Tanner 321, fo. 3^v).

Lord Keeper, 21 April (Hunt. Cal., HM 1554, p. 165).

Charles I, 24 April (H.L.R.O., D.J., pp. 32–33).

Lord Keeper, 25 April (H.L.R.O., Braye MS. 2, fos 65^r–66^v).

[Eliot], ?29 April, note (National Library of Scotland, Neilson MS. 2688, p. 1042).

Lord Keeper, 1 May (H.L.R.O., Braye MS. 2, fos 70^r–73^r).

Bills: Dressed Cloths (H.L.R.O., Main Papers, 23 April 1640).

Clergy and Lay Employments (H.L.R.O., Main Papers, 2 May 1640).

Petitions: Northampton, 17 April (S.P. 16/450/25).

Essex, 18 April (B.L., Harl. MS. 4931, fo 41^r).

Hertford, 18 April (B.L., Harl. MS. 4931, fos 42^r–42^v).

Norwich, 18 April (H.L.R.O., Main Papers, 18 April 1640).

Peter Smart, 22 April (H.L.R.O., Main Papers, 22 April 1640).

Archibald Niccoll, 22 April (H.L.R.O., Main Papers, 22 April 1640).

Oxford Constables, 24 April (H.L.R.O., Main Papers, 24 April 1640).

Henry Presse, 28 April (H.L.R.O., Main Papers, 28 April 1640).

Walter Oke, 30 April (H.L.R.O., Main Papers, 30 April 1640).

INTRODUCTION TO THE SOURCES

OUR knowledge of the Short Parliament owes much to the men who noted its proceedings in their diaries, wrote about it in letters to friends and relatives, and obtained copies of speeches, lists of grievances, and even parts of the Journals. A detailed description of the opening procession, *The Manner of Holding Parliaments in England . . . with the . . . order of Proceeding to Parliament of the most high and mighty Prince King Charles on Monday the 13th April 1640, in the 16th yeare of his Majesties reign, first on horseback from White Hall to Westminster Abbey Church, and from thence on foote to the Parliament house*, was printed in 1641.[1] Accounts of other aspects of parliamentary proceedings were also printed at the time. These sources are part of a larger body of seventeenth-century parliamentary papers and records. Their nature has been discussed in Bond's *Guide to the Records of Parliament*, in other publications of the House of Lords Record Office, and in published volumes of debates such as *Commons Debates, 1621*; *Commons Debates, 1629*; and Foster's *Proceedings in Parliament, 1610*. Despite these very competent aids, an examination of the specific qualities and characteristics of the sources for the Short Parliament is necessary.

The circumstances in which the Parliament was summoned, met, and was dissolved made its history immediately controversial and shaped the nature of that history. Some men probably never committed to paper their ideas, plans, or reactions concerning proceedings. Lady Harley complained to her son that his father said nothing about the Parliament in his letters.[2] Others wrote while stirred by passion or while fearful that, if not carefully worded, their accounts could bring them trouble from the authorities. The loss and destruction of records began immediately following the dissolution. Members were called before the Council and questioned about remarks made in Parliament. Chambers and even men themselves were searched and papers seized. The clerk of the Commons was ordered to bring in Parliament's papers, those who had chaired committees were commanded to turn over petitions that were in their custody, and an official version of proceedings was issued, *His Majesties Declaration to all his Loving Subjects of the Causes which moved him to Dissolve the last Parliament*.

Private individuals were not able to publish and distribute their accounts of Parliament as easily. They could spread dissenting versions of proceedings through petitions of grievance. After the Long Parliament had assembled in November 1640 and parliamentary

[1] B.L., E.157(11).　　　　[2] *Harley Letters*, p. 94.

privileges were in effect, Englishmen could speak there about the events of the preceding spring. M.P.s, such as Pym and Grimston, charged Strafford and other councillors with giving ill advice to the king during the Short Parliament. The parliamentarians argued that the good intentions of the subjects had been misunderstood and that impatience, even malice, prevented a successful conclusion to the assembly. Their tale agreed with that of the king only in so far as it viewed the dissolution with distress.

Later when the Court of Star Chamber had been abolished and the royal prerogative limited, the king's view could be challenged more effectively in print. By that time the Short Parliament had become just one case in a general complaint that the laws and liberties of the kingdom had been infringed. Historical accuracy was less important than political and polemical ends. Speeches from the Parliament were published, but they were not always identified as such. It was the arguments which were considered significant, not the occasion when they were delivered. The printed speeches show signs of editing, in some cases to embellish but in others to eliminate passages which either weakened their claims or had become anachronistic. After 1642 the crises of the Civil War and Interregnum usurped attention from the Short Parliament and took an additional toll from the records of its proceedings.

Subsequent centuries added to losses in evidence and produced further differences of interpretation. After the Restoration some of those who had participated in the events of the 1640s wrote about their experiences. Their reliance on memory and their interest in justifying their actions limit the value of much of their work. Although not uncharacteristic of its age, the earl of Clarendon's *History of the Rebellion* provides details about proceedings in the Parliament which are not available elsewhere and which give his assessments of men and events lasting significance. The years following 1660 saw, in addition to memoirs, more ambitious projects to edit and print the parliamentary papers and speeches from the preceding era. Questions of partisanship arose even here. John Rushworth's *Collections* seemed so defective to John Nalson that Nalson responded with his own edition of some of the same material.

Collections and interpretations of sources continued to appear. The printing of the Lords' and Commons' *Journals* in the eighteenth century, the extensive efforts of S. R. Gardiner in the nineteenth century, and the work by scholars on both sides of the Atlantic in more recent times, have added to our knowledge of seventeenth century Parliaments, including the Short Parliament of 1640. Nevertheless unanswered questions remain. What were the intentions of King Charles, John Pym, or the earl of Strafford? What did

the words 'this kingdom' mean in Strafford's statement to the Council
about where the army in Ireland might be used? Neither Pym nor
Strafford seems to have left many papers relating to the Short
Parliament. Some of Pym's papers were seized after the dissolution
and it was reported that he had burned others.[1] *The Earl of Strafford's
Letters and Dispatches*, ed. Wm. Knowler, ii (London, 1739), includes
accounts of Strafford's general plans for the Irish Parliament, but it
has little to offer concerning the English assembly. The Wentworth-
Woodhouse Muniments, now on deposit at the Sheffield Central
Library, make few additions. Sir Simonds D'Ewes, whose collections
have contributed so heavily to parliamentary history, was not a
member of the Short Parliament. Unable to serve because he was
sheriff of Suffolk, D'Ewes was sufficiently interested in the Parliament to obtain and correct copies of Pym's speech of 17 April, and
that of the king at the dissolution (see below). D'Ewes had offered
some records to John Crewe for use in the Parliament. Crewe
thanked him but replied, 'Your selfe being not here to help me to
understand them and make use of them, I shall not dare to adventure
uppon them.' Crewe concluded his letter with a report about Parliament and the uncertainty of its continuance at that time (1 May).[2]
Accounts from others who might have resolved disputes about
proceedings have likewise remained missing or disappointingly
uninformative. Laud's *History of his Troubles* (London, 1694), which
was written during his imprisonment, is too clearly an *apologia* to
be of much value. His writings which survive among the Domestic
State Papers in the Public Record Office or in the collections of the
Lambeth Palace Library show some of his concerns and activities,
but leave others in obscurity. The letters of the Harley and Oxinden
families, the diaries of Cholmley, Slingsby, and Rous are supplementary sources of limited use.[3] Their authors were too far removed
from the centres of power to add significantly to the standard
accounts of the principal proceedings, and in these they tend to
repeat each other.

Despite the persistence of conflicting views and *lacunae* in the
evidence, a general understanding of this Parliament is possible.
More detailed description of the major sources for its study follows,
first those primarily relating to the House of Lords, then those
devoted to the House of Commons, and finally those which treat
both Lords and Commons. Speeches, bills, and petitions are also

[1] B.L., Add. MS. 11045, fo 116ʳ.   [2] B.L., Harl. MS. 165, fo 4ʳ.
[3] Concerning the Harley Papers, see below, pp. 24–25; *Oxinden Letters;
The Memoirs of Sir Hugh Cholmley, Knt. and Bart. Addressed to his Two Sons*
(printed for private use, 1787); *The Diary of Sir Henry Slingsby of Scriven,
Bart.*, ed. Rev. Daniel Parsons (London, 1836); *The Diary of John Rous*, ed.
Mary Anne Everett Green (Camden Society, lxvi, London, 1856).

discussed. This organizational division is observed where possible, but it cannot be absolute. Parliament was a unit. References to actions in the Lower House appear in sources dealing for the most part with proceedings in the Upper House. The Main Papers in the House of Lords Record Office, which are treated with sources for the Lords, contain miscellaneous papers of both houses. Not all the sources described are printed here. Some add little to material available in other accounts; others give speeches or petitions which were probably never presented.

LORDS
THE LORDS' JOURNAL

John Browne, clerk of the Parliament in 1640, was responsible for compilation of the Journal of the House of Lords. The exact procedure he followed in preparing the Journal cannot be reconstructed from the existing evidence. Among his collections in the Braye Manuscripts and the records of the House of Lords are various papers preliminary to the Manuscript Journal.[1] Braye MS. 16 is his scribbled book of notes taken in the House from the opening of the Parliament until the dissolution. The book includes the motions, orders, and committee lists which ultimately appear in the Journal. With these are Browne's versions of royal and official speeches to Parliament. His rough notes are a record of what was said which can be compared with the many polished copies of these speeches which are available in contemporary hands.[2] His notes of the debates of the Lords are also valuable. On 24 April when the House adjourned into a committee of the whole to discuss the king's request that the Lords urge the Commons to grant immediate subsidies and on 29 April when a similar procedure occurred to consider the Commons' claim that the Lords' action had violated the privileges of the Lower House, the *Journal* reports only that there had been 'long and great Debate and Consideration' or 'long and serious Debate and Consideration' before stating the resolutions taken at the end of the debate,[3] but Browne used fos 21ᵛ–30ʳ in his book for recording the debate of 24 April and fos 35ᵛ–40ᵛ for that of the 29th.

The advantages of the first-hand reporting which Browne does are offset by the difficulty of interpreting his scribbled book. The Short Parliament was the first in which he served as clerk. Inexperienced

[1] The Braye MSS, now at the House of Lords Record Office and in the Osborn Collection, Yale University Library, are described in Bond, *Records*, pp. 269–72; also Hist. MSS Comm., xv, *Tenth Report*, App. vi: Braye MSS (London, 1887).

[2] For example, Braye 16, fos 3–6ᵛ, pp. 53–57.

[3] *L.J.*, iv, pp. 67, 73.

and apparently uncertain how to record procedures, he made many
revisions in orders, motions, and accounts of introductions of new
peers.[1] His method of recording votes by making lines in a vertical
column is cumbersome.[2] No close vote occurred during the Short
Parliament, but calculation of exact totals would have been difficult.
During speeches or debate, he jotted down phrases, using a combination of abbreviations and key words.[3] When he was unable to get
what a speaker said, he left blank spaces. He also sometimes used
blanks within lines to separate thoughts. His notes are not always
as clear as we might wish. Reconstruction of proceedings can be
difficult without recourse to the finished Lords' Journal. Nevertheless Braye MS. 16 provides significant material about proceedings in
the Upper House and has much to offer the student of parliamentary
history.

While the Short Parliament was meeting, Browne took material
from his scribbled book and made a Draft Journal, which a committee
of the House examined each Saturday.[4] The names of the lords on
pp. 15, 38, 52, testify to their performance of their duty on 18 and
25 April and 2 May,[5] but no report survives to indicate whether it was
they who authorized any of the revisions which appear in the text
of the Draft Journal.

Although it amends Braye MS. 16 by giving only the acts of the
House not debate, introducing formal headings, replacing abbreviations and rough notes with full sentences, and listing committees
in order of precedence,[6] the Draft Journal is neither polished nor
complete. The only speeches included are those of the king on 24
April and 5 May. Instead of the others are spaces and Browne's
reminders that the missing material should be entered.[7]

Several volumes contain refined versions of the proceedings in
Braye MS. 16, which were omitted from the Draft Journal but
included in the Manuscript Journal. H.L.R.O., Braye MS. 88,
described as a volume of 'journal extracts',[8] includes fine copies of

---

[1] For example, Braye 16, fo 9, n. 1, fos 10ᵛ, 8ʳ below, pp. 57, 59, 60. For a
general assessment of Browne's work as clerk, see M. F. Bond, The Formation
of the Archives of Parliament, 1497–1691,' *Journal of the Society of Archivists*,
i (1957), pp. 156–57.
[2] Although Robert Bowyer, clerk in the early part of the century, put the
votes in groups of five, Browne's method was used as late as 1713 (Bond,
Records, plate 2).
[3] For example, below, pp. 66, 92, Braye 16, fos 17, 44ᵛ.
[4] The Draft Journal is preserved at the House of Lords Record Office.
[5] The lords signed the Journal on 18 April and 2 May. Their names are in
Browne's hand 25 April.
[6] *Cf.* D.J., pp. 4, 13–15 and Braye 16, fos 3–4, 9ᵛ–10 below, pp. 53–54, 59.
[7] For example that of the Lord Keeper, 13 April (D.J., p. 4); report of
conference, 29 April (D.J., p. 44).
[8] Bond, *Records*, p. 272.

the principal speeches of the Parliament. That of 24 April is directly dependent on the text in the scribbled book, not on that of the Draft Journal.[1] Only the king's speech at the dissolution of the Parliament, is missing.

In Braye MS. 95 (at Yale) is another collection of papers drawn from the rough notes of Braye MS. 16. Here are various resolutions and multiple copies of many of the speeches. Browne himself wrote some of the items.[2] On others, written by assistants, he made corrections and added headings.[3] His memoranda, e.g., 'This relates to the *13° Aprilis* 1640 and there to be entred', show his editorial activity.[4] The notation 'transc.' which appears beside some of the material could be either his direction or an assistant's note of a task completed.[5]

Among Browne's Letters and Papers, 1637–41 (H.L.R.O., Braye MS. 2) are some in Lord Keeper Finch's hand, including rough notes for Finch's speech to the Commons at the conference on 25 April and better copies of his speech at the conference on 1 May and Pym's at that of 28 April.[6] Miscellaneous orders, committee papers, and petitions concerning the business of both Houses can be found in the H.L.R.O., Main Papers, which have been calendared in Hist. MSS Comm., *Fourth Report*, App. pp. 24–26.

Some of this material was inappropriate for the Manuscript Journal which was the finished and official record of proceedings in the Upper House during the Parliament.[7] Its basic framework came from the Draft Journal, but it also includes material, such as speeches and lists of the lords present, which is not entered there. A comparison of texts shows that the compilers of the Manuscript Journal made more than one error in interpreting revisions in the antecedent volume.[8] These errors, the multiplicity of copies of some items in Browne's papers,[9] and the ensuing political turmoil suggest that completion of the Manuscript Journal might not have occurred until after the Restoration of Charles II in 1660, when times were calmer and there was emphasis upon the continuity of Parliament. Regardless of the occasion or manner of its composition, the text of the

---

[1] See Braye 16 (24 April); Speeches, D.J. Charles I (24 April), below, pp. 69–70, 264–65.

[2] *E.g.*, fos 87ʳ, 89ʳ.   [3] *E.g.*, fos 119ʳ, 122ᵛ, 124ʳ.

[4] *E.g.*, fos 90ʳ, 151ʳ.

[5] *E.g.*, fos 87ʳ, 90ʳ; also Braye 2, fos 64ᵛ, 68ᵛ.

[6] See App., L.K. (25 April, 1 May), Pym (28 April), below, pp. 310, 312, 314.

[7] The Manuscript Journal is preserved at the House of Lords Record Office.

[8] When writing about the selection of *receavours* and *triers* of petitions, Browne began in English, but he wrote above the line 'in French' and crossed out his English (D.J., p. 5). In the printed *Journal* (iv, p. 48), the phrase is interpreted as part of the text rather than as an editorial note. See also Braye 16 (24 April); Speeches, D.J., Charles I (24 April) below, pp. 70, 264.

[9] *E.g.*, App., Speeches, Charles I (13 April), below, p. 293.

Manuscript Journal was that which was used when the *Journals* were printed later, in the eighteenth century.

LORD MONTAGU'S JOURNAL

Edward Lord Montagu's journal of proceedings in the Upper House during the Short Parliament is preserved among the manuscripts of the Duke of Buccleuch and Queensberry at Boughton House in Northamptonshire (shelf 13, number 2, North Colonnade). Lord Montagu had sat in many Parliaments in the years before 1640.[1] Prior to his creation as Baron Montagu of Boughton in 1621, he had been a member of the House of Commons. The journals he kept of proceedings and his collections of parliamentary papers show that, whether in the Lords or in the Commons, he took his responsibility and the business of Parliament seriously. For the Short Parliament his journal is not so extensive and comprehensive as are those for earlier assemblies. His age and health may explain this difference, but discretion in the face of anxiety and concern about the state of the realm may also have played a part. Despite its brevity, the journal bears the marks of Montagu's experience and procedural interests. It adds background to the scribbled book of the inexperienced clerk, John Browne.

LEE WARNER 1/2(441x1)

'Bishop Warners diary of the Parlament' has been preserved with others of John Warner's papers among the Lee Warner manuscripts which are deposited at the Norfolk Record Office.[2] It covers the entire session from the opening ceremonies on 13 April to the dissolution 5 May. The initial statement, *'Parliamentum coactum feliciter'* is matched by the concluding one, *'Parl. Infeliciter.'* Warner, who was Bishop of Rochester, gives most of his attention to the House of Lords where he himself sat and where he spoke on two occasions,[3] but he also includes proceedings in the House of Commons and in the Convocation of the clergy. Despite his own

[1] See Esther S. Cope, 'Lord Montagu and his Journal of the Short Parliament', *B.I.H.R.*, xlvi (1973). The journal is not mentioned in Hist. MSS Comm., xlv, *Report on the MSS of the Duke of Buccleuch and Queensberry*, Montagu Papers, i (London, 1899), iii (1926), which describes Lord Montagu's collections and prints his journals for some earlier Parliaments.

[2] We owe many thanks to Professor Mary Frear Keeler, through whom this diary came to our attention. See *D.N.B.*, 'Warner'; Edward Lee-Warner, *The Life of John Warner, Bishop of Rochester, 1637–1666* (London, 1901).

[3] Below, Braye 16 (24 April) fo 22r, Braye 14 (29 April) fo 39v–40r, pp. 72, 88.

prominence in the latter assembly, Warner ignores the Convocation's activity after Parliament's dissolution. He proceeds from his account of Parliament to events in September 1640.

The diary is in a clerical hand, which was probably not Warner's but that of a copyist.[1] Although Warner was new to Parliament in April 1640 and may not have left his account in perfect condition, its errors, blanks, and ellipses seem more like those of a copyist. According to the Lords' *Journal* Warner was absent 18, 24, and 27 April. This could account for his virtual omission of 18 April from the diary, but his coverage of debates on 24 and 27 April suggests that he was present.[2] His precise notation of procedural details in both this diary and that for the Long Parliament is the work of a man who would hardly have erred in references to the Speaker of the House of Commons and the prolocutor of the Convocation.[3] In places, such as his reports of committee proceedings, or the grievances of the House of Commons on 28 April, Warner seems to have relied upon papers.[4] Elsewhere his account is independent. He reorganizes Strafford's longest speech of 24 April and makes that the nucleus of the day's debates.[5] He adds information to that available in other sources for the House of Lords and Convocation.[6] Although he shared some procedural interests with Montagu, they differed concerning religion and support for the king's Scottish campaign. Warner's diary consequently adds a perspective to our understanding of proceedings in the Upper House and furnishes an example of a cleric's attempt at parliamentary reporting.

COMMONS

THE COMMONS' JOURNAL

The scribbled book, presumably kept by Henry Elsyng, clerk in the House of Commons, is not extant. It may have been the 'journall Booke of Parlemt beginning Aprill *13⁰* and ending May *5ᵗᵒ*' which

---

[1] The hand is similar to but not clearly identical with that in Warner's diary of the Long Parliament (B.L., Harl. MS. 6424); see Conrad Russell, 'The Authorship of the Bishop's Diary of the House of Lords in 1641', *B.I.H.R.*, xli (1968), pp. 229–36. See also B.L., Add. MS. 32096, fos 182ʳ–83ᵛ; Bodl. MS. Tanner 49, fo 23.

[2] See below, Braye 16 (24 April), p. 72, n. 3, Lee Warner, pp. 2, 3, 4 (18, 24, 27 April), pp. 108, 109, 110.

[3] Glanville (below, Lee Warner, p. 1; Dr Steiron Cheston (below, p. 106).

[4] *E.g.* Lee Warner, p. 4 (27 April) Comm. of Privileges; p. 5 (28 April), Comm. of Grievances, below, pp. 111, 113.

[5] Lee Warner, p. 3, p. 110.

[6] *E.g.* below, Lee Warner, p. 2 (16 April) Orders, p. 4 (25 April) Convocation, pp. 107, 111.

Elsyng handed in to the Council at the end of Parliament and received back in October.[1] The list of 'such things as [he] brought in . . . immediately upon the dissolution' includes virtually all the records of the Lower House—acts, petitions, messages, reports, committee lists, and notes of his assistant, John Rushworth.[2] Some of these have survived among the Main Papers in the House of Lords Record Office;[3] others have not been found.

If the volume mentioned on the list was not the scribbled book, it was probably the Manuscript Journal of the Commons, now in the House of Lords Record Office. Comparable to the Draft Journal for the Lords rather than to the Manuscript Journal, it shows revisions in some of the orders, names struck out and added, and notes about entering and arranging material. Despite these defects, it provided the text from which the Commons' *Journal* was ultimately printed in the eighteenth century. Its unfinished status can explain imperfections in the printed *Journal*, such as a space left on 2 May for the report of the Lord Keeper's speech at the conference of the preceding day,[4] the entry of a report of the committee preparing for the conference of 28 April instead of the actual report of the conference,[5] and inclusion of fragments of debate.[6]

Two manuscripts in the British Library (Add. MS. 36827, fos 1^r–87^v, and Harl. MS. 4289, fos 58^r–97^r), neither of which is identical with the volume in H.L.R.O., are also versions of the Commons' Journal, but probably not the finished Manuscript Journal. Evidence does not support the proposal in *Commons Debates, 1629*, that they were newsletter compilations.[7] Their provenance and exact relation to the Journal is uncertain. The account in Harl. MS. 4289 had been identified as the 'short minutes taken in the Commons House of Parliament, A.D. 1640' which Humfrey Wanley listed among manuscripts coming from Brampton Bryan in 1725.[8] Sir Robert Harley, master of Brampton Bryan in 1640, was knight of the shire for Hereford in the Short Parliament. The papers and correspondence of his family, especially the letters of his wife Lady Brilliana, show their interest in parliamentary proceedings.[9] It would not be

---

[1] S.P. 16/452/30.
[2] See below, Rushworth, i, p. 41.
[3] *E.g.*, committee papers, orders concerning elections.
[4] *C.J.*, ii, p. 18, *Cf.* M.C.J., pp. 97–98.
[5] *C.J.*, ii, p. 15.
[6] Although Pym's name is not mentioned, a summary of his famous speech of 17 April is recorded (*C.J.*, ii, p. 5; *cf.* M.C.J., p. 22).
[7] *Commons Debates, 1629*, pp. xliv–xlv.
[8] *The Diary of Humfrey Wanley, 1715–76*, ed. C. E. Wright and Ruth C. Wright (London, 1966), pp. 386–87.
[9] *Harley Letters*, pp. 90–95; see also Hist. MSS Comm., xxix, *Fourteenth Report*, App. ii: Portland MSS, Harley Papers (London, 1894), pp. 58–63; *D.N.B.*, 'Harley.'

surprising if they had obtained a copy of the Commons' Journal, but proof that the manuscript was theirs is lacking. Harl. MS. 4289 is a less finished and more interesting copy than Add. MS. 36827. In the Harleian manuscript notes have been made in the margins and spaces are left for the entry of speeches, reports, committee lists, and resolutions concerning some of the grievances.[1] Revisions can be seen in both manuscripts, and both follow the printed *Journal* in some of its variations from the Manuscript Journal.[2] While it cannot be proved that either was the work of the clerk, it seems likely that official sources were important in their composition.

A third copy of the Commons' Journal is that in William Petyt's papers (Inner Temple, Petyt MS. 537/30, fos 1ʳ–55ᵛ).[3] Petyt, a lawyer who served as Keeper of the Records in the Tower for nearly twenty years in the latter part of the seventeenth century, collected many papers concerning parliamentary proceedings. (Another of his volumes, Inner Temple. Petyt MS. 538/11, includes speeches from the Short Parliament.) His Commons' Journal is a fine copy. Working before the Journals were printed, Petyt, like the copyists of the British Library manuscripts, would have had to rely on the Manuscript Journal as the basis for his. Unlike those responsible for B.L., Add. MS. 36827 and Harl. MS. 4289, he omitted some of the clerk's rough notes and marginalia. The result of his discrimination is a carefully composed volume which resembles the printed *Journal*. If they had wished, the editors of the printed *Journal* could probably have used Petyt's text for theirs.

It is tempting to construct a theory about missing versions of the Commons' Journal, particularly one equivalent to the Manuscript Journal for the Lords,[4] but the absence of a finished Journal was not unusual in the early seventeenth century.[5] The brevity of the session and the Council's collecting the clerk's papers on the day of the dissolution may have interfered with work on the Journal. A more finished volume or volumes than the Manuscript Journal extant in the Lords Record Office is not necessary to the existence of the printed *Journal*, Harl. MS. 4289, Add. MS. 36827, Petyt MS. 537/30, or the work of John Nalson (below, p. 44). Individuals edited material they found when preparing their own records.

---

[1] For example, fos 77ʳ–78ᵛ (24 April); *cf.* B.L., Add. MS. 36827, fos 43ʳ–44ʳ.
[2] Neither mentions Pym on 17 April (B.L., Add. MS. 36827, fos 15ʳ–16ʳ; B.L., Harl. MS. 4289, fos 65ʳ–65ᵛ).
[3] Petyt MS. 537 includes 46 volumes of Journals of Parliament, Hen. VIII–Chas. II. See J. Conway Davies, *Catalogue of Manuscripts in the Library of the Honourable Society of the Inner Temple* (Oxford, 1972), ii, p. 611.
[4] We are grateful to Christopher Thompson for some very thought-provoking ideas about this.
[5] *E.g.*, 1610 (Foster, i, p. xxxv).

FINCH-HATTON MS. 50 AND HARVARD MS.
ENG. 982

The journal which has survived among the Finch-Hatton Manuscripts in the Northamptonshire Record Office and also among the collections of the Houghton Library at Harvard provides an account of proceedings in the House of Commons from the opening of the Short Parliament until the dissolution. Both the Finch-Hatton and the Harvard manuscripts appear to be copies. Harvard's volume bears an unidentified armorial bookplate with the motto 'verum atque decens'. It was purchased at Sotheby's in the fourth part of the sale of André de Coppet's library in 1955.[1] Although the Finch-Hatton journal is one of a number of parliamentary papers in that collection, none of these answers questions about its composition.

Like the True Relation of 1628, or the X Diary of 1621, Finch-Hatton MS. 50/Harvard MS. Eng. 982 is a compilation.[2] It incorporates texts of some of the major speeches, which also appeared as separates. Among speeches included are those of the king and Lord Keeper on 13 April, the king, Lord Keeper, and Speaker on 15 April, Grimston, Rudyerd, and Seymour on 16 April, Rous and Pym on 17 April, and the king on 5 May. Herbert's report of the conference of 25 April and Erle's reports of grievances on 24 and 29 April are also given. Although the texts of most of these are similar to those commonly found, both the speech of Seymour on 16 April and that of Pym on 17 April differ from the usual versions.[3]

The compiler seems to have used at least two accounts of proceedings as the framework for the speeches. One of these was probably official and the other private. The initial parts of each day's text, summaries of opinion prior to orders and motions, and the orders, motions, messages, and committee lists all bear the characteristics of the clerk's work. The brief entries such as those on 17 April following Pym's speech may also have come from the clerk's records.[4] It is possible but unlikely that the clerk's scribbled book was the source for some of the debates covered more completely, e.g., 23 and 27 April, 2 and 4 May. If Elsyng used the same method of directly reporting the speakers' words which Browne employed in taking notes in the Upper House, the accounts of debate are probably not his. 'He said' appears frequently in the Finch-Hatton/Harvard manuscript.[5] The absence of any debate from the accounts of 25 and

---

[1] We are grateful to Rodney G. Dennis, Curator of Manuscripts, Houghton Library, Harvard University, for this information.

[2] See *Commons Debates, 1629*, pp. xv–xix; also *Commons Debates, 1621*, i, pp. 15–16. References to the manuscript as a diary are general, not technical.

[3] See below, App. (17 April) Pym; (16 April) Seymour, pp. 297, 299.

[4] Finch-Hatton MS. p. 43, p. 157.

[5] *E.g.*, Finch-Hatton MS. p. 65, Braye 16, fo 22ᵛ, p. 178; *cf.* p. 72.

28 April argues against the compiler's reliance on the scribbled book which should have provided accounts of proceedings on those days just as on any others. Stylistic variations would point to more than one account in addition to the clerk's journal. On 27 April and 2 May 'we' is used to mean the House of Commons, but on 18 April (except in the speeches of Hyde, Strangways, and Rolle) the third person is employed.[1] Differences which may be significant appear in references to the king's councillors. Edward Herbert is invariably Mr Herbert until 4 May when he is Mr Sollicitor.[2] Sir Thomas German (Jermyn) is so called on 18 April and 2 May but is Mr Comptroller elsewhere.[3] Sir Henry Vane, usually Mr Treasurer, is at times Secretary Vane or Sir Henry Vane.[4] Establishing a pattern from these and other variations is difficult. Diarists may not have been consistent; copyists may have attempted to impose regularity upon their texts.

In the Finch-Hatton/Harvard manuscript, speakers expressing differing views are reported. Men who defended the king's interests or felt that his Majesty must be trusted receive rather more space than they frequently do.[5] At the same time Pym, Hampden, and others who spoke for the subjects are not neglected.[6] The extent to which the compiler may have selected his material to illustrate a conflict cannot be determined. Since the speeches of supporters of the court are integrated with others, the account's dependence upon diaries or collections representing differing political opinions seems unlikely.

The speeches of the first week of the Parliament seem better arranged than in many of the sources.[7] Debate proceeds logically and speakers' references to what had been said previously are accurate. The chronology of the period from 25 April to 1 May, which saw conferences one day and reports another seems to have caused the compiler some problems. These difficulties could be explained by his reliance on different kinds of sources. Non-official accounts would place speeches from a conference on the day the conference was held, e.g., 25 April, but the clerk would enter the speech in the Journal

[1] Finch-Hatton MS. p. 65, pp. 46–47, below, pp. 160, 161, 178.
[2] E.g., Harvard MS fos 79, 82ᵛ, below, p. 191; cf. p. 196.
[3] E.g., Finch-Hatton MS. pp. 47, 55, below, p. 161; cf. p. 171.
[4] E.g., Finch-Hatton MS. pp. 56, 58, Harvard MS. fos 75, 80ᵛ, below, pp. 171, 173, 187, 193.
[5] For example, Parry (below, Harvard MS fo 75ᵛ, p. 41); Ball and Jones (Finch-Hatton MS. pp. 58, 66, below, pp. 173, 179); concerning Hyde as possible diarist, see below, Clarendon, p. 141.
[6] For example, below, Finch-Hatton MS. pp. 58, 65, Harvard MS. fo 76ᵛ, pp. 173, 178, 179.
[7] Peyton's account agrees (Oxinden Letters, pp. 162–63).

when it was reported to the House, *e.g.*, 27 April. In this particular instance, Finch-Hatton MS. 50 gives it both places but has the entry for 25 April crossed out.[1] Despite deficiencies and uneven coverage, the Finch-Hatton/Harvard compilation relates the principal speeches, debates, orders, and decisions during the session. It will serve as the basic account of the House of Commons for the Parliament.

H.R.O., M36/1

This diary, now in the Huntingdon County Record Office, was found in 1948, at Kimbolton Castle in a book of devotions which may have belonged to Oliver St John. Valerie Pearl has suggested, on the basis of handwriting, that the diary is that of Robert Bernard, Steward to the earl of Manchester and Burgess for Huntingdon in the Short Parliament.[2]

The diary begins abruptly, apparently in the midst of an account of proceedings in the House of Commons on 20 April, continues for the remainder of the Parliament, and concludes with a description of the Council's action in questioning members and seizing papers from the Parliament. The coverage varies, but it tends to be more extensive as the Parliament progresses. Bernard summarises proceedings concisely on days such as 27 and 28 April. Although he indicates that he was absent from the House on the 30th, he gives a brief statement about the business done that day. He seems not to have relied upon separate copies of speeches as the Finch-Hatton/Harvard diarist did, but got for himself the major points of the official speeches: the Lord Keeper on 21 April at the Banqueting House and on 25 April at the conference; the king at the dissolution.[3] He also noted debate in the House, including some speeches or parts of speeches not recorded elsewhere.[4] The discussions of 2 and 4 May about supply attracted his attention, as did action concerning religion. The proceedings about Convocation on 22 April, Erle's report about religious grievances on 29 April, and the complaint about Dr Beale on 1 May are given at length. Procedure was another area in which Bernard shows interest. He notes many orders of the House: 'None was to be interrupted when he was speaking. Though

[1] See Finch-Hatton MS. p. 60, p. 176 and note 2.
[2] The Manchester Manuscripts in the Huntingdon Record Office are the best source of information about Bernard, whose authorship is not accepted by all scholars. We have examined his letters and believe the handwriting to be the same as that in the diary.
[3] H.R.O., M36/1, pp. 3–4, 7–8, 26–27, pp. 199, 202, 210.
[4] For example, Hampden (below, H.R.O., M36/1, p. 25, p. 209); St John, p. 209.

it pleased not, yet he was to be heard out'; 'It was said, That by leve off ye house, The same man may speake againe to ye sa[*me*] matter, he had spoken before.'[1] He also describes in detail the practices followed at conferences and the way in which messages were sent between the two Houses.[2] As a newcomer he may have been much more impressed by the intricacies of procedure than were many of those who had sat before. His inexperience may also explain the unclear dating of material for the period between 20 and 25 April, but even when confused about dating, Bernard's content is clear. Comparisons with other records of the Parliament indicate that he was observant and precise. His duties as Steward to the earl of Manchester probably demanded the same sort of care and attention which he seems to have given to keeping a journal of the Parliament. The earl himself, then Lord Privy Seal and an experienced parliamentarian, may have instructed Bernard in this respect. Manchester's brother, Edward, Lord Montagu of Boughton, who had likewise sat in many parliaments and kept diaries of proceedings, could also have been a guide for Bernard.[3] Montagu had a passionate interest in procedure and should have found Bernard's diary welcome reading.

WORCESTER COLLEGE MS. 5.20

Worcester College (Oxford) MS. 5.20 (Worc. Coll.) is a compilation It is based on a version of the diurnal of proceedings which appears in the Huntington Library's HM 1554, the Yale Law Library's Glanville manuscript, and in *A Perfect Diurnall* (see below). It seems unlikely that the compiler of the Worcester College volume was also the author of the diurnal even though in that version his notes and the diurnal are in the same hand. The manuscript covers the entire period of the Parliament, from the opening on 13 April to the dissolution on 5 May. A neatly printed title page states, 'Diurnall Occurances or Heads of the Dayly Proceedings of ye last Parliament which begun at Westminster the 13 of Aprill and ended the 5th of May 1640 holding in all but 20 Dayes.' Inserted into the diurnal are separates for virtually all the principal speeches of the Parliament. Those for Seymour (16 April), Pym (17 April), and Waller (?23 April) are printed. The others are handwritten, but most conform to one or more of the common versions.

Several of the compiler's notes to himself about the placing of speeches can be seen on the manuscript.[4] He added to the printed

---

[1] H.R.O., M36/1, pp. 1, 6.
[2] For example, H.R.O., M36/1, pp. 7, 16, pp. 201, 205.
[3] Cope, 'Lord Montagu,' *B.I.H.R.*, xlvi (1973).
[4] For example, below, Worc. Coll. fos 15ᵛ, 20ᵛ, pp. 213, 222, and note 5.

B

copy of Seymour's speech portions at the beginning and end, which appear in manuscript versions but were not printed.[1] His care here would suggest a penchant for accuracy. In his account of proceedings for 27 April he seems to have taken the first portion of Herbert's report from a separate but relied upon a summary for the remainder of the speech.[2] He may have intended to make a complete substitution as he did with the Lord Keeper's speech at the Banqueting House.[3] If so, his failure to execute his plans did not seriously impair the sense of his report. The composite text which appears in his manuscript is probably better than that which a haphazard combination would produce. His dating of some of the speeches, such as Waller's and Digby's, seems less dependable. It is possible that he was working some years after the Parliament although the wording of the title page would date the compilation prior to the end of the Long Parliament.

The manuscript is among the Clarke Papers. Initials, which may be 'G.C.', appear on the title page. Neither George Clarke (1661–1736), son of Sir William Clarke, nor any of the other Clarkes can be tied directly to the volume. The material may have been assembled for John Rushworth, who was associated with the Clarkes during the Civil Wars. The handwriting might be his, but perhaps because he prepared his *Collections* for publication in haste, he does not seem to have relied on this manuscript. There is a memorandum on the title page, possibly in the same hand as the initials, to the effect that, 'There are severall speeches in this MS., which are not printed in Mr Rushworth.' Had Rushworth used the manuscript, he might have avoided some of the errors and omissions noted below.

Bound with the Short Parliament compilation are 'Diurnall Occurances or the heads of the Proceedings in Parliament from ye 8th of November to the 15th, 1641.' Probably in a different hand, these offer no clear clues to the identity of the compiler. Anonymous as it remains, his work illustrates contemporary interest in parliamentary proceedings. The speeches themselves add little to available information about the Short Parliament, but their arrangement with a diurnal and the diurnal itself make the Worcester College manuscript a useful one for the historian.

[1] See below, Worc. Coll. Seymour, pp. 1, 4, pp. 213, 215.
[2] See below, Worc. Coll. fo 21, p. 224.
[3] See below, Worc. Coll. fo 17ᵛ, p. 221.

A PERFECT DIURNALL OF PASSAGES IN THE
LATE MEMORABLE PARLIAMENT BEGUN THE
13. OF APRIL 1640 AND THE DIURNALS OF
WORCESTER COLLEGE MS. 5.20, HM 1554, AND
THE GLANVILLE MANUSCRIPT

These diurnals seem to represent two major versions from a common source, which itself has not been recovered. That source probably contained a very brief entry summarizing proceedings for each day of the session and noting at times principal speakers and their speeches or heads of grievances. The identity of the author is uncertain. It may have been Samuel Pecke, who printed *A Perfect Diurnall of Passages in the late memorable Parliament Begun the 13. of April 1640* (B.L., 195. c. 19) in his newspaper in 1649.[1] This version, however, lacks the sole personal reference which appears in the other three. That reference suggests that the author was probably an observer, as Pecke would have been, rather than a participant in the Parliament. On 30 April the diurnalist comments, 'Itt is generallie doubted that they will shortlie rise without doing anie thinge, yea I heard from a good hand that the Kinge hath beene stronglie importuned to dissolve this Parliament butt as yett denies itt.'[2]

The shorter of the two versions of the diurnal is found in HM 1554 and the Glanville manuscript. It begins with 15 April and, although it closes with a statement that 'This Parliament broke upp on Tewsday the fift of May 1640,' it tells little for the period after 29 April. HM 1554, in the Huntington Library, San Marino, California,[3] includes a collection of speeches in the same clerical hand in which the diary is written, but the speeches (pp. 109–215) are not incorporated with the diary (pp. 252–62). The Glanville manuscript, in the Yale Law Library, is so called primarily because the first two items in the volume containing it are Glanville's speech of 23 May 1628 and his 'Breife and faithful relation.' The journal of the Short Parliament (5 pages, without any accompanying speeches) is the fourth item.[4]

[1] His paper was *A Perfect Diurnall of some Passages in Parliament.*
[2] Worc. Coll. MS. 5.20, fo 23ᵛ.
[3] HM 1554 is not actually part of the Hastings Papers. Some material from other parliaments also appears in the volume. We are grateful to Jean Preston, Assistant Curator of Manuscripts at the Huntington, for information about the volume.
[4] The other three items in the volume are: 3. Hakewill's The Course of Passinge bills in Parliament. 5. Reports of 11 cases in various courts, 6–9 *Jac.* I and one undated. 6. Sherfield's reading in one of the Inns of Court, 1623–24. We are grateful to Robert E. Brooks of the Reference Department of the Yale Law Library for this information. There are photostats of this manuscript in the Folger Shakespeare Library (PR 1405 J6).

Worc. Coll. MS. 5.20 and *A Perfect Diurnall* both give a version of the diurnal which covers the entire Parliament. In printing the diurnal at the back of the 1–8 October 1649 issue of his weekly, Samuel Pecke explained, 'This worke . . . we have the rather undertaken, at the request and importunity of some Gentlemen to reduce to memory the passages of things both before and since the beginning of the late wars, which have not hitherto been so exactly committed to the publique. And because the rise and foundation of all the late proceedings was laid in that memorable Parliament *Anno* 1640. immediately preceding this, we shall first present a Narrative of the passages during that Sessions . . . and from thence go forward. . . .'[1]

Where the compiler of the Worc. Coll. MS. has inserted copies of speeches into the diurnal, the editor of *A Perfect Diurnall* provides a sentence or two of synopsis and comment. Only the lists of grievances of the Commons and the king's speech of 5 May are given *in extenso*. It is impossible to know how many of these variations Pecke himself introduced. Since he had been a writer of newsletters before he started printing his paper, he could easily have had an account of the Short Parliament.[2] Whether or not it was of his own authorship, he probably would have had to make some changes to fit the space available in his paper and consequently omit the more detailed treatment which the other three texts give to the Lord Keeper's speech of 21 April[3] and Mr Solicitor Herbert's report of the conference of 25 April.[4]

Even as printed by Pecke, the diurnal delineates the principal issues of the Parliament. The author describes the dismay of the king's councillors at their inability to guide the House[5] and outlines the Crown's efforts to obtain supply. From the initial complaints of Pym, Seymour and Grimston to the debates of 22 April, the decision to prepare grievances for presentation to the Lords, and the reporting of the heads of such grievances, he follows the Commons' concern about grievances.[6] He concentrates on proceedings in the Lower House, but he does not totally neglect the Lords. He lists the names of those lords who 'voted with the House of Commons' by opposing a

[1] In printing the four-page diurnal of the Short Parliament with an issue of his paper, Pecke was copying the practice of a competitor, Henry Walker, who a few weeks earlier had begun printing a series of summaries of proceedings of the Long Parliament. Joseph Frank, *The Beginnings of the English Newspaper, 1620–60* (Cambridge, Mass., 1961), pp. 182–83.
[2] Frank, *The Beginnings of the English Newspaper, 1620–60*, p. 25; J. B. Williams, 'The Beginnings of English Journalism,' *Cambridge History of English Literature*, vii, p. 394 (eds. A. W. Ward and A. R. Waller, Cambridge, 1911).
[3] See HM 1554, pp. 254, Worc. Coll. fo 19ᵛ, pp. 221, 230.
[4] See HM 1554, pp. 257–58, below, pp. 213–22.
[5] See p. 222, below, Worc. Coll. fo 20.
[6] See below, Worc. Coll. fos 15, 19ᵛ, pp. 212, 221; HM 1554, pp. 252–62; Worc. Coll. 5.20, fos 25ᵛ–26ʳ, pp. 228–29.

resolution about the precedency of supply.[1] Parliament thus appears as it did to contemporaries. It was a body of king, Lords, and Commons whose successful functioning depended on the coordination of its parts. In detail and in general the diurnal reflects an informed view.

LORDS AND COMMONS

B.L., HARLEIAN MS. 4931

The journal of proceedings from the Short Parliament which appears in B.L., Harl. MS 4931 (fos 47ʳ–49ʳ; also marked as pp. 87–91) has the material on each of its pages arranged in two columns, one for the Lords and one for the Commons. The entries are relatively brief although some speakers are mentioned and their arguments noted. The journalist appears to have had Puritan sympathies. Some of the men, such as 'Mr Grimston of Essex,' 'Mr Pim' and 'Sir Francis Seamer' [Seymour],[2] whose contributions he records might be cited in almost any account of the Parliament, but others such as Sir William Masham and 'Sir Robert Harlowe' [Harley], are less likely inclusions.[3] The reports of the Lords' disputes about Convocation days,[4] Bishop Hall's remarks in committee,[5] the arrangements for the fast,[6] the Dell incident,[7] and the presentation of popish pictures to the Commons[8] also suggest an interest in religion. When reporting the presentation of petitions from Middlesex, Suffolk, and Northamptonshire, the diarist refers to the reactions of the 'royalists'.[9] His use of this term may be one example of its early application, but it may mean that he was writing the diary a year or more after the Parliament from sources available to him.[10]

This account may be another variation of the diurnal of which those used by Rossingham and described below are probably the standard type. Unlike the diurnal upon which the Worcester College manuscript was built, Harl. MS. 4931 is not always accurate or clear. The author does not demonstrate an understanding of parliamentary procedure. His comments 22–27 April about the king's demands for supply and the Commons' answers are not precise.[11] The king knew of the Lower House's vote of 23 April but received no answer from

[1] See below, Worc. Coll. fo 26ᵛ, p. 229.
[2] Below, Harl. MS. 4931 fo 47, pp. 233–34.
[3] Below, Ibid., p. 234.   [4] Below, Ibid., p. 234.
[5] Below, Harl. MS. 4931 fo 47ᵛ, p. 236.
[6] Below, Ibid., p. 237.   [7] Below, Ibid., p. 236.
[8] Below, Harl. MS. 4931 fo 48, p. 238.
[9] Below, Harl. MS. 4931 fo 47, p. 234.
[10] O.E.D. gives a date of 1643 for 'royalist', but see: D. H. Willson, *The Privy Councillors in the House of Commons* (Minneapolis, 1940), p. 123, n. 41.
[11] Below, Harl. MS. 4931 fos 47ᵛ–48, pp. 236–39 and notes.

the Commons about subsidies until 2 May, when they asked for more time. If he had received an answer, the question of privileges would not have arisen. His Majesty did not send to the Lower House but to the Lords on 24 April, and it was not the king but the Upper House that sent the Lord Keeper to the Commons on 25 April. The chronology is somewhat confused both during this period and for other days. On 15 April the Lower House, like the Upper, was involved in matters of formality.[1] The Speaker was presented and other business was not done. The discussion of matters ecclesiastical noted for 20 April probably occurred on 21 April[2] and the offer of twelve subsidies on 4 May instead of 2 May.[3] There was no debate on 5 May.[4]

In addition to the journal for the Short Parliament Harl. MS. 4931 contains a journal for the Long Parliament similarly arranged, a description of the opening of the Short Parliament, copies of petitions to the Parliament,[5] various parliamentary speeches, poetry about political and religious affairs, miscellaneous other items, many in the same hand. Some of the material in the volume can be associated with the Reverend John Gauden, one-time chaplain to the earl of Warwick and subsequently reputed author of *Eikon Basilike*, but there is no evidence for linking Gauden to the diary.[6] Regardless of the identity of the author and although the details of its account of proceedings cannot be relied on, the sense of conflict which some contemporaries felt and observed in the Short Parliament is portrayed effectively in this diary.

STATE PAPERS, DOMESTIC

The Domestic Series of State Papers in the Public Record Office includes various items concerning the Short Parliament. Some of the papers bear notations by Archbishop Laud and probably belonged to him;[7] others are in Secretary Windebanke's hand and relate to the activities of the Privy Council.[8] There are a number which deal with parliamentary elections.[9] The newsletters and diurnals described below form another important group. Detailed reports on most items are entered in *Calendars of State Papers, Domestic, 1639–40*

---

[1] Below, Harl. MS. 4931 fo 47, p. 233.
[2] Below, Harl. MS. 4931 fo 47ᵛ, p. 235.
[3] Below, Harl. MS. 4931 fo 49, p. 242.   [4] Below, Ibid., p. 244.
[5] For example, below, Petition, Essex (18 April), Harl. MS. 4931 fo 41ʳ, p. 275.
[6] Christopher Thompson brought the Gauden material, such as that in fo 24ʳ, to our attention.
[7] For example, S.P. 16/441/113; S.P. 16/451/9 (below, Montague Papers, p. 2, 20 April n. 1, p. 99).
[8] For example, below, S.P. 16/450/113, 16/452/9, pp. 290–91.
[9] For example, Hastings (*CSP 1640*, pp. 2–3).

and *1640* (*CSP 1639–40; CSP 1640*), but notice of some papers is entirely omitted from the *Calendars*.[1]

CAPTAIN EDWARD ROSSINGHAM AND NEWS OF PARLIAMENT

Rossingham, well known among contemporaries for his newsletters, was a collector and distributor of information. Both the sources he used and those he compiled testify to contemporary interest in parliamentary proceedings. Unfortunately only the broad outlines of his operations can be established. In return for a fee, 'not under twenty pounds *per annum*' according to one source, Rossingham wrote his clients weekly about events at home and abroad.[2] Those who subscribed to his service included the earls of Northumberland and Salisbury, Lords Say and Brooke, Sir Christopher Egerton, Lord Scudamore, the friend and correspondent of Archbishop Laud who had been ambassador in France from 1634 until 1638, and Lord Conway, the General of the Horse and Deputy General of the Army. The letters to both Scudamore and Conway survive from the period of the Short Parliament. The former are preserved in the manuscript collections of the British Library (Add. MS. 11045); the latter are among the State Papers, Domestic Series, in the Public Record Office.[3] (Lengthy reports appear in *CSP 1640*, pp. 76–79, 108–110).

These newsletters contain detailed and usually accurate accounts of parliamentary proceedings. Although he rarely gave the complete versions of speeches, resolutions, or messages, Rossingham must frequently have had access to copies.[4] The letters themselves tell little about his news-gathering procedure. He says, 'I hear . . .' or 'it is said that . . .' without revealing more about his sources. His occasional confessions that he was unable to learn something, that information in a previous letter was erroneous or that he had not yet seen a specific document show that he was careful in collecting and transmitting information.[5]

Except when catering to the individual interests of his subscribers,

[1] For example, below, S.P. 16/450/113, p. 290.
[2] Bodl., Tanner MS. 65, fo 79ᵛ. A list of correspondents appears there too.
[3] S.P. 16/450/88; S.P. 16/451/16; S.P. 16/451/57; S.P. 16/451/66; S.P. 16/452/20. The comments in *Commons Debates, 1629*, pp. xliv–xlv, need some revision. Copies of the letters of 12 and 19 May (S.P. 16/453/24 and B.L., Add. MS. 11045, fos 116ʳ–17ᵛ) appear in B.L., Sloane MS. 1467, fos 104ʳ–108ʳ, 108ʳ–11ᵛ. The Sloane MS. is a volume of miscellaneous extracts. It includes copies of letters from the period after 19 May but none for that of the Short Parliament.
[4] See B.L., Add. MS. 11045, fos 105ʳ–105ᵛ, 109ᵛ, 116ʳ.
[5] For example, see B.L., Add. MS. 11045, fos 95ʳ, 105ᵛ; but also see B.L., Add. MS. 11045, fo 115ʳ, and Finch-Hatton MS., p. 57, below, p. 172, concerning Peard's speech.

his commentary about the events he reported was limited. Material seems to have been selected and presented with the recipient in mind. Some portions of the letters to Conway are identical to those to Scudamore,[1] but other parts of the letters vary. A detailed statement of the contents of the commissions to the lord general and lord admiral would have been commonplace to Conway but was news to Scudamore. Both receive reports of royal efforts to obtain money from London, but the reports appear to have been composed separately.[2] The letters to Scudamore tend to be more detailed than those to Conway, perhaps because Conway had official and regular sources of information, whereas Scudamore, retired in the country, would have been dependent for news on personal ties, such as that with Laud.[3]

Another explanation for the differences in the letters may be that Rossingham was sending Conway diurnals of parliamentary proceedings. Two manuscripts are now preserved in the Public Record Office: S.P. 16/451/16 notes proceedings during the first week of the Parliament, 13–20 April, and S.P. 16/451/57 continues the account 21–27 April. Two other versions of the continuation, S.P. 16/451/10 and S.P. 16/450/94 are extant. Both have some entries for the period between 27 April and the dissolution of the Parliament on 5 May.

There are some minor variations in the versions of the diurnal. That in S.P. 16/450/94, of which a transcript is printed in *CSP 1640*, pp. 39–40, adds descriptive phrases when referring to individuals. Pym, for example, is described as a 'parliamentman' and Hampden as 'one of the knights from Buckinghamshire,' and Dr Cosin as 'vice-chancellor of Cambridge.' These phrases may have no purpose other than editorial embellishment, but it is possible that they were to aid a reader less familiar with the proceedings and personnel of parliament than was Conway. S.P. 16/451/10 is similar to S.P. 16/450/94 and like it includes some detailed personal identifications. Another feature of S.P. 16/451/10 is its incorporation of the Commons' resolutions about grievances.[4]

Although it is possible that Rossingham himself was the author of these, discrepancies in the chronology and information between the diurnals and the newsletters would argue against his authorship.[5] It

[1] B.L., Add. MS. 11045, fos 109ʳ–109ᵛ, 110ʳ; *cf.* S.P. 16/450/88; see also S.P. 16/451/66 and B.L., Add. MS. 11045, fos 110ʳ–13ʳ.
[2] B.L., Add. MS. 11045, fo 109ᵛ; *cf.* S.P. 16/450/88.
[3] B.L., Add. MS. 11045, fos 111ʳ–13ᵛ, 114ʳ–15ᵛ; *cf.* S.P. 16/451/66 and S.P. 16/452/20. It is possible that they paid different fees.
[4] 25 April (wrongly dated 27 April in MS.); see also *C.J.*, ii, pp. 11–12.
[5] *Cf.* below, S.P. 16/451/16 (21 April), p. 246, and B.L., Add. MS. 11045, fo 111ʳ; also below, S.P. 16/451/57 (23–24 April), pp. 246–47, and B.L. Add. MS. 11045, fos 111ᵛ–12ᵛ.

seems more likely that the diurnals came from one of the sources which he relied upon in collecting material for his newsletters and which could have been used by others. There is no evidence which would link him to S.P. 16/450/94, where the diurnal is combined with a collection of speeches.[1] This manuscript entry book, preserved among the State Papers in the Public Record Office, seems to emphasize religion. It notes the voting of subsidies by the clergy and the Commons' reluctance to approve that grant, items which receive little attention in many of the reports of the Parliament. Manwaring, Cosin, Beale, and Dell are named in the diurnal, but St John, Grimston, and Erle are not. Pym's famous speech about grievances is not included.[2] He and Hampden are mentioned only as participants in an incident involving Dell on 22 April.[3] With the speeches at the presentation of the Speaker and at the dissolution, S.P. 16/450/94 includes two versions of Rous' speech,[4] that of Rudyerd on 16 April and that about the oath *ex officio*, usually attributed to Eliot.[5] Religious grievances are the principal theme of both Eliot and Rous. Rudyerd also mentions religion although he directs more attention to maintaining good relations with the king.

Whether or not directly associated with Rossingham, S.P. 16/450/94 shares at least one source with his work, the brief diurnal. Intended to present the most important information as concisely as possible, the diurnals carried news of Parliament to people not directly associated with it. They could be sent in letters or appended to copies of speeches. Rossingham is probably only the best known of those who publicized Parliament's proceedings in the spring of 1640. Not a direct or an independent account, Rossingham's dispatches can supplement the diaries of debate.

REPORTS OF AMBASSADORS

Foreign ambassadors perceived that the outcome of the Short Parliament was important to them. If the king of England received adequate funds from Parliament, he would be less dependent upon other sources of revenue, such as grants or loans from foreign rulers, to whom he might in return pledge support in the European struggles. Several of the foreign ambassadors reported the events of the English Parliament to their governments. The accounts of the Venetian

[1] But see S. R. Gardiner, *History of England, 1603–1642*, ix (London, 1884), p. 115n.
[2] See below, App., Pym (17 April), p. 299.
[3] See Finch-Hatton MS., p. 54, p. 169.
[4] The second version comes at the end of the volume, after the king's speech at the dissolution, and is in a different hand.
[5] See below, App., Rudyerd (16 April), Eliot, pp. 296, 313.

ambassador have long been available in summary form, in the *Calendar of State Papers and Manuscripts Relating to English Affairs Existing in the Archives and Collections of Venice and Other Libraries of Northern Italy*. Less immediately involved in the continental conflicts and understanding English affairs better than some of his colleagues, Giovanni Giustinian prepared dispatches more valuable than many of theirs. He talked about the strength of the Puritans but paid more attention to complaints about ministers and ship-money than to a Catholic–Protestant division. Controversy in Parliament, he noted, focused upon whether supply should be granted prior to the redress of grievances.[1]

Salvetti, the Tuscan representative, and Rossetti, the pope's agent, devoted more attention to religion.[2] They noted the activities of the Puritans, whom they regarded as the king's enemies as well as theirs, and worried about the fate of the Catholics.[3] Rossetti's close associations with Queen Henrietta Maria may have given him an inside source for his statements about the king and court.[4] Whether blinded by his feelings or hindered by his lack of experience in England, his account contains misinterpretations and misconceptions. Salvetti, whose dispatches show a similar weakness, can hardly be excused on grounds of inexperience. He had been in England for more than fifteen years by 1640. The reports of Von Lisola, the imperial ambassador, are also of limited value.[5] The activities of the three Spanish envoys who were in London at the time were more important to him than the proceedings in Parliament. He makes no reference to the earl of Strafford and mentions the Archbishop of Canterbury only as a target of disturbances which broke out at the dissolution of the Parliament.[6]

Montereul, the French representative, arrived in London only a few weeks before the Parliament opened. Whether prompted by fears of inadequacy, natural diligence, the demands of his superiors,[7] associations with the earls of Holland and Northumberland,[8] or his

---

[1] For example, *CSP Ven. 1640*, pp. 40, 46.
[2] Twenty-one volumes of transcripts of Salvetti's dispatches are among the Additional Manuscripts in the British Library. Those for the Short Parliament can be found in Add. MS. 27962 I. See also Hist. MSS Comm., xvi, *Eleventh Report*, App. i: Skrine MSS, Salvetti Papers (London, 1887), p. 2. Transcripts of Rossetti's dispatches for the Short Parliament are preserved in the Public Record Office, P.R.O. 31/9/18.
[3] For example, B.L., Add. MS. 27962 I, fos 54^r–55^r; P.R.O. 31/9/18, fos 181^r–82^r.
[4] P.R.O. 31/9/18, fos 181^r–82^r.
[5] The reports are preserved among the manuscript collections in Vienna of the Haus-, Hof-, und Staatsarchiv, Englische Korrespondenz 18, fos 54^r–87^r. We used photocopies borrowed from Danila C. Spielman.
[6] Von Lisola, fo 86^r.   [7] P.R.O. 31/3/72, fos 124^r, 129^r.
[8] P.R.O. 31/3/72, fos 4^r–5^r, 136^r.

own interests, he took his responsibility seriously. Apologies about content and form mark his dispatches to Bellievre, his predecessor, and Chavigny.[1] In addition to notes in his regular correspondence, Montereul kept a diurnal of Parliament.[2] It is not clear whether this diurnal was taken from the notebooks (*cahiers*) which he was keeping or whether the notebooks represent another source of information.[3] For him Parliament was not just a part of the larger diplomatic scene. He noted discussion about religion and complaints of Catholic influence, but he did not see the entire Parliament as a battle between Catholics and Puritans.[4]

The diplomatic manuscripts add little to accounts of actual proceedings in Parliament, but both these and others not examined for this project[5] should be investigated for any more general study of the politics of 1640.

B.L., E. 203(1)

His Majesties Declaration to All His Loving Subjects of the Causes Which Moved Him to Dissolve the Last Parliament appeared in print soon after the Parliament had ended. Published 'by his Majesties speciall command' and printed by Robert Barker and the assignees of John Bill, the *quarto* volume of 55 pages provided a brief history of parliamentary proceedings by summarizing each of the principal royal addresses to the Parliament. Although the summaries follow the texts fairly closely in places, they make omissions, additions, and clarifications. Even the king's speech at the dissolution, which is given in full in the *Declaration*, shows some revisions from the version in the Lords' Journal. The only other items whose complete texts are included in the *Declaration* are the Lords' resolutions of 24, 29, and 30 April and the king's messages to the Commons on 2 and 4 May.

In title and purpose the *Declaration* was similar to those issued in 1621, 1626, and 1629.[6] Its content and approach are probably more sophisticated than those of any of its predecessors. Whereas in 1629

---

[1] P.R.O. 31/3/72, fos 4ʳ–5ʳ, 118ʳ, 136ʳ. See also Hist. MSS Comm., ii, *Third Report*, App.: Northumberland MSS, Alnwick Papers (London, 1872), p. 80. Transcripts of Montereul's dispatches are preserved in the Public Record Office (P.R.O. 31/3/72).

[2] P.R.O. 31/3/72, fo 144ʳ.   [3] P.R.O. 31/3/72, fos 124ʳ, 144ʳ.

[4] P.R.O. 31/3/72, fos 119ʳ, 120ʳ.

[5] *E.g.*, the Spanish dispatches (Archivo General de Simancas) or those of the Dutch representative, Heere Van Sommelsdyck. We are grateful to Norah Fuidge for information that the transcripts of Van Sommelsdyck's dispatches in the British Library do not include accounts of the Short Parliament; B.L., Add. MS. 22870 ends in March 1640 and B.L., Add. MS. 22871 begins in January 1640/41.

[6] STC 9241; 9246; and especially 9249, *His Majesties Declaration to All His Loving Subjects, of the Causes Which Moved him to Dissolve the Last Parliament* (London, 1628), B.L., 8122. c. 26; also Rushworth, i, Appendix.

much space was devoted to statements made in the House of Commons and answers to them, in 1640 the emphasis was placed on what the king had said and done. The king's needs and his efforts to fulfil the obligations of kingship were treated at length and in more detail while the House of Commons was dismissed in general terms as having failed to perform what faithful subjects owed their ruler.

The *Declaration* was only one of the measures relating to the dissolution of Parliament which the Crown took in the days following 5 May.[1] A more positive act than the seizure of papers or imprisonment of men, the *Declaration* made use of the official advantages in publishing and distributing information. Law and practice made it difficult for opponents to answer the arguments in print without subjecting themselves to possible prosecution. In his pamphlet on shipmoney Henry Parker seems to have quoted directly from the *Declaration* King Charles' statements about aims.[2] Parker does not, however, specifically cite any source. Authorship of the *Declaration* was one of the charges used in the impeachment of Lord Keeper Finch,[3] but most protests in the Long Parliament about the dissolution of the Short Parliament were concerned with general issues or questions of principle rather than with the *Declaration*.

John Rushworth printed parts of the *Declaration* in his *Collections* (iii, pp. 1160–67). He omitted the speeches between 25 April and the dissolution because he had included them separately.[4] Nalson (i, pp. 345–51) adopted a similar procedure. Since the seventeenth century historians have paid even less attention to the *Declaration*. The publication is more significant for its aims than its achievements.

CLARENDON'S *LIFE* AND *HISTORY OF THE REBELLION*

The Short Parliament was the first for Edward Hyde, later earl of Clarendon. Elected from both Wootton Bassett (Wilts.) and Shaftesbury (Dorset), Hyde chose to sit for the former. His account of 'that Short Parliament'[5] is not only a personal memoir, which records his contributions to debate, giving in the *Life* a detailed report of his speech about the Court of Honour.[6] He also, especially in the *History of the Rebellion*, assesses the Parliament as part of the background to civil war. A comparison of the *Life* with the *History* shows that in the latter Clarendon was aspiring to step beyond the personal. Although

---

[1] See *CSP 1640*, pp. 152–56.
[2] *The Case of Ship Money Briefly Discoursed* (1640), p. 4 (B.L., E.204(4)).
[3] Rushworth, iv, p. 138.
[4] Rushworth, iii, p. 1165.
[5] Clarendon, *History*, I. 166, n. 1, 5. See also *D.N.B.*
[6] See below, App., Hyde (18 April), p. 302.

his sentiments and his knowledge of the subsequent course of events clearly affect his statements, his *History* deserves careful examination The view he presents is his own, and it is not a simple one. He believed the Parliament 'as composed and as well disposed . . . as . . . had met together in any time; . . . there having never passed the least action or word of irreverance or disrespect towards his Majesty during the time they continued together.'[1] At the same time he reports an encounter soon after the dissolution with a smiling Mr St John who stated that some M.P.s were not sorry to see the Parliament end in the way it had.[2]

There are some similarities between Hyde's account of the Parliament and that which appears in the Finch-Hatton/Harvard diary. Hyde refers to speeches including his own which are noted there[3] but not necessarily mentioned elsewhere, but he differs from the Finch-Hatton/Harvard diarist in other respects. The proceedings of 2–4 May show discrepancies in dating and treatment of issues between the two.[4] Missing from the diary are the recriminations and personal animadversions such as Hyde's criticism of Vane's behaviour with regard to the royal request for twelve subsidies.[5]

Both the strength and weakness of Hyde's work is its personal character. Hyde's ability to observe and evaluate the experiences of himself and his contemporaries makes his *Life* and *History* indispensable to the historian of the Short Parliament.

RUSHWORTH

The *Historical Collections* of John Rushworth, who was appointed assistant clerk of the Commons, 25 April 1640, have provided one of the most readily available accounts of the Short Parliament. The value of these *Collections* is not so great as Rushworth's position might lead one to expect. He was not appointed until almost two weeks of the Parliament had passed. In ordering his appointment, the Commons specified that he 'not take any Notes here without the precedent Directions and Command of this House, but only of the Orders and Reports made in this House.'[6] If he took the oath formulated in 1621 for an assistant clerk, he would have bound himself 'neither [to] . . . discover or report' to anyone not a member

---

[1] Clarendon, *History*, I. 166, n. 1, 5.
[2] Clarendon, *History*, II. 78.
[3] His own and Peard, Finch-Hatton MS., pp. 47, 57, below, pp. 158, 172; (Clarendon, *History*, II, 68); Cooke, Harvard MS. fos 82–82ᵛ, below, p. 195; (Clarendon, *History*, II, 71).
[4] *Cf.* Clarendon, *History*, II. 70–75, and below, Harvard MS. fos 75–81, pp. 187–94; see also Clarendon, *History*, II, 166, n. 1, 5–6.
[5] Clarendon, *History*, II. 75–76.
[6] *C.J.*, ii, p. 12; also H.R.O., M36/1, p. 10, below, p. 203.

'anything' he heard in the house 'or read in the journal book.' (The oath is quoted in Foster, 'Elsyng,' p. 12.) The lapse of time between the Short Parliament and the publication in 1679 of the Second Part of the *Collections*, that dealing with the Short Parliament, may also have diminished the significance of Rushworth's clerical responsibilities for the content of the work. The disturbances of the intervening years had taken their toll of papers as well as men and institutions. Rushworth indicates that he still had in 1679 *verbatim* notes that he had taken of arguments in the shipmoney case, of some of the Scottish proceedings,[1] and of cases in the court of honour (he confesses that he could not use these last because he had not transcribed them),[2] but he makes no similar claim with regard to the Short Parliament. He does not even notice in the *Collections* his appointment as clerk.[3] In the Introduction he simply says he will give a 'large account' of the Parliament of the spring of 1640.[4] That account was probably based on the material he was busy borrowing wherever he could.[5]

An examination of the *Collections* shows that none of the speeches he included is difficult to find among the contemporary printed speeches or manuscript copies. Although some of the resolutions entered into his journal follow those in the Commons' Journal, it is hard to believe that he could have had access to the official Journal when constructing his own. His scheme of organization leaves something to be desired. He gives virtually nothing for 23–25 April, when the Commons were busy discussing and voting grievances.[6] The grievances are entered on 29 April when the House voted on the heads concerning religion. He uses a version of these, adds to them the other two categories of grievances as presented on the 24th, and wrongly states that on the 29th following their resolutions, the Commons had a conference with the Lords about the grievances.[7] Another error in his account is his statement that on 30 April while discussing shipmoney, the House by a vote of 257–148 refused a conference with the Lords.[8] The refusal, he thought, was a significant demonstration of the temper of the Lower House. The Commons' *Journal* and other sources make clear that what actually

---

[1] Rushworth, ii, preface. [2] Rushworth, iii, p. 1054.
[3] *Cf.* Bodl., MS. Wood F.39, fo 383ʳ, where Rushworth cites the significance of his clerkship, but does not mention the Short Parliament. The oath of secrecy (above) may explain his silence.
[4] Rushworth, ii, preface.
[5] Hist. MSS Comm., iii, *Fourth Report*, App.: House of Lords MSS (London, 1874), p. 231.
[6] Rushworth, iii, p. 1144; *cf.* Finch-Hatton MS., pp. 54–61, below, pp. 168–77.
[7] Rushworth, iii, pp. 1147–49; *C.J.*, ii, p. 16.
[8] Rushworth, iii, p. 1149.

occurred was much less dramatic.[1] On 1 May while the House was in the midst of dividing on a question about Dr Beale, a message for a conference arrived from the Lords. The Commons replied that they were busy, proceeded with the division, which concerned Dr Beale and not the conference, and then sent to the Lords agreeing to a conference. If Rushworth had relied upon the Commons' Journal or other detailed records of proceedings, his account should not have been so garbled. Nevertheless he seems to have had some parliamentary papers. Without these, even in view of his experience, he would not have been able to give the wording or the details which he does in some instances.[2]

In his Introduction Rushworth apologized for the errors which may have resulted from the haste in which his volume was prepared.[3] Some of the weaknesses cited above can probably be attributed to the hurried assembling of material. Other errors which may have been committed for this reason are the apparent combination of two versions of the Lord Keeper's speech at the Banqueting House[4] and the entry of a second version of Pym's speech of 17 April as the speech of November 1640.[5] Rushworth had received word shortly before he wanted to go to press that he should not include some of the early speeches of the Long Parliament.[6] Pym's speech of 17 April had been circulated in several versions.[7] Under political pressure as well as that of time Rushworth could have taken a second version for a second speech.[8]

For the Short Parliament Rushworth's *Collections* provide various extracts from the proceedings. The *Collections* are not complete or even consistent in their coverage. Rushworth lists certain bills as being read on 29 April[9] but says nothing about bills read on other days.[10] He mentions some of the petitions from the country and omits others.[11] His account can be relied on neither for chronology nor for accuracy of information. Only in a resolution upon the report for 28 April of the committee to prepare a conference with the

[1] *C.J.*, ii, p. 18; H.R.O., M36/1, pp. 14–17, below, pp. 204–05.
[2] For example, Rushworth, iii, p. 1147 (resolutions about privileges), p. 1153 (king's message).
[3] Rushworth, ii, preface.
[4] See below, App. L.K. (21 April), p. 304.
[5] Rushworth, iv, pp. 21–24; below, App., Pym (17 April), p. 299; see also Gardiner, ix, pp. 105–106.
[6] Hist. MSS Comm., iv, *Fifth Report*, App.: Malet MSS (London, 1876), pp. 317–18.
[7] See below, App., Pym (17 April), p. 299.
[8] Hist. MSS Comm., lxiv, *Report on the MSS of the Earl of Verulam* (London, 1906), pp. 82–83.
[9] Rushworth, iii, p. 1149.
[10] Rushworth, iii, p. 1149; *C.J.*, ii, p. 16.
[11] Rushworth, iii, p. 1127; Finch-Hatton MS., p. 43, below, p. 157.

Lords and in the message of 4 May does he seem to have added to material available elsewhere.[1] Despite these limitations and the criticism leveled upon his account in the *Old Parliamentary History*, Rushworth's influence on subsequent study of the Short Parliament has been very great.[2]

NALSON

John Nalson, antiquary and canon of Ely, was among a number of Englishmen who found Rushworth's *Collections* objectionable.[3] Nalson set out with official blessing to prepare an 'antidote to Mr Rushworth'.[4] Although most of the controversy about Rushworth's work focussed on the Long Parliament, Nalson began his *Impartial Collection of the Great Affairs of State* with the 'Scotch Rebellion' and included the Short Parliament. His first volume appeared in 1682; a second which continued the work from May 1641 until January 1642 came out in 1683. More were projected, but Nalson died before he could complete them. For his volumes Nalson solicited and obtained information from a number of prominent persons.[5] Some of the papers which he used were not returned and survive today in various collections, best known of which is that of the Duke of Portland. Examination of the calendar of the Nalson Papers among the Portland Manuscripts offers no help with regard to his sources for the Short Parliament.[6] None of the papers mentioned there concerns proceedings in that assembly.

Nalson's work itself substantiates reports that connections made it possible for him to use official papers, including the Commons' Journal. As a result, he avoids some of Rushworth's errors. He enters the grievances on 24 April as they are in the *Journal*[7] and in general is more accurate in his chronology. Items such as a note that Hyde spoke about the court of honour[8] and Erle moved about the commission to Convocation,[9] not included in Rushworth but appearing in the Commons' *Journal* are entered in Nalson with words similar to if not exactly like those in the *Journal*. In places Nalson's entries taken from a manuscript Journal seem to clarify

[1] Rushworth, iii, pp. 1147, 1153; *C.J.*, ii, pp. 15, 19.
[2] *The Parliamentary or Constitutional History of England*, viii (London, 1751), pp. 458–59.
[3] Hist. MSS Comm., xxix, *Thirteenth Report*, App. i: Portland MSS, pp. iii–v; *Parl. Hist.*, xxiii, pp. 219–31.
[4] Bond, *Records*, p. 278.
[5] Bodl., MS. Tanner 32, fo 65r; Bodl., MS. Tanner 35, fo 56r.
[6] Hist. MSS Comm., *Thirteenth Report*, App. i.
[7] Nalson, i, p. 332; cf. *C.J.*, ii, p. 11.
[8] Nalson, i, p. 322; *C.J.*, ii, p. 6.
[9] Nalson, i, p. 323; *C.J.*, ii, p. 8.

the printed *Journal*.[1] In other places it is difficult to avoid the conclusion that Nalson is following Rushworth without regard to the Journal. Although he does not confess it, Nalson as well as Rushworth may have felt the pressure of time when preparing his work. Like Rushworth Nalson puts the Commons' division on 30 April in the midst of the vote on shipmoney and declares the vote was about having a conference.[2] He also appears to rely on Rushworth for his version of the Lord Keeper's speech at the Banqueting House and the subsequent speech by Waller.[3]

Nalson's compilation includes some notice of proceedings of the Lords and of the Convocation of the Clergy as well as of the Commons. Neither Rushworth, who had omitted the Lords from his enterprise and given only cursory attention to the Convocation, nor other contemporary sources had treated these proceedings in much detail. Nalson's coverage of the Lords, for which he seems to have relied on the Lords' Journal, is itself far from complete but as far as it goes, it is reasonably accurate.[4] His account of Convocation, based on their Journal or Convocation Book, is more thorough.[5]

Nalson, who charged Rushworth with partisanship, is himself guilty of it in his treatment of the Short Parliament. Polemical introductions and comments are somewhat more extensive than those of Rushworth. The accounts of the Commons' response to the king's message of 2 May offer a contrast. Nalson says, 'Notwithstanding all his Majesty could say, the Presbyterian faction, who were secret Friends to the Scots, and had drawn in a great party of loyal gentlemen with their pretences had gained such an ascendant upon the House that all came to nothing . . .',[6] whereas Rushworth simply reports that the House took the king's message 'into consideration, which held debate till almost six at night, but came to no resolution. . . .'[7] Nalson's selection of material also shows some bias. His inclusion of the king's message to the Lords on 24 April[8] adds to the value of the work, but his omission of Pym's speech of 17 April is hardly justifiable in any journal of the Parliament. Lacking too is any note of the action the Commons took about grievances on 29 April.

Nalson's work like Rushworth's must be considered as a collection

---

[1] For example, the case concerning M.P.'s privileges (Nalson, i, p. 331, Thos. Smith; *C.J.*, ii, p. 10, Vincent and Corbet).
[2] Nalson, i, p. 337; Rushworth, iii, p. 1149.
[3] Nalson, i, pp. 324–29; Rushworth, iii, pp. 1137–43.
[4] For example, Nalson, i, p. 318, and *L.J.*, iv, p. 55; also Nalson, i, p. 323, and *L.J.*, iv, p. 61.
[5] See Esther S. Cope, 'The Short Parliament of 1640 and Convocation', *Journal of Ecclesiastical History*, xxv (1974).
[6] Nalson, i, p. 341; also Nalson, i, p. 330.
[7] Rushworth, iii, p. 1153.   [8] Nalson, i, p. 330.

of material about the Short Parliament. It adds information not in Rushworth and in some instances it improves upon Rushworth's work through use of the official journals. In other instances Nalson's volume appears rather carelessly assembled and no more reliable than Rushworth's

SPEECHES

Copies of speeches are among the most common of extant papers concerning parliamentary proceedings in the early seventeenth century.[1] Their provenance is diverse. Although members may have prepared remarks in advance, they did not actually read speeches in the House. The surviving texts may derive from a member himself, either before or after he spoke, or from the notes or memories of other parliamentarians. Depending on its sources and the amount of revision, the written speech may not be an accurate reflection of what was said. Waller's speech which was printed in 1641 may be an example of those which were distributed but never delivered.[2]

The survival of numerous copies of the parliamentary speeches testifies to their circulation. Contemporaries collected speeches, they copied or assembled them into volumes, such as S.P. 16/450/94; Hunt. Cal., HM 1554;[3] Bodl., MS. Eng. Hist. C.199; or B.L., Add. MS. 6411 (the latter two being simply collections of speeches without the extra material of the two former volumes), or used them in compiling a journal of the Parliament, such as Finch-Hatton MS. 50/Harvard MS. Eng. 982[4] or Worc. Coll. MS. 5.20.[5] The content of speeches at times provoked written response such as that in the note about the wine patent.[6] The speeches, whether or not delivered, communicated to people in Parliament and in the country the central issues of the day.

BILLS

Legislation received relatively little attention during the brief session of Parliament in the spring of 1640. The Crown was primarily interested in supply, and members of the House of Commons devoted most of their time to presentation of grievances. Although statutes might prevent future grievances, none of the petitions of

[1] See *Commons Debates, 1629*, pp. xx–xli.
[2] Below, App., Waller, p. 306.
[3] The speeches in HM 1554 are not actually part of the diary; see above, Perfect Diurnal, Intro, p. 31.
[4] Above, Finch-Hatton MS., p. 26.
[5] Above, Worc. Coll., p. 29. Intro.
[6] Below, Trinity Dublin, p. 260.

grievance specifically sought remedy in that form. There are two papers setting forth topics for parliamentary consideration and possible legislation which may date from the Short Parliament. Enumerated in Sir Robert Harley's *'Quaeres* sent to ye parlt. 1640' are 27 concerns, more than half of which deal with religion but which also include proposals for electoral reform and other matters.[1] A list of 43 points has survived among Lord Montagu's papers.[2] With some, such as pluralism, clerical incomes, and alehouses, mentioned on the Harley list, are others such as shipmoney, coat and conduct money, and impositions on commodities, which are not among the 27 *'Quaeres.'*

Some bills embodying reforms were introduced during the Parliament. There were two each about parliamentary elections[3] and clergymen in lay employments.[4] Both the bill about the Queen's jointure[5] and that about the arms of the kingdom[6] appear to have been those left unfinished in previous parliaments. Royal pressure was successful in pushing the jointure bill through the Lords by 2 May,[7] but there is no evidence that any action was taken on the bill which would have brought some relief to recusants. The jointure bill was the only one to get beyond the committee stage. The Parliament was dissolved before proceedings against grievances themselves had produced much legislation. Probably as a result of this limited legislative activity few relevant papers have survived. There is little more than the draft of one bill, the summary of the contents of another, both of which are given below, and the notes, printed in *CSP 1640* (p. 52), about a third concerning recusants, which was apparently never introduced.

PETITIONS

The meeting of Parliament gave an opportunity for Englishmen to petition for relief from distress. Although petitions might be submitted to king and Council at any time, addresses to Parliament during its sessions were another means of seeking remedy. Some suitors presented their cases to Parliament as well as to king and Council.[8] The Lords' position as a court meant that certain petitions were naturally addressed to them. Not a court in the same sense, the Commons were petitioned as representatives of the nation. The

---

[1] B.L., Loan MS. 29/172 (Portland Papers), *'Quaeres* 1639.'
[2] MSS of the Duke of Buccleuch and Queensberry (Montagu Papers), xiii, 17.
[3] *C.J.*, ii, pp. 14, 16.
[4] Below, App., List of Bills, p. 319.
[5] *L.J.*, iii, p. 872; also P.R.O. 31/3/72, fo 139ʳ.
[6] H.R.O., M36/1, p. 24, p. 209; also *L.J.*, iii, p. 696.
[7] Below, Braye 16, fo 45ᵛ, p. 93.
[8] For example, below, Petition, Oxford Constables (24 April), p. 284.

Lower House apparently received an extraordinary number of petitions in the spring of 1640. 'One bundle of petitions 250' is listed in the 'Note of such things as were brought in by the clerk of the parl[iament] immediately after the dissolution.'[1] It is impossible to tell whether that figure represents all the petitions directed to the Commons. Not all of the petitions specifically mentioned in accounts of proceedings have survived, and there are also general references to petitions from the country.[2] The Commons' response to the petitions and the Council's efforts after dissolution to inquire about their preparation and collect those which had been submitted to the Lower House testify to the significance of the petitions.[3]

In some communities petitions were prepared and approved in connection with elections.[4] The petitions were then given to those chosen as members to be taken to Westminster. In addition to the petitions addressed to the House of Commons from freeholders, citizens, or burgesses, were those to either House from individuals, such as Peter Smart,[5] who was engaged in a struggle to free himself from the penalties imposed upon him by ecclesiastical authorities, or Archibald Niccoll,[6] who was trying to recover money lost in a maritime venture.

Both Houses had established procedures for handling petitions. Because of their reliance upon committees for this, our knowledge of the details of proceedings is limited. Among the Main Papers in the House of Lords Record Office are petitions dating from the Short Parliament but not mentioned in the Journals or diaries.[7] Although these may have been prepared and not presented, they may have been handled in committee.

The same circumstances which curtailed the legislative achievements of the Short Parliament affected its activity with regard to petitions. Investigations were initiated, and a few remedial measures authorized. The Commons incorporated some of the complaints in their resolutions about grievances,[8] but the proceedings concerning petitions remained unfinished when the Parliament was dissolved.

---

[1] S.P. 16/452/30.
[2] Finch-Hatton MS., p. 59, below, p. 174; also *C.J.*, ii, p. 11.
[3] S.P. 16/453/24 and S.P. 16/453/52; H.L.R.O., Main Papers, 11 May 1640 (evidence Lords handled petitions after 5 May).
[4] For example, below, Petition, Northampton (17 April), p. 290.
[5] Below, Petition, Smart (22 April), p. 280.
[6] Below, Petition, Niccoll (22 April), p. 283.
[7] Hist. MSS Comm., *Fourth Report*, App., pp. 24–25.
[8] For example, below, Finch-Hatton MS., p. 59; Petition, Essex, pp. 174, 275.

BRIEF CALENDAR OF THE SHORT PARLIAMENT

MONDAY, 13 APRIL 1640

Members of House of Commons take oaths of allegiance and supremacy. Service in Westminster Abbey with the king in attendance. Formal opening: king and Lord Keeper speak to members of both Houses in the House of Lords; letter from the Scots to the French king read.

TUESDAY, 14 APRIL 1640

Neither House sits.

WEDNESDAY, 15 APRIL 1640

Lords and Commons meet together for presentation of the Speaker, Sergeant Glanville, to the king; speeches of the Speaker, Lord Keeper, and king.

THURSDAY, 16 APRIL 1640

Lords:	*Commons:*
Introduction of new lords	Orders about committees; committee of privileges appointed
Committees of privileges and petitions appointed	Secretary Windebanke reports examination of Lord Loudon about the Scots' letter
Lord Cottington reports examination of Lord Loudon about the Scots' letter	Speeches of Grimston, Rudyerd, and Seymour about grievances
Dispute about adjourning for Convocation the next day	

FRIDAY, 17 APRIL 1640

Lords:	*Commons:*
Not sitting (Convocation meets)	Speaker reports Lord Keeper's speech of 13 April
	Speeches of Rous and Pym about grievances
	Petitions of grievances presented

SATURDAY, 18 APRIL 1640

Lords:	*Commons:*
Lord Keeper sick	Speech of Hyde about court of honour
Prince of Wales and others introduced	Other speeches and petitions about grievances

Lords: (cont.)

Questions about Bishop Manwaring

Miscellaneous other business

Commons: (cont.)

Debate about proceedings and dissolution in 1629

Various records sent for

SUNDAY, 19 APRIL 1640

Neither House sits.

MONDAY, 20 APRIL 1640

Lords:

Miscellaneous business

Commons:

Debate about 1629

Miscellaneous other business

TUESDAY, 21 APRIL 1640

Lords:

Message from Commons for joint petition for a fast; Lords agree

Order about Bishop Manwaring

Commons:

Complaint about the commission to Convocation

Other proceedings about grievances

Afternoon: *Lords and Commons* called to Banqueting House to hear speech from the Lord Keeper

WEDNESDAY, 22 APRIL 1640

Lords:

Lord Keeper reports his speech of day before

Miscellaneous business

(Convocation sits; some prelates excused because of Parliamentary business)

Commons:

Lord Keeper's speech of day before reported; debate about it deferred until next day

Afternoon: *Conference* about proposed fast

THURSDAY, 23 APRIL 1640

Lords:

Earl of Strafford introduced

Miscellaneous business

Commons:

Debate about Lord Keeper's speech of 21 April: supply and grievances; [Waller's speech?]

Agree to consult with Lords about grievances

FRIDAY, 24 APRIL 1640

Lords:
King comes and speaks
Long debate about king's speech;
resolve that supply should have
priority and to inform Commons
of the vote at a conference

Commons:
Erle reports heads of grievances
for a conference with Lords;
heads concerning religion and
property approved; action on
head about Parliament de-
ferred

SATURDAY, 25 APRIL 1640

Lords:
Preparations for conference

Commons:
Miscellaneous business

Conference: Lords inform Commons about king's speech
and Lords resolutions concerning supply

(Convocation sits, hereafter repeatedly adjourned without
doing business until 13 May)

SUNDAY, 26 APRIL 1640
Neither House sits.

MONDAY, 27 APRIL 1640

Lords:
Miscellaneous business

Commons:
Mr Solicitor Herbert reports
conf. of 25 April
Debate and resolve privileges
violated; committee to prepare address to Lords

TUESDAY, 28 APRIL 1640

Lords:
King's message about Manwaring
Miscellaneous business

Commons:
Miscellaneous business
Preparation for conference

Conference: Pym presents Commons protest that Lords
violated Commons privileges in conference 25 April

WEDNESDAY, 29 APRIL 1640

Lords:
Lord Keeper reports conference
Long debate about Commons pro-
test
Resolve Lords had not violated
Commons' privileges by voting
supply priority

Commons:
Erle reports particular points
cerning religion for con-
ference about grievances
[Eliot's speech?]
Miscellaneous business

THURSDAY, 30 APRIL 1640

Lords:
Continue debate about Commons
  protest
Resolve privileges not violated by
  hearing king report Commons
  action
Other business

Commons:
Debate about shipmoney
Miscellaneous other business

FRIDAY, 1 MAY 1640

Lords:
Preparations for conference
Miscellaneous other business

Commons:
Discussion of religious grie-
  vances; complaint about Dr
  Beale

Conference: Lords deny violating Commons' privileges
at previous conference

SATURDAY, 2 MAY 1640

Lords:
Miscellaneous business

Commons:
Conference reported
Vane brings message that king
  wants answer that day
  whether Commons will vote
  supply; long debate; resolve
  to ask king for more time

SUNDAY, 3 MAY 1640
Neither House sits.

MONDAY, 4 MAY 1640

Lords:
Miscellaneous business

Commons:
Vane brings message that king
  will exchange shipmoney for
  12 subsidies; wants answer
  that day; long debate; ask for
  more time

TUESDAY, 5 MAY 1640
Both Houses ordered to attend the king in the Lords'
House; the king speaks briefly and then orders the Lord
Keeper to dissolve Parliament.

II. TEXTS: LORDS*

[*H.L.R.O., Braye MS. 16*]   [*13 April 1640, House of Lords*]
[*fo 3ʳ*]   **THE 13 APRILE 1640**
[*See L.J., iv, pp. 45–49*]
The first daie of the Parliament, 16 *Caroli Rex.*

The Kinge being assended his Royall throne in his Regall Roabes made this declaracion to the Lords Spirituall and Temporall of the High Court of parlement and to the House of Commons.[1]

[*LORD KEEPER*].[2] Writt to hould a parlement, gen[*eral*], ancient counsell of this, choice object to regall view; all share in these counsell yt concernes peece of [ye] kingdome.

harts fill with Zeale.

Rejoyce at this dayes meeting, out of [f]atherly affeccon of this people.

those couns[*els*] attend to his Majeste honor and comfort of all.

Beware how to aime at the guiding of the charrit.

he never layes by his fatherly [affeccon] *care.*

His Majest word and great judg[*ment*] hath prevented danger and kept up the [honor of ye] English Crowne. Our fleece is dry [when it hath rained blood]; all other nations [tents are] bloody. To prevent daunger and dishoner yt knocks at our Gates.

A wise K yt made a match with Scotland with his eldest daughter.

K J[*ames*] made his entrance with blood and not by bloodsheed.

His Majest became heire to his vertues as well as to his kingdome. Peace and Plenty dwell in our Streets.

God found out a Gracious [Queene] *patterne* for his Majesties.

[*fo 3ᵛ*] But said Shebas hath blowne ye trompet to ye disersion of *our peace* [his Majestie];[3]

led a mult[*itude*] affec[*tionate*] into a tumult of disloyalty.

Taken armes against ye L anointed and invested themselves with *disloyaltie* [regall power and authority].

[They tooke upon them] to outface his Royall armies with one of their owne.

He choice rather upon their promise to retreate.

---

* See p. 13 for editorial practices in this volume.
[1] The king spoke briefly, but Browne made no notes. See App., Charles I (13 April), Montague Papers, pp. 1–1b, below, pp. 293–96. Rossetti's dispatch says the king's face was very melancholy (P.R.O., 31/9/18, fos 181ʳ–83ʳ).
[2] John, 1st Baron Finch of Fordwich. Below, App. (13 April), p. 293.
[3] 2 Sam. 20.

They have Prevaricated with him, etc. Insteed of performing loyaltie, treated with forreine states to yeild themselves to ther protection. Finde out the Posterne Gates.

Ireland is recovered from distemper; ordered, and Civilized, and gave accept[able] testimonies.[1] Scotland remaines only as [a] distempered body. To reduce them to a modest condition. Not indure his Majestys [honour] should be weighed at a common beame, etc. Charge will amount to a very great some. Most of his owne revenues have ben expended to a publique good.

Parlement called to prevent mutinous behaviour and Common preservation. *Common Particuler* causes maye admitt no deliberacion, but generall not.

Majest desir for awhile [to] lay asid all other busines and hasten the payment. Majest would not propose anything [out of ordinary course if necessity were not yt] 300^m or 400^m,[2] else not secure Carlile nor Barwicke. Tonadge and Poundage only [he] takes *de facto*, untill the Parlement grant it. This with the bill of Subsidies his Majestie expects this session and presently to be levyed and take his [*fo 4^r*] royall worde that afterward [he will] grant [yor] Peticons for ye [graevances of the] Commonwealth etc. and perfect toward winter and then stay untill just grevances [are heard, and redressed] and goe along with ye for a happy conclusion of this parlement.

A letter intercepted to ye French from the Scotts which the K produced.[3]

[Superscription,] *Au Roy* which Style of France is only thus after the French manner. [Is never to any K. but their owne.] Rothes; Montros; Lesley; Mar; Montgom/*ery*/; Louden; Forrester.

I have assigned a war[*ran*]t for Lowden [to be close prisoner]. Colvile did carry ye l[*et*]tre as I think yt.

Commons to present a Speaker on Wednesde next, at 2 *post meridie*.

This daie was reade the names of the Receavours and Triers of Peticions for Engl[*and*], *Escosse*, and *d'Ireland* and *Gascoigne et de autres terres pars de par le mere et des Isles*, etc.[4]

---

[1] The Declaration of the Irish Parliament which accompanied the grant of subsidies (Rushworth, iii, p. 1100); see below, Braye 16, fos 17^v, 24, pp. 67–74.

[2] The king's contribution (*L.J.*, iv, p. 47); *cf.* the *Declaration* (B.L., E.203(1), pp. 7–8); after having 'emptied his own coffers', he borrowed this amount from his servants.

[3] *L.J.*, iv, p. 48, gives the letter. See also Montagu Papers, p. 1b, below, p. 96.

[4] The names appear in *L.J.*, iv, pp. 48–49; also D.J., pp. 1–3; Yale, Stanford (Braye) MS. 95, fos 117^r–17^v. Fo 4^v is blank.

[*H.L.R.O., Braye MS. 16*]   [*15 April 1640, House of Lords*]

[*fo 5ʳ*]   **WEDNESDAIE, YE 15 APRILE 1640**

[*See L.J., iv. pp. 49–54*]

The K assended in his Throne and the Prince on his left hand [uncovered]. The Commons present Sr Glanville, who was brought in betweene Sr Francis Wind[*ebanke*] and Sr Henry Vane,[1] and making his obeyanc, [*blank*].

[*SPEAKER*].[2] Maye it please ye Kts. etc. Councell. The best Guide is ancient priviledge. They have chosen their [mouth] *Speaker* indee[*d*] their servant to steere skillfully, and to present their pet[*ition*]s with truth and lustre to yr Majest. Yr Majest [wisdome], knowledges how to choose. The H.C. is at this tyme to have busines weighty and considerable. Myne Imp[*erfections*] and abil[*ities*] best knowne to my selfe. A learned age wherein we live, and the house of C. a quintescence of the whole Kingdome. I most humbly bes[*eech*] yr Majest as ye father of the Commonwealth.

Ready to faint with feare before ye burden comes upon me. A harty aff[*ection*] to serve, but little abilities, once more to comand H.C. to choose another etc.

LORD KEEPER Answere. [First upon his Knees advised with the K.] His Majest gave a gre[*at*] and Prin[*cely*] Int[*erest*] to yor learned speach of flowers of elloquence and Reason, and finds nothing said to disagree from him. You have set forth soe much of yor owne abilitis; and have moulded it in so apt questions, etc.

[*fo 5ᵛ*] His Majest tooke notice of his private carriage befor him. An occasion to shewe abil[*ities*] and candor and discharge himselfe soe as his Majestie maye [conferre] *deserve* more.

[*SPEAKER*]. My Prof[*fession*] hath taught yt from the high seate of Justice there is no appeale. I beseech Al[*mighty*] God to enable me to conforme to yor good pleasure.

Two enimies I feare: 1. Expect[*ations*]. 2. Jelousis. Not worth ye 1. I contemne ye other. Zeal to serve G[*od*] and my deare Country. I hope no of this nation [an enimie] of an Anti-monarchiall Gov[*ern*]-m[*en*]t. If any, I wish they may be discovered. A G[*ood?*] K. at all tymes, but nowe Great in glory. To behold you thus in peace and safety after 15 yeares, cannot but increase my Joye.

Populo vitando.

Scotland yor birthplace. God make them ever sensible of that

---

[1] The Secretaries of State. Windebanke sat for Oxford University; Vane, also Treasurer of the Household, for Wilton.

[2] Sir John Glanville (Bristol). See below, App. (15 April), p. 294. Extensions are supplied from *L.J.*, iv, pp. 50–54.

hapines. Ireland becomes apace like Engl[an]d. France is in attend-[ance] by yor stile and title.

The temperam[en]t of Law and Justice.

Those commands voide and the K. Innocent for the breaking of his Just Prerogative.

What difference in law betw[een] [no] *a void* command and a voide command in Lawe.

[*fo 6ʳ*] I begg pardon to say these.

1. Set tymes for prayers as yor Majest have done. 2. An other Exceeding to educate child in true Relig[*ion*]. 3. A patent hearer of Justice before. 4. Your Answere to ye Peticon, *soit fait droit*, etc.

Your Majest remembers with tendernes of hart yt they were Christ[*ian*]s.

No Instructions from the House of Comons. [Bps] Relig[*ion*] and [T[*emporal*] Lord[s]] Chivalry. The best way to maint[*ain*] peace, is to be ready for war.

Judges to advance good ould lawes and wholsome good newe stat[*utes*].

Trade and Comerce did furnish us with gold and silver, yt Trades-[*men*] and merch[*an*]ts maye have encouragem[en]ts.

To Knitt such a Knott betweene the head and ye memb[*er*]s and soe ye Jes[*uits*] who would be glad to have division.

And Lib[*erties*]: 1. Serv[*an*]ts and of H. free from Arrest; 2. Freed[*om of*] Speach; 3. Accesse with comp[*etent*] nombers. 4. Grac[*e*] make best construccons and mine p[*ar*]tic[*ular*]ly.

L K[*EEPER*]. Kneeled to the K. and Answered him from the K. as followeth. [*fo 6ᵛ*] Mr. Speaker, Majest no less pleased by yor modest[*y*] then what you have now said.

You lift up your thought aright, next to ye throne for acceptation. Few soules to base to be receave[*d in*]to [an honest] brest.

A monark and hereditary. A large feild to walk in.

Justly and rightly summed all our happines, his Majestys Piety, his Justice. No blood drawne but in petty and p[*ar*]ticuler cases.

Let them be Anathama. A Joyefull acclaim and I mak noe doubt but yor harts doe rejoyce too.[1]

1. Religion is that which must be afore all other things, happ[*iness*] we have soe long enjoyed.

2. Bps. Eliah tooke up his mantle[2] when he had ye Prophets spirit doubled upon him.

3. Judges and Sergeants, etc. less reason to be excused as ever Judges hand have Ex[*cused*] and Lib[*erated*].

---

[1] Members interrupted with humming here (*L.J.*, iv, p. 53; *cf.* Montagu Papers, p. 1c, below, p. 97).
[2] Elisha took up the mantle of Elijah (2 Kings 2:14).

4. Chivaleirs in nomber greater then their Anc[*estors*]. I hope never forget their Anc[*estors*] actions, nor stay theire owne for obed[*ience*] and magna[*ni*]m[*ity*].

5. Trade is the E. and W. Indies of our Nation.

Unity, *Si sumus unanimes, sumus insuperabiles*. There will not [*lack*] talk from abroad, nor at home by [*fo 7ʳ*] peevish and malicious spirits.

Nothing takes a good nature soe much as an Ingenious confession.

As full and as free as ever Predec[*essors*] in any Parlements before.

[*KING*]. Truly to report.

A willing eare to all your just grevances.[1]

Ad[*usque*]; *crast*[*inum*] 8 clocke.

[H.L.R.O., Braye MS. 16]   **[16 April 1640, House of Lords]**

[*fo 8ʳ*]   **AD HUC 16º APRILIS 1640**

[*see L.J., iv. pp. 54–56*]

Praiers.

The Prince was present.

These Ls yt come in by *dissent* [creacon since ye last parlement and are nowe ready] to be brought into the House this day and as many as are not present, the rest the next meeting.

This daie my Lo Mowbraie[2] was brought [betweene the L Strange and Lord North][3] into the House and Garter [who went before] and delivered his writ to the Lo. Keep who delivered it unto the Clerke[4] and he reade it, and it was agreed by *the whole House* that he should take his place *above*[5] *all Barons*.

My Lord Herbert [de Cherbery] was like brought into the House betweene the Lo Newn[ham Paddox] and the Lord Goring [and placed betweene my Lord Powis and Cottington].[6] Garter as above said and the writt, being delivered unto my Lord Keep, he delivered it unto the Clerke and it was reade and he was placed, etc.

The Lord Keep was brought into the House being conducted by the Gent[*leman*] Usher E[*arl*] Ar[*undel*] [and Lo High Chamb[*erlain*][7]]

---

[1] *Cf.* D.J., p. 8, and *L.J.*, iv, p. 54.

[2] William, 10th Baron Mowbray. Many revisions in MS. See also D.J., p. 9, and Montagu Papers, p. 1c, below, p. 97.

[3] James Stanley, Baron Strange; Dudley, 3rd Baron North.

[4] John Browne.

[5] *according* also crossed out in MS.

[6] Edward, 1st Baron Herbert of Cherbury; Basil, Lord Newnham-Paddox, later earl of Denbigh; George, 1st Baron Goring; William Herbert, 1st Baron Powis; Francis, 1st Baron Cottington.

[7] James Maxwell, Gentleman Usher of the Black Rod; Thomas Howard, 2nd earl of Arundel, earl Marshal; Robert Bertie, 1st earl of Lindsey, Lord High Chamberlain.

and betweene the L. Strange and Lord Mowbray and the L Keep was brought up to the chaire of state, and there Garder layd his Pattent which was taken from thence by Mr Maxwell and deliverd to my L Keep who gave unto the Clerke and soe brought to his place as a Baron, and afterwards tooke his place as Lo Keep upon the woolsacke.

[*fo 8ᵛ*] My L COTT[*INGTON*]¹ delivered from his Majest, [that] he and Att[*orney*]² did examine my Lo Louden at the Tower upon diverse Inter[*rogatories*], found him very wary, and said he ought not to be examined here because a Peere of Scotland, but at last he answered, [*that it was*] like his hand *and signet*, In the ende he did confess his hand, *and seale*, and that he did *sende*, and remember [the letter], *the same*, not understanding French did *knowe that it was* to implore aide [conceave it had been for a mediation to the French Kinge].

He confessed that it was to be sent by one Colvile, a servant of the French Kinge, who was then in Edenborough.

[*blank*] by L SAY.³ Order doth preserve substance.

Ordered, that though my Lo Cottingham[*sic*] was not *brought* [introducted] into the House in his Roabes, being upon a speciall occation remitted, yet this shall not be a president *for hereafter*; and [thereupon was admitted to deliver the Ks. message, as a member of the House, concerning Lowden].

The originall lettre in French was reade.

L MOUNTAGUE. Demanded the date and the tyme when the l[*et*]tre was writt.⁴

L COTT[*INGTON*]. Said Lowden confest it was about the same tyme as his Majestie was in Scotland.

Agreed by the Ll. that the orders be reade [first] before the House is called.⁵

[*fo 9ʳ*] The *French* [Scotts] l[*et*]tre in French was delivered againe to my L Cottington.

The L CHAMBERLEINE and other Ls did desire that the l[*et*]tre maye be reade in English.⁶

The Roule of orders was this day reade⁷ and the House is to be called upon Satterday next.

¹ See Harvard MS., fos 20ᵛ–21, Montagu Papers, p. 1c, below, pp. 134, 197; also *CSP 1640*, pp. 29–30 (the interrogatories and answers).
² Sir John Bankes.   ³ William Fiennes, 1st Viscount Say and Sele.
⁴ Edward, 1st Baron Montagu of Boughton. Montagu Papers, pp. 1c–d, below, p. 97; also David Stevenson, *The Covenanters and the Government of Scotland, 1637–1651* (Ph.D. thesis, Glasgow, 1970), i, pp. 145, 207–15.
⁵ See Montagu Papers, p. 1d, below, p. 97.
⁶ Philip Herbert, earl of Pembroke. The letter was not read in English (Montagu Papers, p. 1c, below, p. 97).
⁷ See Lee-Warner, p. 2, below, p. 107.

Committees for the Priviledges, etc.[1] 1 Ar. Cant.; 2 Lo. Treas. B. London; 3 Lo. P. Seale; 6 E. Marshall; 13 Co. Bedford; 25 Co. Clare; 20 Co. Warwick; 18 Co. *Sarum*; 19 Co. Northton; 16 Co. Lincolne; 14 Co. Hartford; 7 Co. Northumberland; 5 Co. Great Chamb; 31 V. Say et Seale; 23 Co. Bristoll; 8 Chamblain; 10 Co. Huntington; 22 Co. March; 21 Co. Cambridge; 24 Co. Holland; 15 Co. Essex; 11 Co. Bath; 12 Co. Southton; 26 Co. Bullingbroke; 27 Co. Barkshire; 17 Co. Dorsett; 9 Co. Ruttland; 29 Co. Newcastle; 30 Co. Portland; 4 Winchester; 28 Co. Cleaveland; 32 Bridgewater.[2] [*fo 9ᵛ*] 2 B. *Sarum*; 1 B. Winchest; 7 B. Ely; 9 B. Chichester; 5 B. Norwich; 6 B. Oxford; 4 B. *Exon*; 8 B. Rochester; 3 B. Co[*ventry*] et Litchfeild. 1 D. Mowbray; 8 D. Kimbolton; 7 D. North; 6 D. Paget; 13 D. Roberts; 23 D. Cottington; 18 D. Howard; 11 D. Mountague; 20 D. Savile; 22 D. Herbert; 12 D. Grey de Werke; 15 D. Lovelace; 19 D. Goringe; 17 D. Maynard; 16 D. Pawlett; 2 D. Clifford; 14 D. Faulkonbridge; 10 D. Brooke; 5 D. Willoughby de Parrum; 9 D. Newnham Paddox; 3 D. Strange; 4 D. Wharton; 21 D. Dunsmore. Mondays, 2 *hora*, p[*ain*]t[*ed*] Chamber. They or any 7 in nomber, Tues[*days*] and Thursdays, p[*ain*]t[*ed*] Ch[*amber*], *post. med.*, 2 *hora*.

Subcommittee 9 E; 7 Barons; 2 Visc; 4 Bps. 1 Co. Privy Seale; 2 Co. Huntington; 4 Co. Essex; 6 Co. Warwick; 7 Co. Bristoll; 3 Co. Hartford; 5 Co. Lincolne; 8 Co. Bridgewater; 8 Visc. Say et Seale; 9 Visc. Campden. 2 Bp. *Sarum*; 4 Bp. Elye; 1 Bp. Winchester; 3 Bp. Norwich. To meete Satterdaies Saterday 2 *hora*, *post. med.*, p[*ain*]t[*ed*] ch[*amber*] [*fo 10ʳ*] 4 D. Montague; 5 D. Grey de Werk; 3 D. Brooke; 1 D. Mowbray; 6 D. Roberts; 2 D. North; 7 D. Falkonbridg.

Committees for Petitions: N. 43; 16 Co.; 16 B.; *2 V.*; 8 B.; 14 Co. Cleveland; 5 Co. Hartford; 6 Co. Essex; 1 Co. Rutland; 18 V. Say and Seale; 2 Co. Bath; 9 Co. Warwick; 7 Co. Dorset; 11 Co. Holland; 15 Co. Newport; 8 Co. *Sarum*; 4 Co. Bedford; 3 Co. Southton; 10 Co. Bristoll; 12 Co. Bullingbrook; 13 Barkshire; 17 Bridgewater; [27]. 8 B. Peterburgh; 2 B. *Sarum*; 7 B. Chichester; 3 B. *Exon*; 1 B. Winchester; 5 B. Ely; 6 B. Rochester; 4 B. Oxford; [8]. D. 11 Howard; 6 Mountague; 5 Brook; 8 Lovelace; 13 Savill; 2 Pagett; 3 North; 16 Cottington; 7 Grey de werke; Kimbolton; 14 Dunsmore;

---

[1] See Montagu Papers, p. 1d, below, p. 98. *Cf.* D.J., pp. 12–13, and *L.J.*, iv, pp. 55–56. Browne used the numbers before each of the names to arrange the lords of each rank in order of precedence. In some of the committee lists he also included the total number in each category, either at the beginning, as in the Subcommittee of privileges and/or prior to the groups as in the Committee for petitions. His figures do not always balance. The additions and deletions of names shown on the manuscript are probably responsible for this discrepancy. See, for example, below, Braye 16 (23 April), p. 69, n. 3.

[2] Browne entered here a note about attendants for petitions, apparently realized his error and crossed it out (see below, p. 60, n. 1).

10 Coventry; 1 Clifford; 12 Goring; 15 Herbert; 9 Maynard; [16].
Attend[*an*]ts: Jus[*tice*] Barkeley; Chife Reeve and such others of
their Lods please to appoint.[1]

[*fo 10ᵛ*] Ordered no peticon to be received, delivered, but by the
Lords sitting [at that Committee] and the Peticons to be subscr[*ibed*]
by [the Peticoners] *those that deliver* them.

Lecta, 1a vice. A Bill concerning the dying and dressinge of
Clothes and Kersies.[2]

Calling the House, on Satterday next.

Ad[*usque*] 9 *hora*, Satterday.

L KEEP.[3] In his place, if it had not been very ill, [desire in regard
of his ill health yt the House might be adjourned untill Satterday].

And the Ad[*journment*] *by reason of my Lo Keep motion. It was
moved that in regard the Convocation sitting the next* [*day*]. *L. Committee
to peruse the Journall books at their pleasures, thus ordered to search
whether it hath ben a custome to adjourn the House because of the
Convocacon sitting.*

Huc. usq. eam 18ᵒ die Aprilis.

[H.L.R.O., Braye MS. 16]   **[*18 April 1640, House of Lords*]**

[*fo 11ʳ*]   *DIE SABBATHI* 18 *APRILIS* 1640

[*See L.J., iv. pp, 56–58.*]

Praiers.

The comission reade to enable Sir John Bramston, Lo Cheife
Justice of England, to suply the Lo Keeps place by reason of his
sicknesse, etc. Enter the commiss[*ion*].[4]

Viscount Camden.[5] L Viscount Campden brought into the House
betweene E[*arl of*] Thanett[6] and Lo Newneham Paddox, his writt of
summons reade, and after he was brought into his place by Garter.

Prince. *Signified by the E*[*arl*] *Marshall that the Prince desired his
writ to be reade.* [The Princes writt was reade.]

[1] *Cf.* note crossed out in Braye MS. 16, fo 9ʳ: 'Ls the Judges and the privie
counsellors to attend the Lords. Attendants for petitions: Just[*ice-*] Barkely,
Reeve, and such other of the Ks learned Counsell as they shall please.'

[2] See below, Bills—Cloth, p. 273.

[3] By the standing orders (4, Hist. MSS Comm., x, New Series, *Report on the
MSS of the House of Lords* (London, 1953), p. 1), the Lord Keeper had to speak
as a baron. Montereul noted the procedure (P.R.O. 31/3/72, fo 146ʳ). See
below, Lee Warner, p. 1 (16 April), Montagu Papers, p. 1d, Harl. MS. 4931,
fo 47, Worc. Coll. fo 17, pp. 98, 107, 219–20, 234; also *Oxinden Letters*, p. 163,
and *Harley Letters*, p. 91.

[4] The commission appears in *L.J.*, iv, p. 57. See also below, S.P. 16/451/16,
p. 245.

[5] Edward Noel, 2nd Viscount Campden.

[6] Nicholas Tufton, 2nd earl of Thanet.

Lo Awdley.[1] Lo Audley *introducted* [was likewise brought in] betweene Lo Strange and Lo Newneham Paddox, and because he came in upon a Restitucion, his Pattent was reade, *Teste tertio die Junii, Caroli Nono.* Placed by Garter, etc, in his place betweene etc. [*blank*].

Creacion. Lo Cottington was alsoe introduced, betweene the Lo Mowbray and Lo Strange, and placed in his due place, his patent not reade.

The house was called, etc.[2] Lo Powis excused *not well* [being sicke] but will come; Lord Boteler, a minor; *Lord Mohun; Lord Coventry;* [*fo 11ᵛ*] Lo Brudnell, desired for 7 or 8 dayes [to be excused], p[*roxy*] Lo Marshall; Lo Pawlett, *not well* [sicke] but will [*blank*]; Lo Lovelace. [excuse for a little while], *his wife ill but* [*blank*]; Lo Craven, K leave [to be absent], *but proxie d Lenox;*[3] Lo Arundl Ward[*our*], K leave to be absent, [Prox[*ie*] shall be sent]; Lo Stanhope, Mother dead; Lo Gherrard, very sicke, Proxie *shall* [will] be sent; Lo Eure, Proxie; Lo Cromwell, Ireland; Lo Windsor, Proxie; Lord Vaux, Proxie; Lo Sturton, E[*arl*] *Marshall*, Proxie; [Lo Dudley, Proxie]; Lo Morley, Proxie; L Bareklie [*Berkeley*], *Proxie* will be sent; Lo Aberg[*avenny*], Sicke, [Proxie will be sent]; Bp Chichester, with the Prince; Bp St Davids,[4] *Leave and Proxie*, Proxie shall be sent; [Bp Lincolne];[5] Bp Carlile, leave of Absence but will be here [within] few daies; Bp Chester, Comes with [Strafford], *L Deputy*; Bp Worster [*Worcester*], Gout and aged, Prox[*ie*]; Bp Durham, K command to goe backe, [being coming for London];[6] *B Yorke, Proxie.* Visc[*ount*] Conway, *Ireland,*[7] Proxie shall be sent; Visc[*ount*] Purbeck, not well but Prox[*ie*] [shall be sent], *coming*; Visc[*ount*] Mountague, Proxie; E[*arl*] Strafford, coming;[8] E[*arl*] Chesterfield, Proxie; Earl Carnarvan, *very ill*, [sicke]; E[*arl*] Kingston, [not in Towne but will come], *he will be in Towne to night*; E[*arl*] Stanford, Proxie; E[*arl*] Newecastle, with the Prince [and will be present as often as he maye]; [*fo 12ʳ*] E[*arl*] Rivers, will be here shortly; E[*arl*] Marlborough, Proxie; E[*arl*] Danby, Proxie will be sent; Earl Mulgrave, Proxie; E[*ar*]l Wemsland [*Westmoreland*], he will shortly come;[9] E[*arl*] Middlesex;[10] E[*arl*] Leicester, Proxie;

---

[1] James Touchet, 13th Baron Audley.

[2] *Cf. L.J.*, iv, pp. 57–58, and *D.J.*, pp. 17–18. The proxy book is missing.

[3] James Stuart, 4th Duke of Lennox and earl of March.

[4] See below, Braye 16, fo 15ᵛ, p. 65.

[5] John Williams. He was imprisoned in the Tower of London; see *CSP 1640*, p. 116.

[6] Thomas Morton. A letter of 23 April reports that he visited troops near Durham (*CSP 1640*, p. 64).

[7] Edward, 2nd Viscount Conway. Letters among the State Papers show that he was in the North of England, not Ireland (*CSP 1640*, pp. 26, 43, 53, 64).

[8] See Braye 16, fo 19ᵛ, below, p. 68.

[9] His mother had just died (*CSP 1640*, p. 22).

[10] See Braye 16, fo 45ᵛ, below, p. 94.

c

E[*arl*] Somersett, Proxie; E[*arl*] Exeter, Proxie; Earl Suffolk, *Gout*, [sicke] but will *shortly* come; E[*arl*] Sussex, Proxie; E[*arl*] Cumberland, Proxie; E[*arl*] Worcester, Proxie; Earl Darby, Proxie; E[*arl*] Kent, Proxie; E[*arl*] Shrewsbury, [will send his] Proxie, *sicke*; Archb. Yorke, Proxie; L Keep, sicke; Prince.

LORD [P[*RIVY*] SEALE. Moved the House yt [he] he observed in the service booke certeine words, which hee conceaved to be improper to be applied to the Church of England], *Chatholicke Church of England improper*, and after [some discourse it was] committed to *vizt*.[1]

E[*ARL*] MARS[*HAL*]. To acquaint the Kinge with it.

ARCHB CANT[*ERBURY*].[2] Yt the K be acquainted and consented to.

E[*ARL*] WARWICKE.[3] For not have it Committed and then reported.

E[*ARL*] MARSHALL. Said every Lo takes oath [of] supremacy.

L VIS[*COUNT*] SAY. To committee.

E[*ARL*] MARSHALL. Only a motion of his owne opinion and no taxe.

L VISC[*OUNT*] [*SAY*]. No taxe, no fund[*amental*] of Religion, but only what concernes this house.

BP NORWICH.[4] He maintaine not cryed downe, for we choke the papists [for it]. It comprehends a holy church.

[*fo 12ᵛ*] [Committed to] 1 Archb. Cant.; 3 Lo Privie Seale; 6 Co War[*wick*]; 4 Co. Bedford; 5 Co. Hartford; 7 E Bristoll; 2 Lord Treas; 8 Visc Say. 4 Roberts; 1 [Kimbolton] *Mandevile*; 2 Brook; 3 Grey de werke. *Archb. Cant* 1 B *Sarum*; 2 B *Exon*. 3 B Norwich. Attend[*an*]ts: C. Justice Crooke; Com[*mon*] Pleas; Crawly; Attorney. Presently; Committy Chamber.

ARCHB CANTERBURY. [Reported, yt the Committees have considered of the words in the Booke of Common Praier appointed for the service and finde yt the wordes are not the Chath. Church, but thy Chath Church, and so it was] agreed to stand as it is without alteracon.

L NORWICH.[5] 2 Sign[*ifications*]: 1. catholic, universall; 2. orthodoxall.

L P[*RIVY*] SEALE. Whether Chal[*sic*] England.

E[*ARL*] BRISTOW.[6] Not to quitt ye chatholique, but whether to England, etc.

---

[1] Henry Montagu, 1st earl of Manchester. See Braye 16, fo 12ᵛ, Montagu Papers, p. 2, below, pp. 62, 98. His remarks caught the attention of Rossetti (P.R.O. 31/9/18, fos 202ʳ–204ʳ).

[2] William Laud.   [3] Robert Rich.   [4] Richard Montagu.
[5] The bishop.   [6] John Digby, 1st earl of Bristol.

E[*ARL*] DORSETT.[1] But one word in, instead of, of, in.

L MOUNT[*AGU*].[2] Observes orders.

Oath for alleageance. The Lords are to take the oath of Allegeance upon Monday next.

D[*r*] Manwaringe. The declaracon of the H.C. against Manwaring, Clerk, was reade, And afterwards was reade the Sentence of the Lls upon Dr Manwaringe.[3]

L VISC[*OUNT*] SAY. Yt he struck at the roots, parliament, Lawes, and Lib[*er*]ties not only touch upon Privileged[*ges*] as Peeres, but trench far upon the Constitu[*tion*] of this House. If Judgm[*en*]ts are overthrowne, it will be worse for ye body of the Peres of this House. It will be thing of great consequence.

That this be remonstrated and presented to his Majestie.

E[*ARL*] MARSHALL. Yt it be tenderly handled.

L P[*RIVY*] SEALE. As a penaltie and personall, Majest may remitt.

L DORSETT. [*blank*].

[*fo 13^r*] Committed to the Grand Privildges upon Monday *2⁰* clocke and moved yt what can be alleadged [on ye Bi[*sho*]ps p[*ar*]te], whether *by* [?] [pardon] or Lycense or otherwise, that it maye be produced and seene at the sitting of the Lls Committees for their full [and cleare] informacion and [better] expedition.

Ad[usque]: Monday, *9⁰ hora*.

[H.L.R.O., Braye MS. 16]   [20 April 1640, House of Lords]

[*fo 14^r*]   *AD HUC* 20th *APRILIS* 1640
                          DIE LUNAE

[*See L.J., iv, pp. 58–59*]

Praiers.

Queenes Jointure. This daie was reade an Act intituled the Queenes Jointure. *1e vice lecta.*

It was agreed the Bill concerning her Majestie jointure should be reade ye second tyme, which was accordingly done. [Committee] 1 Archb Cant; 2 Lo Treas; 3 L Privie Seale; 4 C Bedford; 5 Co. Cambridge; 6 Co March. 1 Mowbray; 3 Goringe; 4 Herbert; 2 Pagett. B. 2 Chester; 3 Co[*ventry*] et Litchfield; 1 Winchester; 4 *Exon.* Att[*endant*]s Com[*mon*] Pleas Barkley; Att[*orney*] Gen[*eral*]. Tyme: Tomor[*row*] 8 a clock, p[*ain*]t[*ed*] ch[*amber*].

[1] Edward Sackville.
[2] He may be speaking about the oath of allegiance; Standing Order 43 (Hist. MSS Comm., x, New Series, *House of Lords*, p. 8) required it be taken. See also Braye 16, fo 14ᵛ, Montagu Papers, p. 2, below, pp. 64, 98.
[3] Roger Manwaring, bishop of St. Davids. See *L.J.*, iii, pp. 855–56 (1628), his impeachment.

D[ominus] Fawconbrid[1] taken sicke.

D[ominus] Marshall sicke.

No mention in the [Lord Stanhope's] letter of meniall nor necessary servant.

Ordered. Lo Stanhope *to sett under his hand* [shall averral upon his honor yt he [*Sanderson*], his meniall servant or solicitor or otherwise imployed in his necessary affaires].[2]

[*fo 14ᵛ*] Whereas it was appointed that the oath of Alleageance should have [*been*] given to the Ls Spirituall and Temporall in the high Court [of Parliament assembled on the 18 day of Aprilis],[3] this referred to the [consideration of ye]Grand Com[*mittee*] for Priviledges [before] *whether* there lordships shall take the oath of Allegeance.

L Visc[*ount*] Campden added to the Grand Committee.

Ad[*journed*] untill to mor[*row*] 9 a.

[H.L.R.O., Braye MS. 16]   [*21 April 1640, House of Lords*]

[*fo 15ʳ*]   *DIE MARTIS 21º APRILIS* **1640**

[*See L.J., iv, pp. 60–61*]

Praiers.

Hospitalls. *1a vice lecta est billa.* An Act for the maintenance of Hospitalls and *measons de dieu*, etc.

2a vice lecta est billa for Hospitalls, etc.

A message from the K to attend him with the Commons at Whitehall at one aclocke.

Bill committed.

Committee for hospitall. 1 Arc Cant; 5 E Warwicke; 4 E Dorset; 3 E Bedford; 2 E Bathon. 1 Bp Winchester; 2 B *Sarum*; 3 *Exon.* D 2 Montagu; 3 Pawlet; 4 Maynard; 1 Strange. Att[*endants*]: Crawley. Wednesday afternoone, 4 a clock, p[*ain*]t[*ed*] ch[*amber*].

Message from the H Co. A message [sent] from the Commons by Mr Secretary Windibanke. [ye Lds desire[*d*]] to joine in pet[*ition*] to his Majestie for a fast [generall for a day, first for both houses and afterwards for the *whole* kingdom [in generall] and hope by humil[*ity*] God will blesse the labours of both houses].

[*fo 15ᵛ*] L ARCHB. Moved that the K might be moved in it [*the fast*] and refer it, the tyme to his Majestie.

Answer. Ans[*wer*] to Commons by the L KEEP. That ye Ls doe

---

[1] Thomas Belayse, 1st Viscount Fauconberg.

[2] Charles, 2nd Baron Stanhope. A petition from Sanderson concerning the letter of protection was read (*L.J.*, iv, p. 59). See also Braye 16, fo 45ᵛ, below, p. 94.

[3] *this day* (D.J., p. 22; *L.J.*, iv, p. 59); see also Montagu Papers, p. 3c, below, p. 104.

assent readily and willing to joyne with them and for the tyme, the Lls will knowe ye Ks pleasure.

The L ARCHB OF CANT[ERBURY] reported the busines at the Grand Committee yesterday.

1. Concerninge the Convocacion that the report concerning ye Convocation be entered.[1] *here enter ye report*

Next was taken into consid[eration] the busines conc[erning] Doctor Manwaring.[2]

2. pardons was produced and upon deliberacon concluded on and it was ordered:

1. Record to be searcht: 1. yt [?] to see priviledges, what they were; 2. and if they did see [what is fitt to present to the Kinge] *yt they had* [yr] *their priviledges.*

Moved that the Lords of the Subcommittee or any of them maye search the records concerning the priviledge of the ho[use].

Ordered that Dr Manwaring, [now B of St Davids], *shall* [not] *come and sitt* [in] *this hon[ora]ble House, nor sende his Proxie unto the House, Proxies further direct* [blank].

Ordered Monday next the records be brought to the House, yt the Lords maye determine the cause.

Ordered that upon Monday yt the Records be brought into the [House] that the House maye determine the cause concerning Dr Manwaring.

[fo 16ʳ] Moved that, whereas a Bp of [the Committee] yesterday lett fall some words [that might reflect upon some Lord of the Committee] *(to the displeasinge of the Lord)* that he maye have an admonicion.

The BP [HALL][3] *what said* [yt if anythinge had fell from him he never intended] *he lett fall to the displeasure of the house. Yt he is sorry.*

BP [HALL] *said that if he did saie soe he is sorry.*

L HARTFORD.[4] [He said the Bp] *comparing the Lds to Covenanters.*

E[ARL] B[RISTOL?] Said the lawes of Scotla[nd] are spoken, but on a sudden and yt acknow[ledg]m[en]t maye serve.

L SAY. If insist, then a great [source] of contentment to the Scotts, for they have the same arguments. You must not then come soe neare them, and admon[ition] to be given.

B [HALL]. *I am sorry to thinke He is very sorry for it and their Lps were sorry for it.*

Ordered: L Arch Cant[erbury] and Lo Chamberleine to waite upon the Kinge to knowe the tyme when their Ll [and Commons] shall waite upon the K about the fast.

[1] *L.J.*, iv, p. 61, gives the report; see also Lee Warner, p. 2 (18, 21 April), Montagu Papers, p. 2, below, pp. 108, 99.

[2] Revisions in MS. See also Montagu Papers, p. 2, below, p. 99.

[3] Joseph Hall, bishop of Exeter. See below, Montagu Papers, p. 2b, Harl. MS. 4931, fo 47ᵛ, pp. 99, 236.   [4] William Seymour, 10th earl of Hertford.

The Committee for Peticons ad[*journed*] untill this afternoone at 3 of the clocke.

Ad[*journed*]: untill to mor[*row*] morning 9ᵃ *hora.*

[H.L.R.O., Braye MS. 16]   **[22 April 1640, House of Lords]**

[*fo 17ʳ*]   *DIE MERCURII* 22ᵗʰ *APRILIS* **1640**

[*See L.J., iv, pp. 61–64*]

Praiers.

The Lo Keep reported the effect of the Ks pleasure at the meeting of both Houses yesterday.

LORD KEEPER.[1] The cause of the causing and the motives were as great as every [*sic*] any K had. Yt the suply was to be speedy for [*blank*] 100 th[*ousand*] a m[*on*]t[*h*][2] [*blank*]. Such a supply for present designes yt they be not lost.

[*His*] Majeste [*took*] notice of some scrupels [in the] ship busines. The King never intend[*ed*] here [?] to make a profitt, but what collected p[*ai*]d to Sr Wm Russell[3] and acco[*unt*] made [*to*] counsell [*of*] every penny spent, besides other ordinary expendsion. To preserve dom[*inion of the*] seas and to preserve trade and comerce. Never intended benefitt to his Majestie.

The mat[*ter*] this yeare resol[*ved*], no writts.

Resolut[*ion*] necess[*ary*] to send Army to Scotland.[4] Preparacon by other neigb[*ouring*] nations. That Algiers makes great prepar-[*ations*], 60 ships. Rebecca worth 260 *m.*[5]

[*fo 17ᵛ*] His Majestie could not have suply soe soone by Parlement as his occasion.

No thought but keep up ye glory of this nation and to be rendred consid[*erable*]. Fe fall [?*faithfull*] to his freinds, and to preserve all in safety, comerce and peace. Not wedded to this way, but yt if any other way might be found to make it up some other way, it shall be dispend[*ed*].

Nothing can be desired of his Majestie hereafter but he will be forward in it.

1. To put obligacons of trust upon his Majestie.

---

[1] See below, App. (21 April), p. 303.
[2] See also Braye 16, fo 23, below, p. 73.
[3] Treasurer of the Navy. For example, see *CSP 1640*, p. 23.
[4] '. . . *during which time it was requisite the seas should be well-guarded*' (B.L., E.203(1), p. 12); *cf.* B.L., Add. MS. 11045, fo 81ᵛ, 'It was never his majesties intention that they should be stopped' (Rossingham to Scudamore, 9 December 1639).
[5] The ship had been lost (*L.J.*, iv, p. 62; also B.L., Add. MS. 11045 fos 109ᵛ, 111ʳ).

2. More secure from feares and jealousi then can otherwise be thought.

3. Agrees with his owne great nature, he stands upon his honor and thinks scorne people should out goe him in kindnes, they cannot expresse soe much, as he will requite.

Example for Incouragment. Ireland gave sub[*sidy*] 2d day, relyed upon his grace and goodnes with advantage. This Parlement alsoe 4 sub[*sidies*] more and his Majests resolu[*tion*] [*fo 18*ʳ] that relying upon them he will be aforehand with them.

He values England befor all ye rest of his K[*ing*]dom.

Lords alone, though suply from the House of Commons.

1. Wittness of important reason. 2. Wittnes of Gracious Express-[*ion*] to all his subjects. Yt if ye H C should faile, yet yor L concur in ye preservacon of yours and keepe up the preservacon of the kingdom.[1]

Tonage and poundage cannot [of itselfe] keepe such a fleet at sea, with[*out*] further supplyes.

LO CHAMBERLEINE reported about the fast. His Majestie likes it well and referres it unto the Lords for ye day and tyme. Moved to acquaint [*H C with*] his Majestie [*answer*].

Conference about ye fast yt 3 clock [this] afternoone, P[*ain*]t[*ed*] ch[amber].[2] L Cheife Justice. Jones. [*Messengers to H C*] Desire a conference with 12 about pet[*ition*] about the fast [1. tyme. and place and other circumstances]. Ye king hath pleased to consent to it and likes it very well.

[*fo 18*ᵛ] Committee of conference with H C about the fast: L Chambl; E Bristow; E Bedford; E Essex; L Treas; B Winchester; B *Sarum*; B Chester; L 2 Kimbolton; 4 Grey; 3 Brook; 1 Pagget.

LO KEEP.[3] That many protections are sould upon downe Towne and conceived to be counterfeited.

Order. Send for the p[*ar*]ty [against] to morrow morning by the officer and to attend the Lo Cheife Justice. Und[*er*] Lo Morleys name.[4] [And such others as Lo Ch[*ie*]f Just[*ic*]e can apprehend.]

A motion moved concerning [abuses of Alehouses and] Pages and Footemen. Those yt keepe tavernes to be sent for to[*morrow*] morning.

An order was reade made *16° Marcii* 1623, *21° Jac.*[5]

---

[1] See Braye 16, fo 21, below, p. 70.
[2] See below, Montagu Papers, p. 2c, Finch-Hatton MS., p. 53, Lee-Warner, p. 3 (22 April), pp. 100, 109, 167.
[3] *Cf.* Montagu Papers, p. 2c, below, p. 100.
[4] Henry Parker, 14th Baron Morley. See H.L.R.O., Main Papers, 22 April 1640, the warrant.
[5] *L.J.*, iii, p. 264; also *L.J.*, iii, pp. 446, 691, and below, Montagu Papers, p. 2c, Lee Warner, p. 3 (22 April), pp. 100, 109.

Lord Cheife [*Justice*] etc. returned an[*swer*]. [*H C would be*] ready at tyme and place with double nomber of committees *according their custome.*[1]

Ad[*usque*] tomor[*row*] 9 *hora.*

[H.L.R.O., Braye MS. 16]   **[23 April 1640, House of Lords]**

[*fo 19ʳ*]   *DIE JOVIS* 23th *APRILIS* 1640

[*See L.J., iv, pp. 64–65*]

Praiers.

L B *Sarum* excused, being sicke.

L STANHOPE. averred under hand and seale, [dated 21 Aprill 1640], yt Sanderson is his meniall servant, etc.

Ordered. The p[*ar*]ties [all] to be sent for, menconed in the peticon.

Bradshaw.[2] The examination of Edward Bradshaw was reade, concerning the counterfeiting of three protections under hand and seale of the Lo Morleys. Bradshaw brought to barr. He confest he did bespeake a seale to be cutt and did [tell] *see Marston,* the seale cutter, that he had lost the Lo Morely seale and soe bespoke another and sould the three to Kynnaston for 3ˡⁱ.

Seale cuttor to be realest and Kynaston. Bradshaw to be bound backe to the [Fleete]; *K. Bench* [Cheape and Westm[*inster*] pillory; bound and restrained to ye House [*of*] Correction untill sufficient suerties [of] good behavior, Fine. 100ˡⁱ men for sureties.] To morrow, 11 a clocke executed.

1 a plaine confession; 2 a plaine forgery.

[*Voting:*[3] *Contents 19; Not Contents 39.*]

Bagshaw [*sic*] kneed at ye barr. Ye Lo Keep pronounced the sentence.

[*fo 19ᵛ*] E[*arl of*] Strafford brought into the [*blank*], E[*arl of*] Strafford brought into ye house betweene the E[*arl*] of Cleaveland and the E[*arl*] of Clare, etc. and brought to his place, next belowe, *vide* the date of the Pattent.[4]

Moved that the earle of Strafford be added to the [*Grand*] *Committee of Privildges.*

Pages and Footemen. Moved that in regard of the disorders of [pages], footemen, and tavernes there might [*be*] consideracon taken

---

1 *manner* (D.J., p. 27).

2 Many revisions in MS. H.L.R.O., Main Papers, 23 April 1640, orders about Bradshaw.

3 The question is not indicated clearly. See also Montagu Papers, p. 2c, below, p. 101.

4 Thomas Wentworth, 1st earl of Strafford, Lord Deputy of Ireland; Thomas Wentworth, earl of Cleveland, cousin to Strafford; John Holles, 2nd earl of Clare.

for preventing abuses. it committed [*to*] these Lords supr[*a*] after to present to ye House. 1 L Chamber[*lain*]; 3 L Vis Say; *Hartford;* *Bedford*; 2 E Dorsett. D 1 Pagett; 3 Mountague; 4 Savill; 2 North. To mor[*row*] after[*noon*], 3 clocke, P[*ain*]t[*ed*] Chamb[*er*]. They or four of them.

L CHAMB[*ER*]L[*AIN*]. Reported confer[*ence*] about [the fast]. [*H C*] Came without order [to appoint a day] and will returne answere this day.[1]

LO PRIVIE SEALE. Report the Q Bill Committee perused the booke and have made some addicons [but little on substance] by the addicons, [amendments] being reade twice, it was ordered to be ingrossed.

[*fo 20*[*r*]] Hospitalls. Added to Com[*mitte*]e for Hospitals. 1 Privie Seale; 2 E Rutland. B 2 Co[*ventry*] et Litchfield; 1 Chester. [D] 2 Dancourt; 1 Pagett. Justice Barekly. To mor[*row*] [afternoone], 3 a clocke. The greater nomber or any seven.

2e vice lecta est billa for dressing of clothing.[2] No place appointed for ordering and government prescribed by the bill. Committed to 16.[3] 1 Arch Cant; 3 P Seale; 2 Treas. 9 Say and Seale; 4 Bath; 5 Harford; 6 Clare; [7 Peterborough]; 8 Strafford. [D] 4 Mountague; 5 Goringe; 3 Willoughby; 2 Wharton; 1 Mowbray. Bp 3 Bristoll; 1 *Exon*; 2 Oxford. Satter[*day*] afternoon: 2 clocke, p[*ain*]t[*ed*] ch[*amber*]. They or any 4. Att[*endants*] *Justice Common pl*[*eas*] Mr Weston; Mr Reeve.

Ad[*usque*]: to[*morrow*] morning *9a hora.*

[*H.L.R.O., Braye MS. 16*]   [*24 April 1640, House of Lords*]

[*fo 20*[*v*]]   *DIE VENERIS 24º APRILIS*

[*See L.J., iv, pp. 65–67*]

Praiers.

The K. present.

[*CHARLES I*].[4] The necess[*ity*] of calling this parlement makes me to come[5] this day contrary to expeditacon[*sic*].[6] You [maye] remember what the Lo: Keep said conc[*erning*] [the meeting][7] and

---

[1] They did not (Braye 16, fo 21[v], below, p. 71; *C.J.*, ii, pp. 10–11). See also Montagu Papers, p. 2c, below, p. 101.

[2] See below, Bills—Cloth, p. 273.

[3] Browne seems to have inserted Peterborough and neglected to change his total to 17. See above, Braye 16 (16 April), n. 1, p. 59.

[4] See below, App. (24 April) p. 308.

[5] . . . *hether* . . . (H.L.R.O., Braye MS. 88, p. 25).

[6] *Cf.* B.L., E.203(1), p. 18, where the action of the House of Commons, not the king's coming, is described as 'contrary to . . . expectation.'

[7] . . . *the first* . . . (H.L.R.O., Braye MS. 88, p. 25).

the 2 day and cheifely on the daye of conference at whitehall. The H.C. have taken it into their Consid[*eration*] but they have in a manner concluded the contrary:[1] To consult innovacon of Religion, and Property in Goods, and priviledges of parlement,[2] and soe[3] putt the cart befor the horse. If it were a tyme to dispute,[4] but the necessitys ar[*e*] soe urgent that there can be[5] no delay.

I will make good what he[6] promised in my name, for Religion my hart and *conscience* [Actions][7] shall goe together, for the shi[*pp*]ing [*blank*].[8] God is[9] wittnes I never [anythinge[10] to my owne profitt but to] the end [to preserve,[11] the] dom[*inion*] of the Seas, but no Eng[*lish*] hart[12] but will consent;[13] *etc. I will give* [*blank*].

Property of Goods[14] is a thinge I never but intended. To be K. of a free and a rich people, and if no Property in Goods[15] no rich people.

[*fo 21ʳ*] This tyme[16] I must be trusted, now whether I or they must be trusted[17] [is the Question]; If they will not trust me first all my busines is lost; and before the yeare goe about I must trust them, for in the winter I must call them to give me a greater Supply.[18]

I conjure [to consider] your owne Honors and mine,[19] and the preposterous course *house* of the hous[*e*] C. yt you will not joyne with them but leave them to themselves, and leave[20] you the way.

1 . . . *and have resolved* . . . (H.L.R.O., Braye MS. 88, p. 25).
2 '. . . *before the business of supply* . . .' (H.L.R.O., Braye MS. 88, p. 25).
3 . . . *they* . . . (H.L.R.O., Braye MS. 88, p. 25).
4 '. . . *I should not be soe pressing* . . .' (H.L.R.O., Braye MS. 88, p. 25).
5 H.L.R.O., Braye MS. 88, p. 25: *there can be* crossed out and *they can beare* substituted.
6 *my Lo Keeper* (H.L.R.O., Braye MS. 88, p. 25).
7 and *my* actions (H.L.R.O., Braye MS. 88, p. 25). B.L., E.203(1), p. 18, adds promises that '*he would give order to his Archbishops and Bishops, that no innovation in matter of Religion should creep in.*' *Cf.* Lord Keeper's speech at the conference 25 April (below, Braye 2, fo 65; Speeches, p. 265).
8 shipping *money* (H.L.R.O., Braye MS. 88, p. 25).
9 . . . *my* . . . (H.L.R.O., Braye MS. 88, p. 25).
10 'never *converted any part of it*' (H.L.R.O., Braye MS. 88, p. 25).
11 'end *of preservation of the*' (H.L.R.O., Braye MS. 88, p. 25). *Cf.* B.L., E.203(1), p. 19, '. . . *which was so necessary, that without it the Kingdom could not subsist, but for the way and means by Ship-money or otherwise, he left it to them* . . .'
12 'seas, *which no Englishman but will*' (H.L.R.O., Braye MS. 88, p. 25).
13 . . . *to* (H.L.R.O., Braye MS. 88, p. 25).
14 '. . . *and liberty of Parliament* . . .' (B.L., E.203(1), p. 19).
15 . . . *there can be* . . . (H.L.R.O., Braye MS. 88, p. 25). '*and liberty of persons* . . .' (B.L., E.203(1), p. 19).
16 '*The* tyme *will come that*' (H.L.R.O., Braye MS. 88, p. 25).
17 . . . *first* . . . (H.L.R.O., Braye MS. 88, p. 25).
18 '. . . *and in conclusion they must for execution of all things wholly trust him* . . .' (B.L., E.203(1), p. 20).
19 B.L., E.203(1), p. 20, gives the remainder of the speech as follows: '*the safety and welfare of this Kingdom, with the great danger it was in, and that they would by their advice dispose the House of Commons to give his supply the precedence before the grievances.*'
20 '*let them not lead*' (H.L.R.O., Braye MS. 88, p. 26).

Desire[1] you [to be] carfull in this point [else there maye be] a breach, I will not say what maye and must follow.[2]

L KEEP. [Delivered from his Majestie which he forgot:] from ye K, that your Lps would determine before you p[ar]te that which his Majestie propounded.

LO CHAMB[ERLAIN]. Said any thing as [the House] doubted of, the Lds of the Privie Councell will informe their Lps soe farr as they know.

Gen[tleman] Usher [sent to tell those that were messengers from the House of Commons], urg[ent] busines now and their Lps will returne them a reason why they did not receive their message now.

[fo 21ᵛ] Mess[age] sent to ye H C by their Lls. Cheife Justices yt upon a Great Considera[tion] [much] concerning his Majeste being they Lps are entred upon a busines which is the cause why their Ll did not receive their message now.

Moved that the house might be putt into a Committee that every Lord may speake his minde, and to be adjourned [during pleas[ur]e which was consented to].

[Committee]

L Dep[u]t[y]. His [Majestie] did expect [his people should now trust him in] their trust in p[ar]te, and after he must [?] trust them, and did expect that untill his Majestie had supply their Lops would not joyne with the [blank].

Report deliv[ere]d ye message unto ye House of Common.

L P[rivy] Seale. 1. Religion 2. Property 3. Liberties of their persons. These the H Co propounded, and his Majestie desires in the first to have his [weighty] occasions [to be] taken into consideracons.

L V[iscount] Say. Hath observed that unlesse both houses have joynd in unity and consent busines hath not soe currantly concluded. The H C have rather fallen into declaracions rather then a progresse, and rather desire to take no notice how ye will proceede, and that both houses may meete and conferre.

E[arl of] Dorsett. Did beleive ye House of Commons may take acceptions; but put this in the ballance that seeinge his Majestie hath conjured this House, and whether to observe is the Question and which of theis 2 waies [fo 22ʳ] we shall take; we in our posterity are concerned in the H C. The Scotts are very ready to be in the field, and if we should disagree it will double their Armie, and [soe hazard] our lives. The Scotts would gladly chainge soiles with us.

E[arl of] Hart[ford]. 1. Busines how the Ks command is to be

¹ *I* . . . (H.L.R.O., Braye MS. 88, p. 26).
² '. . . *I expect that your lordships would determine now before you parte something in this busines*' (H.L.R.O., Braye MS. 88, p. 26).

done. If we refuse to joyne with them unlesse they will doe it, and thinke it fitt to meete them.

Lord Mountague. Ye ques[*tion*] is ye manner of ye carriage lest their be a breach with the House C. A confer[*ence*] and relate to them the effect of ye Ks speach and leave it to them.[1]

L Cott[*ington*]. Q[*uestion*] whether the K.

Besides ye necess[*ity*] there is ye honor of ye K [*which is*] considerable and in ye H C there is a great care had, Meete to confer with the Com[*mons*], but the q[*uestion*] is ye manner how.

Lo Mand[*eville*].[2] We come here to fortifie the trust yt ye King putts in us [rather then] not to banke it. That Ll maye [*confer*] with ye H Commons before proceeding.

B R[3] Not to meete with ye H C before proceeding. Common ordinary ready reason in a body should provide for the greatest necessity.

[*fo 22ᵛ*] Matter: Rel[*igion*], Pos[*sessions*], Lib[*erty*]. Not now proved but supposed but the troubles of Scotland felt and proved first forth. To meete with H C not yet. H C have resolved upon their proposit[*ions*] withoute us.[4] If we meet with them we must begine at their propositions.

L Northto.[5] The K speach hath put a great trust in our honors and persons. Confer not to take notice of their proposit[*ions*] but to propound ye K occasions to them, and soe to have a confer[*ence*] lest they send a mess[*age*] hether.

L Mars[*hal*]. To desire a treaty with ye H C and secondly the manner how; not to tell the H C what we doe, but to consider what is fitt to be said at confer[*ence*] with ye H C.

E[*arl of*] Dorsett. That ye K reade that ye H C had resolved among themselves to prefere their owne busines before his.

L V[*iscount*] Say. Not to make more hast then speed. They give for the whole Countries. If any notice be taken of their busines it must be by their owne members, and their is a statute[6] that no members of that house, yt nothing shall be carrid out of the house without

---

[1] See Montagu Papers, p. 2d, below, p. 101.

[2] Edward Montagu, 1st Baron Kimbolton and Viscount Mandeville, heir to Henry, earl of Manchester.

[3] Probably John Warner, bishop of Rochester, who spoke on 29 April (below, Braye 16, fo 39ᵛ, Lee Warner, p. 88). Although the account of the day's proceedings in his diary was probably written afterwards, its details suggest that, contrary to the attendance list, he was present. See below, Lee Warner, p. 3 (24 April), p. 110. He may have arrived late, after attending Convocation which assembled only to be adjourned until the following day (Nalson, i, p. 363).

[4] Resolution, 23 April, to 'consult with the Lords', Finch-Hatton, p. 58, below, p. 174.   [5] Spencer Compton, 2nd earl of Northampton.

[6] Probably 9 *Hen.* IV, the Indemnity of the Commons, *Rot Parl.*, iii, p. 611; see *L.J.*, iv, p. 73.

their leave, and soe it maye brake them to inquire what member [*fo 23*] did relate it, and moved that Ll would be please to meete and conferr.

E[*arl of*] Dorse[*t*]. To move to a suply in General upon his Majests occasions.

L Say. We doe give our Consents personally, not for Counties as they doe.

L Dep[*uty*].[1] More depends upon the prosp[*erity*] of ye K from this daies debat then any hath done in his know[*ledge*]. To take a viewe of the present cond[*ition*] as the Ks. If now stands if it could endure [or] abate, then ye H C had more reason to debate, but if ye K be not presently suplyd, it will not be in ye power of the HC to restore to the Ks honor.

1. What Insolence, Contumacy and boldnes ye Scotts nation have ben towards his Majeste. Farr from performing [*their duty*], but have gone higher to take ye Crowne; It is not pretence of Religion, but desire better here then at home.

His Majests creditt, sec[*urity*] and revenue of ye Crowne 300[m] *li* issued to prepare else the season lost; by 20th May to march. Issued all these monis as ships, victualls, 30[m] foote, and 1000 horse, 20 May, 8000 foote and 1000, besides Barwick and Carlile [*fo 23*ᵛ] and if not now suply, all this will be lost, the K dishonord; and if H C continued debate but 6[2] week all will be lost.[3]

If H C will for present give such as will 4 or 500[m] *li* this will be gone quickly, and the[*re*]fore the Comons must in the ende have what is reason, and else the busines fall without further suply.[4] It hath ben done before. This toucheth upon no Property nor Privild[*ge*] and in the ende they must trust ye K. This is no new thinge to trust ye K first.

In the 12 *Jacobi*; a busines argued debated in the house upon a grevance, and after came for conference to this house, and this House did at that tyme refuse a Conference.[5]

Likewise in 3⁰ *Caroli* about Pet[*ition*] of Right and includes Property and Privild[*ge*] and H C came for a Conference, and upon voate this house [first] refused to joyne.[6] He was then a memb[*er*] of the lower house.

[1] See Lee Warner, p. 3, below, p. 110.
[2] The six is written over another number, perhaps two.
[3] This is more information about the king's plans than either Lords or Commons had received officially up to this point. *Cf.* Lee Warner, p. 3, below, p. 110.
[4] Windebanke's notes mention 600,000[li] (*CSP 1640*, p. 64).
[5] About impositions; controversy ensued (Hist. MSS Comm., xxix, *Report on the MSS of the Duke of Portland*, ix: Harley Papers (London, 1923), p. 133; *C.J.*, i, p. 496; *L.J.*, ii, p. 707).
[6] There seems to have been no occasion when the Lords refused a conference about the Petition of Right (3 *Car.* I, c. 1). The reference is probably to their insistence on a provision saving the king's prerogative (*C.J.*, i, pp. 901–902).

How much rather nowe, the Conference ye destruction of the Ks affaires, [army] gathered togethered[sic] 20 May, and will not be in the power of the H C to recover etc. Lib[erty of the] Subject is as deare to him as his eyes. [fo 24ʳ] Not to joyne with the H C. If the K affairs would endure it he would advise ye K to heare H C what they can say for 6 weekes.

1. 6 sub[sidies]. 2. 4 sub[sidies]. Ireland hath trusted him, and he hath performed every title, and they had great advantage. They have done nothing but what they will make good. The report is false upon his Honor. Command is given that Irland shall have what is desired, and fitt for them to have.

Upon the breaking of the Treaty of Spaine, the H C brooke with the K.[1]

No ende but the Servise of ye K and the good of his country.

Not to joyne with them unlesse they will suply the K. If not leave them to themselves.

L V[iscount] Say. Not to have it stated, whether ye K or people should be trusted; but how there may be a happ[y] suply, and ye people grieved, releived. It is not in the intencions of the H C to leave [the] King in a desperate estate.

[fo 24ᵛ] If they are ordered etc.

1. How soone to bring the K suply and ye Commons affaires together.
2. Desired Scotts busines to be sett a side and not layd before this house.
3. The K maye please to make Propos[itions] [but it hath ben custom] to leave it to the house.

The treaty of busines until they are concluded are left to the house, and not to say it must be treated upon because the K hath comanded.

Not to come to confer[ence with] H C preingaged.

If Parlement breake of[f] more daunger, if a fraccion, then it is more daungerous.

Whether the Confer[ence] be not a speedier way to expedite this busines.

L Dep[u]t[y]. Far from stirring any deviding Questions H C waies to his apprehens[ion] is such a way as he understands: ye wayes. C H[2] have ben Just and Hon[ora]ble.

H C cannot be exped[ited] in 6 weekes. Shipp mony [only] shall come to voates in houses in 6 weekes. First debate it must H C with deliberacon and injoyne [fo 25ʳ] all the Lawyers [in the] House to deliver the Lawe. This they will aske tyme to doe.

---

1 *L.J.*, iii, pp. 250, 275; *Debates in the House of Commons in 1625*, ed. S. R. Gardiner (Camden Society, New Series, vi, 1873), pp. 2, 31, 143; Robert Ruigh, *The Parliament of 1624* (Cambridge, Mass., 1971), pp. 206–11, 226–27.

2 Perhaps Commons' House. Browne appears to have written originally C.C., then written an *H* over the second *C*, but he may have intended it to replace the first. See also Braye 16 (24 April), fo 29, below, p. 78.

2. To draw up an Erroneous Appeale will aske a tyme.

3. A confer[*ence*] with this ho[*use*] will be

4. Counsell must speake and judges.

5. Come back thither againe and soe tyme spun out, and Majests affaires lost irrecoverably.[1]

Not to debate but advise in a freindly way.

The K did not command, but desire Lls not to joyne with them unlesse they would consent.

L V[*iscount*] Say. He did not say yt Lo Deupt[*sic*] did saie ye K commanded, but he did heare it otherwise. Fraccion at home maye be more daungerous then [any] other.

If Lls tell them unles they give money, their Ls will not joyne that will much disturbe them.

Peticion. 1. Proposit[*ion*] and a debate in this House, but no

Their Lls did joyne with Commons about Peticon of Right.

[*fo 25ᵛ*] Lo Keep. Hath alwaies honord parlements but never feared them.

Necessary for a R[*igh*]t understand[*ing*] between K and people, no malice can have a bitter an influence then upon yoer Lops.

One Reason not yet touched, that the subject should have releife speedily, fully, to their just grevances, and he would let them goe on as far as he could. He would not be overcome with kindnes, but would be aforehand with them.

Blesse G[*od*] for such a K and why not trust such a K. The H Co cannot but spend much tyme in the busines as they goe on. In ordinary Peticons they will advise.

All states aboute us take notice of what we doe. States looke to their owne, and they will aske what the parliament have done. An[*swer*]: nothing but reccon up their Grevances and give nothinge.

That which flyes abroad here in this towne will fly into other countries, and how doth this concern ye K is much to be considered.[2]

To give way to ye weightier occasions.

[*fo 26ʳ*] Not to perswade what to give, but tell them that you would medle with nothing untill then.

E[*arl of*] Hart[*ford*]. None doubts yt ye K will not make good his promise.

None doubts but ye K hath necessity.

How to come to expedite this with the House of Commons.

E[*arl of*] Bristoll. We can but put our best endeavors. They must

---

[1] The lengthy procedure which might be used for shipmoney is not unlike that which the Commons had followed with the Petition of Right (*C.J.*, i, pp. 878ff.). Strafford sat in the Commons at the time.

[2] See Braye 16, fo 36, below, p. 85. On 20 April Peyton wrote of a 'murmure about the Towne that the Parliament will dissolve' (*Oxinden Letters*, p. 163).

give sub[*sidies*] not in our owne power to give; H C are nice in their owne priviledge.

To heare what scruple ye Lower house maye make; *whether we shall heare* Not to goe precommitted, for they maye saye it will be to enjoyne them, and soe not to hurt them.

Not without a confer[*ence*] with them, with fairenes and sweet, reas[*on*] of dutys, gratifie ye K and Presidents are good leaders, but no binders. If hast[*i*]nes may be supos[*ed*] to entrench Lib[*erty*], see how our ends maye be produced with effect.

[*fo 26ᵛ*] To debate how to confer with the House.

E[*arl*] Marsh[*al*]. Not assume that ye power is in them, but injoyne the H C.

To prepare for a Conference. To let [them] know yt ye K hath ben heare and desires exped[*ition*] of his affaires 1st etc.

L Maynard. To begin with the Ks suply. HC did *12⁰ Jac.* resolve that they would not thinke of any other busines untill they had a Confer[*ence*].[1] His Majestie gave *no* touch here concerning Scotland, but take notice in the Confer[*ence*] of Scotland.

E[*arl of*] Dorset. If no mencion at confer[*ence with*] H C of Scotland, then no ground to aske Suply. He hopes and dispaires not of successe with a Confer[*ence*]; some set downe nombers and cary fig[*ures*] in thes [?] matters.

Not for voating.

The K did conjure that we should cooperate with him in this busines.

He thinkes no stat[*ute of*] H L but an Order against false tales with exputcion[*sic*].[2]

[*fo 27ʳ*] If H C will not joyne, soe far to obey K as not to joyne.

E[*arl of*] Southton. 3 great things in quest[*ion*]. There is alleadged not the daunger at home but daungers abroad. Heretofore one countie have secured this k[*ing*]dome against ye Scotts, and not for ye honor;[3] none to thinke that we are worse able now, not knowing the secresie of these affaires and soe in such cause now [to feare as then].

Confer without prelimitacion.

L Brook.[4] 1. resolve whether a Confer[*ence*] or not. 2. what the subject of a Conference not in right.

E[*arl of*] Bridgwater.[5] It cannot be thought the K will be at soe great a charge without feare.

No date of the Scotts l[*et*]tre maye make us suspect there is too

---

[1] William, 1st Baron Maynard, *C.J.*, i, p. 499.
[2] Perhaps a response to the Lord Keeper's remarks (above, Braye 16, fo 25ᵛ, p. 75).
[3] Thomas Wriothesley, 4th earl of Southampton. He apparently exaggerated (*CSP 1639–40*, pp. 295ff. *passim*).   [4] Robert Greville, 2nd Baron Brooke.
[5] John Egerton. See Lee Warner, p. 3, below, p. 110.

much daunger. Have the Scotts given over ther fortificacons? If ever great occasion, now more. *Vis unita fortior.*

They can 6 weekes expresse soe many grevances.

Make meanes to enabled us to hold weapons in our[*selves*] and in good manners ought to give him precedencie.

[*fo 27ᵛ*] This is no new thing. [To prefer ye K busines of war before other grevances]. *H* 5 *R2*, 6 *E* 3.[1]

The ennimie now stands in the Gate.

Stroud was fined, 4 *H.* 8.[2]

If Questions arise at confer[*ence*] rel[*ating*] etc. These *res* cannot be resolved without a [*great*] deale tyme.

The question is but of tyme and order and both maye be soone resolved, what to say when they come to conference.

L Say. Records will be diverse, yt when ye K calls to parlement for war, they parlement hath given divers advises. The Record he spake of was H. 4 tymes. Yt matters in parlement should be *entered* [kept] within themselves[3] and send to desire a conference.

E[*arl*] Marsh[*al*]. Onely mess[*age*] sent by ye Commons but noe desire of confer[*ence*]. The K desire this House to take his busines first into consideracon.

[*He moved that the*] House [*be*] reassumed and [not] entertaine *not* [of any] other conference untill this is resolved.

L Cott[*ington*]. He of opinion yt ye Lo should mediate with the Commons for promoting the K cause, with soe much seriousnes as the 3 tyme.

[*fo 28ʳ*] To resolve what to propound at the Conference. It is now to reduce the Rebells of Scotland, and not as heretofore a privie busines.

The Scotts are able to draw in the Goth and Vandalls and other great Armies; and when the Swedes are quiett for ought I know they may offer them the Crowne of England.[4]

Whether the Kings suply shall be first preferred.

E[*arl of*] Bristoll. If the daunger be soe great a speedy suply must be, and it is not only monie will doe, but the harts must be had to with mony.

Think of all ye Argum[*en*]ts you can and mediate; yet not to crosse our owne ends, nor make our propositions impossible.

---

[1] Perhaps 2 *Hen.* V (*Rot. Parl.*, iv, p. 16 or p. 35); 1 *Ric.* II (*Rot. Parl.*, iii, p. 5) or 4 *Ric.* II (*Rot. Parl.*, iii, p. 89); 6 *Edw.* III (*Rot. Parl.*, ii, pp. 66–67). *Cf.* Lee Warner, p. 3, below, p. 110. Browne has left a note for himself in the margin here.

[2] Stat. 4 *Hen.* VIII, *c.* 8; see also Elizabeth R. Foster, 'Speaking in the House of Commons,' *B.I.H.R.*, xlviii (1970), pp. 48–49.

[3] Probably 9 *Hen.* IV.

[4] See Stevenson, *The Covenanters and the Government of Scotland*, i, pp. 138–45.

De modo is the difference.

If we are in daunger, move them yt their harts maye be united in affeccions which is more then mony. Let the people be somwhat satisfied in the grevances. The right way to compass great busines is, to sett them in a right way.

[*fo 28ᵛ*] E[*arl*] Southton. He did not say there was no feare, but no such feare as we might be thought to be [more] disable now then, we were then.

L Archb of Cant[*erbury*]. Because this is a weighty busines and concernes both houses; so much spoken as very little left.

His Majestie did never make any prohibition concerning Scotland, which is ye maine ground of this busines and meeting.

Great differ[*ence*] betweene Scotland then, and Scot[*land*] now.
1. Heretofore [when] they had another K they had a suply from forrein p[*ar*]tes.
2. Since K James came to this Crown, no nation ever had soe many souldiers bred in forrene p[*ar*]ts as in Poland, Ger[*many*], as the Scotts have had, and now since these troubles all come home with intents to take p[*ar*]tes against the K.
3. They have offered faire pretences to his Majestie, but could make none good.
4. I would make my enemy a bridg of gold soe they will sooner be gone. They looke after ye richnes of this Kingdome.

The trust is mutuall; he must trust them, and they him.

[*fo 29ʳ*] He will never speake against his Conscience. Divers things are in our powers; and what are prefer[*able*] there Lps lib[*er*]ties to make use of that power.

For Innova[*tions in*] Relig[*ion*], Priv[*ileges*], Lib[*er*]tie, Proper[*ty*] and whatsoever lyes in him, he will be a servant to this house and the C H to preserve them.

Proper way not to stay untill they offer a Confer[*ence*] but to offer them a Confer[*ence*] and resolve to send and thinke upon the heads before hand, but to take upon them to appoint what subsidies, but to hould them to what they K desire against his [affaires] precedencie.

L V[*iscount*] Say. Q which [should give] waie to ye K affaires. If a great daunger abroad, set all things right and treate at home, without discontent at home, Questions which is most for the Ks servise.

He thinkes distraccons at home maye be most daungerous.

A confer[*ence*] without prelimitacons.

L P[*rivy*] Seale. Aske a confer[*ence*] which is ye ould way, and the good way.

[*fo 29ᵛ*] L Say desires he maye acknowledge his error concerning the confer[ence]. That that House [not to determine] *not resolve* that the Ks supplyes should goe first.

L Deput[y]. *Rests no more* But state the Questions what to [do] The K commandeth to make an[swer] of this question.

1. Whether we conceave ye K suply should preceed grevances?
2. Whether if [the] C[ommons] will not [departe] *goe* with their grevances their Lops shall not refuse to joyne with them?
3. [Whether] we should not prevent them with a mes[sage] of confer[ence] and to present the Ks desire and occasions to them?

L V[iscount] Say. The Commons will soe much resent the first, as yt it put them to a great stand. Then whether such a voate will not be an Injunction [and none can tell what the newes of the H Commons may be next.].

L Dorsett. It is but an opinion and binds not.

The declar[ation] the rest perswasions.

L Mand[eville]. We have banked all things as maye distructive to our selves and medle freely.

[*fo 30ʳ*] L Goringe. If any doubt, put to the question.

E[arl of] Bristoll. If we resolve and agree aforehand, they will [say why] doe yee come and treate with us. Go to them with strong Arguments and mediate, and if they will not agree, then come and consider further of it.

E[arl] Marsh[al]. To give his Majestie some acc[oun]t of it this daye.

To mediate with them and if not to let them know yt they will not treate of any else, and hopes it will not come to the Questions.

Lord Brooke. 1. Whether a [*blank*].

The House is againe resumed.

[House of Lords]

Whether the Lords will *not* [please to] joyne in the mediation to the H Commons whereby the Ks occations maye [receive] precedence of their Grevances.

[*fo 30ᵛ*] [*Voting: 1: Contents 57, Not Contents 25; 2: Contents 60, Not Contents 21; 3: Contents 67, Not Contents 14.*][1]

[1] The first vote determined which of the two resolutions would be handled first (see below, Lee Warner, p. 3, Harl. MS. 4931, fo 48, Worc. Coll. fo 26ᵛ, pp. 110, 238, 229; also *L.J.*, iv, p. 67; D.J., p. 36). See H.L.R.O., Braye MS. 2, fos 63ʳ–64ᵛ, 'The Two propositions voated in the House the 24⁰ April 1640. Delivered to me by the Lord Keeper under his owne hand.' Rossingham says, 'Some of the Lords and all the Bishops concluding it by their votes that the supply in the first place to his Majesty was to take place and above 20 of the country Lords voting it, that the grievances of the subject were in their judgments the greater and more advantageous service to his Majesty' (B.L., Add. MS. 11045, fo 112ᵛ). Montereul notes that the dissenters were Southampton, Rutland, Say, Brooke, and several others (P.R.O. 31/3/72, fos 133ʳ–34ʳ).

[*fo 31ʳ*] That his Majestys supply shall have precedencie [and resolved of before any other busines be treated of]. Resolved by voate.

As many as thinke fitt to have a conference with the Lower House [to dispose them thereunto]. Resolved a conference to be had.

Whether we should in case [the HC] will not alter from their [orders and parliamentary waies] and take into consideracion the Ks affaires, whether we should joyne with them.

E[*ARL OF*] BRISTOL. To this there must be a presupposicion that the HC will not doe their duties.

E[*arl*] Marshal this day came with a w[*hi*]te staffe as L Steward.

Ad[*usque*]: tomorrow morning 9ª *hora*.

[H.L.R.O., Braye MS. 16]   **[25 April 1640, House of Lords]**

[*fo 31ᵛ*]   *DIE SABBATHI* **25** *APRILIS* **1640**

[*See L.J., iv, pp. 67–69*]

Prayers.

Lo[*rd*] Fawconbridge excused. Ague.

E[*arl*] Marshall came this day with a w[*hi*]te stafe as L Steward.

Message from ye K. LO KEEP delivered from his Majestie as pleased to take notice what yesterday [yor Lops] resolved [concerning the suply of his Majestes affaires and with what] great care and zeale and affeccon to his servise, both for matter and manner and dispatching at this tyme yt his Majest [gives] thankes, nothing more pleasinge then the good relacon betweene [him and yoer lops] and ye shall be allwaies deerest to him, and if it serves not to your harts, yt is my falt.

LO KEEP. Yesterday resolved [it was] his Majests suply to have precedence and conference agreed to send a mess[*age*] by Mr. Justis Jones and Mr Baron Trevor.

Mess[*age*] by the *2 Cheif Justices* [To desire] that upon occasion his Majests being [here yesterday about somewhat his Majests desires] somwhat to referr and that there may be a speedy conference with a *Committee* of both Houses [as a committee] in the P[*ain*]t[*ed*] Chamber with all convenient speed.

Nothing concernes this house soe much as the preservacon of orders and because many stand up together, to give me leave to put yoer Lops in minde who stood up first.

2. Not speake as often as they will when it is a house unless to explaine [motion]; to give me leave to put you in [*fo 32ʳ*] minde to keep the orders of the house.

E[*ARL*] MARSH[*AL*]. Moved to consider the preparacon of the conference and Lo Keep to reduce them to a head.

LO MAYNARD. [*Moved*] Lo Strafford, Lo Archb Canterbury, E[*arl*] Marshall, Lo Privie Seale, Lo Cottington, Lo Bristoll to be added to helpe my Lord Keep in gathering the heads for the conference.

E[*ARL OF*] BRISTOLL. To consider the K speech, who spake not as a K but as a gent[*leman*] in his Trust.

The judges reported yt they [*H C*] taken ye motion into consid-[*eration*] and will give a meeting with a Comittee forthwith.

Moved that L Keep, L Archb Cant[*erbury*], L P[*rivy*] Seale, Earle Marshall, E[*arl of*] Strafford, E[*arl of*] Bristoll, and Lo Cottington doe withdraw themselves and draw up the heads of what shall be thought fitt to propound at the meeting of the committees with the Lower House.

The House is adjourned untill pleasure.

The House is resumed againe.

Headds read:[1]

1. To expr[*ess*] the effect of [*what*] he [*the king*] said here and that conference, ye occation conference which is ye Ks.

2. Put us in mind what was said.

3. necess[*ity of af*]faires [will admitt of] beare no delay in regard of his [*blank*].

4. Distempers of Scotland and tents sett up at Duns.

[*fo 32ᵛ*] 5. Trust to his Majests [now] and he must trust them [hereafter] and he will not breake his word, [and ther is a necessity his Majesty must be trusted in the ende.] *His Majestie cannot be delayed because his affaires*

6. For [the 3 propositions, vizt, Relig[*ion*], proper[*ty*] and privileg] he would [grant] give them as fully as may be.

Prevent innovacions; Religion, his hart and cons[*cience*] should goe together [and yt he would [*live*] and dye in yt religion].

[Shipmoney, never a profitt of his owne revenue, yt it did put ye King into any other way. That to secure the seas he would to heare them.] That these afford unto them to joyne in Relig[*ion*], Lib[*er*]tie of Goods and Privil[*e*]d[*ges*].

If they goe not on presently, all the Ks affaires will be lost.

That we have in our opinions declared yt the Ks busines is preceded all other affaires whatsoever.

The House ad[*journed*] during pleasure.

The House is resumed.

Ad[*usque*]: Monday 9 *hora*.

---

[1] See below, App. (25 April) p. 310.

[*H.L.R.O., Braye MS. 16*]   [*27 April 1640, House of Lords*]
[*fo 33ʳ*]   *DIE LUNAE 27º APRILIS* 1640
[*See L.J., iv, pp. 69–70*]
Praiers.
These Lods were excused: Lo Mountague excused, gout;[1] B Exeter
sick; E[arl of] Kingston[2] excused, sicke.
[*Bill for*] Hospitalls. Committees for hosp[*itals*] tomorrow, 2 *post
med.*, P[*ain*]t[*ed*] Chamber.
[*Bill for*] Pages. Com[*mittees*], Wednesday, for pages, 2 aclocke
and as often as they please.
E[*arl*] Rivers. E[*arl*] Rivers was brought in betweene E[*arl of*]
Rutland and E[*arl of*] Carlile and palced [*sic*] next below E[*arl of*]
Newcastle.[3] His Pattent delivered, etc.
E[*arl of*] Carna[*rvon*]. E[*arl of*] Carnarvan brought into the House
betweene the E[*arl of*] *Sarum* and E[*arl of*] Denbigh. His pattent dd.
[*delivered*] and placed next below E[*arl of*] Peterburgh.[4]
Lo Powis. Lo Powis brought in betwene L Howard and Lo Goring.
Pattent dd [*delivered*] and placed next to Lo Dunsemore.[5]
E[*ARL*] MARSHALL.[6] Moved for the well breeding of the gentry
in riding, etc. that some consideracion might be taken of it.
The busines concerninge Dr Manwaringe is referred untill to
morrow morninge.
[*fo 33ᵛ*] Lo Bp Winchester[7] excuse, taken with a lamenes
Ad[*usque*]: tomor[*row*] 9 *hora*.

[*H.L.R.O., Braye MS. 16*]   [*28 April 1640, House of Lords*]
[*fo 34ʳ*]   *DIE MARTIS 28º APRILIS* 1640
[*See L.J., iv, pp. 70–71*]
Praiers.
L KEEP. From his Majestie [*who*] understood [some] quest[*ion*]
about [Dr Manwaring now Bp of] St Davids. [Majestie hath given]
to give comand [yt ye Bp shall] not *to* come [and sitt in parlement],

---

[1] See Montagu Papers, p. 2d, below, p. 102.
[2] Robert Pierrepoint.
[3] Thomas Darcy, 1st earl of Rivers; George Manners, 7th earl of Rutland;
James Hay, 1st earl of Carlisle; William Cavendish, 2nd earl of Newcastle.
[4] Robert Dormer, earl of Carnarvon; William Cecil, earl of Salisbury;
William Fielding, 1st earl of Denbigh; John Mordaunt, 1st earl of Peterborough.
[5] Edward, 1st Baron Howard, heir to Theophilus, 2nd earl of Suffolk;
Francis Leigh, 1st Baron Dunsmore.
[6] See Braye 16, fo 46ᵛ, Lee Warner, p. 4, below, pp. 95, 111.
[7] Robert Curle.

nor send any Proxie [to the parlement].[1] To be entred soe *and the former order to be suspended.*

Henry Presse.[2] Peticion. The maior and 2 sergeants to be sent for and the pt too.

Bradshaw not to be whipped. Direccons to be given to the W[*arde*]n of the House of Correccion.

Ordered that the Committees of Peticons and Priviledges shall have power to sende for any persons they please to prepare businesses for the House.

E[*arl of*] Dover[3] not well, excused.

Armes. *Hodie lecta est bill,* an *Act* [bill] for Armes of the Kingdome, etc.

Corne. *Hodie lecta est billa,* An Bill for better preserving of Corne.

Message from the Lower House by Mr Secretary Vane. [Knights, Citizens, desire a conference with yor lops etc.] touching something which happened at ye last conference, with [committee of] both Houses concerning the priviledges of parlement [the H] by a committee of both Houses if their Lops [*blank*].

Answ[*er*]: That their Llps will [have been acq[*uainted*]; ready to] meete them presently in p[*ain*]t[*ed*] Ch[*amber*] with com[*mittee*] of both houses, according to [their] *your* desires.

L Keep and ye former assistan[*ts*]: Arch, P[*rivy*] Seal, E[*arl*] Marshall, E[*arl of*] Bristoll, E[*arl of*] Strafford, and Lo Cottington appointed to reporte the conference to this house.

[*fo 34*[*v*]] The House ad[*journed*] during pleasure.

The House is resumed againe.[4]

House ad[*journed*] untill tomor[*row*] morning 9 *hora.*

[H.L.R.O., Braye MS. 16]   [29 April 1640, House of Lords]

[*fo 35*[*r*]] DIE MERCURII VIZT 29º DIE APRILIS 1640

[*See L.J., iv, pp. 71–73*]

Praiers.

Moved that the Lls appointed to report the Conference might retyre and perfect their notes.

House is ad[*journed*] during pleasure.

The House is resumed.

Report. L. KEEP.[5] Conference yesterday was to this effect:

Mr Pim[6] did tell yt he was come to preserve union betweene both

---

[1] See Montagu Papers, p. 3a, Harl. MS. 4931, fo 48, below, pp. 102, 239; also B.L., Add. MS. 11045, fo 114[r].

[2] See below, Petition, Presse, p. 285.   [3] Henry Carey.

[4] The conference was to be reported the next day (*L.J.*, iv, p. 71).

[5] See below, App., Pym (28 April), p. 312.

[6] John Pym (Tavistock).

Houses and to give expedition; that great pri[*vileges*] were not [airy] matters of Pompe but the highest places; ever deare and hoped ever soe; more p[*ar*]ticuler belonging to other House; parliament fountaine of order; on[*e*] great one, yt subsidie ought to begin at the H. C. H. C. did not conceive Lls did vary from yor judgments but somewhat transported, etc. Voated in the house, if yor Llps have voated this, ye have broken the orders and desired reparacion; and desired that Llps would make it. Relig[*ion*]; Prop[*erty*]; Privil[*eges*], there Lps had broken the privil[*eges*], and desire that they would not take any notice of any *res* untill they received informacion from them.

[*fo 35ᵛ*] E[*ARL*] MARSHALL. 1. Advised with subsidie which we ought not to doe, for this to stick upon the clearnes of our intentions; this house was never made such ciphers, but when daungers were to advyse.

2. The taking notice of what was discovered from them. It was resolved by them, and resolutions are not *res* secret; and that H. C. doe question undeservedly and to stand upon what was done.

L GORING. Offinse is taken where none is. Prepare for a conference.

E[*ARL OF*] DORSETT. Q 1. Jealousy of care commendible; 2. Jealousy without cause, though not yet not justified.

L C[*HAMBERLAIN?*] the G[*reat*] Counsell of the K[*ing*]dome. It must have an object to [?] for daunger eminent. If we tell them opinions, this is no breach but rather ought to receive thanks and oblig[*ations*].

Whether they have taken away ours, and no invading of theirs; meddle, transported. We beleive our selves. They doe not, [yt there is] daunger.

Wise pylots shifte their sales.

Let us consider whether we are not [any] more than cir[*cuit*] judges only to serve their turnes.

1. [question] whether in this challenge they have not invaded us.

[*fo 36ʳ*] E[*ARL OF*] STRAFFORD. Proceedings both should be like frends, satisfied fairly, yt unity and the K affaires may be preserved. To come to an issue in a parlementary way, and the H. to be resolved into a committee, that every one may speake their minde and soe prepare for a conference.

H ad[*journed*] into a com[*mittee*] during pleasure.

[*Committee*]

E[*arl*] Marsh[*al*]. To make use of tyme and to propound a generall ground.

1. Challenge of Breach of Priviledge in preferring the suply. [We

never medled with sub[*sidies*], yet never be soe little as in daunger to advise for unity [*?*].]

1. Notice taking; we did take no notice, but it is strange that this house shall not take notice of Resol[*utions*] when it is abroad.

L P[*rivy*] Seale. The fewer *res* stirr the sooner reconsil[*iation*].

E[*arl of*] Stafford. He conceaves yt this silence argues a content and soe yt takes. 1 Q. Whether it be breach pri[*vileges of*] H. C. [*for*] Lps here to deliver an opinion; Had yt goe airely C. kingdom an Illust[*rious*] body, not airy but [*blank*].

There close our mouthes and our harts and gives us both delay and discontent and gives us privild[*ges*] not soe much as breath, airy.

We were very tender, mod[*erate*], and just yt L. would not give an advise. They invade us to ye harte and dom[*inion*] over us yt we shall not deliver our owne opinions here. [*fo 36ᵛ*] There opinion was grevances should preceede, ours yt supply, thus

Let us not make our selves less then we are, nothing can be done; H. C. finally without K. and this H.

Keep that auld station, to have freedome of opinion and speech. They say little lesse then we did not understand what we sayd. They have trespassed highly against yor Lps. I am sensible of the respect of H. C., but I must say it is like unto a child, make a leg, and kisse yor hand. We must finde out a way to repaire them. They can doe nothing without the assent of this House. Nothing invaded, all respect, carefully to proceed, respect, but not neglect our selves.

Soe[1] 1. Q. Whether we have [transgressed] intrenched

2. Whether they have not intrenched upon us.

L V[*iscount*] Say. Both Houses being G[*reat*] C[*ouncils?*], neither can doe any *res* without other, and desire they may be preserved and carried in such way yt though diff[*ering*] yet there may [*be*] a corresp[*ondency*] preserved.

I did feare that this would be ye issue.

Fortifie yor Lops opinion upon such solid grounds, as no accep-[*tions*] may be taken, if yor Lops make yor opinion gen[*eral*].

[*fo 37ʳ*] If resol[*ution*] yt Lops have not broken, fortyfie opinion with reasons yt they may not be repelled.

Floods case;[2] words against Relig[*ion*]; Q Bohemia; they past a censure upon him. The Lds upon this sent downe yt they had broken their Lops Privil[*eges*] and their ans [*wer*] was they were transported.

Take every word in the best interpretacion and soe to goe [*to*]

---

[1] Browne has put an asterisk here in the margin. The practice, which he follows here and in the remainder of the scribbled book, seems to mark points which might be voted upon.

[2] *C.J.*, i, pp. 600–602, 610, 619, 621; *Commons Debates, 1621*, ii, pp. 335, 337, 362–62; iii, pp. 173–74, 237–40, 253–54; *L.J.*, iii, pp. 110, 113, 119, 124, 133.

them that *res* may not be strayned higher, that the breach maye not be made wider.

L Chamb[*erlain*]. That it made be decided whether we have intrenched upon their privileges.

L Keep. In Floods case zeale did transport them, but they [now] voated yt we had broken theirs and desired repar[*ations*]. For ye matter I will [not] [?].

1. Quest[*ion*] how far this H. nor noe tyme needful to search precedents; we have but voated in our opinions.

2. Q. shewes we did not lay an injunct[*ion*] upon them, but to dispose them thereunto.

How can we ans[*wer*] to be meald mouthd when ye preservacon of ye kingedom is concerned. We give ourselves a wound and taxe our selves if we shall forgett our honor, And what to be done to give them a right understanding of what we have done, etc.

E[*arl of*] Dorsett. I hope they will be as modest now as in Floods case. Let us make them see we have not broken their Privil[*eges*] and given them just satisfaction or no.

[*fo 37ᵛ*] E[*arl of*] Strafford. Many *res* belonge to [yor lops], whol[*e*] judicature yor owne; all offences, appeales at this barr; keepe yt dig[*nity*], priority estab[*lished*] in former ages, and to challenge them in a higher degree then the H. C.

I thinke we are upon solid grounds, solid grounds are already laid. We did not resolve the subsidie, but it was our opinion.

He was in his voate against the censure of Floods,[1] and then I told them soe, and they did fundamentally strik[*e*] at the Privil[*ege*] of this House, and saie now if subs[*idies*] are ben granted absol[*utely*] and conclusively, yt came to confer and they waved their error, and I hope will doe soe now, and not persist in their error.

That the Q. may be put, whether we have broken their priviledges or no.

L V[*iscount*] Say. They cannot give without us, nor we give without them; it must be restrayned to that p[*ar*]ticuler.

They did not tell us upon what grounds we have broke their Priviledges.

E[*arl of*] Strafford. The C[*ommons*] cannot [doe] nothing effectively [to ye K] any thing without this House.

L Dorsett. They have allready tould us in three *res* we have broken their priviledges.

[*fo 38ʳ*] E[*arl*] Marsh[*al*]. We are a court of power independant. H. C. voated the Q. before they asked us ye Q. and shewe us since wherein [*blank*] Q. may be putt, whether they have broken ours.

---

[1] Records show he urged accommodation (*Commons Debates, 1621*, iii, pp. 167–68, 208, 238).

L Wharton.[1] To know what their reasons are before ye Q.

L Chamb[*erlain*]. If we put it not to the Q., we are a poore house in my opinion.

L V[*iscount*] Say. They have gone upon our concession, but have not shewed us the reason, and we shall determine it upon the Q. before we heare them.

E[*arl of*] Hunt[*ingdon*].[2] It is cleare our Privil[*eges*] are brook is Ho resumed and to be put to the Q.

E[*arl of*] Bristoll. Whether we shall vote.

[Whereas] that we have broken their Privil[*eges*] in med[*dling*] with their [sub[sidies]]. 2. Notice of any resolution of their houses. We adhere to ours and they to theirs, who shall be mod[*erator*]. To see for a way. Ks supply, let us laye aside debates and thinke of some way of accom[*modation*], yet not to lett our Privil[*eges*] sleepe.

[*fo 38ᵛ*] E[*arl*] Marsh[*al*]. Likes the accom[*modation*], K servise, but the Question to be put whether we have put broke theirs, or no.

E[*arl of*] Bristoll. He values nothing for ye honor of this house, but not to stand upon punctillos, but prefers ye K servise first, yet not to lay aside the honor of this house to the waive it for a tyme.

L Cott[*ington*]. Whether we have broken their Priviledges, they have shew us the reason wherein.

If ye have voated that ye are of opinion, then ye have broken our Privil[*eges*]. That we have taken notice of what is done in their House.

There [maye] be [an] other way besides sub[*sidies*] to suply the K.

To voate whether *we* [they] have [not] broken ours.

L Dorsett. We are wounded; They are not in our opinions. Let us be upon even termes with them.

E[*arl of*] Bristoll. Necessary to breake in the peeces and examine the argum[*en*]ts and see whether we have broken theirs. If the statute[3] mencion K, then some Q.

[*fo 39ʳ*] E[*arl of*] Strafford. If they had said without voated that they did desire a confer[*ence*], then we might a consid[*eration*], but let us be upon even termes. If they will lay aside theirs, then there may [*be a*] conf[*erence*].

E[*arl of*] Bristoll. The less we stirr, the sooner ye Ks busines may be advant.

L Savill.[4] Whether [*blank*].

E[*arl of*] Dorsett. I will not say we may not advise.

[To voate] that we have not broke the Priviledge of the House C.

Lo Mand[*eville*]. All desire unity with H. C. If we goe on thus, I feare conf[*erence*] upon ground they proceed. They take their

---

[1] Philip, 4th Baron Wharton.   [2] Henry Hastings.
[3] Probably 9 *Hen.* IV.   [4] Thomas, 2nd Baron Savile.

grounds from this, that Llps say ye will not medle with matter of subs[*idy*].

If they can make good their reason [beyond ours], we may be of an other mind, else I am not for voating.

L Wharton. To shew them our reasons upon a confer[*ence*], before voating.

E[*arl of*] Dorset. We have heard their reasons.

[*fo 39ᵛ*] E[*arl*] Marshall. They have voated before they have asked us the Question.

L V[*iscount*] Say. I will nothing doe to dismisse the Honor of this House, which is to take such a course as may justi[*fy*].

If we voate, we condemne them before they have given us the reasons. They will fortifie themselves with statutes in their owne and say these *res* we could have given.

E[*arl of*] Strafford. The way to have reason from them is to stand upon our owne reason and [?]wt of that

whether in [our] opinions barely delivered *voated* here etc. be a breach of their Priviledges of H. C.

L North. Voating is to judge before hearing, not ripe yet for a voate; desires a conferrence.

E[*arl of*] Hart[*ford*]. Not to voate before they give their reasons.

Bp Rochest[*er*]. 1. Against confer, against the honor of their Lops as councillors, dishonorable; 2. A hinderance and stop to yor proceedings and a great hinderance [*fo 40ʳ*] to the Ks affaires. Privil[*eges*] will be longe in disputing, etc.

E[*arl of*] Southton. Honor of this H. stands with Justice, not to proceed before their reasons given, which may be contrary to the Justice of this courte.

L Pagett. Will maintaine Priv[*ileges*] ho[*nour?*], as much as any, but not to voate before reasons given.

Lo Cott[*ington*]. [Yt ye Quest[*ion*] is only] whether in yt p[*ar*]ticuler assignd [by us], we have broken their Priviledges.

Lo Brook. [Whether we]: 1. Shall voate [all] what is reasonable. 2. Whether we shall advise them some things are proper to us. Judic[*ature*] proper to us; sub[*sidies*] to them.

L North. Whether voate before the conference.

L P[*rivy*] Seale. Conf[*erence*] with Lo Keep and what they have reported. They have demanded reparacions.

L V[*iscount*] Say. They tooke their grounds upon our concession. To knowe upon what grounds they have charged those p[*ar*]ticulers.

[*fo 40ᵛ*] E[*arl of*] Strafford. Why we should not goe as farr as they. They did not to come to knowe our reasons.

E[*arl of*] Bristoll. If we finde an error in them, why should we [now runne into ye same]. The better were to heare them, but they not done soe first to us. To know whether we should voate before we know their reasons.

L Say. Libertie of voating is free, but whether Lib[*er*]tie of voating concerning subs[*idies*] is [*the*] quest[*ion*].

E[*arl*] Marsh[*al*]. An equall will [*not*] desire reparacon.

L Fawconb[*ridge*]. Desired he may not voate, not being here ye 1 day, and his opinion was not to voate untill ye reasons given.

The House is resumed.

[*House of Lords*]

Q. 1. Whether yt ye voating [in this House] of yt in our Opin[*ion*] is, the [*matter*] of his Majestis supply *ought to preceed all* [should have precedence before any] other *busines* be resolved were a breach of the priviledges of the H. C.

[As many of yor lops as thinke it fitt.]

2. Whether before ye voate [the] Q there should *not* be a conference with H. C. to know their reasons.

[*fo 41ʳ*] 3. Whether ye first quest[*ion*] shall be 1. putt.

Whether [as many] of your Lops [as are of] [*blank*], deliver your opinions [of voating thus] *that yor lordships were of* [we are] opinion that the matter of his Majesties supply should have precedence and be resolved of before any other matter whatsoever [was not] *were* a breach of the priviledges of the House of Commons, say content.

As many of yor lops will have ye question putt, say content.

Whether yor lops will heare the reasons of the House of Commons. Contents carrye it. [*Voting:*[1] *Contents 56, Not Contents 29 (revised in MS. to be 59–31); Contents 60, Not Contents 25.*]

[*fo 41ᵛ*] Resolved thus by their lops, that their thus voting (we are of opinion That the matter of his Majests supply should have precedence and be resolved of before any other matter whatsoever) was no breech of the Priviledges of the House of Commons, say content.

Resolved no breach.

Ad[usque]: to mor[*row*], 9 *hora*.

---

[1] As on 24 April, the first vote was procedural (see below, Lee Warner, p. 4, Montagu Papers, p. 3a, Harl. MS. 4931, fo 48ᵛ, pp. 112, 102, 240; also *L.J.*, iv, p. 73; Yale, Stanford (Braye), MS. 95, fo 77ʳ). Montereul says that the king's party outnumbered the other by twenty (P.R.O. 31/3/72, fo 134ʳ).

[H.L.R.O., Braye MS. 16]   **[30 April 1640, House of Lords]**

[fo 42ʳ]   *DIE JOVIS* 30ᵗʰ *APRILIS* 1640

[See L.J., iv, pp. 73–74]

Praiers.

[Committee]¹

E[arl] Marshall. That we tooke no notice of any thinge from nobody [of their House,] but from the K. himselfe.

E[arl of] Bristoll. That it may passe by voate, whether we shall to accomodation—[to put an ende to dispute]—*or dispute*
All thinke one k[ing]dome is lost, [and a powerfull kingdome], there is discord in one, unlesse accom[modation], there may be fractions at home, which will be most unhappy, whether [*blank*].

E[arl of] Strafford. Takes it to be contradictory to what was done yesterday. To let the H. Co. see that they are mistaken by a confer-[ence], that we have done nothing to their prejudice is the way to bring unity. We are as considerable as they.

E[arl of] Bristoll. If words may be disjoynted, [David may be made to speake Blasphemy in saying there is no God, but it was the foole that said soe in his heart].²
He did not intend any such thinge from his harte and by way of supposicion, and not otherwise.

E[arl of] Strafford. did it only soe by way of carpinge.

Order. Ordered yt the Com[mittee] of Priviledges take into consideracion, whether upon ad[journing] House into a committee [it be necessary] there *may* be one appointed in the nature of a speaker [to gather the sense of the debate to the House].

[fo 42ᵛ] E[arl] Marshall. To [?]deliver H. C. yt for Rel[igion], Prop[erty] and Privil[ege] we did not [*take*] notice of them from any member of theirs, but from his Majestie.

E[arl of] Bristoll. *Not the voating of their lops is ye exceptions* H. C. did not make exception against voating, but transferring of [our opinions] *their resol[utions]* upon them.

E[arl of] Straf[ford]. 1. Breach. H. C. did assigne the reasons [of breach of their Privild[ges],] yt they were transported, etc. 2. Breach. H. C. the taking notice of their proceedings [is their indemnitie]. If his Majestie doe tell Lo. House any [proceed[ings]], they ought to take notice by any person whatsoever, is not included in that indemnitie, and having it from ye K., it is no indemnitie.³

After voating and resolution, notice maye be taken of any matter.

Lo Cott[ington]. 1. Ye K. tells it us and not whosoever. 2. Ye K.

---

¹ See below, Braye 16, fo 43, p. 91.   ² Psalm 14:1.   ³ 9 *Hen.* IV.

tells us what use we shall make it, *vizt.* that ye K. is resolved to give them satisfaccion and 2 will joyne with them.

L V[*iscount*] Say. Their indemnitie is this, that they meant is, yt nothing be carried out of their house, but by their Speaker, and by their declaracon. Whosoever, is meant, yt none whosoever shall carry it out of the House.

To heare first what H. C. can say and afterwards determine. They can [*cite*] some ordinances [of Parlement and statutes] in ye same cases.

[*fo 43ʳ*] E[*arl of*] Dorsett. Records must stand upon their owne leggs and their whole bodies considered.

E[*arl of*] Strafford. Sub[*sidy*] is to begin at the House of Commons. 1. and by bill it must first be begun, not yt the Lo House may not treate of it first.

L V[*iscount*] Say. The Q. is, whether upon ye K. speach it be not a breach of to ground a proceeding upon it.

Sub[*sidy*] and supply will be construed all one to them.

E[*arl*] Marsh[*al*]. The Lo maye wish that sub[*sidy*] maye be given, and no breach.

Lo Wharton. Who tould the K of it.

E[*arl of*] Bristoll. The H. Co. to finde out and right themselves upon him yt tould the K. But the privil[*eges*] of H. C. have not ben broken by us, seeing the K. tould us of it.

E[*arl*] Marshall. That the K. spoke it openly to both Houses at the Banq[*ueting*] House.

E[*arl of*] Bristoll. The [K.] spake the words here.

The House is resumed.

[House of Lords]

[*fo 43ᵛ*] Whether [we have broke any Priviledge of H. C. by hearing report] or taking notice what his Majestie sayd here, and by reporting the same [to] House of Comon[*s*] by the K direccion.

That it was no breach of the priviledges of H. C. for Los to heare what his Majests declared to [*blank*].

[*Voting:*[1] *Contents 80, Not Contents 2.*]

[*fo 44ʳ*] Resolved upon the Q. by their Lops: As many of yor Lops as are of opinion, that it was no breach of the Priviledges of the House of Comons for yor lops to heare what his Majestie declared to your lops and thereupon to report the same to the [House] of Commons. Cleerely resolved no breach.

Moved that Nicholls[2] had a letter of marke and did enter upon a

---

[1] *Cf.* Montagu Papers, p. 3b, below, p. 103; also *L.J.*, iv, p. 74; Yale, Stanford (Braye) MS. 95, fo 77ʳ.

[2] See below, Petition, Niccolls, p. 283.

ship yt had done him wrong and Sr John Apsley afterward sesed for ye K. 50000^{li} which 2000^{li} was paid to Nicholls. Ye rest remains unpaid by his Majestie, yt the K. may be moved.

The Lo. committees are to meete this afternoone at the Counsell Chamber, at Whitehall to draw up the heads of conference with the Commons.

To send notice to the Keep of the Records of the Tower to bring to mor[*row*] morning the record of 9 *H*. 4 of the Indemnity of ye Commons.[1]

Ad[*usque*]: to mor[*row*] 9 *hora*.

[*H.L.R.O., Braye MS. 16*]   [*1 May 1640, House of Lords*]

[*fo 44*^{v}]   *DIE VENERIS 1° DIE MAII* 1640

[*See L.J., iv, pp. 74–77*]

Praiers.

Report of ye heads of the conference [prepared by the Lls appointed who] yesterday and nowe ye Ll com meete.[2]

The correspondence is entertayned with all respect and what belonge to ye House C., Lo doe no[*t*] challeng, what belongs to ye Ll, their desire to keepe intire, no desire to impeach and will be carefull of there owne.

Majestie took into cons[*ideration*] the great [and necess[*ary*] [?]portent] of cal[*ling*] parlement and the great dangers that are now on foote—if by sup[*ply*] his Majestie doe not prevent; Majests notice of Rel[*igion*], Pro[*perty*], and Pri[*vilege*] and will give willing eare [and just releife], to which is a just greevance and graciously this sess[*ion*] as much [as ye season of the yeare will permitt].

Their Ll are [in rank and honor ye nearest unto him] *Willing to beleive that their resol*[*ution*] *was a mistake* 1. Q this did no[t] intrench upon any priviledges as H. C. did pretend.

Their [Llps] doe acknow[*ledge*] yt the bill of sub[*sidy*] must come first from them by their Speaker. But to give their Lops advise in sub[*sidy*], they doe not [as by naming sums or tyme. Ll. did not. They did not, but to advise among themselves is no breach.]

Lo not unacquainted with the [[?] in parliament nor] record of 9 *H* 4 at Glost. Their was a confer[*ence*].

1 10th etc.

1 subsidy etc. ton[*nage*] and pound[*age*].

Lords and Commons among themselves may treate of any daungers.

1 Also 2 *Ric.* II (*L.J.*, iv, p. 74), probably *Rot. Parl.*, iii, pp. 55–56, 61.
2 See below, App. (1 May) p. 314.

The H. C. have no reason to demand reparacons.

2. Obj. How his Majestie knew of yt [3 p[ar]ticulers belongs not to their lops to inquire and in the duty unto his Majestie, they could doe noe lesse but rather merretts your good affeccons].

To take into H. C. confer[ence], the K. supply and [blank].

[fo 45ʳ] Mess[age]. Mess[age] to H. C. about a Conference, p[ain]t[ed] Ch[amber], with all convenient speed to cleere somewhat which fell from them at the last conference with a comitte of both Houses. L C[hief] Justice and Mr Justice Jones.

Answer by ye Judges. The judges *returned* this ans[wer] from H. C., [that they have the mess[age] from the Ll and at] this tyme [they are imployed upon] important busines and cannot now returne [their answere], but will by [messenger] of their owne [withall convenient speed] which they hope will be this morning.

The Queenes [counsell] to report the Bill of the Queenes Jointure before it be reade againe in the Houses.

The Bill of Fees.[1] The Bill of Fees was this day reade in the House, being reported by the e[arl] of Warwicke, from the Grand Comittee [to be approved by them and ye L subcomittees] and agreed to by all their Llps, *nemine dissentiente.*

Answ[er]. The H. of C. by mess[engers] of their owne H. returne an Answere to the mess[age] sent to them, *vizt*, the H. C. are ready to give a meeting presently if [it stand with your] *their* Llps *please* [occasions], P[ain]t[ed] Ch[amber].

LO KEEP, from ye [Lods], yt their Lops will presently give them a meeting, P[ain]t[ed] Ch[amber].

Ad[journed] Ho. during pleasure.

House resumed.

Ad[usque]: to mor[row] morning *hora* 9.

[H.L.R.O., Braye MS. 16]   **[2 May 1640, House of Lords]**

[fo. 45ᵛ]   *DIE SABATTI 2º DIE* **MAY 1640**

[See L.J., iv, pp. 77–79]

Praiers.

[*Message from K.*] Graciously interpret your loves and forwardnes in his busines concer[ning] his supply with the H. of C., and his Majestie this morning hath sent to [H. C.] desire they will take it into consid[eration] for expedition.

Nicholls.[2] It was the opinion of the H. yt the E[arl] of Dorsett should present to his Majestie the case of Archbold Nicoll.

Queenes bill. The Queenes bill reade being *3a vice* and dd [*delivered*]

[1] See H.L.R.O., Main Papers, 30 April 1640, list of fees.
[2] See below, Petition, Niccolls, p. 283.

D

to the Lo Keep, who demanded the voate of the House for the passinge it, and [being] put to the Question and generally consented to.

E[*arl of*] Midd[*lesex*]. It was moved[1] in behalfe of the E[*arl of*] Middlesex yt he is become an humble suitor to their Lops that they will extend their grace and remission towards him, that he may come and sitt amongst them. He hath his writt of sommons. Committed to the Grand Committee for Priviledges on Monday, the first thinge handled.

Joseph Roberts brought to the bar for arresting Sanderson [at his suite] and being charged [whether he saw ye protection], he said the protection was not shewed him nor did not know he was the Lo Stanhopes servant.

[*fo 46ʳ*] Redfort Bayly arrested him in St. Dunstan.

[Comp[*laint*]] Sanderson shewed him a pap[*er*].

The jaylor will not obey the *habeas corpus* for to sende Sanderson.

LO STANHOPE confest Sanderson hath ben his servant but 2 mo.

Lo Stanhope did withdrawe himselfe.

L KEEP. No intencon to Q. priv[*ilege*] nor ye Averm[*en*]t [of L Stanhope], nor ye men to lie in prison.

No protections shewed but only a paper and not reade nor to terme it protection but priviledges.

All the p[*ers*]ons set at large and the prisoner.

The contempt of the jaylor to be ex[*amined*] by the *sub*Committee of Priviledges [for] either refusing to dd [*deliver*] or to sende him up.[2]

Ad[*journed*]: untill Monday 9 *hora*.

[H.L.R.O., Braye MS. 16]   **[4 May 1640, House of Lords]**

[*fo 46ᵛ*]   *DIE LUNAE VIZT. 4⁰ DIE MAII* 1640

[*See L.J., iv, pp. 79–80*]

Praiers.

Hospitalls. Bill for hospitalls being *sine die* this morning after the House is up to meete.

1 By the earl of Bristol (*L.J.*, iv, p. 78); Lionel Cranfield, earl of Middlesex, had been impeached in 1624. See also H.L.R.O., Main Papers, 2 May 1640, draft motion; D. J., pp. 51, 58 (report of committee of privileges); and Montagu Papers, p. 3c, below, p. 103. Rossingham reports, 'Their lordships tooke this petition to hart, knoweing all was certainely true, which was inserted in the petition. And their lordships were the more willing to restore his lordship, because hee haveing receavd the Kings writt to repaire to the Parliament his lordship had not only forborne, but had forborne alsoe to send his Proxie. This petition is to be taken into consideration by the Committee of Priviledges to drawe upp his lordships restoration according to former Presidents, thereby to preserve the priviledges of their house' (B.L., Add. MS. 11045, fo 115ʳ).

2 *Cf.* Montagu Papers, p. 3c, below, p. 104.

Acadamy. E[ARL] MARSHALL. For a body pollitique for an academy to [traine up young noblemen and gentlemen, etc] It [referred] comitted to the Committee for Priviledges.

E[arl] Hartford excused, not well.

L Bp of Exon. excused, not well.

Lo Brudnell.[1] Lo Brudnell bought [sic] in betwene Lo Mowbray and Lo Audley and dd. [delivered] a constat of his pattent, being date xxvi Marcii tertio Caroli and placed next below Lo Deinecourt.[2] Ad[usque]: to mor[row] 9 hora.

[H.L.R.O., Braye MS. 16]   [5 May 1640, House of Lords]

[fo 47ᵛ]   DIE MARTIS 5º MAII 1640

[See L.J., iv, pp. 80–81]

Praiers.

The Bp of Oxford[3] excused.

His Majestie being in p[er]son in his roabes, and the Lods being [in] their roabes, the House of Commons and their speaker were called in, and after his Majestie had made a short speach[4] to them, the Lo Keeper by the Ks comand signified unto them that the Kinges majestie do dissolve this parlement.

[Montagu]   [13 April 1640, House of Lords]

[p. 1]   A JOURNALL 1640. 16: CAROLI

Tuesd[ay] I sett oute from Boughton towards London last time.

Thursd[ay] the 2 March[5] I came to London.

Tuesdy the 7 March[6] I went to the courte to do my duty to his Majestie. That After noone the Lord Keep: Finch was created Baron of Fordish in the presence chamber wher[e] the Queene was And a greate presence of Lords and Ladies. He made a very fine Elegant speach touching all his preferment by the Queene.[7]

MONDY 13 APRILL

The King rid in [?]state to the parliament [with the prince].[8] The Queene had a stage provided upon White hall garden, who afterwards went to the parliament house.

[1] Thomas Brudenell. See H.L.R.O., Main Papers, 27 April 1640, certificate of date of patent.   [2] Francis Leake, 1st Lord Deincourt.
[3] John Bancroft.   [4] See below, App. (5 May) p. 316.
[5] Probably April.   [6] Probably April.
[7] Finch had been the Queen's Attorney General (D.N.B.).
[8] See also Oxinden Letters, pp. 161–62; The Manner of Holding Parliaments

The King lighted att the west end of the Abbey Church. Wren Bishop of Ely preached—[(his text psalms 68:17: the letters read)] made a very good sermon [(I could wish it in printe)].[1] After pryers endes we lords went according to our degrees before the King to the parliament house on foote.

When the King came to the house, he went unto the Lord Treasurers side, [which I never saw before], And sent for all the privy councell where he sate with them alone halfe an howre and then came from thence, being sett.

[CHARLES I].[2] His Majeste told us that never king had so much cause to call a parliament as he had had but for the p[ar]ticulars he would refer them to be delivered by the Lord Keep.

The LORD KEEPS[3] speach bending alltogether to the Scottish business

[(I then present)] but so as the King would have no mercie As for them but should alltogether proceed to occasions.

[p. 1b] Account unto us what the Irish had done and what they professed (But left [?]oute these wants In parliamentary way).

Told us aboute the tonnage and poundage, that the King had taken yt de facto [as other kings had done], but claymed yt not but by grant of parliament and to that end there was a bill drawn as yt was in his fathers time with this to have from his fathers time.

And for subsidies that yt might be first moved with a speedy sequal of the same and though the King should give his Royall assent to yt yet it should be no conclusion of the session but they might proceede to there other petitions wherein they should have a gracious answer after this speach.

The KING drew oute a letter in French which was written by the Scotts to the King of France but intercepted and never came to the kings [(of France his)] hand which letter he caused to be read by the clerke [Lord Keeper] in French and After in English with these names subscribed: (Rothes, Montrosse, Mountgomery; Lowden; Lesly and Mountgomery and other whose names I remember). And then the King told that one of them being here (Lord Lowden) he had committed him to close prisoner in the Tower.

And so that done business moved. The Speaker to be presented on Wednesday.

---

in England . . . with the . . . order of proceeding to Parliament of the most high and mighty Prince King Charles on Monday the 13th of April. . . . (1641) (B.L., E.157(11)).
[1] See Lee Warner, p. 1. below, p. 105. We have not been able to find it among Wren's printed sermons. See also Harley Letters, p. 90; Hist. MSS Comm., Fourteenth Report, App. ii, p. 62.
[2] See below, App. (13 April), p. 293.
[3] See below, App. (13 April), p. 293.

[*Montagu*]　　　　　　　　　　　　[*15 April 1640, House of Lords*]

[*p. 1c*]　　　　**WEDNESDY 15 APRILL**

The SPEAKER was presented: made his excuse, but the King accepted of the style: and then he made his speach, a very good one, and desires the old [grace and privileges for them].[1]

The LORD KEEP made an Answer and held that the King granted all the privileges.

The KING made a short speach to this effect that if they would proceede with the supply: they should have all their just favors, Att the which there was a greate hum.[2]

The house adjourns [by the Lord Keeper] to 8 the next morn.

[*Montagu*]　　　　　　　　　　　　[*16 April 1640, House of Lords*]

[*p. 1c*]　　　　**THURSDY 16 APRILL**

The house mett at the howr where the prince was come at the first.

After pryers and some lords were introducted: the Lord Mowbry, the Lord Herbert, and the Lord Keep. After they had delivered up the patents and the writt, the writts of all of them was red which to my remembrance I never observed befor.[3]

Then the orders of the House wer called for to be read. But the LORD COTTINGTON rose and told us [*he*] had some thing to deliver for his majestie. That he with Mr Secretary Windebank and Mr Attorney Generall wer sent to the Lord Lowden to examine him uppon the letter. That the Lord Lowden stood uppon yt att the first that he was not to [*be*] examined. And many dilating uppon the question [*he*] denies assent. But att last confessed yt to be his hand.

The Letter was delivered to the Clerke who read it in French: many desire to have had [*it*] in English but because yt cleared to us, yt was lett alone. The time when yt was written was not so well expressed. [*p. 1d*] but my self coming oute of the house with my Lord Cottington, I asked him whether yt was written before the Kings going to Scotland had say no.

The orders of the house read and being donne yt was moved that the house should be called but Inquiry upheld that in my observance the committees of privileges and other busines was appoynted before the calling of the house because that myght be done [when

---

[1] See below, App. (15 April), p. 294.
[2] See below, Harvard MS., fo 29ᵛ, p. 143.
[3] *Cf.* Henry Elsyng, *The Ancient Method and Manner of Holding Parliaments in England*, 3rd ed. (London, 1675), pp. 97–98.

there Lops pleas[*ure*] for adjourning the house did nott assent att this time.

It was moved fill them over. I saw yt and Yt was forbade. And the [great] committees for privileges was named And likewise the sub-committee, and likewise the committees for petitions. These done, I was on them all.

A bill was read aboute transporting of clothe.[1]

And then the LORD KEEP desired to know the pleasure of the house for adjourning the same, whether till to morrow because yt was a convocation day or till Saturday but that was not approved of being a division whereupon the ARCHB made a speech to hold us according to ancient custome and to desire yt might be till Sater-day but that took no pleas[*ure*]. Then the LORD KEEP went to his place: shews his indisposition of health and how that morning he had been so ill that he had sent to the King by my lord mayor for a commission to supply his place but finding himselfe somewhat better he came but desired that the house might be adjourned till Saterday which was presently yielded unto and so adjourned to 9 that morning.

[*Montagu*]   [*18 April 1640, House of Lords*]

[*p. 2*]   **SATERDY 18: APRILL**

The Lord Keep being sick there was a commission to the Lord Cheife Justice to supply his place, And so as often as he was not well this parliament.

Lords Introduced. The Lord Audley being a restitution his patent read, The viscount Camden, the Lo Cottington.

The House was called.

After the calling, the LORD PRIVY SEALE, desires an explana-tion of the words—Chatholicke Church of England which did abide some debate but yt was committed to some few presently in the committee chamber, but before they went oute the EARLE OF ESSEX moved the house being a thing concerning us to all in Doctor Manwarings cayse, but some opinion being delivered, it was com-mitted to the committes of privileges.[2] Then the lords aboute the pryer [*book*] went out and agreed quickly: for the pryer to stand.

The subcommittee for privileges to sitt this afternoone and to view the journall booke which we did.

The house adjourned till Monday 9 clock.

---

[1] See below, Bills—Cloth, p. 273.

[2] It is hard to see how Rossetti might have interpreted this motion as one in favour of the Catholics (P.R.O. 31/9/18, fo. 197r).

[Montagu]   *[20 April 1640, House of Lords]*

[p. 2]   **MONDY 20 APRILL**

Little done but a long bill for the Queens jointure twice read.
The adjournment till to morrow.

That afternoone the greate committee for privileges mett and in
regard of the greate number they removed into the parliament
house. Where two things was handled. First for the sitting of the Convocation. And an old order being read in yt King James that the
Lord Keep every Tuesday and Thursday should move the house
whether they had any busines that the Convocation might then sitt
on Wednesday and Friday.[1]

But there fell something from the Lo of Cant[er]b[ury] that they
were a third estate that bid some debate but yt was layd by.[2]

The second busines was concerning Doctor Manwaring, his censure
he sent in his pardon that had greate debate how far his preferment
would trench agynst the privileges but referred to search some
records what had been done in the like case.

[Montagu]   *[21 April 1640, House of Lords]*

[p. 2b]   **TUESDY 21 APRILL**

A bill read aboute reforminge of abuses in hospitalls and *maisons
de dieu* twice read and committed.

The report of convocation business assented unto and ordered that
for Manwaring putt yt [*off*] till Monday.

His Majestie sent us commande to attend him att White Hall att
1 of the clock: the Commons had the like message.

The lower house sent us a desire to joyne in petition with them for
a fast: ii daies later for the Lords and Commons and then for all the
Realme which we assented. They desire the time, our answer was
that we must first know his Majesties pleysure. [The Archb and the
Lord Chamberl[*ain*] were ordered to do it.]

Then [the LORD [?]MANDEVILLE] was moved aboute a speach
used yesterday by Hall, Bishop of Exeter, att the committee: aboute
the three estates that yt would much Incourage the Scotts I can not
remember the words but they were offensively taken and he made a

---

[1] See S.P. 16/451/9, endorsed by Laud, 'Received April 20, 1640. Journall
of Parliaments Concerning Convocation Dayes.' *Cf.* Elsyng, *Ancient Manner*,
pp. 111–12.
[2] Montagu may have been confused. *Cf.* below, Montagu Papers, p. 2b,
p. 99.

kinde of sorrow for them which satisfied the house, but there was much speach aboute them in a [?] contrary question.

There was a motion to adjourn the house till Thursday because to morrow was the first day of the terme: but because his Majestie had sent to us to wyght on him and could tell what business might fall oute, it was thought to adjourn but till to morrow, and so yt was.

In the after noone, both the houses attende the King. The Lord Keep[1] made a speach but yt was long and my memory fyles me in nature. It is like many to come oute in print, and some menn sniph of yt: but yt all tended to quicken a supply: And the matter is to be quickly done and the speaker to Informe him.

After this I went to the committee of petitions, but court was sett befor I came in and there I saw the Attendants sitt with their [?] Hatts [?]onn I told some of the Lords but they said they gave the leave.[2]

[*Montagu*]   [*22 April 1640, House of Lords*]

[*p. 2c*]   **WEDNESDAY 22 APRILL**

The LORD KEEP reported the tenor of his speaking to [*the*] speaker when we attended his Majestie yesterday.

The LORD CHAMBERLINE returned his Majestie pleasure for a fast leaving the time to us. And so a conference was appoynted with the Lower House that after noone att 3 clock, the Lords were xii the Commons, according to the old count, 24.

This day the order formerly writ against the abuses in Taverns of the pages, footmen, and coachmen and their disorder was commanded to be putt in execution.

The LORD CHEIFE JUSTICE[3] delivered us the abuses of protections and 2 that he had committed, one for a counter fitter who was apoynted to be brought to the house to morrow.

The adjournment to 9 a clock next morning.

The afternoon the committee [mett] aboute the time on the fast. we having agreed to be Saterdy come sevennight, if their voices are [not] otherwise; and to lett us know to morrow that so we might wyght on the king for his pleasure.

---

[1] See below, App. (21 April), L.K., p. 303.
[2] Hist. MSS Comm., x, New Series, *House of Lords*, pp. 3–4, Standing Order 23.
[3] Probably the Lord Keeper.

[*Montagu*]   [*23 April 1640, House of Lords*]

[*p. 2c*]   **THURSDAY 23 APRILL**

Little done but putting the Queens joynture to Ingrossing.

And setting one Bradshaw on the pillory att Westminster and
Cheap side, fined a hundred pounds, and to the house of correction
to be whipped and sett on work till he can finde sureties of the good
behavior. It was putt to voting whether he should be nayled or no,
but the non contents carried yt by far.

The Lord Strafford introducted but no writt was red.

The House adjourned till 9 to morrow.

[*Montagu*]   [*24 April 1640, House of Lords*]

[*p. 2d*]   **FRIDAY 24 APRILL**

The KING came into the higher house, made a speach unto us.
Vide what yt was and the debate of yt.[1]

We concluded upon 2 questions to *confer with the lower house. Vide*
the questions *inde**

*The questions

As many of your Lops as are of opinion that the matter of his
Majests supply should have precedence and be resolved of before
any other matter whatsoever, say content:

As many of your Lops as think fitt ther should be a conference
desired with the House of Commons to dispose them thereunto, say
content.

The contents carried yt.

[*Montagu*]   [*25 April 1640, House of Lords*]

[*p. 2d*]   **SATERDAY 25 APRILL**

The King sent us thanks by the Lord Keep: and we presently sent
[to] the Commons for a speedy conference, for a committee of both
houses they came up presently and st[a]yed a goodwhile befor we
went to them because we had not thoroughly sent downe what to
say to them and being ready: the Lord Keep[2] spake to them of the
busines and whatt we had voted. they came up only with there eares
but appoynted to consider of the thing proposed on Mondy.

---

1 See below, App., Charles I (24 April), p. 308.
2 See below, App., L.K., (25 April), p. 310.

[*Montagu*]   [*27 April 1640, House of Lords*]

[*p. 2d*]   **MONDY 27 APR[IL]**

I went not to the House the Lo: Dorsett made my excuse being
lame. The Committee for privileges sate that afternoone. *Que.* what
was done.

There was that dy, these Lords introduction: the erle of Carnarvon,
and the erle Rivers and the Lord Powis.

[*Montagu*]   [*28 April 1640, House of Lords*]

[*p. 3a*]   **TUESDY 28 APRILL**

The Lord Keep delivered us a message from his Majestie concerning the Bishop of Saint Davids that he should neither come into the
house nor send any proxi: the Lords tooke this well and willed yt
should be entered into the Journall book.

The Commons sent to us a message for a conference [of the committees of both houses] aboute the conference we had with them on
Saterdy.

We presently yeilded unto yt, to have yt presently done.

The Lord Keep and some other Lords to assiste him was appoynted
to prepare what they delivered unto them and to reporte yt. The
reporte was putt off till to morrow and so the house adjourned till
9 a clock.

[*Montagu*]   [*29 April 1640, House of Lords*]

[*p. 3a*]   **WEDNESDY 29 APRILL**

The LORD KEEP[1] made reporte of that which was spoken for the
Commons Att which was taken much exception, especially that they
had voted that we, in voting the question of our opinion, had broken
there privileges and some things else [?]gi.

Gett what the speach was.

This did abide a greate deale of debate amongst us, for myntyning
what we had done to be no breach of there privilege. And so att
length yt was voted. The contents 59 the not contents 31.

What will be the issue of this.

[1] See below, App., Pym (28 April), p. 312.

[*Montagu*]   [*30 April 1640, House of Lords*]

[*p. 3b*]   **THURSDY 30 APRILL**

We fell into debate aboute the 2 exceptions the Commons tooke
for breach of their privileges saving there second resolution. After
much arguing we concluded of this question.

That the King making knowne to us those things which they had
concluded and desired us to make yt known to them, this we concluded to be no breach of the privileges by us, which we voted all
content but one.[1]

The lords that had the drawing of the other matter into heads wer
appoynted to draw them along together, this after noone and to
reporte what they had done to morrow morning: and so the house
adjourned till then att 9 a clock.

[*Montagu*]   [*1 May 1640, House of Lords*]

[*p. 3b*]   **FRIDY 1 MAY**

The Lords brought yt [*in*] writing what they determine which was
twice read by the Lord Keep and a message was sent to the Commons
for a conference and as they occasioned, we to sett downe a time.

The[*y*] returned by our messengers that they wer in handling of a
weighty busines and would send us an answer by messengers of their
owne this morning, and so within a little while the[*y*] sent unto us
that yf we wer att leysure yt might be presently in the pynted
chamber.

So they and the lords mett and what the lord Keep had read unto
us was repeated by the Lord Keep with helpe of his pap[*er*] unto
them and so uppon returne the House was adjourned to 9 a clock
next morning.[2]

[*Montagu*]   [*2 May 1640, House of Lords*]

[*p. 3c*]   **SATERDY 2 MAY**

The Lo Keep delivered unto us a message from his Majestie of his
good acceptance and our cariage, the busines of his supply and gave
us thanks for yt. And that his Majestie had sent a message to the
Commons [(*quaer*) to quicken them].

The ERLE OF BRISTOW delivered unto [*us*] a desire from the
Lord of Middlesex aboute taking him into the house agyne and

---

[1] 'who mistooke the question' (B.L., Add. MS. 11045, fo 114r).
[2] See below, App., L.K. (1 May), p. 314.

would have had yt presently voted, but the house thought yt fitt to be first committed to lords and privileges and so yt was agreed on to [be] on Mondy, the first cause.

The Queens bill for her joynture was passed.

There was some approval aboute the Lo Stanhope protection, but no fault found and so the men were discharged in some respect to the Lo; his man was likewise to be sett att liberty.

The House adjourned till Mondy 9 clock.

And After this message delivered the Commons sitte all that day till 6 a clock and in the end putt yt of till Mondy. (*quaer*).[1]

[*Montagu*]   [*4 May 1640, House of Lords*]

[*p. 3c*]   **MONDY 4 MAY**

Little to do in the House and so yt was adjourned to 9 a clock to morrow.

[The Lord Brudenell Introducted.]

The house rising so soone, yt was appoynted to sitt [*in the* Rolls Office] upon the bill of Hospitalls which was drawn but not reported.

We heard that the King had sent to the Commons for 12 subsidies and so of his grace in voting yt the ship mony. This held them in debate till 6 at night and not any thing concluded but referred to the next morning.[2]

The committees for privileges sat that after noone.

First was the Lord of Middlesex his coming into the house.[3]

Secondly upon the Lords to be uppon Honor and not on oath.[4]

Thirdly aboute the oath of allegeance.

[*Montagu*]   [*5 May 1640, House of Lords*]

[*p. 3d*]   **TUESDY 5 MAY**

As I was going to the house, one of the gromes mett me and told me I was to be in my Robes for the King would come into the house. This drew me [?] doubting as I sett oute.

---

[1] See below, Harvard MS., fos 74ᵛ ff., pp. 187ff.

[2] See below, Finch-Hatton MS., p. 81, p. 197.

[3] A copy of a committee report in favour of his admission appears in D.J., pp. 58–59, following the proceedings for 5 May.

[4] The point was discussed in 1628 (*Notes of the Debates in the House of Lords, 1621, 1625, and 1628*, ed. Frances H. Relf (Camden Society, Third Series, xlii, 1929), pp. 143ff). Registrars of the Court of Delegates, Auditors of the Court of Wards and the Examiners of the Court of Star Chamber were ordered to appear (H.L.R.O., Main Papers, 4 May 1640).

We were all in our Robes. And After pryers the Commons were sent for to come but before they came, the King was sett and stayed a pretty while till they wer come up.

[*Charles I*] And made a short speach. Gett what it was.[1]

And when he had done he bad my LORD KEEP speake which was no more but this. This Parliament is dissolved.

[*Lee Warner 1/2(441x1)*]   [*13 April 1640, House of Lords*]

[*p. 1*] **BISHOP WARNERS DIARY OF THE PARLAMENT**
APRIL. 13⁰. 1640.

Parlamentum coactum feliciter.

Concionatur coram Rege Episcopus Eliensis super psal. 68: 17.
Dominus est in illis in Sinai in Sanctuario.

In illis [*blank*].

In [?] *Sinas ubi Sol et Judicium. In Sanctuario* for Gods Worship; and then When *Dominus* is in all these; and without *Dominus* in all is nothing.

The KINGS[2] Speech. Never King had a more weighty cause of a Parlament then I have; the Keeper shall deliver the particulars.

[*LORD KEEPER*].[3] 1. That the King had sequestred ye ill usage of ye last parliament and in grace called this.

2. That ye Scotts who had Invaded England in both[4] . . . days. . . . honour and wealth never turned heel against all.

3. Ireland had given largely and promised more, if need be.

4. The Supply will admit no dispute but present.

5. The King in ye act of Subsidies [will acknowledge] that hitherto he had taken tonnage and poundage *de facto* onely, but . . . by parliament as his father did.

6. After which they shall sit and he hear their just petitions to all greevances.

7. [*blank*]

in relieving distressed princes and states that he would [*blank*] and to give credence to the bearer.

---

[1] Among his papers there is a copy, endorsed in his hand 'The Kings Speech upon Dissolving ye Parliament' (Montagu Papers, XIII, 75). See also below, App., Charles I (5 May), p. 316.

[2] See below, App., Charles I, L.K., (13 April), p. 293.

[3] See below, App. Ibid., p. 293.

[4] The copyist occasionally uses a series of dots to show an omission in his text. At other times he simply leaves a blank space. We have used ellipses where the copyist did, and have tried to indicate whether or not a sentence ends in the gap.

[*Lee Warner 1/2(441x1)*]   **[*14 April 1640, House of Lords*]**

[*p. 1*]   *14º APRIL*

[*CONVOCATION. See Nalson, i, pp. 356–57*]

Dr. [*Turner*][1] *ad clerum*
commisso 2º in medio luporum [*?*]*disertinen 3. estote prudente* . . .
munera, seu requisita.[2]

That day Dr. Steiron Cheston[*sic*][3] prolocutor who deane of
[*Chichester*] . . . and clerk of the [*Closet*] . . . Dr Sheldon of all
[*Souls*][4] . . .

[*Lee Warner 1/2(441x1)*]   **[*15 April 1640, House of Lords*]**

[*p. 1*]   *15º APRIL*

SRJANT CLANVILLE[5] in the afternoon presented [*as*] Speaker
who in his speech presented as—his owne [*desires: 1.*] the care of
Religion (or [*blank*] on right side) 2. [*blank*].
3. Justice, Judges. . . 4. [*blank*].
5. concerne for trade.
In Name of the house [*desired*][6] 1. liberty. . . 2. voices 3. [*blank*].
All which the King granted.

[*Lee Warner 1/2(441x1)*]   **[*16 April 1640, House of Lords*]**

[*p. 1*]   *16º APRIL*

[*UPPER HOUSE*]

A Comittee of 40 for priviledges of the [*blank*].
The Commission for petitions
8 persons. . . 7 of these . . . sit and . . . in sitting . . . to verifie
petitions and present them to yor [*blank*].
[Theusd. and Thursdays] in the afternoon at 2. a. clock in ye painted
chamber.[7]

[1] Rev. Thomas Turner, D.D., Canon Residentiary of St Paul's, preached
(Nalson, i, p. 357). We have made references to Nalson when material appears
both there and in the MS. Convocation Journals (Lambeth, Conv. I/1/1).

[2] Turner proposed that the theme for the Convocation be that of Matthew
10:16. *Cf.* Lambeth, Conv. I/1/1: '*Fece mitto vos ut oves in medium luporum
esotote igitur prudentes sicat serpentes et innocentis vi columbae.*'

[3] Richard Steward, Dean of Chichester and Clerk of the Closet to Charles
I (Nalson, i, p. 357; *D.N.B.*).

[4] Gilbert Sheldon, D.D., Master of All Souls, Oxford, presented Steward as
prolocutor (Nalson, i, p. 357).

[5] Glanville. See below, App., Speaker, L.K. (15 April), p. 294.

[6] MS.: destined.

[7] This is the order for the Committee of Privileges.

[*ARCHBISHOP OF CANTERBURY*] His Grace yt after ye Instant, Wednesday, and Friday may be allowed for the Convocation.

To which L. SA[Y] . . . against the Custome: which pleased.

[*ARCHBISHOP OF CANTERBURY*]. Whereon his Grace [against] Leave to Interpret and that ye records might be inquired: which granted.

[*p. 2*] After this the L. KEEP. Moved that the house, for his [*blank*] sake might be adjourned to Saturday (this being thursday) which granted so that. . .

This day many former orders were read.[1] 1. that Barons coming after prayers should pay—[*barons or bishops*] 1 [*shilling; those above*] 2 [shillings.] absentees [*pay five shillings for the poor*[2] *without*] . . . the excusation 3. for speaking without naming [*names*] or . . . [*offending*] persons. 4 not [*blank—privileges for any*] but . . . [*followers and*] servants or such as imployed in ye [*blank—persons and estates of the nobility*] 5. that Judges should [*not sit or be covered*] 6. Judges called to speak in house or at committee to stand bar[*e headed*]

In the upper house a bill [*once*] read for an Act that no wool should be transported; that [*blank*] clothes [*blank*] and late manufactures might be warranted and the impeditors punished.[3]

[*LOWER HOUSE*]

In the Lower House Sr Benjamin Ruedies Rudier[4] moved for subsidies: but Sr Fr. Seynor[5] questioned [*blank*] of priesthood for not [*blank*] and that they might know what was their own to give.

[*Lee Warner 1/2(441x1)*]   [*17 April 1640, House of Lords*]

[*p. 2*]   17⁰ APR.

[*CONVOCATION. See Nalson, i, pp. 358–61*]

Dr. Steward presented and the L. Archbishop caused ye King grant to be made 1. whereby with a *nonobstante* to the statute of 25 *Henr. 8. c.* 19. he gives leave to alter, add, Interpret Canons of the Church with a proviso not to meddle with the Articles, Common prayer book or Rubrick therein: at that time declared that the records in Queen Eliz. time granted Wednesday and Fridays for

---

[1] Hist. MSS Comm., x, New Series, *House of Lords*, pp. 1–11.

[2] Hist. MSS Comm., x, New Series, *House of Lords*, 44 (25 Feb. 1625); *cf.* 16 (28 May 1624) whereby there was no charge.

[3] The bill provided for the transportation of dyed cloths. See below, Bills—Cloth, p. 273.

[4] See below, App., Rudyerd, p. 296.

[5] See below, App., Seymour, p. 297.

convocation in [blank] and thereon parliament records to be en-
quired and [blank] the Convocation adjourned to Wednesday following in the fornoon at 8 in morning; so that If need be were [blank].
Some canons to be prepared for the restraint of popish swearing and
seducing the people. An advise to all clergy to be prudent, moderate
and united.

[*Lee Warner 1/2(441x1)*]   [*18 April 1640, House of Lords*]

[*p. 2*]   *18° APR.*

[UPPER HOUSE]

. . . [*An order*] of parliament in 1620. and 18. of K. Henry that it
was a custome to let the convocation sit
[*blank*]

[*Lee Warner 1/2(441x1)*]   [*20 April 1640, House of Lords*]

[*p. 2*]   **20 [APRIL]**

[UPPER HOUSE]

to [*blank*]. [*Bill*] for 99 years in trust for the Queen and her life
twice read and committed to 12.[1]

[*Lee Warner 1/2(441x1)*]   [*21 April 1640, House of Lords*]

[*p. 2*]   **21 [APRIL]**

[UPPER HOUSE]

A bill twice read for bettering hospitalls and setting poor on work.
The Commons desire the pears to repair with them for a fast to the
King for 2 days. the 1. for the tow houses together; the other
through the land; which was assented by the pears.
The King [*sent word*] the Lords to wait upon him, with the Com-
mons at Whitehall at 1. a. clock. in the banqueting house.
An order entered for the Convocation to sit if they will, on Wednes-
days and Fridays in the morning, but [*blank*].

[*p. 3*]   [*Banqueting House*]

[*Lord Keeper*][2] In the afternoon the [*Lord*] Keep spake and
repeated—his first days speech with hastening to subsidies [*blank*]
that as in Irland, so the King would be more gracious to requite
[*blank*] 2. that tonnage and poundage were not [*blank*] 3. [*blank*]

---

[1] The Queen's jointure.   [2] See below, App., L.K. (21 April), p. 303.

4. that the King bad them find how—he should be maintained as their King and defend the Land; he would make no benefit by shipmoney ([blank]) but be content, and thereupon bad them consult and resolve (the Speaker of Commons . . . graciously, we are made). . . . the assistance of us was desired for the Shipmoney this year, which the King cannot spare.

[*Lee Warner 1/2(441x1)*]   [*22 April 1640, House of Lords*]

[*p. 3*]   22⁰ [*APRIL*]

A Committee of 12 Lords and 24 Commons to resolve of a day for the parlament fast, thereby to present it to the Kings approbation.

[*LOWER HOUSE*]

The Subsidies moved but not a word spoken to it.[1]

[*UPPER HOUSE*]

The Order viewed and commended to be executed against [blank] other servants goods in taverns and no taverner to be in the parlament pay'd.

[*CONVOCATION. See Nalson, i, pp. 361–63*]

In Convocation sitting in fornoon (half the Lords there, the other half in parlament) 6 subsidies granted, and more if ever more were granted by cleargy.[2]
The first entire to be paid in [blank] following, the other five yearly by half payements.
One Canon made against papist, recusants, and seducers to popery.[3] After this the Convocation [to] sit in afternoon Wednesdays and Fridays.

[*Lee Warner 1/2(441x1)*]   [*23 April 1640, House of Lords*]

[*p. 3*]   23⁰ [*APRIL*]

[*UPPER HOUSE*]

One [blank] to be [blank] and put into the house of correction for forging the [blank].
[blank]

[1] See Finch-Hatton MS., p. 53, below, p. 167.
[2] Nalson, i, pp. 361–63; see Rossingham's report (B.L., Add. MS. 11045, fos 111ʳ–11ᵛ) and below, S.P., 16/451/57 (25 April), p. 247.
[3] Canon 3, *Constitutions and Canons Ecclesiastical Agreed upon at London and York, 1640* (London, 1640).

[*Lee Warner 1/2(441x1)*]   [*24 April 1640, House of Lords*]

[*p. 3*]   24º [*APRIL*]

[*UPPER HOUSE*]

[*CHARLES I*][1] The commons having concluded not to traite of subsidies, till 1. Innovations in Religion 2. propriety of goods. 3. Liberty of person and parlament were presented to the Lords. Thus moving his Majestie by his own tongue presented the necessity required and civility—that he should be first heard and supplied, calling God to witness he never Intended to gain by shipmoney, and that though they trust him more, yet he [*blank*] for this supply cannot serve him ever.

After the Kings desire the Commons sent to hold a Conference, which by [*blank*] was denied, untill the Lords first consulted about this supply.

[*Committee*]

[*Earl of Strafford*] 12. [*Jac.*] the Lords house denied conference with the Commons about the right of Impost which is a greater cause then the other first supplied or the subject first heard.
2. in the petition of right the Lords refused Conference with the Commons.

The whole army 42000, whereof 38000 foot 4000 horse of these from Ireland 8000 foot, 1000 horse. The Charge 100 thousand a month. Ireland hath given four subsidies, each above 600 thousand pounds; and if the King [*blank*] to have 5 subsidies more, which granted to, and all things granted then which the King promised or they desired: peccant humours within the body give eternall (heat and cold) their advantage to hurt the body.

[*Earl of Bridgewater*]. In *Henr.* 7[2] *Ric.* 2. *Ed.* 3. often first they gave subsidies then [*blank*] remedie to greevances.

[*House of Lords*]

After a long debate it was resolved that all should be put to those questions. 1. whether the Kings supply may be first considered before all other businesses. 2. whether the Lords shall have a Conference with the Commons.

Then first the question is which of these tow questions shall be first voted. and by plurality of vots the first question was to go first, and then [*blank*] was also granted.

[*p. 4*] A question whether [*blank*] dispose the Commons to the Kings supply in first place and granted.

[1] See below, App., Charles I (24 April), p. 308.
[2] Probably Henry V.

[*Lee Warner 1/2(441x1)*]   [*25 April 1640, House of Lords*]

[*p. 4*]   **25 [*APRIL*]**

[*UPPER HOUSE*]

The King gave thanks by his Speaker[1] for the speedy resolution of the Lords.

The KEEPER that he might tell who stood up first, desired order in speaking, and one to speak but once in a question.

They sent 2 Judges to the Commons for a Conference, which presently came together, the Speaker assisted by his Gr[*ace*] . . . [*blank*],[2] Bristoll, Lord Cottington repeated to the commons all the King had before spoken for subsidies.—

[*CONVOCATION. See Nalson, i, p. 363*]

In the Convocation a latin prayer for the peace and prosperity [*of Parliament*] and synod to follow St. Chrysostoms prayer.

An act that no Bishop under pain of synodical monition, nor other clergy under pain of 3 mon[*ths*] suspension shall [*give*] out the whole or any part of the Canon made for suppressing popery, until it be agreed on and presented to his majesty.

A Canon to be thought on for the Suppressing Books tending to Socinianisme.[3]

The Bishop of *Sarum*[4] would have the like against Arminianisme and Remonstrances, etc., but . . . of his majesties Injunctions sufficient 2 and that we might know what they say no Latin books popish or Arminian to be prohibited, but onely English.

[*Lee Warner 1/2(441x1)*]   [*27 April 1640, House of Lords*]

[*p. 4*]   *27⁰* [*APRIL*]

[*UPPER HOUSE*]

Annotation by [*blank*] for an Academy to withdraw young Nobles from drinking Gaming, etc.

At the Committee for privileges it appeared that a Baron at his admission is to pay 6.10.0—*viz.* to the Usher 2.10.0. to the Clerke 2.10.0. to the [*blank*] 20*l* and to the [*blank*][5] then and then the rolls 1628 declare that no peer is to swear but upon his honour, but in

---

[1] The Lord Keeper.
[2] Warner gives all the names on 30 April, Lee Warner, p. 4, below, p. 112.
[3] Canon 4, *Constitutions and Canons, 1640.*
[4] John Davenant.
[5] He owed ten shillings a piece to the clerk's chief clerk and to the yeoman usher (Hunt. Cal., Ellesmere MS. 34/A/2). He also paid two pounds to the doorkeeper (*L.J.*, xxii, p. 627), and something to the Lord Keeper (*L.J.*, iv, p. 77). The total would exceed £6. 10*s*.

his own cause rather then loose it to swear *super Sacramentum* and after to Complain. Yet at the Counsails board *Rege presente* it is ordered that they sweare in Chancery, Exchequer, Wards *super sacramentum*.[1] At that time the Lord Brooke say'd openly in the time of *Interregnum*, now in parliament it may be etc.

At the comittee for petitions it was urged that the high Commission Court had no power to much less Imprison but that we should excommunicate, and so a writ *de excommunicato* etc.

[*blank*]

[Lee Warner 1/2(441x1)]   **[29 April 1640, House of Lords]**

[*p. 4*]   **[29 APRIL]**

[UPPER HOUSE]

A general Comittee to debate 1. the breach of the commons priviledge 2. whether we may not take notice of their resolutions without a breach of priviledge that the first [?] should go first say'd 59 voices, on the other 31. nothing [*blank*] of either side. It was debated long and after put to question whether the delivery of our opinions that the Kings supply should precede all other businesses were a breach of the priviledges of the Commons, who pretend their right first to grant subsidies: which by 31 voices was affirmed to be a breach and by 59 voices denied.[2]

[Lee Warner 1/2(441x1)]   **[30 April 1640, House of Lords]**

30 [APRIL]

[UPPER HOUSE]

After debate de[*sic*] question was put whether that the Lords taking notice from the King that the Commons had voted (first to begin with reformation of greevances 1, in Religion 2 propriety of good. 3 liberty of persons and parliament) were a breach of the priviledges of the Commons right, that nothing under debate or resolved should be carried from them, but by their assent and by all votes [*blank*] of the Lord Brooke it was denied. Thereupon the former committee of Cant[*erbury*], Keeper, privy Seal, Earl Marshall, Earle Bristoll, Stratford, Lord Cottington were to Confer with the commons.

---

[1] Hist. MSS Comm., New Series, *House of Lords*, 53; also *Notes of the Debates in the House of Lords, 1621, 1625, and 1628*, pp. 144–47.
[2] Warner seems to be repeating himself here.

[*blank*][1]

[*Lee Warner 1/2(441x1)*]   **[*28 April 1640, House of Lords*]**

[*p. 5*]   **APR. 28. 1640**[2]

The head of the greevances to be consulted of with the Lds of ye upper house.
1. How to prevent Innovations in Religion 2. Concerning propriety in ye goods 3. priviledges in parliament the better to prepare us to give a present Supply to his majesty.
Inducements upon these heads
Concerning the first head 1. The Commission to the Convocation house 2. the complaint brought into the house against Innovations in Religion 3. the molestation of Conformable Ministers concerning their restraint Not to preach in their own Churches. 4. The divulging and publishing of popish Tenets.
Concerning the 2d head: 1. Monopolies and restraint of trade 2. Shipmoney 3. Forest business 4. Military Charges, arm coats, conduct mony, horses, carts, and harness for soldiers.—5. denying of Justice in courts of Justice 6. the frequent Imprisoning of persons for not paying of unwarrantable Monopolies.
Concerning the 3d head 1. to prevent punishing, or questioning of things out of parliament. 2. the not holding of parliament every year according to ye statute. 3. the sudden dissolution of parliament before ye businesses of parliament be perfected. 4. the pressing of trayne bands out of ye [*counties*][3]

[*Lee Warner 1/2(441x1)*]   **[*1 May 1640, House of Lords*]**

[*p. 5*]   **1° [*MAY*]**
[*UPPER HOUSE*]

The report to the Commons . . . [*blank*] of the houses and their priviledges, that the [*blank*] of tithes is in ye [*blank*] but the Lds to treate of the. . . .
The Lds sent to the Commons for a Conference; which was granted, thereupon presently met and the report in painted chamber was for fear of mistaking. . .

---

[1] A space is left at the top of the page, as if Warner intended to enter something prior to the list of grievances.
[2] See below, App., Grievances (24 April). p. 308.
[3] MS.: Comitees.

[*Lee Warner 1/2(441x1)*]   [*2 May 1640, House of Lords*]

[*p. 5*]   **2⁰ [MAY]**

[*UPPER HOUSE*]

His majesty thanked the Lds for their resolution to ye disposing ye Commons to his secure[*ty*] and say'd this day he would send to ye Commons to speed them which he did.

The Earl of Midlesex, and the Earl of Bristoll desired restitution to the house, the King having pardoned and sent him his writt.[1]

[*LOWER HOUSE*]

It was Committed to ye Commitees for priviledges on Munday next that they might report what held [*blank*] whereas many things are objected against Dr Beale, [*blank*] of St. Johns in *Cant.*[2] which he preached [*blank*] 27 March 1635. (Concerning the Kings propriety In subjects goods, etc.) [*blank*] by a pursuant it is Intimated [*blank*] him by the Commons that he appear before them at their house by thursday next if he please.

[*Lee Warner 1/2(441x1)*]   [*5 May 1640, House of Lords*]

[*p. 5*]   **5⁰ MAII 1640**

The Earle of Midlesex to be restored to the Lds house upon his petition, but upon the dissolution. . .

This day the King came and both houses assembled,

[*CHARLES I*][3] his Majesty gave the Lds thanks and promised that out of parliament as well as in he would preserve the unity of the Religion in ye Church of England, and the propriety of goods, and liberties of his people. [*p. 6*] but for ye cunning and ill affection of many of ye Lower house, who delayed which [?] worse then denial, he commanded ye Keeper to dissolve ye parlament which he did. *Parl. Infeliciter.*

---

[1] Bristol presented Middlesex' request for restoration.
[2] Cambridge. See below, Harvard MS., fos 73ʳ–74ʳ (1 May), p. 186.
[3] See below, App. (5 May), p. 316.

TEXTS: COMMONS

[Finch-Hatton MS. 50]   *[13 April 1640, House of Commons]*

[p. 1]

A JOURNALL OF THE PARLIAMENT HELD AT WEST-
MINSTER BEGUNNE ON MONDAY THE 13th DAY OF
APRILL IN THE SIXTEENTH YEARE OF THE RAIGNE
OF KING CHARLES *ANNO DOM.* 1640

DIE LUNAE 13⁰ APRILL

[See L.J., iv, pp. 46–48, and C.J., ii, p. 3]

After the usuall solempnity of the daie[1] the sermon being ended
and the Kinge together with the Lords spirituall and Temporall and
the Knights, Cittizens, and Burgesses had addressed themselves to
the upper howse; the Kinge said, My Lords and Gentlemen:

King.[2] There was never kinge had a more greate and weighty cause
to call his people together then myselfe. I will not trouble yow with
the particulars; I have informed my Lord Keeper, and commanded
him to speake; and desire yor due and serious consideracon.

Whereupon the Lord Keeper said:

Lo Keeper. My Lords and yow the knts cittizens and Burgesses of
the howse of Commons. Yow are this day assembled by his Majeste
gratious writt and Royall comand to hold a Parliament, the generall
antient and greatest counsell of this renowned kingdome. By yow
as by a select choyse and abstract of the whole kingdome is presented
to his Majeste Royall viewe, and made happy in yor beholding of his
most excellent and sacred person. All of yow not onely the Prelates,
Nobels and Grandees, but in yor persons that are of the howse of
Commons every one even the meanest of his Majeste subjects are
graciously allowed to participate and share in the honor and in the
councells that concerne the greate and weighty affayres of kinge and
kingdome.

Yow come all armed with the votes and suffrages of the whole
Nation; And I assure myselfe that your hearts are filled with that
zealous and humble affeccion to his Majeste person and gover-
[n]m[en]t that soe just, soe pious and soe gratious a kinge hath
reason to expect from all his subjects.

I doubt not but that you doe rejoyce at this dayes meeteinge. And
me thinks the sunne doth seem to doe soe too, And good reason have
wee soe to doe and with all humblenes of heart, to acknowledge the

[1] See above, Montagu Papers, p. 1, p. 96.
[2] See below, App., (13 April), p. 293.

greate goodnes of his Majestye who sequestring the memory of all former discouradgm[en]ts in precedeing Assemblyes is nowe out even not of a fatherly affection to his people and a confidence [*p. 2*] that they will not be faileing in their dutye to him who is pleased graciously to invite yow and all his loving subjects to a sacred unitye of heart and affeccions in the service of him and of the comon wealth; And in the execution of those councells that tend onely to ye honor of his Majestye and the good and preservation of yow all.

His Majestyes kingly resolutions are seated in the Arke of his sacred brest; And it were a presumption of too high a nature for any Uzzah uncal'd to towch it.[1]

Yet his Majestye is now pleased to lay by the shineing beames of Majesty as Phoebus did to Phaeton that the difference betwixt soveraignety and subjeccion might be discerned, but might not barre you of that fillial freedome of Accesse to his person and councells; Only let us beware howe with the sonne of Achimenia we Ayme at the guideinge of the charriott.[2] As if that we were the onely testimonye of fatherly affeccion. And let us ever remember that thowgh the kinge sometymes layes by the beames and rayes of his Majestye he never layes by Majestye itselfe.

In former Parliaments yow have beene advised with for the preventing and diverting of those dangers which by forregn and remote councells might have tended to the ruine and dishonor of this nation. Therein his Majestes greate wisdome and providence hath for many yeares eased you of that trouble.

His Majesty haveinge with greate judgment and prudence not onely foreseene and prevented or dangers but kept up the honor and the splendor of the English Crowne; of which wee all at this daye find the happye and comfortable experience; God haveing vouchsafed such successe to his Majestyes councells That or fleece is drye when it rayneth blood in all other Neighbouring States, but what avayleth this to the kingdome *si hostem foris non inveniet si domi inveniet*.

You are nowe summoned to councells and resolutions that more neerely concernes you to prevent a danger and a dishonor that knocketh at or gates, And that moves from such from whome we had little reason to suspect it.

It is well knowne upon what happie and sollid councells one of or wisest kinges made a match with Scotland for his eldest daughter (wee cannot forgett I am sure we should not) the blessed successe

---

[1] 2 Samuel 6.
[2] Harvard MS. Eng. 982, fo 2ᵛ, continues to the end of the paragraph without beginning a new sentence.

[*p. 3*] that wayted upon those councells when the Crowne of England descended upon K: James of ever blessed memorye, who with the fulnes of joye to all English hearts made his entry by blood not by bloodsheed.

The wall of separation was thereby taken awaye And that glorious kinge to make his words good *Faciam eos in gentem unam* made all England rejoyce and Scotland I am sure had noe cause to be sorry for it.

They participated of English honors. The wealth and revennues of the Nation they shared in; and noe good thinge was withholden from them; such was the largnes of hearte of that most excellent kinge; And such was the comfort we tooke in that fraternitye or rather unitye when nowe both of us had but one brazen wall of fortification to looke unto the Sea, And all things soe equally and evenly carryed betweene us that [*blank*] *nullo discrimine habetur.* His Majesty or most gratious sovereigne became heire as well to his fathers virtues as to his kingdomes. [*blank*] *Paccatumque*[1] *patris virtutibus orbem* And in his tender and gratious affeccion to that Nation hath given[2] as many indulgent testimonyes of love and benignitye as they could expect.

Thus became we both like a land floweing with milke and honey, peace and plentye dwelt in or streetes; Wee have had all or blessinge crowned with the sweete hopes of perpetuitye.

God found for my Lord the Kinge a companion meete for him his Royall consort or most gratious Queene, who as shee is not to be parralleld for her person[3] and virtue, soe hath shee made his Majestye and his whole kingdome most happie and blessed in the sweetest pledges of their love and or hopes that ever stood like ollive branches about the Throne or Table; but for which I sorrowe *Civiles furores Patriae nimia infelicitas*, When his Majestye had most reason to expect a gratefull returne of loyaltye and obedience from all the Scotish Nation some men of Belial some of Sheba have blowne the trumpet there and by their insolencyes and rebellious accions drawne many after them to the utter dissertion[4] of his Majeste gover[*n*]m[*en*]t.

His Majeste and his kingly fathers love and[5] bountye to that nation quite forgotten, his goodnes and pietye unremembred, they have led a multitude after them into a course of disloyaltye and rebellious Treasons such as former tymes have not left in mention nor the present age can any where equall.

---

[1] Peccatumque (Harvard MS. Eng. 982, fo 3ᵛ): . . . *regit* . . . (B.L., Harl. MS, 6801, fo 3ᵛ).   [2] Harvard MS. Eng. 982, fo 3ᵛ, omits: his . . . given.
[3] *reason* (Harvard MS. Eng. 982, fo 3ᵛ).
[4] *distruction* (Harvard MS. Eng. 982, fo 4ʳ).
[5] Harvard MS. Eng. 982, fo 4ʳ, omits: love and.

[*p. 4*] They have taken up Armes against the Lords annoynted their[1] rightfull Prince and undoubted soveraigne and followeing the wicked councells of some Achitophells. They have seized on some tropheyes of honor and invested themselves with Regal power and authoritye such and soe many acts of disloyaltye and disobedience as let their pretences be what they will be. Noe true English nor Christian heart can but acknowledge them to be the effects of fowle and horrid Treason.

The last Summer his Majestye at his owne charge and at the vast expence of many of his faithfull and loving subjects of England went with an Armye, And then they tooke upon them the boldnes to outface and outbrave his Royall Armye with another of their owne raiseinge.

Yet for all this his Majestyes goodnes was not lessened by that nor could his gratious nature forgett what hee was to them nor what they were to him, but considering with himself they were such *quos nec vincere nec vinci gloriosum* out of his piety and clemencye chose rather to passe by their former miscarriadges upon their humble protestacion of future loyaltye and obedience, then by just vengeance to punish their rebellions.[2]

But his Majestye who is ever awake and vigillant for the good and safetye of all his hath since too playnelye discovered that they did but prevaricate with him to divert the storme which being over their heads and by gaineinge tyme to purchase to themselves more advantage for persueing their rebellious purposes.

For since his Majestye came from Barwicke it is come to his certeyne knowledge that instead of performinge that loyaltye and obedience which[3] the Lawe of God of Nature and Nations they owe unto him. They have addressed themselves to forreigne states And with them treated to deliver themselves up to their proteccion and power.

As by Gods great providence and goodnes his gratious Majestye is able to shewe under the hands of the prime ringleaders of that faccion, then which nothing could be of more dangerous consequence to this and his Majestyes other kingdomes.

Whosoever they be as doe or shall wish England ill, They may knowe it to be of too tough a complexion and couradge to be assaulted in the face or to be sett upon at the foredore. And therefore it is not unlikelye but they may as in the former tymes find out a posterne gate.

---

[1] *this* (Harvard MS. Eng. 982, fo 4ʳ).
[2] '. . . *Hereupon the armies retourned in peace and his Majestie came home with good hope that they would by their future dutie and humilitie regaine his gratious affection and good opinion*' (B.L., Harl. MS. 6801, fo 4ᵛ).
[3] *with* the lawes (Harvard MS. Eng. 982, fo 4ᵛ).

There were before two of them Scotland and Ireland[1]
[*Harvard MS. Eng. 982*]
[*fo 5ʳ*]
through his Majestyes just and prudent governem[en]t which is not
only reduced from the destiny of former times but setled in such a
condicion of peace and during his Majestyes raigne soe altered and
civillized that instead of being a charge to him (as it was to his
predecessors) hath yeilded to him some revenue. And his subjects doe
dayly give very acceptable testimonyes of their loyall and dutifull
affeccions both to his person and Governem[en]t. And now lately at
their Parliament assembled they have not only with one free consent
made his Majesty a chearfull aide towards this present preparacion
to reduce his disaffected subjects in Scotland to their due obedience.

But they have also protested and promised that they will bee
ready with their persons and Estates to their uttermost of their
Abillityes for his Majestyes future supply as great occasion by
continuance of his forces against the distemper shall require so that
the hopes of hurting England that way is only extinct. [*fo 5ᵛ*]
Scotland only remaynes whether (as to a weake and distempered
p[ar]te of the body all the veines of fluxes of faccions and seditious
humors make away).

His Majesty hath taken all these and much more into his princely
consideracion and to avoid a manifest and apparant mischeife
threatned to [*t*]his and his other kingdome hath resolved by the
meanes of a powerfull Army to reduce them to the just condicions of
obedience and subjeccion.

It is a course his Majesty takes no delight in but is forced unto it
for such is his Majestyes grace and goodnesse to all his subjects and
such it is and will bee to them how undutifull and rebellious soever
they now are, that if they putt themselves into a way of humillity
becomeing them his Majestyes piety and Clemency will soone appeare
to all the world, but his Majesty will not endure to have his honor
weighed at the comon beame nor permitt any to stepp betweene
him and his birthright.

And therefore as hee will by no meanes admitt the mediacion of
any person whatsoever soe hee shall Judge it high presumption for
any to offer it as that which hee must account most daingerous to his
honor to have conceipt that the sollicitacion of others can by any
possibility better incline him to his people then hee is and ever will
bee of his owne grace and goodnesse.

[*fo 6ʳ*] The charge of such an Army hath been throughly advised on
and must needes amount to a very great summe such as cannot bee

---

[1] pp. 5–36 missing from Finch-Hatton MS. 50; Harvard MS., Eng. 982, fos
5ʳ–35ᵛ, substitutes.

Imagined to bee found in his Majestyes Coffers which how empty soever have never yett been exhausted by unnecessary triumphes or sumptuous building or other magnificence whatsoever but most of his owne revenue And whatsoever hath come from his subjects hath been by him imployed for the common good and preservacion of the kingdome and like vapours ariseing out of the earth and gathered into a Cloude hath fallen downe in sweete and refreshing showres upon the same ground.

Wherefore his Majesty hath at this time called the Parliament as the second meanes under Gods blessing to subverte those publique calamityes threatned to all his kingdomes by the mutinous behavior of[1] them and as his Majesty now offers you the honor workeing together with himselfe for the good of him and his and for the common preservacion of yourselves and your posterity.

Councells and deliberacions that tend to benefitt and profitt may indure their disputes and debates because they seeme only accustomed with persuasions, but deliberacions that tend to persuasion are waited upon by necessity and cannott endure either debate or delay, [fo 6ᵛ] of such nature are the bleeding evills that are now to bee provided against.

This summer must not bee lost nor any minute of time foreslowed to reduce them of Scotland left[sic] by protraction here they gaine more time and advantage to frame their projects with forreine States.

His Majesty doth therefore desire upon these pressing and urging reasons that you will for awhile lay aside all other debates, And that you would passe an Act for such and so many subsedyes as you in your hearty affeccions to his Majesty and to the common good shall thinke fitt and convenient for so great an Accion.

And withall that you would hasten the paym[en]t of it so soone as may bee with a provisoe in the Act, That his Majestyes Royall assent shall not determine this session, His Majesty assures you all that hee would not have anything proposed out of the ordinary way, but such is the streightnesse of time that unlesse the buisness be forthwith past, it is not possible for him to putt in order such things as must bee prepared before soe great an Army can bee brought into the feild, and indeed had not his Majesty upon the creditt of his servants and security out of his owne Estate taken up and issued betweene three or 4 hundred thousand pounds,[2] It had not been

---

[1] '. . . *many* of *that nation* and as his Majestyes *predecessors have accustomed with your forefathers, he* now *in like manner* offers . . . posterity *His Majesty resting most confident that by Gods assistance and your tymely and needfull supply he shalbe inabled to wade through all difficulties whatsoever and to vindicate and make shine that soveraigne power which is entrusted to him by God for the protection and government of these kingdoms'* (B.L., Harl. MS. 6801, fos 6ʳ–6ᵛ).

[2] *Cf.* below, Harvard MS. (2 May) fo 80, p. 192.

possible for his Majesty to have provided those things it began with, which was [*fo 7ʳ*] necessary to so great an Enterprise and without which hee could not have secured Barwick or Carlislle or avoid those affronts, which the insolency of that faccion might have putt upon us by injureing the persons and fortunes of his loyall subjects in the Northern p[*ar*]ts.¹

To avoide all Questions and disputes that may arise touching his Majestyes taking of Tunnage and poundage his Majesty hath comanded mee to declare that hee hath taken it only *de facto* according to the example of former kings from the death of the past predecessors untill the Parliament had past an Act for themselves.²

That in like manner his Majesty desires to claime it by graunt of Parliament. For this purpose his Majesty hath caused a Bill to bee preferred in the same forme as it passed from his royall father of blessed memory, adding only words to give it him from the first of his Majestyes reigne.

This and the Bill of subsedy his Majesty expects (for the pressing reasons before delivered unto you) may bee dispatched with all speede which his Majesty commanded mee to tell you hee shall gratiously accept as the welcome pledges of loving happy and dutifull affeccions to him his person and government.

[*fo 7ᵛ*] And his Majesty is gratiously pleased to give you his royall word that afterwards he will give you time for considering of such peticions as you shall conceive to bee good for the commonwealth, even now before you desp[*ar*]te according as the season of the yeare and the great affaires in hand will permitt.

And what is now omitted his Majesty will give you time to perfect towards winter when your owne leasure and conveiency may better attend it, hee knowing well that these Subsedyes can but bee of little use without that more ample supply which he expects upon the happy conclusion of this Session.

And therein his Majesty is gratiously pleased according to the auntient way of Parliament to stay till your just greivances bee heard and redressed. And his Majesty doth assure you hee will goe along with you for your advantage through all the gratious expressions of a just pious and gratious king to the end there may bee such a happy conclusion of this parliament, that it may bee a cause of many more meetings with you.

I have now delivered what I had in comand from his Majesty.

[*fo 8ʳ*] The Lord Keeper having ended the King said:

The King. My Lords you shall see hee hath spoken nothing by

¹ *Cf.* B.L., Harl. MS. 6801, fos 7ʳ–7ᵛ, where variations in wording and organization occur in the remainder of the Lord Keeper's speech.
² See his list of precedents in the *Declaration* justifying the dissolution of the preceding Parliament (B.L., 8122.c.26, pp. 16–17).

perbollically[*sic*] nor nothing but what I will make good one way or other, and because hee did mention a letter from my subjects in Scotland who did seeke to draw in forreine power for aide, here is the Originall letter And which I shall command him to read unto you. And because it may touch a neighbour of mine I will say nothing on but yt which a just God forbidd I should for my p[*ar*]te. I thinke it was never accepted by him. (Indeede it is a letter to the French K.) but I know not that ever hee had it for by chance I interrupted it as it was going to him and therefore I hope you will understand rightly in that.

His Majesty delivered the letter to the Lord Keeper, his Lordshipp beganne to read and observed as followeth:

The supersciption of the Letter is thus: *Au Roy*.

Lo Keeper. For the nature of which superscription it is well knowne to all that knowe the style of France That is never written by any Frenchman to any but to their owne king so in effect they doe by that superscription acknowledge [*fo 8ᵛ*] Then his Lopp read the letter in French being the Originall Language wherein it was written.

The l[*et*]tre being read in French his Lopp added, his Majesty hath comanded mee to read it in English unto you as it is translated, for that is the Originall under their owne hands.

The Scotts l[*et*]ter to ye Fr. K. Sr. Yr Majesty being the refuge and sanctuary of Afflicted princes and States, Wee have found it necessary to send this Gentleman Mr Colvile by him to represent unto your Majesty the candor and ingenuity as well of our accions and proceedings as of our intentions which wee desire should bee engraven and written to the whole world with the beames of the sunne as well as to yr Majesty. Wee most humbly beseech you therefore to give faith and creditt to him and of all that hee shall say in our parte concerning us and our Affaires being most assured of an assistance equall to yr accustomed clemency heretofore and so often shewed to this nation which will not yeild to any other whatsoever the Glory to bee eternally. Yr Majestyes most humble Obedient and affectionate servants. Roches [*Rothes*], Marr, Moungumy [*Montgomery*], Lowdon, Leslye, Forrester.

[*fo 9ʳ*] Then the King added:

The King. Of these Gentlemen that have sett their hands to this l[*et*]tre here is one and I beleive you would not thinke it very strainge if I should lay him fast, and therefore I have signed a Warrant to lay him in the tower close prisoner, My Lords I thinke but I will not say positively because I will not say anything here but I am sure of I thinke I have the Gentleman that carryed the l[*et*]tre fast enough but I know not I may bee mistaken.

Lo Keeper. And then my Lord Keep concluded, Gentlemen you of the house of Commons his Majestyes pleasure is that you doe now repaire to yr owne house there to make choice of yr Speaker whom his Majesty will expect to bee presented on Wednesday next at 2 of the clock in the afternoone.

Serjeant Glanville Speaker. The Commons departed and being come together in the Lower house according to the antient and accustomed [*manner*] Serjeant Glanvile was nominated Speaker and chosen who having taken his chayre.

Bill read. A Bill after the antient manner was read which concerned the abuse of clothes in the Excesse in embroidery in silver and gold with provisoe nevertheless to tollerate the King Queene and Royall blood in neare degree.[1]

[*fo 9ᵛ*] After this the house was adjourned till Wednesday at 2: of the clock.

[*Harvard MS. Eng. 982*]   [*15 April 1640, House of Commons*]

[*fo 9ᵛ*]   **DIE MERCURII 15 APRIL**

[*See L.J., iv, pp. 50–54, and C.J., ii, p. 3*]

The King being seated on his throne and the Lords in their severall places in the upper house the commons were admitted in who then and there presented Serjeant Glanvile their speaker, who being called to the barr after the accustomed reverence done spake as followeth.

Mr Speaker.[2] May it please your majesty:

The Knights Cittizens and Burgesses of the Commons house of parliament in conformity of an antient and most constant usage, the best guide in great solempnity according to the well knowne priviledges a sure warrant for their proceedings, and in obedience to yr most gratious councell and comand a duty well becomeing loyall Subjects have mett together in their howse and chosen a Speaker one of themselves to bee the mouth[3] indeed the servant of all the rest to steare watchfully and prudently in all their weighty consultacions and debates, to collect faithfully and readily the votes and genuine sense of [*that*] numerous Assembly to propound the same seasonably [*fo 10ʳ*] in apt questions for their finall resolucions, and to represent them and their conclusions their Declaracions and Peticions upon all urgent occasions with all truth and light with life and Lustre, and with free advantage to yre most Excellent Majesty with what

---

1 '*lecta 1⁰ vice* Apparel' (M.C.J., p. 7, 15 April 1640; also C.J., ii, p. 3).
2 See below, App. (15 April), p. 294. *Cf.* especially B.L., E.198(32) and B.L., E.199(43).
3 Marginal note: *officium prolocutoris* (Folger, X.d.23).

Judgement what temper what spirit[1] what elocucion hee ought to bee endowed and quallifyed, that with any good successe I should undergoe such an Imploym[en]t. Yr Majesty in your great wisdome is best able to discerne and judge both as it may relate to your owne p[ar]ticular and just important affaires of Estate and governem-[en]t, and as it must relate to the proper worke and businesse of the howse of Commons which was never small nor meane and is likely at this time to bee exceeding weighty.

Had yre howse of Commons been so happy in their choice as they were regular well warranted and dutifull in their proceedings myselfe which stand yett elected to bee their Speaker and am now presented by them to your Majesty for yr gracious and royall approbacion, I should not have medled to have become troublesome to yr Majesty[2] and care for the prosperity and good successe to yr affaires. I hold myselfe obleiged to make [fo 10ᵛ] myne Imperfeccions and disa-billityes which are best knowne to myselfe and to yr Majesty not altogether I suppose unknowne before whom in the Course of my practise and Profession such hath been the goodnesse towards the meanest of your Subjects, that I have divers times had the honor and favour to appeare and beare a p[ar]te as an ordinary pleader. [blank] It is a Learned age wherein we live under yr Majestyes most peaceable[3] and most flourishing Government. And yr house of Commons as it is now composed is not only the [re]presentative but the abstracted Quintesence of the whole comonalty of this yr noblest Realme of England.

There bee very many amongst them much fitter then I am for the place, few or none in my opinion soe unfitt as myselfe. I most humbly beseech yr Majesty as you are the father of the Comonwealth and head of the whole Parliament to whom the care of all our welfare cheifely apperteynes, have respect to yr interest, have regard unto yr house of Commons have compassion on mee the most unworthy member of that body, ready to faint with feare before the burthen Sight[sic] upon mee, why then should [fo 11ʳ] they in mee or yr Majesty in them through my defact stand exposed to any hazard of disservice. I have only a hearty affeccion to serve yow and your people little abillityes for performance. In the freenesse therefore of yr kingly power and piety and your goodnesse be gratiously pleased to comand ye house of Commons once more to meete together to consult and deliberate better about their Choice of a meete Speaker till they can agree on some such person, as may [bee] worthy of their choice and chooseing and yr Majestyes acceptacion.

---

[1] Marginal note: *munera prolocutori* (Folger, X.d.23).
[2] '. . . *in this Suit of my Releasement and Discharge which now in Duty to Your Majesty* and care for the *Preservation* and good . . .' (*L.J.*, iv, p. 50; B.L., Harl. MS. 6801, fo 40ʳ).   [3] *powerful* (Folger, X.d.23).

Unto which the Lo: Keeper by direccion from his Majesty replyed as followeth.

Mr Speaker:

Lo: Keep. His Majesty with a princely attencion and a gratious care hath listned to your humble and modest excuse full of flowers of witt of flowers of Eloquence,[1] many reasons from yourselfe hee hath taken to approve and agree to the choice and eleccion made by the house of the Commons. His Majesty finds nothing from any thing that you have said to disassent or disagree from it you have sett forth your inabilityes with so great abilityes yow have so well deciphered and delineated the parts dutyes and office of a good Speaker, which is to collect the some of the howse judiciously [*fo 11ᵛ*] to render it with fidelity and sume it up with integrity[2] and to mould it up into fitt and apt questions for resolucions. And those as occasion shall serve to present with vigor advantage and humility to his Majesty, hee doubts not but that you that are so perfect in the Theorye will with great ease performe the practicall p[*ar*]te. And with no lesse commendation, his Majesty hath taken notice and well remembers yr often wayting of him in private causes wherein you have alwayes so carryed yrselfe and wonne so much good opinion from his Majesty as hee doubteth not but that yow now when yow are called forth to serve the pub[*l*]ique yr affeccions and the powers of yr Soule will bee sett on worke with more zeale and with more alacrity.

It is that for which the Philosopher calls a man happy when men that have ability and goodnesse doe meete with an object fitt to bring into an Act, And such at this time is yr good fortune an occasion being ministred unto yow to shew your ability and goodnesse and to your fidelity to his Majestyes service to the shew the candor and clearenesse of your hearte towards those of the house of Commons. In all which his Majesty nothing doubting but you will soe discharge yourselfe as hee may to his former favour find occasion to add more unto yow.

[*fo 12ʳ*] That this house of Comons may rejoyce in this Eleccion of theirs and that the whole kingdome by your good cleare and canded service may receive fruites and effects that may bee comfortable to all: His Majesty therefore doth approve and confirme the choice of the house of Commons and ratifyes you the speaker.

After that my Lord Keep had thus by his Majestyes direccion confirmed Serjeant Glanvile in the place of a Speaker, the s[*ai*]d Mr Speaker addressed himselfe to his Majesty as followeth.

---

[1] *Judgement (L.J.,* iv, p. 50; B.L., Harl. MS. 6801, fo 42ᵛ).
[2] *Dexterity (L.J.,* iv, p. 50; B.L., Harl, MS. 6801, fo 43ʳ).

E

Mr Speaker. Most gratious Soveraigne:

My profession hath tawght mee that from the highest seate of Justice there lyes no Writt of Error noe Appeale. Your Majesty in full parliament hath been pleased by the mouth of your Lord Keeper to declare your royall Judgement in affirmacion of the Eleccion of your howse of Commons, thereby I am become their Speaker and their Servant. What is there left unto mee but in the first place devoutly to beseech Almighty god the author and finisher of all go[o]d workes to enable mee by his blessing to discharge honestly and Effectually soe great a taske. [*fo 12ᵛ*] And in the next place humbly acknowledge (as I doe) the great grace and favour that is done unto mee by your Majesty and readily to conforme myselfe to your good pleasure and command to which I now submitt with all possible chearefulnesse lest else my too much diffidence to undertake the service might add a further disadvantage to my performance then peradventure would rise out of my other imperfeccions. Two enemyes I might feare, the commons enemyes of such services, Expectacion and Jealousy. I am not worthy of the former and contemne the latter.

Time which tryes the truth shall lett the world see and knowe I am and will bee found equall free man zealous to serve my gratious King, zealous to serve my dearest country.

Monarchy Royall and hereditary is of all sorts of governement the most compleate and excellent (whether wee regard the glory the wealth the Justice[1] of the Governor and of the people or of both) and I hope there are not any of this nation that are of antemonarchiall spiritts or resolucions, noe nor disposicions nor freinds to such as are so If there bee I wish noe greater honor to this parliament then to discover them[2] or to confound them.

[*fo 13ʳ*] Yow are a great king at all times but sitting now attended by your prelates your Lords and people in free Parliament yow are in the highest State of Majesty and glory and now I remember well that I heard yr Majestyes royall father our late deare Soveraigne King James of ever blessed memory speake to that purpose of himselfe and of kings in generall, his Majesty sitting then in parliament upon that throne which by dissent from him and from inumerable and Royall Ancestors is now become yr Majestyes Royall seate and rightfull inheritance.

To behold you thus in peace and safety upon this great and good occasion after full 15en yeares experience of your most peacefull governem[en]t yeildes most compleate joy to all yr Majestyes most Loyall and well Affected subjects who cannot but concurre with mee

[1] *Safety* (L.J., iv, p. 51; B.L., Harl. MS. 6801, fo 46ʳ).
[2] '. . . *and by all good Means possible to assist Your Gracious Majesty to suppresse . . . them . . .*' (L.J., iv, p. 51; B.L., Harl. MS. 6801, fo 46ᵛ).

in this desire[1] and prayer *caelum cetusding letus Populi Britania* England is yr seate of residence not made a province nor Governed by ViceRoy God open all or eyes and understandings soe to discerne and value the greate and mediate influence of life and chearefulnesse of all the p[*ar*]ts of this yr noblest kingdome.

[*fo 13ᵛ*] Scotland is your birthplace and therein hath the advantage your other Realmes, God make them and ever keepe them ever sensible and worthy of that honor.

Ireland begins apace to imitate England by a great and quick progression in civillity of manners and consultacions of many schedulous[*sic*] plantacions and enacting the more wholesome Lawes and Statutes of this Kingdome and many other effects and fruites of peace and blessed governem[*en*]t.

France is still attendant in yoer royall title, the prerogative of a king is as necessary as it is great without which hee should want power and Majesty which is and ought to bee inseparable from the Crowne and Scepter, nor can there any dainger result from Such prerogative in the King by the liberty of the subject so long as both of them admitt of the temperam[*en*]t of Lawe and Justice, especially under such a king as your Majesty who to your immortall glory among the printed Lawes have published this to the whole world for yr example.

The Liberty of the people strengthens kings prerogatives And the kings prerogative is to defend the peoples Libertyes, Apples of Gold [*fo 14ʳ*] in Pictures of silver, Kings as they are kings are not said to erre, only the best may bee mistaken by informacion[2] and the highest pointe of prerogative is the king can doe no wrong. If therefore by the subtilty of misinformers by their spetious false pretences of publique good by cunning and close contriving of these wayes to reduce the sacred royall person shall not at any time bee circumvented or surprised or wrought or drawne to command things contrary to Lawe and that the same bee done accordingly this comand will bee void and the king Innocent even in his very person defended by his prerogative. Nevertheless the Authors of such informacion and actors in these abuses will stand lyable and exposed to strict examinacion and Just Censures as having nothing to defend themselves but the Collour of a void command made void by just prerogative according to fundamentall and true reason of State and Monarchy or what difference is there or can there bee in Lawe betweene a void command and no command at all.

---

[1] '. . . *servus in* caelum *redeas diuque* laetus *in terris populo* Britannia' (B.L., E.198(32), p. 5; *cf. L.J.*, iv, p. 51).

[2] . . . abused by *misinformation* (B.L., Harl. MS. 6801, fo 49ʳ); *abused* by information (*L.J.*, iv, p. 51).

If religion, Justice and mercy all happily assemble and gratiously lodge togeather in your royall brest may give to you[r] well affected subjects a good hope of the good successe [fo 14ᵛ] of this Parliament. I knowe not why wee should not all of us expect it with much confidence some few p[ar]ticulers perteyning to these generall heads I humbly begg¹ of your sacred eares. I may have to mention and observe to the further comfort of myselfe and all that heare mee.

What Prince of this Land was ever known to keepe his howres and sett time for prayer and service of almighty god with that regularity and constancy as your Majesty, nay more you have ever since yr accesse to the Crowne had one day in every weeke besides the Lords day dedicated and applyed to preaching and devotion. I may not stay here there is another perticuler way much excelling both the former, and that is yr Majestyes great care to educate those pledges of conjugall and most abundant mutuall Love that is betweene yr Majesty and yr most gratious consorte the best of Queenes and women and the foundacion of our future hopes that most illustrious Prince Charles and the rest of yr royall projeny in the true religion of Almighty god publiquely professed and by Lawe Established in this Kingdome, what tongue is able to expresse the great joy and consolacion which all yr Majestyes most Loving Subjects doe derive to themselves in contemplacion of your great piety and providence in this one Act considered extending [fo 15ʳ] itselfe not only to the present time but to the good succession of all other after ages.

Touching Justice there is not any more certaine signe to discerne an Equall Judge then by his patience to bee well informed before hee give sentence, and I may boldly say that all your Judges throughout all your kingdomes may take Example by yr Majesty and learne their duty from yr practise in this kind, my selfe have often been a Wittnesse of it to my noe little Admiracion and contentm[en]t.

From yre patient heareing lett mee passe unto yr righteous Judgem[en]t and therein bring out an instance but it shall bee a greate one When your Lords and yre people the last parliament presented to yr gratious Majesty a Peticion concerning divers rights and Libertyes of yr subjects, the peticion being of noe small weight and importance as by the same may well appeare, yr Majesty after meete deliberacion in few but in most Effectuall words *soit droit faict come est desira* made them such an Answere as shall renowne you for yr just Judgem[en]t in this age and to all posterity.

I make hast to come unto yr mercy whereof I cannot but to have neede againe and againe before I have finished [fo 15ᵛ] that service

¹ '. . . of *Your Majesty that without Offence to* your Sacred Ears' (*L.J.*, iv. pp. 51–52; B.L., Harl. MS. 6801, fo 50ʳ).

to which I am enjoyned and not altogether in dispaire of obteyning it, Neverthelesse the mercy which I meane to celebrate is not only concerning single or p[ar]ticular persons but whole Nations.

That unexampled mercy which in yr wisdome and abundant goodnesse hath happily met together yr majesty vouchsafed to shew to us and o[th]ers who by this meanes are still in peace and tran-quillity not without good hopes of long continuance.

A blessing peradventure undervallued by us who have had so much of it under yr Majesty and yr most gratious and blessed Governem[en]t. I have yett no instruccions from yr house of Commons and therefore can propound nothing as by warr[an]t from them. But if I may have leave to present yor Majesty with my owne most humble and most hearty wishes and desires they bee directed upon Religion, Chivalrye, Justice, Commerce, and Unitye.

That this parliament may bee famous for the care and advance-ment of Gods true Religion, the only meanes to make us happy in this world and that to come.

And to that purpose that the most reverend prelates your Majes-tyes Archbishops and Bishopps sitting on the right hand of yr throne will bee therein most forward to whom it is most proper.

That the Lords temporall guirt with their swords in their Creation as may especially bee rewarded or prepared for accions military would call to mind the most noble and [*fo 16ʳ*] most valiant of their Ancestors whose lands and honours of their inheritors and how famous this land hath been at home and abroad for Deedes of Armes and Acts of Chivallry and to labour to restore it by all meanes to its antient glory, the best way to preserve peace is to bee prepared ready for warr.

That yr Majesty would bee pleased to command your grave and learned Judges whose observacions should exceede other mens (though they bee but Assistants in the service) to contribute the most and best they can to explaine, to execute, to advance our good old Lawes and to propound such things for the enacting of whole-some and plaine new Statutes that every Subject of this realme may bee enabled to know and understand himselfe clearely both what hee hath to doe; and what hee may possesse and what not.

Their are no[1] considerable Mines Royall in this kingdome, the expectacions of our woolls in Manufactures and native comodityes is that which furnisheth us with gold and silver the mettalls of other kingdomes and hath only power to enable us to supply your Majesty for the defending of orselves and the offending of our enemyes.

That Merchants and Tradesmen therefore should have all meet encouragem[en]t which is a most notable and spetiall Interest of this

---

[1] *two* (B.L., Harl. MS. 6801, fo 55ʳ).

Island, but were wee never so valiant, [*fo 16ᵛ*] never so wealthy, if love and duty bee not amongst us, what good will our wealth doe your Majesty, Hee that comands a hearte in love, hee even hee only commands assuredly the purse to pay and the hand to fight.

I Pray God therefore wee may all endeavour to knitt such a knott of love and true affeccion betwixt the head and the members that Jesuited forreigne States who looke perchance with envious and malignant eyes upon us and would bee glad to rejoyce in our divisions may see themselves lost and defeated of all their subtill plotts and combinacions and of all their wicked hopes and expectacions to render as, if their endeavors might prevaile, A people inconsiderable at home and contemptable abroad.

Religion hath taught us *si deus nobiscum quis contra nos si sumus inseperabiles sumus insuperabiles*. It was wont to bee and I hope ever will bee the tenent and position of our house of Commons That the good of the king and his people cannot bee severed. And cursed bee everyone that shall goe about to devide it.

I feare I have adventured too farre on yr Royall patience though yett I must confesse I never knew it wearyed Neverthelesse I will heare conclude only first I beseech yr gratious Majesty in the names and rights of yr house of Commons That in yr Justice you would bee pleased to graunt and confirme to them for their encouragem[*en*]ts (to proceede in their [*fo 17ʳ*] great businesse) this their antient and Just Libertyes which tyme out of mind they have had. That them their Servants and necessary attendants together with their goods may bee freed from all Imprisonm[*en*]ts, Arrests and molestacions during the Parliament.

That they may enjoy fredome of speech in all their propositions and debates which I hope they will bee carefull to use within the bounds of loyalty and duty.

That upon all necessary occasions they may have Accesse to yr Majesty with such number of competent members and at such seasonable times and places as yor Majesty shall appointe.

And last of all that yr Majesty would hee pleased gratiously to make the best construccion of all their words and accions and mine in perticuler.

To which speech the Lo: Keeper replyed as followeth.

Lo: Keeper. Mr Speaker:

His Majesty is no lesse pleased with yr humble and chearefull submission to his pleasure then hee is with your modesty and yr excuse of it before neither doth hee the lesse commend what yow have now said. As that which is full of both Judgem[*en*]t in dividing the parte of it and of sharpenesse and eloquence in the Expressions of it you lift up yor thoughts and direct your devocion [*fo 17ᵛ*] aright.

First to the great throne of heaven next to his throne upon Earth
to the first for devine Assistance to the other for gratious Exceptacion
being armed with this confidence you neede feare none enemy And
yett I must tell you Mr Speaker as smoot[h]ly as I looke upon yow
there was entertained and lodged within or breast that great enemy
of yr expectacion but now yow have lost it and discovered it I will
not feare to name him to you for the other Jealousy it is too base a
companion to retaine admittance into any Noble or magnanimous
hearte and I will leave it with yow to the greatest contempt and
disdaine that may bee.

You have sett forth the blessednesse and happinesse of this
kingdome in the frame of Governem[en]t that it is Monarchiall in
the nature of it That it is hereditary and certainly it was a wise and
true saying.

It is a large feild to walke in and such a one as to speake any thing
to the purpose would take up more time then ether yor employm-
[en]t or mine will permitt.

And yett you have brought mee into a large feild for Monarchyes
in Generall are but happinesses that a man cannot fix upon unlesse
wee receive the joy, the comforte, and fruite of them in p[ar]ticular,
soe certainly in the person of his most excellent Majesty yow have
Justly and rightly summoned up all our blessings and all our happinesses in one But in one [fo 18ʳ] Great and eminent example his
Majestyes piety the world cannot doubt it you have well observed it,
his Justice is knowne to all his Subjects his Clemency beyond Expression when[1] did ever king in this kingdome sitt in his white robes for
fifteene yeares together and scarce any man to feele the sensible
stroake of the Axe nor blood to bee drawne but in petty and perticular causes.

It was a good wish and I will joyne with you with all my hearte
That they may bee accursed and Anathemised by this parliament
by all the kingdome and all succeeding ages that goe about in the
least manner to innovate or alter anything in this happy Governem[en]t under which wee live.
THE COMMONS APPLAUD HIS LOPPS EXPRESSIONS BY
    A GENERAL HUMM.
HIS LOPP PROCEEDETH.

It is a Joyfull acclamacion and I doubt not but that yr hearts
are full and certainly yow my Lords and yow of the house of
Commons will easily knowe that those that are of Spiritt and dis-
posicion will quickly resolve all their debate and all their accions
into Cates and Cades[2] principles which is to ruine the nobility, to

---

[1] B.L., E.199(43) begins here.
[2] Robert Kett (1549) and Jack Cade (1450) led popular revolts.

ruine the Gentry, to ruine Learning, and devoure and eate up one another.

[*fo 18ᵛ*] Mr Speaker you have lifted up yr contemplacions and raysed them upon 5 excellent pillars That of Religion you doe well in the first place to begin with for certainely it is that[1] wee ought to ascribe to the great judgem[*en*]t and discretion you fix yr eye and your care upon the reverend Prelates that assist his Majesty on his right hand certeynely to them and [to] their predecessors wee owe the preservacion of the Gospell in that purity and sincerity wee now enjoy it Lett any man looke back from the first of Queene Elizabeths raigne and somewhat before and see to whom wee owe it most.

The prophet Elisha when hee had Elishas spirit doubled upon him hee tooke up his mantle[2] There are golden candlesticks and there are Gates of Saphire and Onix and other with Stones spaken of as well in the new testament as in the old and god forbidd that wee should live to see That God which is the god of Order, the god of Glory, the God of decencye, served in such sorte and manner as plowmen come home from their plow.

Mr Speaker you shall not neede to doubt but that his Majestyes pious example unpresidented by any king If I should say by any man I should not say amisse.

I will give you of the house of Commons and all the world cause to rest confident and most assured of his zeale and constancy in the [*fo 19ʳ*] Religion hee professeth which nothing with in or without the kingdome hath ever found to shake or move.

In the next place yow looke upon the Judges and sages of the Lawe and well yow may persons for gravity and learneing certainly not exceedes in any age And for justice and integrity I am sure if any of them bee guilty of the least defect therein they have the least reason to bee excused for it. Whatever Judges had in any tyme or age more; first they have the example of the king, they have the freedome of his royall eleccion, they have rec[*eive*]d from time to time charge and command that they should with equallity[3] and indifferency distribute that Justice Committed and so discharge the trust by God laid upon his Majesty and by him transmitted to their dispensacion.

For Chivalrye the next pillar on which yow sett your trophies of honor the Grandees and great Lords of this Kingdome yow behold them in number I thinke greater than ever their Ancestors were and

---

[1] '. . . *to which* we ought to ascribe *the great Happiness that we have so long enjoyed; in that with* great Judgement and *Discretion* . . .' (*L.J.*, iv, p. 53; B.L., E.199(43)).

[2] 2 Kings 2: 8–21.   [3] *equity* (B.L., E.199(43)).

I doubt not but their Courage is every way equall And I assure myselfe they will [*fo 19ᵛ*] never forgett the famous Acts which they have left them honourable to all posterity nor doe the least thing that may either deface the monumentall name and accions of them their ancestors or that may in the least kind stayne their owne honor ability[1] and magnaminity.

For Commer[c]e it is most certaine Mr Speaker that it is the royall mine of this Kingdome, the East and west Indies of our nation And in that wee have all great cause to blesse God and to give humble thanks to his Majesty that hee takes such care to maintaine and encourage it yett it never more flourished since the conquest then now it doth.

There remaines but unity and as you said well without it noe man can ever be happy. I will but turne yr saying yow have said *si sumus inseparab[i]les sumus insuperabiles*. I will but say (it is a borrowed one but it is a true one) and I will as soone borrow that as any *si colligimur[2] frangimur*.

Mr Speaker Lett all the world avoid distrust, assure yourselfe there will not lack malignant and ill affeccion, there will not lack pestilent and peevish endeavours to make their accions, there will not lack malitious and ambitious Spiritts that may disjoyne and unknitt his Majesty and his house of Commons. Yow see his Majesty hath gratiously invited yow hither and left mee to putt yow in mind that yow forgett not what was said to yow the last day howsoever and that you remember that there is nothing doth take a gratious and good nature so much [*fo 20ʳ*] as humble sweete and chearefull expressions out of affeccion.

For yr peticions his Majesty hath heard them all and hee grants them all as fully and freely as ever himselfe in other Parliaments did or have any his predecessors before him. And therefore there remaynes nothing now but that you goe on with those expressions yt may rejoyce the hearte of soe gratious soe just and soe good a King that you may more than showres in the drought and heate of summer refresh and cheare the kingdome and all his Majestyes other dominions.

Afterward his Majesty spake as followeth.

The King. Mr Speaker: I will only say one word to yow now that yow are the Speaker I command yow to doe the office of a Speaker which is faithfully and truly to reporte the great cause of this meeting that my Lord Keeper in my name did represent to yow the last day with this assurance that yow giving mee your willing eare to all yr just greivances.

---

[1] honor, *nobility* . . . (B.L., E.199(43); *L.J.*, iv, p. 53).
[2] *Collidimur* (*L.J.*, iv, p. 53); see also Hunt. Cal., H.M. 1554, p. 252, below, p. 230.

Lastly the Lo: Keeper adjourned the house till the morrow at Eight of the clock.

[*fo 20ᵛ*] Having thus finished in the upper house the Commons went to their owne house and there read a Bill.

Bill 1st read.¹ Against the Common recoveryes made by Infants under the age of 21 yeares.

[*Harvard MS. Eng. 982*]   [*16 April 1640, House of Commons*]

[*fo 20ᵛ*]   *DIE JOVIS 16° APRILL*

[*See C.J., ii, pp. 3–4*]

This day immediately after the coming of the Speaker the last mencioned Bill was read the same being the first time of reading thereof, The body and provision thereof being that all such common recoveryes suffered by Guardians wherein Infants under the age of 21 yeares were either the Tennts or Vouchees should bee to all intents and purposes void as well ag[ains]t such infants as ag[ains]t them in revercion or remainder were made p[ar]tyes thereunto.

This passed the first time *nullo contradicente.*

SECRETARY WINDEBANKE.² Mr Secretary Windebanke acquainted the House with the Kings desire of their sudden handling of the Scotish busines as farr as it had relacion to the Covenanters l[ett]re written to the French king, for that perhapps some of the house heard it not soe well the other day when it was read in the upper house, He asked whether hee should read the l[ett]re, which [*fo 21ʳ*] they wished him to doe both in French the originall as likewise in English which nowe hath declared that by direccion and order from his Majesty my Lord Cottington, himselfe and Mr Attorney Generall were yesterday sent to the Lord Lowden in the Tower (whose hand was subscribed to ye said l[ett]re) to examine him thereof. And they having made examinacion of the Lo: Lowden, his confession extended, hee said, to the acknowledgem[en]t of his owne hand and *in fine* to the knowledge of all the other hands, his excuse only was hee knew not what the l[ett]re conteyned in regard that hee understood not the French tounge. Taking the contents of the l[ett]re (as hee was made to believe) to conteyne only a desire that the French king would bee a Meadiatour betweene the King and the Scotts. Mr Secretary seemed not to like this excuse, urging his breeding, quallity, parts and as hee thought educacion in France or travells at least, so with a desire of the houses pleasure Mr Secretary sate downe.

¹ *Cf. C.J.*, ii, p. 3 (16 April 1640).
² *Cf. C.J.*, ii, p. 3; Rushworth, iii, p. 1127.

Whereupon Mr Grimston stood up and spake to this effect—
[*fo 21ᵛ*] MR GRIMSTON.¹ Mr Speaker wee are called by his
Majesty to consult together of the great and weighty affaires of the
State and Kingdome.² There hath now a greate and weighty
businesse been presented to the howse by the noble Gentleman that
spake last and a l[*ett*]re hath been read importing (according to the
interpretation which hath been collected out of it) a defeccion³ of
the Kings naturall subjects.⁴

Mr Speaker there is a great cause and very worthy of the consideracion and advisem[*en*]t of this great councell. But I am very
much mistaken if there bee not a case here att home of as greate a
dainger as that which is already putt, the one stands without at the
back dore for soe daingers from thence in all our Historyes have ever
been termed. But the case I will putt is a case already upon our
backes. And in these great cases of dainger which so much concernes
the welfare of the body politique, Wee ought to doe⁵ in them like
skilfull phisitians that are not ledd in their Judgements so much by
outward expressions of a disease as by the inward sumptomes and
causes of it. For it fares with a body politique as it doth with a body
naturall. It is impossible to cure an ulcerous body unlesse you first
cleanse the veynes and purge the body from these obstruccions and
pestilentiall humors yt surcharge [*fo 22ʳ*] nature and being once done
the botches, blaynes and scabbs which grow upon the superficies and
outside of the body dry up, sheed and fal away of themselves.

Mr Speaker, the dainger which hath now been presented to the
house, it standeth at a distance, and I heartily wish it were further of
yett as it stands at a distance, it is so much the lesse daingerous.

But the case that I shall putt is a case of greater dainger here at
home domesticall, and is therefore so much the more daingerous
because it is home bredd⁶ and runnes in to the veynes.

Mr Speaker, if the one shall appeare to bee as great as the other I
hope it will not bee thought unreasonable⁷ at this time to putt the
one soe well as the other.

Mr Speaker, the case is this the⁸ Charter of our Libertyes called
magna charta was graunted unto us by King John which was but a

¹ Harbottle Grimston (Colchester). See below, App., Grimston, p. 296.
Peyton reported, 'One fault was observed to be committed in the Lower
House by one Mr. Grimston, who first spake in the House and jumped upon
the grievances of our state untimely and too early' (*Oxinden Letters*, p. 162).
² *Church* (B.L., Harl. MS. 6801, fo 32ʳ; B.L., Sloane MS. 1200, fo 13ʳ).
³ *disertion* (Bodl., MS. Rawl. A.103, fo 19ʳ).
⁴ '. . . *in the Northern parts*' (B.L., Harl. MS. 7162, fo 229ʳ; Worc. Coll. MS.
5.20, fo 28ʳ).
⁵ *deale with* (Worc. Coll. MS. 5.20, fo 28ʳ).
⁶ *humored* (Hunt. Cal., HM 1554, p. 150).
⁷ *unfitt nor unseasonable* (Hunt. Cal., HM 1554, p. 150).
⁸ . . . *great* . . . (Worc. Coll. MS. 5.20, fo 28ᵛ).

renovacion and restitucion of the auntient Lawes[1] of the kingdome. This charter was afterwards, in the succession of severall ages confirmed unto us above 30: severall times. And in the third yeare of his Majestyes raigne that now is wee had more then a[2] confirmacion of it, for wee had an act declaratorye past and that to putt [*fo 22*v] it out of all question and dispute for the future, his Majesty by his gracious answere *soit droit fait come est desira* invested with the title of Petition of Right.[3]

Mr Speaker, it may bee some may object that *partiriunt montes* etc. That I promised to present the howse with a case of very great dainger here at home, But the mountayne at last hath brought forth nothing but a mouse.

That this case if it were worth the name of a case, yett it is a case without doubt and soe not worth the putting. And truly for my owne parte I should have been of the same opinion had not some exposicions contrary to the Lawes of God the lawes of man and reason, and I am confident that[4] the dictamen of their owne consciences marrd the text with their exposicions, undermining[5] the Liberty of the subject with new invented subtill distinctions and assumeing to themselves a power I know not where they had it, out of Parliament to superseade, annihillate[6] and make void the lawes of the kingdome. What sad effects those[7] wayes and opinions have produced I am as confident his Majesty hath never seene nor heard as wee have felt them. And it is now his Majestyes goodnesse and piety to give us leave to speake them and present them with our greivances which are not a few.

[*fo 23*r] Mr Speaker, the Commonwealth hath been miserably torne[8] and massacred and all property and Liberty shaken, the Church distracted, the Gospell and the professors of it persecuted and the whole nation is over runne with multitudes and swarmes of projecting cankerwormes and caterpillars, the worst of all the Egyptian plagues.[9]

Then, Mr Speaker as the case now stands with us I conceive there

---

[1] *liberties and privileges* (B.L., Harl. MS. 7162, fo 230v; Worc. Coll. MS. 5.20, fo 28v).

[2] ... *bare* ... (Worc. Coll. MS. 5.20, fo 28v).

[3] 'come *il* est *desire* ... our Petition of Right' (Worc. Coll. MS. 5.20, fo 28v). Rushworth, iii, p. 1128, summarizes the following section: '*What* expositions contrary *to that Law of Right have some men given to the* undermining the Liberty of the subjects. . . .'

[4] ... *even contrary to* ... (Hunt. Cal., HM 1554, p. 151).

[5] *ruining* (Worc. Coll. MS. 5.20, fo 28v).

[6] *violate* (B.L., Harl. MS. 7162, fo 231v; Worc. Coll. MS. 5.20, fo 28v).

[7] ... *new* ... (S.R.O., DD/MI, Box 18, 97). Rushworth, iii, p. 1129, omits this sentence and the following one.

[8] '... *tormented* and *macerated* and *the law of* propertie shaken . . .' (Worc. Coll. MS. 5.20, fo 29r).   [9] Psalm 78: 46; also Exodus 10.

are 2: points very considerable in it, the first is what hath been done any way to impeach the Liberty of the Subject contrary to the Peticion of right, the second is who have been the authors and causers of it.

Mr Speaker, the serious examinacion and discretion[1] of these 2: questions doe highly concerne his Majesty in point of honor and the subjects in poynte of interest,[2] and all that I shall say to it are but the words that Ezra used to King Artaxerxes of the settlem[en]t of that state, which at that tyme was as much out of frame and order as ours is at this presente. That which cured theirs I hope will cure ours. His words are these [fo 23ᵛ] Whosoever (saith hee) hath not done the Lawes of God and the King, lett Judgement bee speedily executed upon him. Whether it bee unto death or unto banishment or to confiscation of goods or to imprisonm[en]t.[3]

Mr Speaker, it may bee some doe thinke this a strainge text and tis possible some may thinke it to bee as strainge a Case. As for the text every[4] man may reade it as will, And as for the case I am afraid there are but few here that doe not experimentally know it as badd as I have putt it. And how to mend a badd cause I take it as parte of the busines wee now meete aboute.

Mr Speaker, his Majesty yesterday did gratiously confirme unto us[5] our great and antient priviledges of freedome of speech, and having his kingly word for it, I shall rest as confident of it as the greatest security under heaven, whilst I have the honor to have a place here, I shall with all humillity be bold to expresse myselfe like a freeman.

Mr Speaker, the disseases and distempers that are now in our body are grown to that height that they pray for and importune a cure, and his Majesty out of a tender care and affeccion to his people like a nursing father hath now freely offered himselfe to [fo 24ʳ] heare our greivances[6] and complaints.

Mr Speaker, wee cannot complayne yt wee want good Lawes, the witt of man can not invent better then are already made there wants only some Examples that such as have been the Authors and Causers of all our miseryes and distraccions in Church and Commonwealth contrary to these good Lawes might bee treacle to expell the poyson of mischiefe out of others.[7]

---

[1] *discussion* (Hunt. Cal., HM 1554, p. 151); *decision* (B.L., Harl. MS. 7162, fo 232ʳ); *division* (Worc. Coll. MS. 5.20, fo 29ʳ).

[2] *proprietie* (Worc. Coll. MS. 5.20, fo 29ʳ).

[3] Ezra 7: 26. Rushworth, iii, p. 1129, omits: death.

[4] *anie* (Worc. Coll. MS. 5.20, fo 29ʳ).

[5] '. . . *by his royall word* . . .' (Worc. Coll. MS. 5.20, fo 29ʳ).

[6] *prayers* (B.L., Sloane MS. 1200, fo 15ʳ; B.L., E.199(25), unnumbered; Worc. Coll. MS. 5.20, fo 16ᵛ).

[7] *Cf.* Hunt. Cal., HM 1554, p. 152: '*but we may justly complaine* there wants

But my parte is but to *ostendere portum*[*sic*] therefore having putt the case I must[1] leave it to the Judgem[*en*]t of the house whether our daingers here att home bee not as great and considerable as that which was even now presented by the Noble Gentleman that last spake. And soe I conclude.

SIR BEMA RUDYARD.[2] Then Sr Bem Rudyard said, Sr there is a[3] dore now opened to us of doeing good if wee take the advantage thereof.

Wee are here mett by the blessing of god and our King parliaments have of late dayes become unfortunate. It is our duty by or good temper and Carriage to restore Parliaments to their auntient Lustre. [*fo 24ᵛ*] There bee some here present who can remember the breaking up of the last parliament, a buisnes certainly from which the papists are not exempt, who now by the discontinuance of Parliaments are come to that arrogancy and boldnesse that they intend[4] who are the greatest subjects. Their envy[5] I like, but their presumption is not to bee borne with. I wish them no harme but god[6] for I desire their conversion and the way to doe that is to sett up better lights who have warmth in them and are not lukewarme in Religion Surely they that quarrell betwixt preaching and prayer and would have them contend never meant well to either[7] but both must have their due. And yett I know not how it comes to passe that happneth to us which is no other Religion in the world that a man may bee too religious in and many a one by yt scandall is frighted into a deepe dissimilacion.[8]

Heretofore the distempers of the house have been imputed to the papists but the happy Successe of this parliament seemes to bee the Generall power of all, And therefore it is wisdome in us to preserve[9] temper and moderacion.

---

equall even and due execution of them which is a great part of our misery and causers of all our distractions *both* in Church and Commonwealth, whereas contrarily those good lawes might be treakle to expell the poyson *of our daylie corruptions and errors.'* Also B.L., Add. MS. 6411, fos 38ᵛ–39ʳ.

[1] portam . . . *shall now* (Worc. Coll. MS. 5.20, fo 16ᵛ).

[2] Sir Benjamin Rudyerd (Wilton). See below, App., Rudyerd, p. 296. Peyton reported that Rudyerd had tried to moderate Grimston's attack on grievances (*Oxinden Letters*, p. 162).

[3] . . . *great* . . . (Hunt. Cal., HM 1554, p. 193; S.R.O., DD/M1, Box 18, 98; Worc. Coll. MS. 5.20, fo 15ᵛ).

[4] '*contend with us, who are the better Subjects*' (Rushworth, iii, p. 1130; see also B.L., Add. MS. 6411, fos 60ʳ–61ʳ; Worc. Coll. MS. 5.20, fo 15ᵛ).

[5] *emulation* (Hunt. Cal., HM 1554, p. 193; S.R.O., DD/M1, Box 18, 98); *persons* (B.L., Add. MS. 6411, fo 61ʳ).

[6] *good* (Hunt. Cal., HM 1554, p. 193; S.R.O., DD/M1, Box 18, 98; Rushworth, iii, p. 1130; Worc. Coll. MS. 5.20, fo 15ᵛ).

[7] S.R.O., DD/M1, Box 18, 98, adds: '*both are the way under God to rectifie us and bring us to salvation. Some say* that a man may bee too religious. . . .'

[8] Rushworth, iii, p. 1130, omits the following sentence; B.L., Add. MS. 6411, fo 61ʳ, ends here.   [9] *use* (Worc. Coll. MS. 5.20, fo 16ʳ).

[*fo 25ʳ*] Breakings of Parliaments makes daingerous wounds in the body politique and if these splinters bee not pulled[1] out with a Gentle hand we may hereafter dispaire of cure.

In the 14 *E*: 3: Subsedyes were given to the King for his Expedicion into France, but by the ill managing of his treasure here, hee was so low that hee was glad to make truce with the French King.

In the 15 *E*: 3: hee returned and summoned a Parliament wherein they were nothing but jealousyes and distempers.

In the 17th hee called another Parliament to procure an attonement with his Subjects, which tooke Successe by their humble Carriage to him and his willingnesse to ratifye their Libertyes whereby all breaches were then made up.[2]

A Parliament is the bedd of reconciliacion betwixt King and people And therefore it is fitt for us to lay aside all exasperacions and carry ourselves with humility[3] howbeit the Kings Prerogative may goe farr, yett if they bee swayed with equanimity, it may bee the better borne.

Princes are and will bee as Jealous of their power as people of their Libertyes, though both are the best when kept within their bounds.[4] [*fo 25ᵛ*] Leavying of moneyes are a great disturbance to the subjects, And so will the Scarcity of the Kings revenues untill they bee supplyed, and where the power[5] and necessity meete in one hand, hee will not bee disappointed.

But before the ending of this Parliament, the untymely breaking whereof would bee the breaking of us, I doubt not but his Majestyes revenues may bee so setled that hee may live plentifully at home and abroad and without taking any thing from his Majesty[6] save that which of it selfe would fall away and which wee desire to restore before the Parliament ends wee thought his Majesty would redresse our greivances and should wee[7] now otherwise then thinke better of an Imaginarye then of a reall Parliament.

In former Parliaments the carriage of some have been so hauty

[1] *drawn* (B.L., Sloane MS. 1200, fo 17ᵛ).

[2] Worc. Coll. MS. 5.20, fo 16ʳ, adds: 'The King is the husband of the commonwealth and if there bee anie difference (as in the most perfect union there is sometimes some) then. . . .' *Cf.* Elsyng's 'Memorandum for the Earl of Dandy' (Elizabeth R. Foster, 'The Painful Labour of Mr. Elsyng,' *Transactions of the American Philosophical Society*, lxii (1972), pp. 60–63).

[3] '. . . *to submit to the Kinges prerogative according to lawe and justice*' (S.R.O., DD/Mɪ, Box 18, 98).

[4] '. . . *of the general action of moderation*' (S.R.O., DD/Mɪ, Box 18, 98).

[5] '. . . *of a King* . . . *not longe* be disappointed' (S.R.O., DD/Mɪ, Box 18, 98; Worc. Coll. MS. 5.20, fo 16ᵛ).

[6] *subjects* (S.R.O., DD/Mɪ, Box 18, 98). Rushworth, iii, p. 1130, ends paragraph: fall away.

[7] 'should *it be* otherwise nowe, *shall* wee thinke . . .' (Hunt. Cal., HM 1554, p. 195; Worc. Coll. MS. 5.20, fo 16ᵛ).

as though Parliaments would last alwayes and the carriage of others as if there would never bee any againe and therefore a moderacion if wee love our selves is requisite.

The delayes whereof are knowne how daingerous it is to the Commonwealth and religion seeing during this vacacion of parliaments so many disorders have been committed in the violacion of Lawes, such invasions upon oer Libertyes. To sett all which [fo 26ʳ] aright is now our taske and if in these tempting provacacions wee beare a moderacion[1] wee shall not misse of our end but shall vindicate God in his religion, the King in his honor, and the common wealth in its Gasping Extremityes.

All these things bee respected by us. Lett us beware of having the race of parliaments rooted out.

Men and Brethren what shall wee doe If I were to speake for my life, (as I doe for more) I would desire nothing more than that wee proceede with such moderacion as the parliament may bee the mother of many more happy parliaments and that no dismall events may happen to any for when parliaments are gone, wee are gone.[2]

SR FRANCIS SEYMOR.[3] Upon this said Sr Fran: Seymor, his Majesty, I believe hath as greate affeccion to parliaments as ever and I hope hee shall find us as affeccionate hearted to serve him. But wee must not doe him a disservice in neglecting the Commonwealth, and now Espetially for Subsedyes, what time is fitt for the granting of them, that is the question, for If wee should graunt the King Subsedyes before our Greivances are debated and [fo 26ᵛ] redressed our Judgem[en]ts may very well bee questioned, and it may give the Country (whom wee serve) cause to blame the men whom they have chosen as consenting to their Sufferance and it may likewise bee taken as a Confirmacion of our Greivances.

This great Councell as Tully said of the Senate,[4] is the Soule of the Commonwealth, wherein his majesty may heare and see all the greivances of his subjects. And in the multitude of such Councellors is Safety, the place and time to speake of them is allready proper and seasonable (the greatest priveledge here being Liberty of speech)

---

[1] Rushworth, iii, p. 1130: 'so many Disorders have been committed, by Innovations in Religion. Violation of Laws and intruding upon Liberties.' See also, B.L., Sloane MS. 1200, fo 18ᵛ; Worc. Coll. MS. 5.20, fo 16ᵛ.

[2] Hunt. Cal., HM 1554, p. 196: 'proceed with moderation that soe wee may have many happie Parliaments and that noe dismall events may happen to any, for when Parliaments are gone, then wee are lost.' See also, B.L., Sloane MS. 1200, fo 18ᵛ; Worc. Coll. MS. 5.20, fo 17ʳ; B.L., E.178(28), p. 4.

[3] Sir Francis Seymour (Wiltshire). See below, App., Seymour, p. 297. Peyton noted 'that Rudyerd's warning had not stopped Seymour from saying 'as much agen' as Grimston and comparing 'our affayres to the bondage of the Israelites in Egypt' (Oxinden Letters, p. 162).

[4] Perhaps Cicero, De Republica, 3:25.

if the dainger that of late yeares hath followed freedome of speeche did not deterre men. And therefore I humbly offer it unto you what wrong hath been done herein, what Judgem[en]ts have been against the members of this house for speaking nothing but what concerned the good of the Commonwealth,[1] which Judgments have been ag[ains]t Lawe; and reason and without president: daingerous, it is that those censures and Judgem[en]ts upon the former members of our house should rest upon record which were acts and Consequences [fo 27ʳ] wholly against the priviledges of the house. I know not whence Judges assume to themselves that power of censuring of Parliaments. What Lawe or reason is there that a parliament which is the highest of all courts should bee questioned by Inferior courts and judges. Surely they themselves will not like that the Common Pleas should conclude the Kings Bench or either of them, the Courte of Chancery. Sure I am that the Parliament is the Superior Courte of any and consequently not to bee censured by any, But surely the Judges did this to make way for themselves to evade the like (it touching every man to looke to preserve himselfe) that perhapps made them condemn that and those men which otherwise would condemn themselves, and such things have been done not onely which trench upon the Libertyes of parliaments, but upon the Liberty of the whole Commonwealth. And though the Gentlemen that late suffered were an ill Example, and I know not how soone it may bee our case, yett had I rather suffer herein for speakeing the truth, then that truth should suffer for want of my Speaking.

[fo 27ᵛ] Whereas evermore piety in a prince and more loyalty in Subjects. And yett what Common wealth ever suffered more then this. It is a riddle but easily answered. His Majesty is the sunne, which though it alwayes shines alike in it selfe Gloriously, yett by reason of cloudes it may not soe appeare. If Majesty by the reason of badd members appeares not in such splendor, what will it avayle us if the fountayne bee cleare, if the streames that Issue therefrom bee not so alsoe, soe though the King bee never so Just, his badd ministers may corrupt his Justice.[2]

I will instance in some Perticulars, if wee looke into the face of Religion (that is almost outfaced) [they][3] come boldly into our houses as if they had concealed tolleracions, I meane the Seminary preistes, who though they have lesse power, yett have they not lesse malice but more, so long as the pope hath his Agents amongst us.

See wee not how they goe to Somersett House and to St. James

[1] See *State Trials*, iii, 305–10.
[2] Montereul thought the Archbishop of Canterbury and the Lord Keeper were the principal targets of these complaints (P.R.O. 31/3/72, fo 118ʳ).
[3] Phrase probably omitted from MS. *Cf.* Worc. Coll. MS. 5.20, p. 3 (below, p. 214).

with too much Countenance, these are the Enemyes of the church without the Church.[1]

Wee have alsoe Enemyes within us which are:

[*fo 28*ʳ] 1. Nonresidents, who though they pull no churches downe I am sure they build none upp amongst us who oversway by worldly preferments and many Livings, our Savior Christ made it the touchstone of Peeters Love to feede his Sheepe and Lambs,[2] but these men regard not that but their private gaines, mistaking the Apostle as if in saying that ministers are worthy of double honour,[3] hee meant of double Livinges what more ag[*ains*]t reason or nature, then for one man to have above one wife and for shepheard to have more then one Shepefold.

2. Others hee said were dumbe doggs and cannot speake a word for God, covetous are they and ignorant of whom the people may seeke spirituall food, but can find none, and yett they cannot endure that their flock should feede elsewhere or abroad. Those are complayned of by the Prophett Jer[*emiah*] saying these steale the word from the people.[4]

3. Others there are that can speake and preach but it is not the Gospell but themselves and the Kings prerogative that the King hath an unlimitted power and that the subjects have no property [*fo 28*ᵛ] in their goods. These are badd devines and more ignorant Statesmen, applying their doctrine to the tyme and not to the Text, who under the name of puritans condemn all who truly professe Religion, there are surely many who under a forme of godlinesse cloake impiety, but to teach that a man can bee too holy is a doctrine of Devills.

Enemyes being thus within and without us, wee had need have a care of our Religion. Israell prospered while they kept close to their God, but when they fell from him, they were all scattered.

And now I feare I have been over longe. I shall a little speake of the greivance of the subject in poynt of Priviledge, when I remember what was confirmed to us by word of a King, and God forbid that I or any other should Imagine that the King did intend otherwise then hee granted us. But some there bee who have betrayed the King to himselfe and soe committed worse treason then those who betray him to others, who tell him his prerogative is above all Lawes and that his Subjects are [*fo 29*ʳ] but slaves to the distruccion of property

---

[1] Montereul mentions bitterness against the chapel at Somerset House but greater moderation than previously appeared in references to the Queen Mother's chapel (P.R.O. 31/3/72, fo 119ʳ); Rossetti thought there was some reason for the Catholics to hope when he wrote his dispatch of 28/18 April (P.R.O. 31/9/18, fos 181ʳ–83ʳ), but he was less optimistic when reporting grievances in the following dispatch (P.R.O. 31/9/18, fos 184ʳ–86ʳ).
[2] John 21:16.   [3] 1 Timothy 5:17.   [4] Jeremiah 23:30.

And it can passe their Judgements whereby the King is neither preserved in honor nor the Commonwealth in safety. If all that the Judges shall say (who have but their places at will) though contrary to the Lawe, experience, and presidents shall find us and by their doomes, wee of this house shall suffer Imprisonment[1] I know not what that in tyme may come to for such power will not stay there nor hath it, for they have taken upon them to send away some and remitt others as they should thinke fitting.

How unfitt a thing it is that the Lords of the Councell should rate the Country towards the shipmoney at their pleasure.

The abuses of the Sheriffs in Leav[y]ing of the said moneyes are most intollerable, who send out men in favour or mallice and are as greivous a plague as the task masters of Egipt.[2] They employing in most places none but Rogues, to execute their warfares, as one of them hath said unto mee, none else can bee procured to serve if this bee tollerated I know not but that the Lawe of Villany were better to be in force. In all these things I doubt not of his Majestyes Justice and proteccion.

[*fo 29ᵛ*] SR HEN: MILDMAY.[3] Sr Henry Mildmay spake ag[*ains*]t humming as undecent, then hee said hee thought wee had hitherto been a little out of the way and told us the parte of Musick was keeping of tyme, hee thought it fitt to beginne with God, *A Jove Principium*, advised after the manner of the house to thinke of a tyme for a fast and receiving of the communion and choice of ministers.[4] Hee likewise thought it fitt that Mr. Speaker should deliver to the House the effects of the Kings speech before hee fell upon other businesse.

SR HEN VANE: Sr Henry Vane excused the humming saying soe many young men being of the House were ignorant of the indecencye of it as yett.

Hee said that as for or greivances, hee thought it fitt for us to chuse a Committee of greivances and to bring them to them urging that wee had hitherto been out of Order, yett hee said hee hoped the King and country would receive content.

MR PIMME. Mr Pimme said that for a Committee of Greivances, it was to bee the whole House for not any subcommittee must conclude the house hee said for his p[*ar*]te hee wished not the retarding of the Kings affayres and thought the sooner the better.

[*fo 30ʳ*] Wherefore ordered by the House.

Committee for Religion—Monday; for Greivances—Wednesday;

---

[1] Montereul noted talk of punishing those who participated in the judgment (P.R.O. 31/3/72, fo 119ʳ).
[2] Exodus 1:13–14; 5:6–19.   [3] Sir Henry Mildmay (Maldon).
[4] A committee was appointed (*C.J.*, ii, p. 4; see also H.L.R.O., Main Papers, 16 April 1640, and Rushworth, iii, p. 1127).

for Courts of Justice—Friday; att two in the afternoone and the place in the house.

This day also a committee of priviledges was chosen the same by the direccion of the house not to bee above 60,[1] whereof Competent number of Lawyers to bee not all the Lawyers of the house as some would have had it, nor yett too few.

The time of this meeting was to bee thrice in the weeke, Tuesday, Thursday and Satturday at 2: of the clock in the Starr Chamber, the committees according to the auntient priviledges thereof to have power to send for all records and witnesses as should bee thought necessary for them.

1. It was Ordered that noe man should name but two Committees.
2. That none whose Eleccion was disputable should bee of the Committee.
3. That after a competent number were named, the Clearke should read openly after that to proceede to name more.

Order touching Eleccions. That p[ar]tyes greived by any Eleccion to peticion and make knowne their greivances within [fo 30ᵛ] ten dayes or else to bee concluded and Debarred from this Committee.

That if any more then two bee chosen Knts and Burgesses for one place that in such case none of them presume to sitt in the house upon cirtificatt of priviledges before they have setled the eleccion.

Whereupon divers withdrew themselves out of the house this day by comand and amongst them one Mr Bisloe,[2] whose case was the clearest to witt 23 freemen, which were all of the towne returne him, 12 of the same men returne a second, and 11 of them returne a third, yett by Order hee departed the house, only before his going a question was moved whether hee might not speake in his owne case or noe.

MR PYMME. If a member of a house bee accused of any crime or if any Exception taken to him, in such case hee may speake for himselfe, but not when his case concern the right of his house.

MR CHAR: JONES.[3] Mr Jones said as this case is hee may speake for himselfe and therefore hee may Justly prosecute it.

MR WINDHAM. Mr Windham said our Lord High Steward gave it as a charge the other day that none should presume to bee sworne unlesse hee were without question returned Justly and where none but 2 were returned.[4]

[fo 31ʳ] MR GODOLPHIN.[5] It was moved by Mr Goldolphin,

---

1 Probably 90. 89 were named 16 April, 9 were added 17 April (C.J., ii, p. 4; Yale, Stanford MS. I (Box 27, 5), fos 417ʳ–17ᵛ).
2 Edward Bysshe (Bletchingly) (Official Return, p. 483). See also, C.J., ii, p. 4 (17 April 1640); M.C.J., p. 9.
3 Charles Jones (Beaumaris).
4 Edmund Windham (Bridgewater). C.J., ii, pp. 2–3.
5 Sidney Godolphin (Helston).

whether (if: 4: were returned for one place all might sitt. Hereupon the former discourse arose.

This day all those who were chosen for more places then one named the places, and made their Eleccion for one and waivd the other and thereupon it was Ordered that new writts should Issue.

Maior chosen Burgesse. It was alsoe moved whether a writt being directed to a Sheriffe of a Citty that is a County to make Eleccion who choose the maior if such Eleccion were good or noe.

Divers were sited on both sides.

Mr BALL. Mr Ball being Recorder of Exeter when the Maior was now chosen held that the Maior of the towne could not bee returned. That hee hath power by Charter to take Statutes and Recognizances and to doe Juditiall Acts wherein hee cannot make a Deputy and so are the Charters of that towne.[1]

MR PYMME. Its matter in fact whether hee hath power by the Charter to make a Deputy or noe but I conceive if hee may make a Deputy and hee returne not himselfe but the Sheriffe returnes him in such case the Eleccion is good.

[fo 31^v] This was referred to a Committee And whether the Maior was Chosen of that or any other place, the house conceived it all one.

MR SPEAKER. Yesterday it pleased his Majesty to confirme mee your Speaker and amongst other things comanded mee to deliver fait[h]fully and reporte truly those things to the house which were delivered by my Lord Keeper by direccion from his Majesty touching the disorders of Scotland. I had not then pen, Inke, and paper with mee to take p[ar]ticuler notes of the passages, but by such helpes as I shall endeavour to promise I will at such tyme as the house shall appointe deliver the same faithfully unto you, whereupon the house appointed the morrow morning to heare the same.

[Harvard MS. Eng. 982]   **[17 April 1640, House of Commons]**

[fo 31^v]   **DIE VENERIS 17° APRILL**

[See C.J., ii, pp. 4–6]

MR SPEAKER. The first thing was Mr Speaker reported to the house the effect of the King and Lord Keepers speech to him on the Wensday before in the Lords House.[2]

MR ROWSE.[3] I find in yr reporte that it hath pleased his Majesty

[1] Peter Ball (Tiverton). Sir William Masham and Sir Robert Harley also spoke. See below, Harl. MS., 4931 fo 47, p. 234.

[2] See C.J., ii, pp. 4–5.

[3] Francis Rous (Truro). See below, App., Rous, p. 298. Peyton wrote, 'One Mr. Rous, whether out of some daunt at the assembly, or zeale to his cause, or abundance of matter, made a good butt a confused speeche, declaring the grievances of the state' (Oxinden Letters, p. 162).

or greivances should be shewed[1] and remedy given unto them.
[*fo 32ʳ*] And albeit some worthy members of this house have shewed
some of them yett they have left roome for others, for further discovery, for there yett remaynes two maine and weighty Consideracions:
1. The one is the roote of our Greivances.
2. The other is the Order and propagacion[2] of them.
For even in disorder there is some Order. The roote of all or
greivances I thinke to bee an intended[3] union betwixt us and Roome.
I speake it not without booke for there is too many bookes of it,
And one who is no little one saith if hee knew where the poynts[4] laye,
hee would not shew[5] them.

Another saith that the poynts in controversy are of an Inferior
way[6] and may be held this way or that way without Rapacye[7] which
if it were true wee can hardly bee excluded[8] of Romish Schisme.
True it is that for the union of Christendome, all the Blood of this
house were of too low a price though I value it a very[9] high rate.

But lett us agree with Roome in all points and differ in one which
is the popes supremacye the agreem[*en*]t to all others is to noe
purpose, but if wee agree to that,[10] wee are sworne at the threshold
and forsworne when wee come into the House. [*fo 32ᵛ*] And now as
Zim and Gym doe send a like answere one to another in the defects[11]
soe doe those of Roome answere those amongst us.

One called Santa Clara, though hee have another name, undertakes
to turne all or Religion enacted in this house into an Agreem[*en*]t
with Popery, but the printer hath confuted him well, for whereas hee
should have printed [*scabritiem*] *subjecti*, hee printed *scabiositatem
Egipti*[12] and indeed the scabb of Egipt is upon it which hath an

---

[1] *heard* (S.P. 16/450/94, 1).
[2] *concatination* (Hunt. Cal., HM 1554, p. 161; S.P. 16/450/94, 2); *continuation* (Worc. Coll. MS. 5.20, unnumbered); '*order, concatination, and continuation* (Bodl., MS. Rawl. A.346, fo 165ʳ).
[3] *endeavour of* union (S.P. 16/450/94, 2).
[4] points *of division* (B.L., Add. MS. 6411, fo 39ᵛ; S.P. 16/450/94, 1; Worc.
Coll. MS. 5.20, unnumbered); *the division* (Hunt. Cal., HM 1554, p. 161).
[5] *tell* (Hunt. Cal., HM 1554, p. 161; S.P. 16/450/94, 2).
[6] *allay* (Hunt. Cal., HM 1554, p. 161); *indifferent nature* (B.L., Add. MS.
6411, fo 39ᵛ).
[7] 'without *perill of perishing forever*' (Hunt. Cal., HM 1554, p. 161; S.P.
16/450/94, 2; Worc. Coll. MS. 5.20, unnumbered).
[8] *exposed* (Hunt. Cal., HM 1554, p. 161); *excused* (S.P. 16/450/94, 1);
excused of schism (S.P. 16/450/94, 2).
[9] S.P. 16/450/94, 2, omits: very.
[10] 'but if we *shall shake hands with them in* that . . .' (B.L., Add. MS. 6411, fo
40ʳ); '. . . we agree to *all, and then* we are sworn . . .' (Worc. Coll. MS. 5.20,
unnumbered).
[11] '*King* and *King* do answer one another' (Hunt. Cal., HM 1554, p. 161);
'*Hin* and *Gin* answere one another in the *desarts*' (S.P. 16/450/94, 2; Bodl.,
MS. Rawl. A.346, fo 165ʳ; cf. Worc. Coll. MS. 5.20, unnumbered).
[12] Christopher Davenport, *Deus Natura, Gratis Sive Tractatus de Prae-*

itching desire to scratch but there comes forth such corruption from it that though the savour pleased themselves yett to us it was displeasing wee heare of some trading into Roome so that a member of this house who loves Roome but a little[1] and I thinke had as little businesse there of his owne is said to have been there, and hee can tell best what his businesse was.

Yett further for the setling[2] of this worke the word puritan is an Essentiall Engine, a word that must not bee considered only as consisting of a few letters, but according to the manifold use the divell makes of it.

For this word in the mouth of a drunkard doth meane a sober man, in the mouth of an Arminian, an Orthodox man, in the mouth of a papist, a Protestant. [*fo 33ʳ*] And so it is spoke to shame a man out of all Religion, if a man will bee ashamed to bee saved.

And if once this name bee putt upon a man, you may lay upon him as on St Paul forty stripes save one,[3] and yett it is well if hee scape with his Limbes and members whole.

Another Advancem[en]t of this union is the laying of illegall burthens upon conscionable ministers, who if they had no conscience might beare them well enough but because they are conscionable, therefore they must bee driven away, a course in tyme sufficient to produce an unconscionable ministry.

To this end a booke[4] concerning Mortice[*sic*] Danceinge on the Lords Day is enjoyned to bee read by ministers, though the clerke may serve turne.

If it bee true which one minister spake that hee needed not to read it at all for his parishoners could play on Sundayes without Booke, but this conscionable and religious Minister suspended, excommunicated, and driven away.

Which course, if it should continue, might in tyme drive them all away and all religion with them[5] but lett [*fo 33ᵛ*] us see the

---

destinatione (1634), printed with the privilege of the king and the approval of the doctors. In Kenelme Digby's copy (B.L., 4378.1.12), p. 277, the error, which is listed in the printed *errata* is corrected by hand. Not all the *errata* are corrected.

1 *not* a little (Hunt. Cal., HM 1554, p. 162).

2 *setting on* (B.L., Add. MS. 6411, fo 40ʳ); 'further *tends* for the *settling* . . . an *espetial* engine . . .' (S.P. 16/450/94, 2).

3 2 Cor. 11: 24.

4 *pamphlett* (B.L., Add. MS. 6411, fo 40ᵛ; Hunt. Cal., HM 1554, p. 162). *The King's Majesties Declaration to his Subjects Concerning Lawfull Sports* (1633) (STC 9257).

5 '. . . If God be God lett us feare him and endeavour (as it is our duties) not thus to hault before him and connyve at the enimies of his Church but seeke to redresse such abuses and no doubt but God will prosper the worke that is intended for his glory and root out all those that thus contumeliously abuse his saints, therefore lett us bee couragious for the truth' (Hunt. Cal., HM 1554, p. 163).

propagacion, consequence, and order of others greivances issueing from this[1] to setle this worke of parliament to bee made needlesse and that this may bee Effectuated.

The property of the Subject in their goods must bee taken away by Iniquity[2] and thus breakes in the swarmes and innundacions of Monopolies and projectors and the like caterpillars of Egipt upon which plague this other plague is attended, that little of money they bring in is to bee seene.

Hence all the shippmoney goes out which disables us to give a fitt supply to his Majesty.[3] For if [*I have*] a bowle [*and the bailiff*] cometh in [*and I offer*] to make the bayliffe drinke hee takes the bowle with him for so did one to a freind of myne and putt it into his pockett.

Now if a man bee to pay his Lord a Rent and to raise his paym[en]t hath a feild of Corne, if the cattle breake into his Corne, hee must drive them out to preserve his corne that hee may pay his rent. Lett us therefore take care to drive these cattle in like manner out of our corne, thus wee see the rootes of our miseryes and the traynes and chaines that follow it.

Therefore I conclude as the Isralites did concerning the fact Gibeah — there hath not such a thing been done since Israell came from the Egipt of Roome.[4]

[*fo 34ʳ*] Consider it, take advice, and speake yr mind.

MR PYMME.[5] Hee that takes weights and impedim[en]ts from buisnesse doth as much good service as hee that gives it wings. I thinke it very pertinent that the proposicions made for taking of those rubbs out of the way that hindred the Kings buisnesse should bee furthered. Agents must worke after a patterne; our many

---

[1] '. . . grievances from this *roote, which is* this worke of Parliament must be made needles . . .' (B.L., Add. MS. 6411, fo 41ʳ); '. . . from this work. Parliaments *must* be made . . .' (S.P. 16/450/94, 2); '. . . grievances issuing from this, *as* Parliament *must* be made needless, And that this may be *effected* the *proprietie* of the subjects . . .' (Worc. Coll. MS. 5.20, unnumbered).

[2] *divinity* (S.P. 16/450/94, 2; Bodl., MS. Rawl. A.346, fo 166ʳ).

[3] In S.P. 16/450/94, 2, the sentence is underlined and *N.B.* written in the margin by a hand which may have been Laud's. The two stories which follow are variously worded in the MSS.

[4] Judges 20.

[5] See below, App., Pym (17 April), S.P., 16/451/16 (17 April), p. 299; also *C.J.*, ii, p. 5, and below, p. 245. Peyton reported, 'Mr. Pimme, an ancient and stoute man of the Parliament. . . . as yett only made the full complaint of the Commons, for he left nott anything untouched . . .' (*Oxinden Letters*, p. 163). Montereul mentioned only the religious issues. He noted that Pym spoke boldly against innovations in religion, the excessive power of the high commission, the number of priests permitted in London, the boldness of the English papists in entering the chapels, especially that of the pope's resident at St. James, and the open communication between the pope and the English (P.R.O. 31/3/72, fos 144ʳ–45ʳ). Conrad Russell, *The Crisis of Parliaments* (Oxford, 1971), pp. 310–22, gives more information about many of these grievances.

Greivances I take to bee first in Order and shall therefore offer you a modell of them which afflict us and the Commonwealth and which have disabled us to Administer any supply untill they bee redressed and will still disable us. I will recite them as breifely as may bee and as truly as my memory will permitt mee.

I shall ranke these Greivances under these 3 Generall heads: Greivances: 1. Ag[ains]t Libertyes of Parliament

2. In matters of Religion

3. In Affaires of State or matters of propertye.

In all these I shall take care to maintaine that great prerogative of the King that hee can doe no wrong.

[fo 34^v] As for the first which concernes the Liberty of parliaments, wee all know that the Intellectuall parte which Governes all the rest ought to bee kept from distempers.

The Parliament is as the soule of the common wealth, that only is able to apprehend and understand the sumptomes of all such diseases which threaten the body pollitique. It behoves us therefore to keepe the facultyes of that Soule from distemper. And although Religion is in truth the greatest greivance to bee lookt into, after and alsoe should claime the precedence in that respect before either of the other Generalls, yett insomuch [as] that verity in Religion receives an influence from the free Debates in Parliament and consequently from the priviledges in Parliament without which men will bee afraid to speake I thinke it fitt in order to priviledges in parliament to have prioritye.

I shall breifely therefore give yow a view of such occurrences as have altered the happy and healthfull Constitucion of it and in the first place remember [fo 35^r] the breaches of our Liberty and priviledges of Parliament and that divers wayes:

1. As namely the Speaker of the last Parliament was comanded to putt noe question and the house comanded that they should not speake these were conceived to bee the very ground and source of the ensueing evills of whatsoever fell upon those Gentlemen which so lately suffered it is true that the house was then breaking being commanded to adjourne presently, yett there were peticions left not heard.[1] It was hard to take away the last will of a dying man and to debarre us of our last Sighs and Groanes to his Majesty.

Here hee applyed it some way to the present Speaker in telling him the rights that appertaine to the house even at a dissolucion of a Parliament.

2. That the Judges presume to question the proceedings of this howse and that inferior courts have touched the Courte of parliament.

---

[1] *Commons Debates, 1629*, pp. 103–106, 239–44.

It is against nature and Order that inferior things should undertake to regulate superior. The Cort of parliament is a Courte of the highest Jurisdiction [*fo 35ᵛ*] and cannot bee censured by any Lawe or sentence but its owne.

Then that divers Gentlemen were imprisoned for such passages as proceeded from them in Parliament till they had putt in Security for their good behaviour and being caused to appeare in the Kings Bench were not admitted to make their defence.[1]

3. Lastly and as I conceive it the greatest that the Parliament was punished without being suffered to make its owne defence. I call the dissolucion of the Parliament a punishm[en]t and consequently the breakeing up of the Parliament to bee as a death to a good Subject thus much

[Finch-Hatton MS. 50]
[*p. 37.*]
of the first Generall.

The second generall head is of those greivances that concerne Religion, established by the Lawe of God and man.

1. The encouradgm[en]te given to them of the Popish Religion; divers of them might be of themselves I confesse of peaceable disposicions and good natures, but wee must not looke upon them they are in their natures for the planetts of themselves are of a slowe and temperate motion, weare they not hurried about by the rappid motions of the spheares, and they carryed about by the violence of the *primum mobile*; soe are all these Papists at the Popes command at any tyme, who onely waytes for blood. I may Instance in Hen. 3 and 4 of France, that were both taken away for alloweinge of Protestants. I desire noe newe lawes, nor a rigid execucon of these wee have but onely soe farr forth as may tend to the saftye of his Majestye. 2dly I observe a suspension of those lawes made against the Papists which are not either executed at all, or are onely so farre used as to make a proffitt by them whereas the said lawes were not made for the Kings revenue, but for distinction.

3dly There is an unrestrayned and mutuall communication of or Counsell with them.[2]

4thly They are encouradged by admittinge them to greate places of trust in the church and commonwealth (I crave pardon for the last slippe of my tongue), but I wish with all my heart that it neither be soe nowe nor at any tyme hereafter.

---

[1] See W. J. Jones, *Politics and the Bench* (London, 1971), p. 79.

[2] '. . . *by the frequent accesse of those who are active men, amongst them, to the tables and company of great men, and under subtile pretences and disguises, they want not meanes of cherishing their owne projects, and of indeavouring to mould and biasse the publike affaires to the great advantage of that partie*' (B.L., E.78(12), p. 6).

5thly The employm[en]t of a *Nuncio* from Rome, whose Councell and businesse is to reduce our land to the Pope.[1]

2) The second head of the second Generall is an Applying of us towards a conversion to Rome.[2]

First by the printing and publishing of many ill Popish bookes with priviledg; the publishing and preachinge [*of*] many Popish poynts in Pulpitts and disputed in schooles in the Universityes and there maynteyned for sownd Doctrine.

2dly The Introduccon of Popish Ceremonyes such I meane not as the Constitucon since the Reformed Religion continued unto us; But we must introduce againe many of the superstitions and infirme ceremonyes of the most decreppid age of Poperye, [*p. 38*] as the setting up Altars, boweing to them, and the like.

3). Next I shall observe the dayly discouradgement[3] of those that are the best professors of or Religion, for not doinge something that were against their consciences. The Manner of howse of Commons usually hath been to reconcile men of nice Consciences to their Bpps,[4] thereby to hide the weaknesses of others, but this was a meanes [to publish] the disgrace yt may be to all the world, as these good men for the most part feele.

Now Ceremonyes as bowinge at the name of Jesus rising up at *Gloria Patri* are imposed upon the consciences of men and required as dutye and the omission thereof punish without all grownd. And many Ministers likewise without any ground of Lawe questioned [for not reading] the Booke of Libertyes on the Saboth a booke which I must needs affirme hath many thinges faultye.[5] And for not doing of it have beene deprived of their livings, etc. This is a very greate greivance being ag[ains]t the foundacon of gover[n]m[en]t.

4. The fowrth thinge is the encroachm[en]t of the Authoritye of Ecclesiasticall Courts, assumeing to them more then the Lawe gives them.

As first the High Comission to fine and Imprison, to administer the oathe *ex officio*, with many the like usurpations.[6]

---

[1] Montereul wrote that there was bold talk against Count Rossetti, the pope's resident (P.R.O. 31/3/72, fo 119ʳ).

[2] Harvard MS. Eng. 982, fo 36ʳ, omits this sentence.

[3] B.L., E.78(12), p. 7, notes also the encouragement of the innovators.

[4] B.L., E.78(12), p. 7, cites practice in Queen Elizabeth's time and also 'one of our petitions delivered at Oxford to his Majestie that now is.'

[5] B.L., E.78(12), p. 7, lists among the practices for which men were punished: '*not removing the Communion-Table, to bee set Altarwise at the East end of the Chancell, . . . not coming up to the railes to receive the Sacrament, . . . preaching the Lords day in the afternoone, . . . Catechising in any other words and manner than in the precise words of the short catechisme, in the Common Prayer booke.*'

[6] See below, Worc. Coll. MS. 5.20, fo 22ᵛ (Eliot), p. 225. Montereul says they were debating doing away with the Court of High Commission which was new in England and an invention of the Archbishop of Canterbury (P.R.O. 31/3/72, fos 119ʳ–20ʳ).

2dly, In that the Bpps[1] disclaime jurisdiccon from the Kinge, but would have it from heaven, *jure divino*, contrary to many Acts of Parliament in that poynte, which wee are all bound to mainteyne as or owne Acts.

3dly, A very greate greivance it is that many Ordnaryes should take upon them the power to set forth newe Articles,[2] yea and every Chancellor assumes to himself synodicall power in Ecclesiasticall government.

Third Generall Hed Civill Goverment. From hence I come to the 3d Generall head, towching Civill gover[n]m[en]t wherein there are many Greivances, but I will moderate sharpe matters with fidellitye to the howse. 1. The takeing of Tonnage and Powndage without graunte from the Parliament. I am not ignorant, but some were due of themselves, but others were not, but the right hereof was ever in the howse and they many tymes have given different order herein; sometymes they have given it to the Kinge for certeyne yeares, some-tymes to his Tre[asure]r for 2 yeares, to be imployed in the howse. But nowe of late dayes, the affeccons of the people groweing stronger and stronger to their Princes, what [*p. 39*] before was given them for yeares, they give them nowe for life, But it was always given by the Parliament and by the Princes received, as the peoples kindnes,[3] But noe burthen layd upon the comoditye, never any charge upon the Marchandize, This will spoyle all Trade if Kinges may impose. There was a case in King James his tyme in ye comoditye of curran[t]s whether the king might impose; but the Judges were different in their opinions, this hath since beene a president to all Imposicions ag[ains]t Lawe taken in barring all proceedinges.[4]

The great excesse of Impositions taken makes the charge exceede the comoditye, which not nowe claymed by the King as he is keeper of the Ports, but but [*sic*] as graunted to him in poynt of prerogative (as in the Case of shipmoney) And in that it is not used according to the intention for which it hath beene alwayes given; it is a Greivance in the employm[en]t.

2. The second head of these greivances is knighthood; and though it be past, it is not forgott when the defence of the kingdome stood upon service and soccage, it dilated it self but to a fewe, but nowe it is extended to all; every one was forced against lawe to compound,

[1] Salvetti mentions parliamentary opposition to the bishops but does not think the king will abandon them (B.L., Add. MS. 27962 I, fos 45ᵛ–47ʳ).

[2] '... upon which they inforce the Churchwardens to take oathes' (B.L., E.78(12), p. 8).

[3] *Cf.* B.L., E.78(12), pp. 8–11, where the argument is expanded and specific precedents cited. See F. W. Maitland, *The Constitutional History of England* (Cambridge, 1963), pp. 182–83.

[4] Bate's Case (*State Trials*, ii, 371–94); see below, Harl. MS. 6801, fo 63ᵛ, p. 257.

and those that paid not were sued to their great vexation and those that have desired to answere for themselves have beene sent for up to attend the counsell Board; and have beene there delayed from day to day to their greate charge and inconveniencye And notwithstandinge the just defence they have made for themselves, Greivous distresses have beene laid upon them and, for any thing that I knowe, men may be still fined for it.

3. The third greivance is the greate inundation of Monopolyes, where-of we have a multitude; that lay and leave a burthen upon all things in or kingdome, as soape, salt, bread, beare, etc. which much differs the case from that of forraigne comodityes;[1] All men have beene much greived herein, it being soe common that it is knowne to all.

4. The fowrth is ship money. It is true it hath the countenance and coullor of a Judgm[en]t for it, but such a Judgm[en]t as is contrary to all other Judgm[en]t of the Lawe; being ag[ains]t all lawe and have-ing noe one booke for it,[2] besides kings heretofore have beene in very great dangers, yet never any one practised it before, And besides it is left at [p. 40] large both for the Tyme, frequencye, and pro-porcon. I say it is Judgm[en]t without any coullor at all of Lawe. I desire to prove it, And if any here shall endeavour to defend it, he must knowe that his reputacon and conscience lye at stake in the defence.

5. I had almost forgott it But nowe I recollect my selfe. It is the Proceedinge in the forrest busines; And noe marvaile I had neere lost myself, a man may soone loose himselfe in a wood; The old bounds[3] are taken awaye and they are enlarged with newe ones, our Predecessors have without question given sattisfaccion, yet upon the very same grownds wee are condemned.

I shall excuse that Noble man[4] that was commissioner in the service what hee did, hee did not of himself, but as he was guided by the Judges.

6. The sale of Publicke Nusances that they should be matter to

---

[1] See below, Finch-Hatton MS., p. 40, p. 154. B.L., E.78(12), pp. 12–13. describes the 'principal undertakers' in the soap business as popish recusants seeking 'their private gaine,' division of king and people, and destruction of Parliament. Among the results are increased prices, 'subjects deprived of their ordinary way of livelyhood,' and 'a great number of persons . . . unjustly vexed by Pursevants Imprisonments, Attendance upon the Councell-Table, seisure of goods, and many other wayes.'

[2] Cf. B.L., E.78(12), pp. 13–14. 'I see no book, nor know of any authority that doth maintain this writ' (State Trials, iii, 1129, Croke).

[3] B.L., E.78(12), p. 14, cites 27 and 28 E. III and the Charter of the Forest. See Precedents, p. 322.

[4] Probably Henry, earl of Holland, who was Chief Justice in Eyre. Finch may have been the target of the complaint about the judges; see the charges against him (Rushworth, iv, p. 137); cf. B.L., E.78(12), pp. 14–15, for more details.

rayse money by; Men are questioned for them, but upon composition the same things become noe Nusances. It is of dangerous consequence when Lawe is made but a couller for private men as may be instanced in buildings, depopulacons, etc.[1]

7. The Millitary charges or Imposicons on the people, raysed by Princes l[*ette*]rs or by Lords of the Councell, as Armour money, conduct money, and the like; these are Impositions ag[*ains*]t all Lawe, which as they are very burthensome soe is the consequence very dangerous.[2]

8. The extrajudiciall declaracions of Judges without heareinge as in the case of shipmoney, men were anticipated in their Judgm[*en*]ts;[3] In many cases we have Appeale, but this greate greivance prevents us thereof. This is *contra morem majorum*.

9. The next greivance is that the greate Courts doe countenance these opressions, as I may instance in the greate Courte of Star Chamber concerninge the Monopolye of soape.[4] This is a greate greivance for such a courte to countenance these things, for the nature of the Star Chamber is to protect not to bee a courte of Revenue.

10. That the Lords of the Counsell should countenance these things is a very greate greivance And whereas they are bownd by the Stat[*ute*] of *Magna Charta* to doe justice to all,[5] they spend that pretious tyme uppon plotting of Monopolyes, which should be bestowed upon the good and saftye of the kingdome. A projector heretofore hath beene accompted a name of contempt; It greives my [*p. 41*] very heart to thinke that persons of greate dignitye and trust should not onely countenance, but owne them. I shall shewe that the Lords of the Counsell had their originall from the howse of Commons, who did humbly beseech the Kinge not to manage the greate affayres of the State singly, but to admitt of some grave Counsellors to advise with him; this was accompted as greate securitye that Kings were pleased not to goe alone,[6] but for this Counsell nowe to allowe of Monopolyes is much beneath them. Howe illegall these Monopolyes are our lawe determines which enforces us to fly for proteccon to the Kings power and prerogative.

11. The Royall power warrants Monopolyes as by proclamations and gard of the greate seale, I confesse the Kinge hath a transcendent power in many cases, but that power ought to be em-

---

[1] See details in B.L., E.78(12), p. 15. Also Foster, ii, pp. 260–61.

[2] See below, Harvard MS., 79ᵛ–80 (Hotham), p. 192. B.L., E.78(12), p. 16, gives some Elizabethan and Jacobean background.

[3] *State Trials*, iii, 842–46.

[4] Rushworth, ii, pp. 189–90, 252–53; also below, Speeches, Holland, p. 262.

[5] *Magna Carta, c*. 40.

[6] See A. L. Brown, 'The Commons and the Council in the Reign of Henry IV,' *Historical Studies of the English Parliament*, ed. E. B. Fryde and Edward Miller, ii (Cambridge, 1970), pp. 31–60.

ployed to preserve the subjects And not to countenance illegall courses.

I am nowe gone as high as I can upon earth, and yet I will goe higher. Not onely the Kings prerogative is wrested for the maintenance of these oppressions under which wee all suffer.

12. But the bond of conscience hath beene applyed to countenance many of these greivances wee knowe that it hath beene preached for sownd Doctrine that what property the subject hath in any thinge may be lawfully taken awaye when the Kinge requires it. Dr Maneringe I remember for publishing these and the like Tenents was questioned and censured in this howse the last Parliament I sawe him as lowe in this place as ever I sawe anye, and little then did I thinke, that he would have leapt soe soone into a Bppricke, his preferment I am sure hath done much hurt, and beene the meanes to encouradge many others.

And though I cannot goe any higher I will yet goe more compasse.

13. The intermission of Parliaments have beene a true cause of all these evells to the Commonwealth, which by the Lawe should be once everye yeare;[1] Wee must therefore desire them humbly for the Kinge truely hath the choyce.

Nowe after these perticular greivances I shall undertake to demonstrate them to be as prejudiciall to the Kinge as to the subject and that I shall prove by these followeinge reasons.

1. First it keepeth the Kinge and people from understandinge one another, for if an interruption happen [*p. 42*] betweene the head and the members; howe can the whole body subsist.

2. It keepes the King from supplye of Subsidyes which could not be given away as his land hath beene.[2]

3. Losse of his reputacon abroad and had it not been for this, I beleive the Palatinate had not nowe been in whose hands it is.[3] Queen Eliz never did things on her private purse. Moreover the Kings of England had as greate advantage over the Howse of Austria as any Prince whatsoever, and I thinke it may bee recovered still.

4. Losse in regard of Religion which hath lost us much allyance. We have not that intelligence and partye as before we had, because our change is feared.[4]

5. It hath lost the King many of his subjects and soe the Kingdome much weakened, they being fledd into the desarte of another world,

[1] 4 *Edw.* III, *c.* 14, and 36 *Edw.* III, *c.* 10.
[2] B.L., E.78(12), p. 20, refers to recent efforts to reform revenue collection in France.
[3] The Elector Frederick had lost it to the Catholic powers in 1622. See C. V. Wedgewood, *The Thirty Years War* (New York, 1961), ch. iv.
[4] Probably the statement questioned below, Finch-Hatton MS., p. 54 (Dell), pp. 168–69.

because they could not injoye the libertye of their consciences here in indifferent things.[1]

6. Losse by the discouradgm[en]t of vallor and industrye, men being loath to take paynes since the[y] worke for others, And there are but fewe nowe that applye themselves either to doe well or deserve well, finding flattery and complyance to bee the easier waye to obteine their ends and expectacions. It alsoe makes bad men gratious with their Kinge and soe they have an easy way to pre-ferm[en]t, whosoever will but sell their consciences.[2]

7. It makes a way to distempers. It breeds jealousyes betweene the Kinge and his people; To consider the trouble and charge that one summers distemper will put the Kinge to may suffice to enforme us withall howe dangerous it is to the state to have such intermissions of Parliaments. It is true that Religion keepes us from Distempers; But I observe that those Kings that have beene greatest with their people have ever beene most happye.

I forgott one thinge which is a newe course. they are nowe about to lay charges upon commodityes imported from and into foreigne kingdomes as from France into Spaine and the like a course before this tyme never heard of.[3]

One thinge more I shall onely remember, which is this these imposicions come not all into the Kings purse, what becomes of them I knowe not much. I [p. 43] beleive, stickes by the waye, I will instance in the Monopolye of wynes, the Kings customes and other perquisites amounte but to 30000^{li} per annum. The 2^{li} upon each Tunne by computacion of Marchants comes to at least 230000^{li} per annum soe that the King receives but 30000^{li} for that which the subject was dampnifyed 230000^{li}, which is a shamfull thinge.[4]

I shall nowe humbly[5] pray That these greivances (being cleere in fact) may bee voted, if any thinge in the vote bee stucke upon, that it may be layde aside to be debated and drawne accordinge to the

---

[1] B.L., E.78(12), p. 20, cites in particular the departure of clothiers. The 'Great Migration' to New England occurred 1630–40; see Carl Bridenbaugh, *Vexed and Troubled Englishmen, 1590–1642* (New York, 1968), chs xi, xii.

[2] B.L., E.78(12), p. 21, cites a 'westerne man, much imployed while he lived' as an example of those who profitted personally from office.

[3] Perhaps the issue in the petition of Spanish Merchants (*CSP 1639–40*, p. 161).

[4] *Cf.* Harvard MS. Eng. 982, fo 42^r: 'comes to at least 20000^{li} p. annum . . . the K receives but 20000^{li} . . . the subject was dampnified 230000^{li}.' See below, Trinity, Dubl. MS., 623, p. 260. Alderman Abell, chief farmer, was apprehensive about parliamentary complaints (B.L., Add. MS. 11045, fos 105^r–105^v). Montereul reported that the Marquis of Hamilton had an interest in the wine business from which he made a considerable profit (P.R.O. 31/3/72, fo 119^r).

[5] *only* (Harvard MS. Eng. 982, fo 42^r).

course of the howse, into a Remonstrance, with an humble Peticon of both howses for Redresse.

And I hope the wisdome of this howse will prepare such a remedye as will make the Kinge a greate Kinge and the people happye.

Dabit deus his quoq[ue] finem.

SR GILB PICKERING. Presented a Petition from the countie of Northoun which he desired showld be reade, wherein there was peticioned for releife in many greivances in Innovations of Religion and against Shipmoney and Militarye charges.[1]

SR GILB GARRARD. Presented another Petition for Middlesex and to the same effect.[2]

MR BALL. Hereupon moved that it was unseasonable to present any of these petitions to the howse and advised that they might be delivered to the Committee of Greivances.[3]

SR WAL EARLE. Answered That if any Petitions were presented by any without dores it was fitt for such to be delivered to the Committee; But he was of a different mind, where the Petitions came from members of the howse.[4]

SR NATH BARNSTON. Presented a Petition for Suffolke.[5]

MR KIRTON.[6] Moved that some present remedyes might be thought on for these greivances that soe wee might afterwards fall with more allacritye on the Kings affayres.

SIR JOHN HOTHAM.[7] Thought good to fall on the preparacion of them the next daye.

SIR GILB GARRARD. Seconded that mocon and wisht we might meete earlye, and because that worke was of consequence not to parte till finished.

Hereupon it was ordered by the howse That the next morninge the Greivances named showld be discussed.[8]

---

[1] Sir Gilbert Pickering (Northamptonshire). See below, S.P. 16/450/25, p. 275.
[2] Sir Gilbert Gerrard (Middlesex). See below, Harvard MS., fo 81, p. 194; also S.P. 16/453/52–55, reports of an investigation about a petition from Middlesex. We have been unable to find the petition. Rushworth, iii, p. 1127, dates the presentation 16 April.
[3] See below, Harl MS., 4931, fo 47, p. 234.
[4] Sir Walter Erle (Lyme Regis). Erle also moved that the previous Parliament's remonstrance concerning religion be brought in (*C.J.*, ii, p. 4).
[5] Sir Nathaniel Barnardiston (Suffolk). See Rushworth, iii, p. 1131. We have not found the petition.
[6] Edward Kirton (Milborne).
[7] M.P. for Beverley.
[8] Vassall and Crispe also spoke (below, Harl. MS., 4931, fo 47, p. 235).

[*Finch-Hatton MS. 50*]   [*18 April 1640, House of Commons*]

[*p. 44*]   SATTERDAY *18º* APRILL

[*See C.J., ii, p. 6*]

Hertfordshire. A peticion presented by the knts of Hertfordshire.[1]
Essex. Another presented for Essex.[2]
Cittye of Norwich. The Cittye of Norwich peticon presented with 300 hands subscribed to it.[3]
MR HIDE.[4] Stood up and said that a worthy member of the howse had omitted yesterdaye one greivance and as he thought noe way lesse then any hee had named; wished (hee said) that it had beene inforced by his tongue; yet rather then it showld be forgotten; he would be bold to name it. Itt was the Courte of Honour.

This Courte is risen, said hee to that height as never Courte did in soe short a tyme. I[*t*] assumed power to fine and imprison what it listed. Nowe he said if he owed his Taylor moneye he could provoke him and pay him with his badd manners. Hee graunted the Courte was old, but the customes of it were newe.

Besides he said this Courte is attended by a Pageantrye of Herraulds. They require portions out of our estates, nay they lay Imposicions on or dead carkasses. Hee hath heard (he said) that a knt could not live soe cheape as a gentleman, but nowe he said, they could not dye soe cheape as other men, for it would cost him 5^{li}[5] more then a Gentleman; hee spake of the severity of that courte in case any showld refuse to pay this fee. A gentlewoman, hee said that had beene sollicited by the Herralds for their fees for her husbands corpes asked but a Lawyers advise, whether it was due, hee replyed not, that he knewe by Lawe, for this the Lawyer was summoned to that courte, and being he would not there recant his opinion and make submission, hee was find, imprisoned, and not dischardged in a long tyme.

Another sufficient man was undone by that courte onely for his jest mistakeing a swanne for a goose, therefore he concluded that while this courte had such a power; for ought he knewe noe man but might be fined to his ruine and fewe dayes before to have spoke thus much would have undone him.

Towne of Northton. A peticion from Northton Towne.[6]

---

[1] See below, Petition, Harl. MS. 4931, fo 42, p. 277.
[2] See below, Petition, Harl. MS. 4931, fo 41, p. 275.
[3] See below, Petition, HLRO, Main Papers (18 April), p. 279.
[4] Edward Hyde, later earl of Clarendon (Wootton Bassett). See below, App., Hyde, p. 302.
[5] *s* (Harvard MS. Eng. 982, fo 43ᵛ).
[6] *C.J.*, ii, p. 6, We have not found the petition.

[*Committee*]

Mr Grimston in ye chayre. Mr Speaker quitted the chayre and the Howse was dissolved into a committee And Mr Grimston was chosen to the chayre.

The order made concerninge the discussion of Greivances was read.[1] Sr John Stranguage.[2] Said that the first he conceived necessary was [*p. 45*] liberty in Parliament accordinge to Mr Pymme, for without that we sate there in vayne (he said).

Hee graunted that the Kinge may out of Parliament question Treason or felony in the Howse, but not misdemeanors, the howse was to be the sole judge hereof and if those members of the howse that were imprisoned committed any thing the last daye of the Parliament, the King should question them the first daie of the next Parliament.

Hee read the Informacion against Sr Jo Elliott and those who were committed and shewed the manner of their committm[*en*]t by the Judges; if these thinges were suffered, wee could not treate of any thinge for feare.[3]

Hee shewed that divers greate personages have beene referred to the censure of Parliament as the Duke of Lancaster, Ed. 3 sonne,[4] the Duke of Suffolke, and in King James his tyme to his greate praise Chancellor Bacone and the Duke of Buckingham.[5]

The next thing to be questioned (he said) was whether he had anything to give or not, for if the Kinge be judge of the necessitye, wee have nothing and are but Tennants at will.

The Judges they give their opinions that all is the Kings and the Ministers preache it and therefore he did much extoll the Kinge for his mercy to us; (said) he having consulted with the Judges and Divines herein, it argued much grace in him in suffering it to be argued after oppinions delivered, he concluded not doubting but that the Kinge in grace and favor called this Parliament to settle these greivances which done (he said) for his part he thought fitt to helpe the Kinge.

Sir Ric Hopton.[6] Said that he perceived his owne thoughts were spoken onely he would that Religion should be remembred.

Mr. Jones.[7] Mr Jones recited the manner of ye proceedings with

---

[1] Probably that made the preceding day (*C.J.*, ii, p. 6).
[2] John Strangways (Weymouth).   [3] See *State Trials*, iii, 293–310.
[4] In the Good Parliament of 1376 (*Rot. Parl.*, ii, pp. 323ff.).
[5] These precedents had been cited in 1629 (*State Trials*, iii, 295); see also *Rot. Parl.*, v. pp. 176–83; *L.J.*, iii, pp. 53–55, 570, 576–77.
[6] Here and below, Sir Ralph Hopton (Somerset).
[7] Here and below, probably Charles Jones, son of the judge, who spoke 16 April (above, Harvard MS., fo 30ᵛ, p. 144), although Richard Jones (Radnor) and Gilbert Jones (Wareham) also sat.

the members of the howse [th]at were committed after the last
Parliament and wished the howse for a more ample sattisfaccion
therein to send to the Kinges Bench for the originall informacion
there putt against them.

Sr Sam Roe [Rolle].[1] Sir Samuell [Rolle] made complaynte to the
howse that whilst he served his countrye in giveing his attendance in
the howse, the sheriffe had distrayned his goods for Shippmoney and
added that if there might [p. 46] not be priviledge for or goods as well
as or persons, it would dishearten men from the service of the
countrye. Hereupon some would have had the Sherrife sent for, as a
delinquent; but the major parte were for moderation. And soe it
was for borne.

Hereupon the howse returned to the persuite of the last question,
Whether the Records in the Kings Bench showld be sent for or to
take notice of the Judgm[en]t; greate debate hereof arose, but the
howse seemed inclined (it being allready soe well knowne) to proceede without sendinge for any Record, thinkeing that a meanes
onelye to loose tyme.

Sir Hen Vane. Wherefore Sr Hen Vane spoke and told the howse
that as they were tender of their priviledges soe must the[y] expect
the Kinge to be of his. Confessd he was very unwilling to venture
upon his memorye and that he was ignorant of the particulars till
that morninge and soe he thought were many more; Why therefore
the howse should make this pressure, he knewe not; but desired
information in particulars before the howse proceeded to Judgm[en]t.

Mr Vaughan.[2] Recited what was before recited, and accorded with
Sr Hen Vane to se[e] first the Records.

Mr Wilde.[3] Mr Jones playnely declared that the first breach given
was that of the Speakers in offeringe to adjourne the Parliament
without the howses leave which was against Lawe.

Ordered by the Committee that the first thing handled showld be
that Greivance in the aforesaid judgm[en]t And therefore It was
thought fitt and ordered That the Records in the Kinges Bench and
Starr Chamber showld first be browght.[4]

Mr Lewknor. After this order Mr Lewknor pressed it further that
the dissolution of the former Parliament, he said he served of it, and
desired the leave of the howse to make use of the notes he (then a
member) tooke, which obteyned, hee read.[5] That at that dissolucion

---

[1] M.P. for Callington, Cornwall, and brother of John Rolle, the merchant
who had complained in 1629 that his goods had been seized for failure to pay
tonnage and poundage (Commons Debates, 1629, pp. 7–9).
[2] Henry Vaughan (Carmarthenshire).
[3] John Wilde (Droitwich).
[4] H.L.R.O., Main Papers, 18 April 1640, drafts of orders.
[5] Sir Christopher Lewknor (Chichester). See C.J., ii, p. 7. Montereul says the

fewe, if any, were consenting thereunto of the members of the howse, but the Speaker did it of himselfe. 2. That he was pressed by some of the howse to keepe the chaire, the Speaker replyed he was the Kings servant and desired not to be ruined, adding that he left the chayre not to dissobey the howse, but to obey the Kinge. [*p. 47*] Twas urged further by the Howse That the Speaker was their servant, He replyed in being the Kings servant he did not cease to be the Howses alsoe; And when he was asked whether or noe he would put the question; he answered that he would not say, he would not put the Question; but he would say he durst not. Mr Lewknor, after this recitall, concluded in advise to the howse not to interfere with the Kinge in judging whether he may forbid the putting of the Question; But whether, being the Speaker was the Howses servant he owght not to obey them?

Sir Thomas German.[1] Said that if the king did manifest his intentions (as then hee did) of dissolveing the Parliament, the Speaker did not transgresse.

Sr Hugh Cholmely.[2] But Sr Hugh Cholmely moved that 3 things showld presently be putt to the Question. 1. Whether the Speaker may leave the chayre; 2. Whether being called, he owght not to repayre againe to it; 3. Whether hee may dissolve a Parliament.

Mr Kirton. Said it never was the manner of the Speaker to bring commands from the Kinge without the Greate Seale, but the honorable counsell ever did.

Sr Hen Vane. Sir Henry Vane replyed he conceived it very familiar for the Speaker to bring commands from his Majestye, hee instanced in Sr Rob Phillips, his father, who being Speaker often did it.[3]

Sr Miles Fleetwood. Hee once remembred that Phillips did declare a command from the Kinge, but that hee thowght owght not to be the Question.[4]

After longe debates and yet not able to come to the Question.

It was ordered That a Subcommittee showld be chosen to search the matter in fact which was esteemed for the best meanes to knowe

---

Speaker had said only what the king commanded, that his Majesty wanted the Parliament put off to another time. He (the Speaker) asked them if they would be willing. Montereul added that this was a point of some importance since they wanted to infer from it that it was up to the king to assemble Parliament but not to dissolve or adjourn it (P.R.O. 31/3/72, fo 120ᵛ).

[1] Sir Thomas Jermyn, Mr Comptroller (Bury St. Edmunds).
[2] Sir Hugh Cholmley (Scarborough).
[3] Sir Edward Phelips, Speaker, 1604–10; see Wallace Notestein, *The House of Commons, 1604–1610* (New Haven, 1971), ch. 7.
[4] Sir Miles Fleetwood (Hindon). Probably the incident of 12 May 1610 (Foster, ii, pp. 85–86). Fleetwood was in the House in 1610.

the cases of the violation of the priviledges, the place chosen was the Courte of Wards, at 2 in the Afternoone.[1]

Sir H Cholmely. This beinge thus settled, returninge to the complaynt of Sr Samuel [*Rolle*] said that since that Gentlemans goods were taken away in this manner, he thowght it the best waye before the howse showld rise to laye a brand upon shippmoney.

Mr Herbert.[2] Stood up saying that the Gentleman that used [*p. 48*] the words of laying a Brand, he feared was a boldnes might prove unfortunate; he said that the Kinge in a case of such danger tooke the severest course he could in the judgm[*en*]t, wished the howse to looke to their oathes they had taken to the Kinge and not rashly to doe it without weighing the causes, the Judges went upon, leass that the whole proceedinges should thereby prove over hastye.

As for claymeinge priviledge of Parliament in not haveing or goods distrayned, he said he was utterly against that opinion; since if the Kinge have right the howse protects noe man in doeing wronge; his heart went he said for the howse to proceede, but not out of tyme.[3]

[*Finch-Hatton MS. 50*]   [*20 April 1640, House of Commons*]

[*p. 48*]   *DIE LUNAE 20° APRILL*

[*See C.J., ii, pp. 6–7*]

SR H CHOLMELY.[4] Sr Hugh Cholmley moved That the Sheriffs showld be stopped in distraininge till the matter of shipmoney showld bee adjudged.

MR PIMME. Mr Pimme seconded the suspence thereof.

Committee. A committee chosen to receive greivances.[5]

MR TREASURER. Being of the Committee[6] made Relacon to the Howse of the particulars received at the Committee concerninge the manner of the Speakers behaviour upon the dissolucion of the preceding Parliament. The Howse upon this Report inclined to the

---

[1] H.L.R.O., Main Papers, 18 April 1640, list and order. Peyton wrote, 'And first upon Saturday they did little, because they could not agree where to begin their greivances, butt in the end elected a committee which is to prepare and prefere the businesse to the House' (*Oxinden Letters*, p. 163).

[2] Edward Herbert, Mr Solicitor (Old Sarum).

[3] Records concerning shipmoney were sent for (*C.J.*, ii, p. 6; H.L.R.O., Main Papers, 18 April 1640). With the motion of 20 April (below, Finch-Hatton MS., p. 48, p. 162) for a select committee is a note struck out which may have related to Rolle's issue (M.C.J., p. 28).

[4] He had refused to pay shipmoney (*Cholmley Memoirs*, p. 60). See below, Harvard MS., fo 81, Worc. Coll. MS. 5.20 fo 17ᵛ, pp. 194, 220.

[5] H.L.R.O., Main Papers, 20 April 1640, list and order; see also M.C.J., p. 28.

[6] That appointed Saturday (above, Finch-Hatton MS., p. 47, p. 162, n. 1); see also below, Worc. Coll. MS. 17–17ᵛ, pp. 220–21.

putting of it to vote, whether that carriadge of the Speaker and manner of dissolveing the Parliament was not ag[ains]t the libertye of the subject and a Greevance.

MR HERBERT. Said that since at the dissolucon some of the Howse would have a question put and others would not, he conceived it noe fault in the Speaker, for he said till the howse be unanimous, the Speaker owght to put any Question, And as concerning the manner of the Kings dissolveinge he desired the howse to forbeare, told them they were putting the greatest Question that ever was putt in a Parliament and said it manifestly trenched upon the Prerogative. He would have it quallified, putt to a committee first to examine presidents, And concluded that he wished neither the matter of fact nor of right to be layd by but onely wished tyme for soe greate a case.

MR ST JOHNS.[1] Hereupon said that he did not beleive this Question [p. 49] any way against the Prerogative. He urged that the matter of fact was proved; and as for the matter of right, hee shewed that the Kinge called Parliaments by his Greate Seale and not by bare command of word, and therefore he held it might not be adjourned with a bare command, Nay hee said it was a Question whether the Greate Seale could adjourne it, for the courte must adjourne it selfe. Hee concluded therefore that the adjourneing was not legall, etc.

Much tyme and long debates were herein spent. At length it was put to the howse Whether the adjournment of the howse by a verball command of the Kinge from the mouth of the Speaker bee not a breach of Priviledges And voted that it was after long delayes on both sides, some rather desireing a Peticion to the Kinge before a declaration, others to stay the declaration till Presidents were searcht that might make for the Kings verball adjournment but the proposicions were overruled.[2]

[Finch Hatton MS. 50]   [21 April 1640, House of Commons]

[p. 49]   DIE MARTIS 21mo APRIL

[See C.J., ii, pp. 7–8]

2d Reading. A bill read to restrayne the use of gold and silver to beginne the March followeinge and to continue a yeare for probation.[3]

---

[1] Oliver St. John (Totnes).
[2] 'That there 3 waies of seeking redres from ye King for a greivans in breach of privilege of parliament as by petition, Remonstrans, protestation' (H.R.O., M36/1, p. 1). A committee was appointed (C.J., ii, p. 7); also see below, S.P., 16/451/16 (20 April), p. 245.
[3] Probably the apparel bill (C.J., ii, p. 8).

2d Reading. Another Bill read concerning comon Recoveryes by Infants. Both bills were Committed.[1]

SR WALT EARLE. Acquainted the howse with the large extent the Commission bore which was graunted to the Convocation Howse[2] insomuch, as he said; some of the Convocation gave out that they were never soe strong these 40 yeares as nowe, wherefore hee said since their commission was soe large and they by virtue thereof about to make newe Canons, hee judged it most fitt for the howse to looke to the settlem[en]t of Religion.

The best meanes thowght upon by the howse was the chooseing of a committee, who had power given them by the howse to search the commission graunted to the Convocacion under the Greate Seale, and consequently to make a report of it to the howse the next morninge.[3]

The Rolls were brought in of the Judges opinion of shipmoney and alsoe the Record of Elliotts busines according to a former order herein.[4]

It was moved that the Instruccions likewise [*p. 50*] of the Lords of the Counsell to the Sheriffe touching ship money should be looked into.

A Committee chosen for bringing in of ye Records concerning Bells case of curran[*t*]s.[5]

[Banqueting House]

The howse attended the King in the Banquetting Howse where the Lord Keep made a speeche to excite the howse to supplye the Kinge as followeth.

Lo Keeper.[6] First he remembred them of the greate and weighty causes that moved him to assemble this Parliament, which he had declared unto them: The first was for his Ayde towards his reduceing

[1] H.L.R.O., Main Papers, 21 April 1640, list and order; see below, S.P., 16/451/16 (21 April), p. 246.
[2] See below, H.R.O., M36/1, p. 2, Harl. MS. 4931, fo 47ᵛ, pp. 199, 236; S.P. 16/450/95, copy of the commission; P.R.O. C.82/2190/132, warrant for the Great Seal. Rossingham gives Scudamore details of the commission: '. . . It is said there shall be canons made for the more decent service of God hereafter and that he shall be served no longer so slovingly as of late yeares' (B.L., Add. MS. 11045, fo 105ʳ).
[3] M.C.J., p. 35, shows a draft order which refers to the commission 'for introducing and establishing new ceremonies'.
[4] The House had been informed of difficulties in obtaining these the preceding day: 'It was moved, That ye records of ye Kings bench ought not to goe out of ye Cheife Justice his hands. Bookes were cited for it. Mr. Speaker said, There was dis[*tinction*] betwixt a perusal and a removal, they might send to peruse them. And he signed a warrant for yt purpose' (H.R.O., M36/1, p. 1); see also C.J., ii, pp. 6–7, and below.
[5] Bate's Case, also those in Vassall's case (C.J., ii, p. 8).
[6] See below, App., L.K. (21 April), p. 303.

into his obedience the Rebellious Scotts, That if this supply were not speedye it would bee of noe use to him, The reasons wereof were:

Because his armye was nowe on foote and marchinge and that the charge of it amounted to 100000^{li} monthly which was more then he could furnish out of his owne coffers.

That if the supply was not answereable, all the charge hee had beene at would be cast awaye and the designe lost.

That he required not at this present a greate or absolute supplye but such as might be sufficient and answereable to the worke but onely soe much as might keepe the designe on foote from being lost.

That the designe was undertaken upon weighty reasons of State and the end of it for the honor of this Nation and for the assurance of or selves, our wives, and children.

That this supply being graunted his Majestye would give free scope to present unto him all our just greivances, and would heare and give a gratious answere unto them And himself [*assist*][1] in the redresse of them.

Then he tooke notice of the shipmoney and told us that he never had soe much as a thought to make it an annuall revenue; noe nor at any tyme any private benefitt to himselfe, but it was for the consideracon[2] of the glorye, dignitye, and splendor of the English nation; And that every particular person had his share in the benefitt of it[3] without which wee should by this tyme have found the woe of it.

That as his intention was to make noe private benefitt of it to himself his practise had [*p. 51*] beene accordingly, nay that he had added divers summes out of his owne coffers to cooperate with us.

That truthe of which might appeare for that the whole money had beene delivered over to Sr Wm Russell who had made the accompts to the Counsell Table where any that dowbted might see howe it had beene disposed of.

That his Majests intention was that noe writts should have issued this Yeare but that he was compelled to it for these weighty considerations.

1. That there was a necessity for him to prepare an Army to reduce his disaffected subjects in Scotland whereunto his owne private coffers were not sufficient.

2. All Neighboring Princes were prepareing greate fleetes And that his Majests dominion over the seas which was soe much to the honor

1 Worc. Coll. MS. 5.20, fo 18^r; *cf.* B.L., E.203(1), p. 11, the king asked for only enough for three or four months and 'expected no further supply till all their just grievances were relieved'.

2 *conservation* (Worc. Coll. MS. 5.20, fo 18^r); *conservation* of *his Kingdom and for* the glorie . . . (Bodl., MS. Rawl. A.346, fo 157^r).

3 Worc. Coll. MS. 5.20, fo 18^r, omits the remainder of the sentence.

166 PROCEEDINGS OF THE SHORT PARLIAMENT

and splendor of this Nation would have beene lost; And trading much impayred, if the whole kingdome and the danger of the danger of the seas had not beene guarded.[1]

3. Thirdly those of Algiers were going to have 60 shipps to sea to infest our Marchants tradinge into the streights And that lately a shipp had beene taken by them called the *Rebecca* valued worth 260000^{li}.

His Intentions of shipmoney were soe still that he might be able to live like a kinge of England, to defend us with safety and honor.

Wee not withstanding might be masters of or owne waye soe to settle the shippmoney, as that wee might be assured it showld not come to his private use, but be wholly expended for the defence of the kingdome and guardinge of the seas.[2]

That for the proprietye of or goods and liberty of or persons, he would be as forward to graunte us them as wee could be to aske.

That he would nowe tell us the best meanes how to make this Parliament the happyest Parliament that ever was in England, which was by putting an obligacon of trust and confidence upon the Kinge (and that good manners did require we should goe this waye) and that his Majestye much scorned to be overcome with any kindnes by his people.

That this kingdome ought to bee and is the [*p. 52*] dearest unto him of all his kingdomes.

That his kingdome of Ireland in the last Parliament before this had given unto him 6 subsedyes the second day of the Parliament and had relyed on his Majesty for redresse of their greivances, which before the end of that Session had beene performed unto them with advantage.

That at this Parliament they had graunted him 4 Subsedyes and that a Subsedye in Ireland amounts to betweene 50 and 60000^{li}.

That the freenes and alacritye where with they had given the 4 subsedyes were more acceptable to his Majestye then the Guifte itselfe.

Then he spake to the Lords sayinge that the Lords were called to be wittnesses of his intentions to the howse of Commons hoping not to find them backward. And that though the most proper and naturall waye of subsedyes was to arise from the howse of Commons, Yet his Majestye would expect that they showld give their assistance.

He came then to answere an objeccion (which he said he had forgotten) which might be made.[3]

---

[1] '. . . the whole kingdome *in* dainger if the seas had not been guarded' (Worc. Coll. MS. 5.20, fo 18ᵛ).

[2] '. . . for the *use* of the kingdome *and* defence and guarding of the seas' (Worc. Coll. MS. 5.20, fo 18ᵛ).

[3] '*The Lord Keeper* had forgotten to answer an objection *that* might bee made, *and thereupon repeated itt after all which was this objection* . . .' (Worc. Coll. MS. 5.20, fo 19ʳ).

That it might be objected that Tunnage and Poundage were taken for guarding the seas and therefore noe neede of the ship money.

To which he answered that Tunnage and Poundage were for the ordinary charges at sea but not for extraordinarye And that as the forces of all neighbouring kingdomes were increased soe it was necessary his Majestyes forces showld be augmented,[1] unto which Tunnage and Poundage were not nowe sufficient.

Lastly the King himself required the Speaker to make a Report of this to the Howse and give him a speedy accompt of the Howses resolucion.[2]

[*Finch-Hatton MS. 50*]   [*22 April 1640, House of Commons*]

[*p. 52*]   *DIE MERCURII 22ᵈᵒ APRIL*

[*See C.J., ii, pp. 8–9*]

A Peticon of Peter Smart, prisoner in the Kings Bench was read. It was against Neale, then Bpp of Duresme.[3]

A committee whereupon chosen to examine the causes and by what authority the Peticioner lay in prison and soe to report it to the howse.

[*p. 53*] MR SPEAKER. Mr Speaker asked the howse whether hee showld make them a Report of what my Lord Keeper delivered to the howse the day before, some were against a Report, till the King showld warr[an]t that [*which*] he had delivered in writeing or by testimoney of some noble persons neare the chayre but the pluralitye of voyces inclyned to a report which was made.[4]

MR KIRTON. After the Reporte wished the howse to take till next day to consider and then to fall uppon the busines.[5]

Twoe of the Judges came from the Lords and acquaynted the howse that the Lords had upon speech with him [*the king*], found him readye in alloweinge of a fast and further that the Lords desired a meeteinge of both howses in the afternoone at 3 of the clocke in the paynted chamber. Answere was returned by the Judges that the howse would give their Lopps a meeteinge at the howre and place appoynted. Mr Secretarye Vane[6] was chosen to make reporte to the Howse.

---

[1] '. . . *in* the *like proportion* . . .' (Worc. Coll. MS. 5.20, fo 19ʳ).

[2] '. . . *therein and of all their proceedings thereupon*' (Worc. Coll. MS. 5.20, fo 19ʳ); see also below, Finch-Hatton MS., p. 53, p. 167.

[3] See below, Petition, Smart, p. 280.

[4] The report does not appear in *C.J.*

[5] It was so ordered (*C.J.*, ii, p. 9); see also below, Worc. Coll. MS., fo 19ᵛ, p. 221. A draft of the deferring order stated that the House should 'pursue it with all ex[*pedition*] not to adjourn till they are come to some resolution . . .' (M.C.J., p. 38); *cf.* B.L., Add. MS. 11045, fo 111ʳ: 'But they have not tied themselves to prepare it in one day.'

[6] Windebanke (*C.J.*, ii, p. 9; H.L.R.O., Main Papers, 22 April 1640).

MR HOBORNE. Gave an imperfect accompt to the howse concerning the Commission of the Convocation Howse.[1]

Feared it was by the Howse least the Convocation showld have to greate a power in their commission.

MR PYMME. But Mr Pymme said that they could onely bind themselves not the layity without the assent of the howse of Commons urged 21 *E.* 6 and 6 *R.* 2 by both which it appeared that the Convocation cannot bind the layitye.[2]

Yet he said he nowe much feared what might bee attempted except their power should be somewhat restrayned by the Howse. That it cannot be that they showld bynd any but the clergye, for nowe they come without any legatine power from the Pope or the Archbpp of Cant[*erbury*] as heretofore and therefore there was noe reason for the clergy to seeke more.

It was by many desired that some committee chosen might goe to the Lords and desire them to joyne with the Howse of Comons in peticon to the Kinge to stoppe the proceedinges of the Convocation.

MR ST JOHN.[3] Concurred with Mr Pimme that the Acts of the Convocation could not bind the layitye or make Canons universall since the words of summons made against them, and for the howse of Commons. For the writt to the Clergy runnes *ad consentiendum* but to the Commons *ad tractandum de rebus ad Ecclessiam pertinentibus*, urged further howe dangerous it were for the Convocation to make cannons to bind the Layitye and shewed the danger of [*p. 54*] Excommunication that would then lye upon a man; and howe merciles the common lawe was to a person excommunicated he wished the howse therefore presently to repayre to the Lords; And moved for an order in it.

MR JONES. Moved hereupon That the commission to the Convocation (which the day before could not be seene) showld bee lookt into at my Lord keepers before a conference with the Lords in this poynte because as yet the Howse knewe not of what particulars to complayne of.

MR DELLE.[4] Mr Delle said hee perceived the howse very jealous of innovations in Religion, but he believed they had noe great cause

---

[1] Robert Holborne (Southwark). The committee had not seen the commission (*C.J.*, ii, p. 9); see below (24 April), p. 175, n. 2.

[2] The precedents should be 51 *Edw.* III (*Rot. Parl.*, ii, p. 368) and 6 *Ric.* II (*Rot. Parl.*, iii, p. 141). See H.R.O., M36/1, pp. 5–6, Finch-Hatton MS., p. 60, below, pp. 201, 175.

[3] See H.R.O., M36/1, p. 6, below, p. 201. St. John understood that the commission was issued on the basis of the writ. '*Nota*', perhaps in Laud's hand, is written in the margin of the king's writ for Convocation beside the words of summons (S.P. 16/445/73). The wording was discussed in the Long Parliament (Notestein, *D'Ewes*, pp. 153 and note, 156 and note).

[4] William Dell, Secretary to the Archbishop of Canterbury (St. Ives).

for it, he said he wondred to heare a member of the howse say that the churches beyond sea were about to forsake us because wee did forsake or Religion.

MR PIMME. Mr Pimme said hereupon that the words were fowle, and desired the howse that Mr Delle might name the man for hee knewe not those words were spoken by any man. Hereupon called uppon him to name the man; And after much unwillingnes he named Mr Pimme who recited what before he had delivered much blameing the gentleman for his mistake; And after the Howse by vote cleared Mr Pimme of those words.[1] They were inclyned to have Mr Delle come to the Barre and make his recognition, but Mr Pimme did intercede for him takeing his acknowledgm[en]t of sorrowe, not as a delinquent but in his place; desireing him to acquaint his Lord alsoe of his mistake, for he said he doubted not but he had misinformed him herein.

MR PEARD.[2] Mr Peard called the accusation of Delle murther because he said it was done in cold bloode.

Ordered ag[ains]t Delle. Hee was therefore ordered to aske forgiveness and to recant it wherever hee had told it.

In fine it was putt to the Question whether without further Inquisition the howse showld repayre to the Lords concerninge this commission of the Convocation and it was voted affirmative.[3]

[*Finch-Hatton MS. 50*]   [*23 April 1640, House of Commons*]

[*p. 54*]   *DIE JOVIS 23tio APRIL*
[*See C.J., ii, pp. 9–10*]

The Howse assented to the Lords for a fast for ye howse, the daye being Satterday sevennight. Preachers were chosen.[4]

The howse was dissolved into a committee for the [*p. 55*] consideracion of the Kings busines.

[*Committee*]

Lentall[5] in ye Chayre. Mr Lentall chosen to the chayre.

Sr Ben Ruddierd. Sr Ben Ruddierd said the howse had done wisely

---

[1] See above, Finch-Hatton MS., p. 42, p. 155, and below, S.P., 16/451/57 (22 April), p. 246.

[2] George Peard (Barnstaple).

[3] A committee was appointed (*C.J.*, ii, p. 9; also H.L.R.O., Main Papers, 22 April 1640).

[4] The House did not succeed in delivering the assent to the Lords. Bernard, who was one of those attending Windebanke with the message, notes that the Lords answered, 'That they were busy but they would send for us, when they w[ere] at leasure' (H.R.O., M36/1, p. 6); *cf. C.J.*, ii, p. 9.

[5] William Lenthall (Woodstock), speaker in the Parliament of November.

in takeing the Kings busines into present consideracon, the advantage would be to or selves trust him that hee may trust us. The common wealth was, he said, a miserable spectacle, but we had the Kings word for redresse which as it was sacred soe likewise inviolable and therefore wished the howse to bringe thinges to an happie conclusion.

Sr Ric Hopton.[1] Sr Ric Hopton said that it nowe was with the King and his people as with a M[aste]r and his servant; the M[aste]r sends his servant to a place and bids him make a speedye returne, but the servant askes some reasonable things first, this capittulacon he said was not fitt; But if a Master sends his servant and the servant desires onely tyme to pull out a thorne first, whereby he better enables him selfe to serve his M[aste]r, this is no delaye but an advancem[en]t. He said we had many Thornes to pull out before we were able to serve the Kinge, named divers greivances, which he called those thornes.

As for the charge which my Lo Keeper delivered the daie before; that the Kinge was at the charge of 100000^{li} a moneth, he said it was a summe that if ye land were united would serve to sett upp the Kings standard in any Princes Countrye in Christendome and if the ordinarye expense were soe greate, the extraordinary may be thought twice as much. He concluded first to pull out the thornes and then to the Kings bussines.

Mr Comptroller.[2] Sayd we came to heale the wownds of the kingdome which by Gods grace he hoped we showld effect. The King hee said desired the howse to repose a confidence in him and that greivances may have their consideracon in tyme, hee urged the Kings hast and his gracious speeches to confide in him.

The King he said told us that any other meanes to doe the worke without shippmoney should content him, told us that when first he came into the Howse, hee expected soe happye a Parliament as that we might have counted from the tyme as from an Epocke and that his wishes showld still goe for it.

Sr Fr Seymor.[3] Said that tyme was pretious, his Majestyes supply and or greivances lying both before us, which putt him in a greate streight, In the one side his dutie (he said) [p. 56] to the Kings commands the precedence on the other the Trust the countrye hath laid on him, forbade him to relye on future hopes. He said, he would not care for trustinge the Kinge if that were all, but when or busines shall have false glosses putt upon it, by ill Ministers about him, He thought fitt or Greivances to bee first and then his Majestyes supplye.

[1] See H.R.O., M36/1, p. 5, below, p. 200.
[2] See H.R.O., M36/1, p. 4, below, p. 200.
[3] See H.R.O., M36/1, p. 4–5, below, p. 200.

Sr Hen Stranguage.[1] S[ai]d the first institutions of Parliaments were to represent greivances and urged the fittnes thereof in Parliament, s[ai]d the thorne in or feete disabled us to stand, lett us but bee inabled to goe and wee will runne, wee will trust the Kinge if he will inable us to And therefore concluded greivances must precede.

Sr Jn Wraye.[2] The part of the greatest Monarch was to doe noe wrong, which he said King Charles would verifye; The poynte of propertye once cleared he said we showld doe Parliament miracles.

Mr Kirton. S[ai]d the vote of the Howse was to serve both king and Countrye wisht therefore the Howse to move a Conference with the Lords about these 3 poynts: 1. Religion; 2. Property in goods; 3. Libertye in Parliament. This done wee showld be enabled for the Kinges worke.

Sr Wal Earle. Seconded Mr Kirtons motion concerning the Conference about these 3 poynts and desired it might be put to the question.

Mr Herbert. Urged the order made by the Howse which was to take a present consideracon of the Kings affayres, not that he deserted the greivances but wished the Kings busines first considered.

Sr Harb Grimston.[3] Said that if before releife in our Greivances we showld send downe a Bill for subsedyes, the Countrye would not agree to it and they would give but a badd welcome to us.

Mr Tre[asure]r. Said that the worke of the daye was a supplye And though wee conceived we had many Greivances, yet the waye for their redresse was by the Kinges releife, pressed the unhappines that must needes befall our kingdome upon a disjunction nowe when the catholicke Princes were united; urged there were presidents in Parliament which gave priority to a supplye as *60⁰ E. 3*: when he said a breach was conceived of the subjects libertye; Nevertheless the[y] beganne with a supply.[4]

Sr Humph May.[5] Would have the supply take precedence.

Mr Glinne.[6] Said that all agreed to give supplyes, the Question rested only whether wee showld graunte supplyes till some emminent dangers were releived, saying it was no lesse [*p. 57*] necessarye for the releife of Greivances then that of supply. This might, he said, stand with the Kinges intentions, for the Kinge he said looked not

[1] Probably Sir John Strangways; Giles Strangways (Melcomb Regis) also sat.

[2] Sir John Wray (Lincolnshire). See below, App., Wray, p. 305.

[3] Harbottle Grimston, M.P. for Essex, and father of Harbottle Grimston (above, Harvard MS., fo, 21ᵛ, p. 135).

[4] Probably 6 *Edw.* III; see below, H.R.O., M36/1, p. 4, p. 200.

[5] Perhaps Sir Henry Mildmay (above, Harvard MS., fo 29ᵛ, p. 143); Sir Humphrey May died in 1630. Thomas May (Midhurst) was a member of the Parliament.

[6] John Glyn (Westminster).

for a full plenarye supplye nor wee nowe for a perfect releife and therefore concluded for Mr Kirtons motion.

Somewhat he answered the President urged by Mr Tre[*asure*]r said he thought Presidents dangerous and that the collour of Presidents had drawne the sword of shipp money over our head in which there was not one Booke, etc. Hee dowbted not he said, but the Kinge would be as glorious and free from these greivances as any of his predecessors and desired the honorable persons neare the chaire to acquaynt the Kinge that the Howse was ready for supplye, onely wished their greivances first.

Mr Peard.[1] Said that there was a greate Question about the manner of supplye slaves he said did but restore; but free men give Shipp-money hee said invaded the propertye of or goods and that it was necessarye to settle the poynte whether he had any thinge to give or not. Said a president of it nowe might hurt the child unborne and if ship money should nowe be gathered it would become a President. Hee held it therefore necessary first to determine the propertye of goods and soe take away yt abominacion of Ship money; Libertye (he said) was the salt that seasoned all; if that be not likewise settled; wee were in greate misery shipp money he further said tooke away not onely our goods but persons likewise shewed how difficult and heard it was to obeteyne a *Habeas Corpus*, etc. Then he spake of Religion of all other not to be neglected, without which wee were to be accounted Heathens, etc.

Mr Herbert. Interrupted him and tooke exceptions at the language that fell from Mr Peard. Wondered, he said that any should offer to call shipp money abomination, remembringe them with howe much gravitye the Kinge proceeded in it, howe solemnely it was debated by the Judges; and therefore required the Justice of the Howse upon Mr Peard, as alsoe for speakeinge of Religion, whereupon Mr Peard cald those that lived without it Devells. This language Mr Herbert thought very punishable.

Mr Controller. Seconded the complaynt against Mr Peard said though he looked upon shipmoney as a dyinge thinge yet that phrase of Abominacion, he thought deserved reprehensions, etc.

[1] See *C.J.*, ii, pp. 9–10. Rossingham reported in connection with the ship-money debates of 30 April, 'One Mr Peard, a Lawyer of the Middle Temple made a speech in this case of the shipp mony which offends the Judges, which was, That the Parliament was the only creator of lawes, and the expounder of those lawes. The Parliament was the Phisitian to prescribe remedy to the diseases of the commonwealth, and the Judges were as the Apothecaries (not to putt, or add to any newe ingredient but such onely as the Phisitian, the Parliament had before prescribed) wherefore hee concluded the Judges had done beyond their Commission in giveing Judgment in this businesse of shipp mony, although the necessity were never soe greate' (B.L., Add. MS. 11045, fo 115ʳ).

Mr Peard. Hereto seemed to answere and said that they yt had noe Religion had the Religion of Divells and he desired [*p. 58*] soe to be understood; And for his calling shipmoney an Abominacion he retracted confessing himselfe to bee sorry for it adding that himself had an English heart and he hoped others had English eares.

Mr Pymme. Was for the releife of Greivances first, wished it to be put to the Question which should have precedence.

Secr[*etary*] Vane. Said that there were 2 greate workes in hand together; but he feared if wee did not supplye the Kinge first wee showld doe neither of them.

Mr Jones. Urged the *21⁰* of K James where a declaration was made of the intentions of the Howse to the Kinge, though noe subsedy past,¹ and wished the Howse to looke thereunto as to a moderate waye.

Sir Ph Manering.² Made relacon to the Howse of the love of the Irish to the Kinge and alsoe recited some particuler expressions both in their last and former Parliaments stirringe upp the Howse to followe their example.

Mr Pymme. Dissented from Mr Jones in sheweing a greate difference betweene the present case and that in the 21th of King James for then, he said, the Kinge declared the busines to the Howse and desired their advice concerninge the Palatinate.³ The Howse after consideracion had delivered their opinions with a declaracion to assist him with money for supplye if he pleased to followe their advice, but nowe he said the Kinge hath not pleased soe farre to impart his affayres to the Howse or to demand any Councell from them.⁴ 2. For trusting the Kinge (he said) he conceived it noe way necessarye; for Justice was oweing to the subject by dutye, and we desired noe more; But in case wee showld desire any favor; then to expresse our gratitude in that way were most fittinge. 3. For to make a bare declaracion would be dishonorable for the Howse to breake and noe way profittable for the Kinge, besides (he said) heretofore it had an ill event being pressed and gathered contrary to the intentions of the Howse.

Much debate whether we showld goe to the Lords or not, concerning a Treatye of or Greivances spent all this day, and at length this Question was putt to the House.⁵

¹ See *L.J.*, iii, p. 275; *C.J.*, i, p. 679. A subsidy was passed later, 21 and 22 *Jac*, I, *c*. 23.
² M.P. for Morpeth; he was Strafford's Secretary of State in Ireland.
³ See *L.J.*, iii, pp. 209–10.
⁴ Montereul reported that it had been noticed that in the entire speech the Lord Keeper had hardly named Scotland once (P.R.O. 31/3/72, fo 121ʳ).
⁵ Waller may have spoken in the debate. See below, App., Waller, p. 306.

[*House of Commons*]

As many as are of opinion that we shall consult with the Lords to prevent innovacions in matter of Religion concerning propertye of Goods and Priviledges of Parliament, say I.

A Conference hereupon was voted.

[*p. 59*] A Committee chosen for to meete in the afternoone to expedite the busines of the Conference.[1]

[**Finch-Hatton MS. 50**]   [**24 April 1640, House of Commons**]

[*p. 59*]   **DIE VENERIS 24º APRIL**

[*See C.J., ii, pp. 10–12*]

SR WR EARLE.[2] Sr Walter Earle made report of the Heads for Conference with the Lords which were agreed on by the Committee as inducements to Innovation in matter of Religion, of propertye of Goods, of Libertye in Parliament.

Those heads which concerned Religion were these:

1. The Commission graunted to the Convocation conceived as a Greivance, the rather because of the practise of those men to whome the Commission was graunted.
2. The complaynts of the Countryes in their petitions.
3. Disturbing of godly Ministers complayned of for not doing things enjoyned without Lawe, being conformable otherwise.
4. Popish poynts preached and printed.
5. Restrayning conformable Ministers, etc.

These were the Inducements which the committee thought fitt at the Conference with the Lords to represent as inducements in matters of Religion.

The next that followed were such as concerned the breach of Governm[en]t, which were these:

1. Monopolyes.
2. Shippmoneys.
3. The enlarginge of forrest bounds.
4. Coate and conduct money with the rest of millitary chardges.
5. The deniall of Justice in Westminster to the subject.
6. The frequent imprisonm[en]t of such as failed to pay unwarrantable taxes.

Those that concerned the Libertye of Parliament were these:

---

[1] This is the same committee as that appointed 22 April concerning Convocation, with some additions. See *C.J., ii*, pp. 9, 10.

[2] The many extant copies of the report show slight variations. See below, App. Grievances, p. 308.

1. The punishing of men out of Parliament for things done in Parliament.

2. The vote which allready the Howse had passed concerninge matter of fact (*vizt*.) That Libertyes of Parliament have beene infrindged.

3. The Dissolveing of Parliaments without redresse of Greivances.

4. Not holdinge a Parliament yearly accordinge to the statute.

The Committee left it as a *Quere* to the Howse whether the trayned Bands goinge out of the Countie showld not at the Conference with the Lords be represented as an inducement.[1]

Some dispute arose whether the Comission granted to the Convocation showld be represented or not, Whereupon a Gentleman said that *2do, Jac.* a comission was graunted in the same words, which he desired the Howse to consider. The present Comission was read and parralleled with that of *2do Jac*.[2]

[*p. 60*] MR HAMDEN.[3] Mr Hamden hereunto said that though the like was graunted *2do* K James, yett not any before in 60 yeares. He urged the practise of the men to whome it was graunted and the largenesse of the Comission extendinge to alter and amend and alsoe to make newe Canons.

2. The extent that it includes all persons that may lawfully be concerned, which he said must intend the Layitye insomuch that the Clergie were before named.

3. The Limittacion he said served to make it faire in poynt of Lawe; but how farre it might be interpreted was the danger; (he said) and therefore he concluded it fitt to be represented for an inducement.

MR CONTROLLER. Mr Controller said that since nothinge was newe in it, he thought it most unfitt to be complayned of by the Howse.

MR PYMME. Mr Pymme shewed how that Comission *2do* K James was complayned of; our Ancestors protested then they would not subject themselves to the Clergie more then their Ancestors had done;[4] he hoped (he said) we were of the same mind. Hee shewed that the Clergye could not bind us. And moreover that those canons made by virtue of that comission had produced ill effects And therefore the Howse should nowe be more vigillant.

---

[1] See below, Harvard MS., fo 81, p. 194.

[2] *C.J.*, ii, p. 11, adds some details. For 2 *Jac.*, see D. Wilkins, *Magna Concilia*, iv (London, 1737), pp. 378–79.

[3] John Hampden (Buckinghamshire), the man of the shipmoney case. Rossingham reported that although 'the late commission for the making of canons . . . bee the same granted in the second of King James, yet nowe they present it as a grievance by reason of the late practice of innovations' (B.L., Add. MS. 11045, fo 112ʳ). 'A book of divers notes and matters concerning the Convocation House and ecclesiastical government' was among the papers of Hampden's seized at the end of the Parliament (Bodl., MS. Tanner 88*, fo 116ʳ).

[4] For example, *C.J.*, i, pp. 199–200, 327, 329, 348, 417, 418, 421; Hist. MSS. Comm., *Buccleuch and Queensberry*, iii, pp. 87, 89.

After some debate whether this Comission graunted showld be one poynte of Conference it was voted to bee one.

1. All the poynts one by one concerning Religion were voted for the Conference.

2. All poynts concerning propertye of goods voted for a Conference. These passinge by vote, the House thought fitt to rise, before they had voted the poynts of the third head.[1]

[*Finch-Hatton MS. 50*]   [*25 April 1640, House of Commons*]

[*p. 60*]   *DIE SABATI 25⁰ APRIL*

[*See C.J., ii, p. 12*]

Conference. A conference desired by the Lords in the painted Chamber.

[*Conference*]

Lo: Keeper.[2] Both howses being mett, The Lord Keeper declared to the Howse of Commons The cause of the Conference That the King had beene the day before in the upper Howse and that he there used many gratious speeches and expressions to the Lords, and howe the Kinge was pleased to put the Lords in mynd of the Lord Keepers speech, from which he told them he was resolved not to parte. Howe that the King told the Lords that his affayres would beare no delaye, delaye being as destructive [*p. 61*] as a denyall, his honor was at the stake which was as deare to him as his life; And that he thought that in all civillitye as well as necessitye he was first to bee trusted, and in conclusion the trust was to be in him, beginne it with whome it would. That the King further declared that he desired but a present supplye to goe on with the busines in hand; and that a little tyme would be to him a greate losse, Moreover the danger which nowe was greate, for of late the Kinge was informed that the warre was begunne; and that the Scotts had pitched their tents up at Dunce, and further that they had taken some of Sr Wm Brunkards troopes, etc.[3] Besides all which that it did appeare by the letter that they intended to put themselves into a forreigne defence; He said the King told the Lords that these reasons made it impossible that

---

[1] A committee was authorized to prepare the grievances (*C.J.*, ii, p. 12; H.L.R.O., Main Papers, 24 April 1640).

[2] The speech is crossed out in MS. (only in the Finch-Hatton version, not in Harvard MS. Eng. 982, fos 63ʳ–65ᵛ), but see below, App. 25, 27 April, pp. 310–11.

[3] 'Last Saturday Sir Wm Brunkard came to court from Berwick he tells his Majesty that divers of his troops are run away' (B.L., Add. MS. 11045, fo 110ʳ, Rossingham to Scudamore, 14 April 1640).

the matters of greivance showld have precedence and that otherwise he would be contented; Neverthelesse he would lett the Howse goe on as farre as possible nowe; and hereafter would give them a full tyme and releife.

That the King did gratiously listen to the 3 poynts in Question and That he declared himselfe, for Religion that he would live and dye in it, and that none showld be more carefull in matters of Innovation in Religion then himselfe and that he would speake to his Bopps about it.

As for shipmoney, That he never desired any proffitt by it, but had expended divers thousands out of his owne Treasure; That if the Parliament would thinke of anye other waye to secure the sea; (since shippmoney was soe displeasinge), His Majestye for his parte would be contented and joyne with them in it, without which neither his Majestye nor we can subsist.

He further told the Howse That the Lords hereupon considered of what his Majestye had delivered and that they all resolved to trust him and said they would take the word of a Kinge, and that some alsoe added of a Gentleman. He said that the Lords would not meddle with supply as appertayneing properly to the Howse of Comons; Neverthelesse as fellowe members and subjects equally interested in the good of the kingdome, they gave their advice; To which end the Lords had by vote held it fitt that supply should have the precedence before any other matter whatsoever And therefore the Lords desired this Conference, And that afterwards they would freely joyne with the Howse of the Commons [*p. 62*] in any thing for the comon good as the 3 poyntes spoken of this followed (Hee said) their Lopps hoped a good and happy Parliament would succeede.

[*Finch-Hatton MS. 50*]   [*27 April 1640, House of Commons*]

[*p. 62*]   *DIE LUNAE 27⁰ APRIL*

[*See C.J., ii, pp. 13–14*]

Bill read. A bill was read That English men showld onely bee needlemakers. And this to begin after the 20th of Dec. next.

A Report was made to the Howse of the Lo: Keepers speech on Satterday at the Conference with the Lords, by Mr Herbert.

Mr HERBERT. . . . [*pp, 62–64, see above, pp. 176–7; also C.J., ii, p. 13.*][1]

[*p. 64*] SIR WR EARLE. Sr Walter Earle spake against the Lords

[1] See below, App., Herbert, p. 310. 'This conference was no sooner reported in the House of Commons than their whole temper seemed to be shaken' (Clarendon, *History*, II. 69); 'The House took greate offense' (B.L., Add. MS. 11045, fo 113ʳ).

directinge of the Howse of Comons; he said the libertyes of Parliament were our inheritance; cited divers statutes for to prove the right of the Howse herein; And further added The Howse had ever one priviledge, (*vizt.*) to order their owne busines in prioritye without any directions therein.

Then he shewed how the Lo: Keeper trenched upon this libertye when he said the Lords declined the matter of Subsedys as proper to the Howse of Comons, and yet they thowght fitt the supply to have prior\itye; this he said was highly trenching upon the libertye of Parliament, to remedy which he advised for a conference [*p. 65*] with the Lords or some other way of redresse.

MR GRIMSTON.[1] Mr Grimston said howe farre the Lords trenched upon the Libertyes of the Howse he knewe not, But as for the Arguments used for a supply as that the Kinges affayres could be frustrate; And his present necessityes, this he said was none of or faults, for the King if he had beene pleased might have called us sooner and therefore we were not guiltye of the Kings streight.

Then he fell upon shippmoney (which dissabled us he said) for the Kinge might as well take all this yeare as a part and therefore: *ex nihilo nihil fit et nemo potest dare quod non habet.* Let therefore first or propertye be settled; and all, he said would serve the Kinge for the preservation of the kingdome. He concluded therefore, that he would not say that he would not give, but would say that hee had nothing to give.

SIR BEN RUDIERD.[2] Said the Kinge was in necessitie and that was an ill Councellor, it was therefore our part to remove it from him, for which wee should have both thanks and leave wished wee would trust the Kinge with a curse upon those that wrought dissidence betweene the Kinge and his people. He said since wee must trust the Kinge, let us doe it at first which we must doe at last.

MR PYMME. Seconded Sr Walter Earles motion: Said the danger of a President for the Lords to direct us was of much consequence, for the Lords had he said, a Clarke of Register, That if the Lo Keeper had onely told us, what the King delivered to the Lords in the upper Howse, this had been fayre, but to tell their votes and opinions this was greevous for, he said noe authoritye should presse us, and he said this was the greatest libertye we had, and advised the Howse therefore to protest against it. Another thinge observable he said was their direccion of an order, this he said was an unthankefullnes in them, to send an answer before the question was put to them; left it therefore to ye Howse, either to goe to the Kinge with a Petition or to desire another Conference with the Lords to redresse this.

[1] See below, Worc. Coll. MS. fo 19ᵛ, p. 221.
[2] See below, Worc. Coll. MS., fo 22, p. 224.

MR GLINNE. Mr Glinne assented with Mr Pymme.

MR CONTROLLER. Hereunto answered that necessity must have prioritye above any Lawe, wished the Howse to listen to the Kings gratious promises and then he doubted not, but wee should accompt from this tyme as from an happye Epocke, even as the Isralites did from their migration out of Egipt.

MR HOLBORNE. Agreed herein with Mr Pymme, saying that subsedyes were the guifte of the Howse of Commons, by this [*p. 66*] meanes he said wee showld loose the thanks from the King and yet retayne the anger of the Countrye. He said yt in 25 Q *Eliz*.[1] the same thing was practised by the Lords and the Question was then put whether the Howse showld conferre with the Lords and the Howse declined it; true (he said) it was that afterwards that afterwards [*sic*] the Howse conferred with them about the danger; but not about any subsedye. Breake a rule and or libertyes are gone. The Lords showld tell us the danger and not what we should doe; for then wee have not a free conference; and therefore he wished us to give the same answere as in the Queenes tyme.

MR BALL. Mr Ball justifyed the Lords and said our libertyes were not broken; that of [*35*] *Eliz*. he said was not right cited; he cited 50 *E*. 3 and 1 and 4 *R*. 2,[2] in which tymes hee said the Lords conferred with the Howse of Commons and then a supply was graunted; more then these he said might be browght; and noe breach of Libertye in it; for hee said the Lords appoynted nothing in particular.

MR JONES. Answered that [*35*] of the Qu: was right cited, and for the other presidents, he said the Kings told then the occasions of warre abroad, and expressed them in the writt,[3] That there was a Conference then had by both Howses and was mutuall to the dishonor of neither Howse. But for the Lords to tye us to an order, and then to conferre, these records did noe waye warrant the action of the Lords in bidding us beginne with Subsedyes or else to deny a Conference.

MR ST JOHN. Likewise answered Mr Ball and concluded it for a greate violation in the Lords; s[*ai*]d there was an Act in *H*. 4 not printed; That noe man showld speake to the Kinge or any other of what passeth in the Howse.[4] And finally said that whosoever acquaynted the Kinge with the intentions of the Howse deserved not to sitt there.

[1] Probably 35 *Eliz.*, here and in subsequent references (Simonds D'Ewes, *The Journall of all the Parliaments during the Reign of Queen Elizabeth* (London, 1682), pp. 480–94 *passim*; J. E. Neale, *Elizabeth I and Her Parliaments*, ii, pp. 298–307).

[2] 50 *Edw.* III (*Rot. Parl.*, ii, p. 322); 1 *Ric.* II; 4 *Ric.* II.

[3] For example, see Elsyng, *Ancient Manner*, pp. 69–71; Foster, 'Elsyng', p. 51.

[4] Probably 9 *Hen.* IV.

SR FRA SEYMOR. Said it stucke much with him that the Lords showld thinke we owed more to them, then to the King and therefore they showld have the thanks and wee doe against our duetye to the Kinge.

It was called uppon to be putt to the question; whether this of the Lords was not an infrindgment of the libertyes of the Howse.

MR HERBERT. Interrupted the puttinge of the Question, sayinge what the Lords spoke was by way of advise onely and desired the question to be declined.

SR MILES FLEETWOOD. Said he was sorrye that rocks were dayly cast in or waye; said it was a breach of Priviledges in the Lords; [*p. 67*] wished it voted and for the Howse to protest it for a Wrong.

At length it was put to the Quest[*ion*] and resolved by the Howse for a violation of the Priviledges; and left to a Committee to consider a meanes of Redresse.[1]

[*Finch-Hatton MS. 50*]   [*28 April 1640, House of Commons*]

[*p. 67*]   DIE MARTIS 28⁰ APRIL

[*See C.J., ii, pp. 14–15*]

A Report made to the Howse of the Conference made by the Howse to the Committee concerninge the redresse of ye breach of Priviledge by the Lords on Satterdaye. The Committee thought fitt that a Conference showld be desired with the Lords, thereby to desire them to take noe more notice hereafter of any thinge that the Howse shall intend till they shall declare it themselves; and to take some present order for what was past by way of redresse.[2]

[*Finch-Hatton MS. 50*]   [*29 April 1640, House of Commons*]

[*p. 67*]   DIE MERCURII 29 APRIL

[*See C.J., ii, pp. 15–16*]

SR WALTER EARLE[3] made a report to the Howse of the Particulers that the Committee had chosen for the Conference with the Lords upon the 3 Generall heads. Hee said that the 3 heads after

---

[1] '2 Waies off remedy were propounded. 1 by protestation. 2 by going to ye Lords' (H.R.O., M36/1, p. 10). See *C.J.*, ii, p. 14; also H.L.R.O., Main Papers, 27 April 1640, list and order.

[2] See below, Finch-Hatton MS., pp. 69–70, App. Pym (28 April), pp. 182–83.

[3] The many extant copies of the report show slight variations; see below, App. (24 April), p. 308.

the usuall manner were assigned to 3 worthy members to prepare for conference by the Committee: That of Religion to Mr Pimme; That of Property to Mr St John; That of Lib[*erty*] of Parliament to Mr Holborne.

Some interruption was made by complaynte of the newe Commission Whereupon after small debate, The Howse did by order protest themselves not bownd by any Canons made by the Convocation without the approbation of the Howse of Commons.

SR WR EARLE. Proceeded to the particulers that the Committee thought fitt to offer to the Howse upon each severall Generall. Those poynts which they thought fitt to complayne of concerninge Religion were these:

1. The removeing the Communion Table and placeing it to the East Altar wise; to this the Howse gave assent by vote.

2. Concerninge settinge up of Crosses images and cruicifixes in Cathedrall Churches and Parochiall churches and chappells in the Universitye and other places. This passed by vote for the Conference.

3. The refusall of Ministers to give the Communion to such as will not come up to the rayles and excommunicateing men for not doeing soe. This passed likewise.

4. The makeing and enjoyning Articles at the Visittation without other authoritye then the Bpp of the Diocese. This passed etc.

[*p. 68*] 5. The disturbing of Ministers for not reading the Booke and things enjoyned without Lawe. This passed.

6. Preaching and printeing of Bookes concerning Popery. This passed.

7. The enjoyning to bowe to the Altar and enquireing who did not.

8. Restrayneing conformable Ministers from preaching in their owne charges. All theis Poynts passed by vote.

It was questioned whether the Howse showld make use of these complaynts as of crimes or grievances or both.

MR PIMME. Hereupon advised the Howse not to be afraid to call Crimes Crimes if they be soe; and further that the Howse may proceede against any person hereafter if any bee fownd guilty or criminall; And added that if wee were faynt in this place, wee showld discouradge all others.

MR HOLBORNE. Was of a contrarye opinion because he said if they were called crymes, wee bring all that are criminall into a *Praemunire*.

SR ROB HARLYE.[1] Said It was noe matter if crimes were called crimes though the guiltye fall into a *Praemunire*.

[1] M.P. for Herefordshire.

Neverthelesse the Howse was pleased to take notice of those not as Crimes but as Greivances onely and soe voted it.

SR THOMAS LITTLETON.[1] Spoke against a Nurserye of Jesuites, which he said was tollerated here in England; instanced in Oxford and further added That a Preist said a Monasterye was tollerated in a cheife place of the kingdome.

MR PIMME. Seconded the complaynt affirmeing it to bee a greate shame, and that he heard that Masse was said in Oxford and complaynt being made to the Vice-chancellor thereof, he replyed he durst doe nothinge in it because it received countenance from above, this (he said) was told him from a very good hand.[2]

Some would have had this complayned of at the Conference, but the Howse thowght fitt not soe to doe, but to leave in themselves a power of Reservation for hereafter.

The 2d Generall head next followed whereof the first particular was shipmoney; But the Howse was tender in passing it by vote for a greivance and therefore first appoynted a Committee to examine all Records and Rolls in This case and soe to reporte.[3]

Mr Pimme was chosen by the Howse in behalfe of the Howse to acquaynte the Lords at the desired conference howe sensible the Howse was of the breache of their Priviledges by their Lopps.[4]

[*Finch-Hatton MS. 50*]   [*30 April 1640, House of Commons*]

[*p. 69*]   ***DIE JOVIS 30º APRIL***
[*See C.J., ii, pp. 16–17*]

The Lords assented to a Conference: And Mr Pimme very learnedly discharged his trust in letting the Lords knowe what sense the Howse had of their invadeing our libertyes.

[*Conference*]

Mr Pimme.[5] Said, My Lords, I am commanded by the knights, [*citizens*][6] and burgesses of the Comons in Parliament to represent to yor Lopps their desire and care to preserve such an union and correspondencie with yor Lopps as might not onely expresse the honor and respect which they beare to this illustrious bodye of the

[1] M.P. for Great Wenlock. See H.R.O., M36/1, p. 12, Harl. MS. 4931, fo 48ᵛ, below, pp. 204, 240.
[2] Richard Baylie, a protege of Laud was probably the vice-chancellor in question.
[3] A committee had been appointed 21 April (*C.J.*, ii, p. 8); see also *C.J.*, ii, p. 16.
[4] Probably the conference 28 April.
[5] 28 April 1640; see below, App., Pym (28 April), p. 312.
[6] Worc. Coll. MS. 5.20, fo 23ᵛ.

Nobillitie and the greate and high courte of Peeres[1] but might be effectuall to give expedition to both Howses in the greate and urgent affayres for which his Majestye was pleased to call this Parliament. The greate Priviledge belonging to this [high] Courte of Parliament are not drye and matters[2] of pompe, but have in them reallity and substance whereby this great Councell of the kingdome is called to performe all those hon[ora]ble[3] accons which belonge to them in respect of power and concillary [power].[4] And as they are the greatest and highest courtes of Record in the kingdome and these priviledges have beene ever deare and I hope shall ever be soe to both Howses.

As there are greate priviledges belonging to the whole bodye, soe are there others more particular belonginge to either Howse And of these wee shall ever be tender; for the Courte of Parliament is not onely a rule but a founteyne of order; and if any confusion showld be browght in here, there would be danger, that might be from hence derived to inferiour Jurisdiccions of the kingdome. Amongst these perticular Priviledges there is one greate Priviledge, which was acknowledged by yor Lopps in the last conference.[5] That the matters of Subsedyes and supplye owght to beginne in the Commons Howse.

This I have noe direccion to prove by Argum[en]t or president because it was admitted by yor Lopps.

The Howse of Commons doe not conceive yow to[6] varye from yor Justice or from or good intentions though in the proceedings of that Conference yor Lopps have beene transported beyond those bounds which yor Lopps had sett to yorselves.

Your Lopps in the last conference were pleased to affirme that the matters of Subsedye and supply naturally and properly belonginge to the Howse of Commons, yor Lopps would not meddle with it, noe not soe much as to give advise, soe yor Lopps expresst it.

Yet after you were pleased to declare that you had voted in yor Lopps Howse that it was most necessary and fitt that matters of supplye should have the precedencie[7] of all other businesses And being done your Lopps would [p. 70] freely joyne with us in all things concerninge matters of Religion, Propertie of goods and Libertye of Parliament.

Nowe, my Lords, if you have voted this you have not onely

---

[1] *Parliament* (Worc. Coll. MS. 5.20, fo 23ᵛ).
[2] 'matters *and businesses* of pompe . . . in them *solid* . . .' (S.R.O., DD/M1, Box 18, 96, unnumbered).
[3] . . . *services and* action (Worc. Coll. MS. 5.20, fo 24ʳ).
[4] Worc. Coll. MS. 5.20, fo 24ʳ.
[5] 25 April 1640, see below, App., L.K. (25 April), p. 310.
[6] . . . *differ or* vary (S.R.O., DD/M1, Box 18, 96, unnumbered).
[7] *preheminence* (Worc. Coll. MS. 5.20, fo 24ʳ).

meddled with matter of supplyes, [but] (as farre as in you lyes) have concluded both the matter and order of proceedings which the Howse of Commons takes to bee a breach of their priviledges; And for which I am commanded to desire reparation from yor Lopps.

The Howse of Commons hath not directed me to propownd any way of reparacion; not dowbting but yor Lopps wisdome and Justice will find out a way to make up theis breaches and to provide that this president may not bee prejudiciall to the Howse of Commons for the future.

I am further commanded to lett your Lopps understand that from the[1] propoundinge of these 3 particulars: 1. Religion; 2. Proprietye of Goods; 3. Priviledge of Parliament, The House of Comons doe collect that yor Lopps have taken notice of some[2] proceedings in this Howse concerninge those particulars, which is a breach of another Priviledge of that Howse sollemnely established in Parliament and called the Indempnitie of the Commons.[3]

Thereupon they have commanded me to desire yow for the maynteyneing of a good understandinge betweene both Howses, your Lopps would forbeare to receive any Information concerninge the proceedings and the conclusions in the Howse of Commons till they shalbe browght to yow by themselves, not doubting but all their Resolucions shalbe such as shall manifest to yor Lopps and to the whole world their Zeale and faithfull endeavours to maynteyne the greatnes and the lustre of his Majestyes throne, the saftye and prosperitye of the kingdome, and the comfort and contentment of both Howses.

[House of Commons]

MR MAYNARD.[4] Mr Maynard chosen in the Committee to the chaire reported to the Howse what was done by the Committee concerninge the search of the matter of Shippmoneye.

First therefore he read to the Howse the Kings letter to the Judges in requireing their opinions of shippmoney in case of danger and necessitye. Hee read alsoe the Judges replye to his Majestye That hee might; Then were read the proceedings in the issueing forth of the writts and Mr Hamdens Judgm[en]t.[5]

The Howse was here at a greate debate, concerning puttinge the Question whether shipmoney were not unlawfull which

---

[1] '. . . House of Commons these 3 particulars were considered and insisted upon' (S.R.O., DD/Mi, Box 18, 96, unnumbered).
[2] several (Worc. Coll. MS. 5.20, fo 24ᵛ).
[3] 9 Hen. IV.
[4] M.P. for Newport and Totnes. The report does not appear in C.J. A note to enter it and a space appear in M.C.J., p. 80.
[5] State Trials, iii, 825–1316; see also below, Petition, Oke, p. 285.

[*Harvard MS. Eng.* 982]

[*fo 72ᵛ*]

was much opposed and desired that the Kings Councell might bee
admitted.

Many statutes were cited to shew the illegallity hereof in so much
that many of the House would have putt it to the Question forthwith affirming that it was contrary to soe many statutes that every
man could judge of it.[1]

MR ST JOHN.[2] Added further that the case hath been already
judged and therefore thought it not for the Honor of the house to
admit any further Arguments in it. Hee shewed how in the matter
of Loane, this of shipp money was likewise Judged compared that
Commission with this which was in a manner the same words,
desired the House that both Commissions might bee read, which hee
said being the same was not fitting for the house to admitt of fresh
debates.

MR TREASURER pressed it so much for the King that the house
was contented to give a day to the Kings councell.

[*Harvard MS. Eng.* 982]   [*1 May 1640, House of Commons*]

[*fo 73ʳ*]   *DIE VENERIS 1ᵐᵒ DIE* APRIL [*sic*].

[*See C.J.*, *ii*, *pp. 17–18*]

MR PYMME. Made compl[*ain*]t of a sermon preached by Dr Beale[3]
at St Maryes in Cambridge *anno* 1635; (upon the Kings Coronacion
day) being master of St Johns Colledge and Vice Chancellour.

The p[*ar*]ticulars were these:

[*1*]. That the King might constitute Lawes what, where, when, and
ag[*ains*]t whom hee would and that it is onely his Royall benignity
that hee will admitt of the consente of the Parliament.

---

[1]'Much was said against ship money, and presidents brought of ordinances
in ye higher house and lower house against such demands. . . . It was said.
It had beene a fit answeare off ye Judges to have referred so great a cause
betweene ye King and his people to Judgment off Parliament. And not to have
medled with binding all our interests. Judges heretofore have done ye like,
in causes of lesse consequence' (H.R.O., M36/1, p. 13).

[2] St John, Hampden's counsel in the shipmoney case had some of his papers
concerning shipmoney seized at the end of the Parliament (Bodl., MS. Tanner
88*, fo 117ʳ). Rossingham says, 'they indeavoured to prove the shipp writt to
bee against all lawe, or costume, and that it was against the petition of right
that ther kinge should leavy any monye upon the subject without concent in
Parliament upon any necessity, or pretended necessity whatsoever' (B.L.,
Add. MS. 11045, fo 115ʳ).

[3] William Beale, D.D., was also attacked in the Long Parliament (B.L.,
873.g.28, *Articles exhibited in the Parliament against William Beale* . . . *Aug.
6 1641* (1641); also *D.N.B.*); see H.R.O., M36/1, p. 14, Harl. MS. 4931, fo 48ᵛ,
below, pp. 204, 242; *CSP 1640*, p. 40.

2. Noe conformity with the Tertullians, Ambroses, Origens, Ciprians[1] of old, ye very Language of antiquity must bee disused as of preists, Altars, etc. and now transmarine termes of pastors and teachers must bee used.

3. Or parsons, vicars, and curates dare take upon them to refuse the reading of the Kings Declaracions for the lawfull use of recreacions on Sundayes and holy dayes.

4. The silenced ministers yt cry downe, forsooth sabbath breaking and civill honesty, these must bee extolled, these calves must bee worshipped from Cam to Beersheba.[2]

[fo 73ᵛ] 5. It may bee said of us as Augustus did of his tyme, that hee had 2 adverse daughters, *Juliam et Rempublicam*.[3]

6. Taxes and subsedyes, tonnage and poundage now must bee tyed to yfs and ands and to condicions of Justice, whereas they are the Kings Absolutely, defend hee the seas or defend them not they are his as absolutely as his crowne and likewise or selves our goods our servants, our children And hee may call for his owne when hee will.

7. The Parliament gives the King a subsedy or two and takes away 2 or 3: Royall priviledges as Tonnage and poundage and gives him a subsedye but first call him to an accompt what hee did with the former and what hee will doe with the latter [so] they feede him as men use[d] to feede apes. Give him a bitt and a knock they give to him the Supremacy but joyne to him [a] *coadjutur* to witt the people, the body of the Parliament without whom hee must doe nothing and by this meanes his Royall proclamacions are of noe authority and this is to bind him under Lawes that [fo 74ʳ] can bind the consciences of men.

8. The house of Parliament, both the Upper House and Lower House cannot make a member, nay not a hayre, an excremt of a King.

The House upon this misdeamenor of Dr Beale (though they were unwilling to send for him as a delinquent in regard hee was a member of the Convocation House) Neverthelesse ordered that hee should have informacion att his lodgeing given him; That the house had taken notice of such allegacons against him and that if hee desired to purge himselfe hereof hee might before the Thursday following repaire to the House of Commons to heare what should be objected.[4]

---

[1] Early Church Fathers. Rossingham notes Beale 'is alsoe accused, to have inforst at the same tyme some perticulers concerning those, that crye downe Alters, as that they had brought into the Church [blank] words: noe more Alters, nor Preist, but table, and minister. Paster and elder, and such like terms, which the purer Primitive tymes were not acquainted with' (B.L., Add. MS. 11045, fos 115ʳ–15ᵛ).

[2] Exodus 32.   [3] Macrobius, *Saturnalia*, II, 5.4.

[4] The House divided on the question (see H.R.O., M36/1, pp. 15–16, below, p. 205, and *C.J.*, ii, p. 18). Rushworth, iii, p. 1149, wrongly indicates that the division concerned supply.

Conference. A Conference was desired by the Lords in the Painted Chamber, to which the house of Commons gave a present assent.

[Conference]

[Lord] Keeper.¹ Both Houses being mett, the Lords by the mouth of the Lord Keeper told the House of Commons that the Lords would not attempt or invade any of our priviledges, nor yett loose any of their owne, as they would not exceede their owne bounds, soe would they not narrow or lessen those of the House of Commons, But their Lopps tooke some distast in that the House of Commons should [fo 74ᵛ] say their Lopps were transported beyond their grounds and said they were not transported, nor had done any thing ag[ains]t our priviledges; ever confessing that matters of Subsedye must beginne with the House of Commons and that the Bill of subsedye is to bee presented by the Speaker of the House of Commons and therefore they thought they had said nothing derogatorye to the House of Comons.

The Lo: Keeper further said that their Lopps as persons moving in an Orbe nearer the Kings person then the House of Comons and as persons at least equally interested with the House of Commons in the good of the kingdome could not but more tymely discerne and alsoe as interested give their advice.

Wherefore having thus justifyed themselves their Lopps said they must returne to their first councell, vidzt, their desires that the Kings supply should have the prioritye.

[Harvard MS. Eng. 982]   **[2 May 1640, House of Commons]**

[fo 74ᵛ]   **DIE SABATI 2ᵈᵒ MAII**

[See C.J., ii, pp. 18–19]

MR JONES. Mr Jones made reporte of the Lo: Keepers speech in the painted chamber the day before.²

[fo 75ʳ] MR TRE[ASUR]ER.³ Mr Treasurer acquainted the House that hee had somewhat to deliver to the house from his Majestie hee desired yt hee might read it in regard of his memory which the house graunted. The contents of the Paper were these:

That his Majesty had often told us of his dainger and yett had received no answere at all hee doth now againe require a present

---

¹ See below, App., L.K. (1 May), p. 314.
² The report is noted and a space left for it to be entered in C.J., ii, p. 18.
³ The message is given at greater length in C.J., ii, pp. 18–19. Concerning its receipt, M.C.J., p. 97, notes, 'Not to stand without farther order of the House.' See also Rushworth, iii, p. 1153; P.R.O. 31/3/72, fo 138ʳ; and below, S.P., 16/452/9, p. 290.

answere of his Supply and p[ro]mises all that before hee had p[ro]-mised, adding that a delay was every way as distructive as a deniall.
MR PRICE.[1] Mr Price hereupon moved that the House would present the King with a peticion and a Bill of Supply togeather.
MR PYMM. Mr Pymme moved that a Committee should bee chosen to examine the Records in the difference betweene the Lords and the House of Commons. A Committee was for this purpose chosen.[2]

[Committee]

Mr Lentall in ye chaire. The House was putt into a committee for consideracion of the Kings message which was to bee debated for answere. Mr Lentall was chosen to the chaire.

[fo 75ᵛ] Dr Parre.[3] Said hee had read of a man yt was dumbe all his life tyme yett spake when the K: was in dainger. The like was his case who had not thought to have spoke. As farre as hee p[er]ceived, hee said, it was or Greivances yt retarded our mocion to the K. supply yett wished the House to consider for hee said it might bee that the lyon was not so great as hee was painted for those Greivances which concerned the church hee said many of them which were complayned of hee beeleived might bee obteyned in poynte of Lawe and many denyed in poynt of fact. Wished therefore or feares not to bee greater then our dainger as for property of goods hee beeleived hee should find the farmer and his Asse equally oppressed and bid remember that wee live not in an utopia but *in faco Romuli* yett hee said hee did not wish that wee should thus rest in the lee, but wee must looke for a reformacion wished us therefore to excell orselves. Lucius Crassus hee said was commended by Cicero for the best orator, who speaking of him one day saith *eo die excessit seipsum.*[4] But hee said that hee died within few dayes after having it seemes broke a veine.

Desired the house to consider likewise yt a councell may erre That in Queene Eliz [fo 76ʳ] tyme The Lords and house of Commons joyned (which now differed) in desireing the Queene to nominate her Successor, yett for all that the Queene continued obstinate and that hee said was accompted afterwards the greatest wisdome in her.[5] Wherefore hee wished the house to consider though late that his Majesty cannot bee lesse then a King and that hee hath made

[1] Probably Charles Price (Radnorshire). Herbert Price (Breconborough) and John Price (Montgomeryshire) also sat.
[2] The committee was that 'formerly appointed for preparing and giving directions for managing the business of the Conference to be had with the Lords' (*C.J.*, ii, p. 19).
[3] Dr. George Parry, Chancellor of the Diocese of Exeter (St. Mawes).
[4] *Cf.* Cicero, *De Oratore*, III. 1(3).
[5] In 1563 the Lords and Commons petitioned separately, but in 1566 they cooperated (D'Ewes, *Eliz.*, pp. 103–104; Neale, *Eliz. Parl.*, i, pp. 106, 109, 141).

gratious p[ro]mises. That hee deserves Love and requires not money, but wee must not pay him with a Complement. And soe *exoneravi animam meam.*

Sir Fr Seymor. Sr Fran Seymor said that hee p[er]ceived the Message could receive no delay and on the other side the common wealth that lay groaning alsoe for his parte hee said hee should bee as zealous to serve the King as to live yett must not deceive the trust putt in him by the Country for there is an impossibillity putt upon us to give satisfaccion to the King, for to speake of supply before wee have what to give was improper, besides whiles shippmoney was gathering and souldiers billiting in our houses this were to give countenance to what was already done. Hee spake of the Lords directions soe as it [*fo* 76ᵛ] was not now what wee must but what wee cannot doe the streight was therefore greate and therefore a mutuall trust was best. The King to trust his people and they their King. And therefore his opinion was that if hee had sattisfaccion for shipp money hee should trust the King with the rest and hereof to acquainte the King concluding that the conclusion of the Parliament must make both King and people happy.

Sr Ro North.[1] Sr Roger North and divers of the House approved of this mocion.

Mr Strowd.[2] But Mr Stroud urged the 3: Generall heads saying if wee would lay aside one, lett us lay aside all and proceede to the K: supply.

Mr Hamden. Mr Hamden said many remoras lay in order to bee first removed affirming that till wee had freedome of speech setled wee cannot meddle with any thing, that being first necessary and said hee knew not but that wee might humbly represent these impediments to the King and yett continue constant to our owne way and order.

Mr Tre[asure]r.[3] Mr Treasurer said hee should deliver what hee spoke with as much affeccion as any and with the same candor judged so of others; [*fo* 77ʳ] desired of the house to consider of the Ks gratious speeches who desires to bee clearly understood and thought it very unhappy that the King and house agreeing in the same and should neverthelesse through misconstruccions make the many other things impossible to bee handled all in soe shorte a tyme. Hee approved of Sr Franc: Seymors mocion hopeing that this day should produce some good effect for his parte hee was unwilling to move any thing rather desireing it might arise from the country concluding that if a Rupture should happen, hee did beleive that the Country would not thanke us.

---

[1] M.P. for Eye.   [2] William Strode (Beeralston).
[3] Probably the speech noted below, H.R.O., M36/1, p. 21, p. 207.

G

Mr Pymme. Said that there was a demand for supply and an answere required hee wisht that such an answere could bee given as might respond to the King and countryes affeccion, and since the King did require an answere hee thought most fitt to give his Majesty a resolute one the taking away of shippmoney hee said were not enough for (hee said) wee might bee as much opprest by millitary charges as with shipp money hee would therefore have it published that no charges should bee laid upon the people without consent in parliament.

[*fo 77ᵛ*] But hee said there was another thing which hee would deliver which was greater and more nice and feared hee said least hee should bee mistaken and therefore hee desired the House to observe what hee said 3: things hee ever graunted for undoubted principles:

1. That ye K hath power to make warr and peace.
2. That it rested in his Majestyes wisdome and Justice to determine of the causes of warre.
3. Not bound to seeke any Councell for ye making or managing of the warre.

As these things were his Majestyes Prerogatives, soe hee said the priviledges of the house of Commons have ever been not to bee bound to the maintenance of any warre except upon his Majestyes calling them to his Councell they shall give their Assent thereto.

Hee said this warre with Scotland was of daingerous consequence and since wee were not obleiged to maintayne a warre hee thought as yett wee had not proofes enough to engage our selves and the Country and that it was daingerous in consequence for tyme to come for the Commons to bee engaged in a warre upon the Ks word etc.

Sr Tho German. Sr Tho German said hee expected not what was last spoken of.

[*fo 78ʳ*] S[er]jeant Godbolt[1] wished yt Supply and shippmoney might goe hand in hand urging that in a calme and a storme the case was not the same and therefore such a combustion being abroad, it was fitt to fill the Kings coffers wished therefore wee would peticion for shippmoney, and for as much as was already collected hee would have it goe in parte of supply.

Mr Kirton. Said shippmoney was not enough; for others could [?] invent as well as Mr Noye[2] and wee must expect new oppressions.

Sr Rob Crane.[3] Spoke ag[ains]t shippmoney and [as] for giving supply to the King lett us give it to the King without examining what hee will doe with it.

---

[1] John Godbolt (Bury St. Edmunds).
[2] William Noy, Attorney-General from 1631 until his death in 1634.
[3] M.P. for Suffolk.

Mr Bridgman.[1] Said to deferre supply till or 3: poynts were discussed and releived were to putt off his Majesty for this Quarter of
a yeare Supply hee said noe way related to the warre and was not
engageing of men but if men will will [sic] engage themselves why
should they bee debarred hee liked not shipp money yett thought it
an ill argument that wee had nothing to give or because our goods
may bee taken away therefore they are wished therefore that both
shippmoney and supply might goe hand in hand.

[fo 78ᵛ] The Lo Fawkland.[2] The Lo. Fawkland answered yt
though or goods were not taken away yett ye p[ro]p[er]tye was.

Lo: Digbye.[3] The Lo: Digbye said that there was scarce a clowne
in the country but would wonder and say; if wee had prop[er]tye in
or goods to give a subsedye why not p[ro]perty enough to keepe or
goods from shippmoney much they comended the Justice of ye
King but that hee said was not enough, for great councells must
provide for the future and urg'd what the consequence might bee of
an ill Kings reigne, and kings hereafter would not bee sattisfied with
[saying] shippmoney was graunted in a good K reigne, for present
Ks are always best.

Hee further added yt if subsedyes were graunted to his Majesty,
yt was not sufficient for hearts were as necessary to the warre as
money.

Mr Jones. Mr Jones s[ai]d the danger of ye danger of Scotland was
the discontent at home, and therefore the best way for the K was
to redresse them first the posterne dore was to bee looked too but
cheifely the greate gate wished us to thinke of an answere to the K
saying yt though wee were trusted with ye purses [fo 79ʳ] of the
country; yett they were not to bee used but upon occasion and
therefore the occasions of the warre must bee open or the Commons
are not bound.

Mr Tre[asure]r. Mr Treasurer s[ai]d if the House was violent in
soe many things, the country would not thanke us and therefore
p[er]suaded the House to dispose themselves for an answere.

Mr Herbert. Mr Herbert said hee found ye house much devided,
and for the further avoynding of multiplicity of questions wished it
to bee putt to the Question whether wee would give the K: a supply
or not? Hee s[ai]d it was as direct an answere to say Sir wee will not
supply yow till our greivances are redressed as wee will supply you
first Hee concluded yt for aught hee could perceive the case stood
thus That unlesse the King would releive us in shippmoney without

[1] Orlando Bridgman (Wigan).
[2] Lucius Cary, Viscount Falkland (Isle of Wight). His was a Scottish
peerage.
[3] George Digby, heir to the earl of Bristol (Dorset). Probably the speech
which circulated as a separate; see below, App., Digby, p. 316.

a due debate wee would not supply ye King for his owne p[ar]te hee said hee desired not yt shippmoney should receive any countenance by or graunt of supply but rather in the graunt of it to reserve all such right in our selves.

[*fo 79ᵛ*] Mr Jones. Mr Jones answered yt the house desired not ye King to parte with his right that were inglorious for ye King to graunt and injust for us to require. It was Justice which wee desired.

Hee said yt in five dayes wee might have damned the councell and opinion of the Judges wee wanted or Ancestors witt to find this was a Lawe created not declared. Hen: 6 required advice of his Judges concerning the crowne but they refused it as a thing of too high a nature for them to judge of desireing his Majesty to take councell of his Parliament[1] applyed it to our Judges in shewing how well such a modestye might now have become our Judges in soe great a case as shippmoney.

Hee s[ai]d hee did not doubt but wee should give subsedyes in due tyme but yt the consideration thereof was of greater consequence then all the subsedyes since [?][2] of the Queene gave therefore advice to represent to the K or sence of shippmoney and after to proceede to the matter of supply.

Sr Jo. Hotham.[3] Said yt releife ag[ains]t shippmoney was not enough for in his owne country hee was sure yt millitary charges lay heavyer on the commons for whereas the last yeare shippmoney was but [*fo 80ʳ*] 120000ˡⁱ,[4] Millitary charges cost ye country above 40000ˡⁱ therefore hee should unwillingly give money till shippmoney, millitary charges and matters of Religion were redressed wished those therefore to bee putt to the Question.

Mr Tre[asure]r. Mr Tre[asure]r for shipp money s[ai]d the K had spent 230000ˡⁱ above what hee had received out of his owne coffers and that hee knew nothing of the relinquishing thereof for hee said if a rupture should happen wee must not expect yt the K would quitt shipmoney.[5]

Mr Pymm. Mr Pymme advised the House to give an answere to his Majesty and to present or cheife Greivances first further declaring yt wee will supply the K if it may noe way tend to the breach of or priviledge in not knowing ye councell of ye Scottish busines.[6]

Much it was urgd by the Kings councell to have it putt to the

---

[1] *Rot. Parl.*, vi, pp. 375–76, 39 *Hen.* VI.

[2] The binding makes it impossible to tell whether a date is given.

[3] Rossingham reported that Hotham was preceded by Sir William Savile and Henry Belasyse, knights for Yorkshire (*CSP 1640*, p. 154).

[4] The figure should be £12,000 (*CSP 1640*, p. 155; J. T. Cliffe, *The Yorkshire Gentry from Reformation to the Civil War* (London, 1969), p. 315).

[5] See H.R.O., M36/1, p. 21, below, p. 207.

[6] See also *CSP 1640*, pp. 144–45; Gardiner, *History*, ix, p. 116.

Question whether the house would supply the King or not? but the House did wholly decline yt question.

Mr Hamden.[1] Mr Hamden would have had this question putt whether ye committee was as yett ripe to give their full resolucion to the matter of ye Kings supply, but much debates hindred the putting of any Questions till it was so late, that the House thought fitt to deferre the resolucion for a further day.

[*fo 80ᵛ*] It was much questioned whether ye Munday (in regard the Kings councell were Assigned that day for the Argument of shippmoney) or Tuesday should bee appoynted for an absolute answere to his Majestyes answere.

[House of Commons]

In fine it was resolved Munday should bee the day unlesse his Majestyes councell did offer themselves for the Argum[en]t of shippmoney.[2]

[Harvard MS. Eng. 982]   **[4 May 1640, House of Commons]**

[*fo 80ᵛ*]   **DIE LUNAE 4 MAII**

[*See C.J., ii, p. 19*]

SR HEN VANE.[3] Sir Hen Vane brought a declaration from his Majesty whereby the King pr[o]mised upon 12: subsedyes presently passed to bee gratiously pleased to parte with shippmoney in regard yt hee p[er]ceived that to bee the maine stopp in our passage to his supply.

His Majesty demanded that 12 subsedyes to bee p[ai]d in three yeares and those to bee graunted with provisoe not to determine this present session.

His Majesty hereunto required a present answer, urging againe the great necessity of his Affayres.

[Committee]

Committee. Mr Lentall to ye chaire. Hereupon the House putt themselves into a committee and Mr Lentall was chosen to the chayre.

---

1 Clarendon, *History*, II. 71–72, gives a somewhat confused account of the debates of 2 and 4 May and puts Hampden's call for the question 4 May. Montereul says Vane was asked insolently about what the king meant when he asked for a present answer (P.R.O. 31/3/72, fo 138ʳ). He also notes in the debate a proposal that the Commons ask the king that the Lord Keeper be punished for his part in the shipmoney judgment (P.R.O. 31/3/72, fo 139ʳ).

2 Mr Treasurer, Mr Comptroller, and Mr Secretary Windebanke were ordered to acquaint the king with the action of the House (*C.J.*, ii, p. 19).

3 See H.R.O., M36/1, p. 22, below, p. 208; the declaration does not appear in

Sr Benj Rudd[*yerd*].[1] Sr Ben Rudder said hee counted it a great happinesse yt wee had a Parliament to give our money in which might bee otherwise taken away [*fo 81ʳ*] from us; wherefore hee accounted this not as a Gift but as a purchase and thought wee could not lay out or money better and therefore advised the House soe to supply ye King that hee might grow in Love with Parliaments.

Sir Gilb Gerrard. Sr Gilb Gerrard hereupon desired the House to consider that the county of Middlesex, for which hee served, were at three subsedyes for their shippmoney as much for military charges, and moreover that 1200 of their trayned band were appointed to goe out of their country and therefore offered it to the House to consider the charge as well as dainger that county was in who desired him as (hee said) to acquainte the House with as much with hopes of Releife herein which made him thinke subsedyes untymely as yett.

Sr H Vane. Sr Hen Vane answered that the Armyes were not to goe out of the county and as for their men they might as well spare them as any other county in regard that the Citty had 8000: men of their trayned band.

Mr St John: Mr St John s[*ai*]d that shippmoney millitary charges and Monopolyes out of parliament came to above 12: subsedyes.

Sir H Chol[*mley*].[2] Sir Hugh Cholmley s[*ai*]d yt if shippmoney were legall wee much bound to his Majesty for his gratious offer but if illegall hee knew noe reason to buy it out, for millitary charges for ought hee knew might have a Judgment the next yeare.

[*fo 81ᵛ*] Mr Controller.[3] Mr Controller said that the execucion not ye Legallity was yt which pressed us and further yt his Majesty quitted it out of Grace and contract.

Mr Rigby.[4] Mr Rigbye said it plainely appeared to bee a contract because the condicion of graunting 12: subsedyes is expressed wherefore he thought it most fitt that the Legallity bee first [*looked*] into, for if it were Legall 12 subsedyes were too little.

Mr Holborne.[5] Mr Holbourne said for the Legallity to bee first searched for his Majesty could not Alien[*ate*] it from the crowne if it were Legall for the Judges in their Argum[*en*]ts delivered it to bee soe inherent to the Crowne as not to bee quitted.[6]

C.J., ii, p. 19. Montereul attributes the message to Strafford, who he thought made the condition so high that it would never be accepted so that he (Strafford) would enhance his own position with the king and bring the king to make terms with the Spanish (P.R.O. 31/3/72, fo 141ʳ).

[1] Also H.R.O., M36/1, p. 22, below, p. 208.
[2] After Parliament the Council questioned him concerning remarks about shipmoney (*Cholmley Memoirs*, pp. 60–61; *CSP 1640*, p. 155).
[3] Also H.R.O., M36/1, p. 23, below, p. 208.
[4] Alexander Rigby (Wigan).
[5] Also H.R.O., M36/1, p. 23, below, p. 208.
[6] For example, *State Trials*, iii, 1235.

Sir Fr S[*eymour*].[1] Sir Fran Seymour said that since 12: subsedyes were demanded, if hee must needes affirme yt without betraying the trust of the country hee could not doe it. Hee wished therefore an humble Remonstrance to the King of the impossibillity of it for his parte hee could not.

Serjt Gl[*anville*].[2] Sarjeant Glanvile said that since some of the Judges were of opinion that shippmoney was soe inherent to the crowne hee would with leave of the house deliver his opinion which at a committee hee thought hee might which was to goe by way of declaratorye Judgem[*en*]t that shippmoney never was due and wished yt damned and impious opinion of the Judges (in saying yt shippmoney was soe inherent in the crowne yt a Parliament could not take it away) to bee more infamous to posterity, by laying a brand upon it.

[*fo 82ʳ*] Insomuch for his owne parte hee said though hee was not a Judge, yett he was the sonne of a Judge And in his conscience shippmoney was not Legall wished the house to give their opinions freely of it. As for—Monopolyes wee could not make a better Lawe then already was made and therefore wee were in a better condicion for that[3] And if hee had been of councell, hee should have given his Advice Than [*sic*] an accion should have been brough[*t*] upon the Statute and not upon the Common Lawe[4] and s[*ai*]d it were well if wee could roote out those Caterpillars out of ye commonwealth.

As for the charges of subsedyes yt was nothing hee for his p[*ar*]te p[*ai*]d for 5: subsedyes one yeare but 10ˡⁱ but shippmoney cost him 20ˡⁱ and therefore wished yt wicked hatefull opinion of shipmoney branded but as for 12 subsedyes to give to soe gratious a King and in 3 yeares this was nothing 5 the 1st yeare 4 the 2d and 3 the 3d was nothing to stagger or gratuity to soe good a King.

Sr Ro. Cooke.[5] Sr Ro Cooke advised to have them questioned that delivered their opinions for ye shipmoney hee added further how ill opinion ye Country had of the warre and yt his Majesty stood in greater needs of hearts then of men that it was a warre yt reflected

---

[1] Also H.R.O., M36/1, p. 23, below, p. 208.

[2] Also H.R.O., M36/1, pp. 23–24, Harl. MS. 4931, fo 49, below, pp. 208–209, 243. *Cf.* Clarendon, *History*, II, 73–74; writing that Glanville had 'delivered his opinion freely, as a member of the House against yt [*shipmoney*], speaking more bitterly against that judgment and the judges declaration at the assizes then all those that had spoaken against yt during the Parliament,' Rossingham thought that the speech was probably a reason why Glanville had not been permitted to go to the Commons on the following day (S.P. 16/453/24).

[3] See Elizabeth R. Foster, 'The Procedure of the House of Commons against Patents and Monopolies, 1621–23,' *Conflict in Stuart England*, ed. Wm. A. Aiken (New York, 1960); Glanville was a member of Parliament at the time.

[4] See *State Trials*, iii, 857–58.

[5] M.P. for Gloucestershire. *Cf.* Clarendon, *History*, II. 71, which places the speech in the debate of 2 May.

onely upon Religion and yt some of the Bishopps themselves [*fo 82ᵛ*] called it *bellum Episcopale* And hee said since wee must not peticion hee thought it fitt that wee should peticion to peticion.

Serjt Gl[*anville*]. Sarjeant Glanvile said that it was not expected the House should engage themselves in a warre but to give money for ye Kings pleasure of calling us togeather as or Ancestors did before us.

Mr Jones. Mr Jones inclined to have subsedyes without any relacion to the Scottish businesse, onely shippmoney first suppressed.

Mr Soll[*icitor*].[1] Mr Sollicitor s[*ai*]d hee p[*er*]ceived ye House was much out of the way hee feared the Message which his Majesty thought would have fallicitated [*sic*] the worke did much retard the Kings businesse, and as for the Judges opinion of shippmoney being inherent in the Crowne

[Finch-Hatton MS. 50]

[*p. 81*],

he thought it unfitt to be spoke of; The question onely was whether or noe the House would supplye the Kinge.

[*Sir*] Wr Earle. Sʳ Walter Earl: said those speeches of some of the Judges, (that if there were a thousand acts of Parliament against shippmoney they were all voyde) were spoken by some of the Judges in most parts of the westerne circuits.[2]

[*Mr St*] John.[3] Mr St John moved for the legallitye of shippmoneye to bee putt to the question, and much debate was in the Howse about the puttinge of it, many likewise would have had militarye charges alsoe putt to vote.

Mr Tre[*asure*]r. Mr Tresurer hereupon desired the Howse to forbeare the putting of both questions, in regard that he knewe the Kinge had much to saye for millitarye charges; urged that Sr Edw Cooke delivered that his Majestye might in case of danger throwe downe any howse to build a castle;[4] And that there was the Lawe of H. 4 though not printed yet still in force and wished us to consider it.[5]

Mr Slingsby. Mr Slingsbye urged the grace of the Kinge in his offer of remittinge shippmoney; for as long as his Majestye hath a judgment of his side, it was rebellion in any to withstand the paym[*en*]t of it.

---

[1] *Cf.* Clarendon, *History*, II. 75.

[2] Perhaps in the incident at the Assizes in Exeter, August 1639, which Finch reported to Laud (S.P. 16/427/31 and 32); see also the charges against Finch (Rushworth, iv, pp. 137–38).

[3] Also H.R.O., M36/1, p. 25, below, p. 209.

[4] *Cf.* Sir Edward Coke, *The Twelfth Part of the Reports* (London, 1656), 12–13 (Saltpetre Case).

[5] Perhaps 13 *Hen.* IV (*Rot. Parl.*, iii, pp. 662–63). See Wm. Holdsworth, *History of English Law* (Boston, 1922–32), iii, p. 377; vi, pp. 49ff.

He was much call'd upon to the barre for that language, but the Howse was pleased to take his recognition in his seate.

It was much urged by many in the Howse to have this Question putt. As many as are of opinion that the legallitye or illegalitye of shipmoney be first debated and voted, before we give an answere to the Kings busines say I.

This Question though much pressed to be putt, yet by reason of the difference of opinions was delay'd till it grewe soe late that the Howse thought fitt to rise.[1]

[Finch-Hatton MS. 50]   *[5 May 1640, House of Commons]*

[p. 81]   *DIE MARTIS 5° MAII*

[See L.J., iv, p. 81, and C.J., ii, p. 19]

His Majestie by his black rod commanded the Howse of Commons to attend him in the Lords Howse where His Majestie said as foll[oweth].

The Kinge.[2] There can noe occasion of comeinge to this Howse be soe unpleasant to me as this at this time. The feare of doeinge what I am to doe to daye made me not longe agoe to come into this Howse where I exprest these feares and remedyes I thought necessarye for the escheweing of it. I must needs confesse and acknowledge that you my Lords of the Higher Howse did give me soe willinge an eare and such affeccion that you did shewe yorselves accordingly there-after; soe that [p. 82] certeynly I may say if there had been any meanes to have had a happie end of this parliament[3] it was not yor lopps faults that it was not soe. Therefore my Lords in the first place I must thanke you for yor good endeavours.

My Lords for my owne parte I hope yow remember what the first daie of the Parliament; my Lo Keeper said unto yow in my name; What he said in the Banquetting howse at Whitehall, and what I said to yow my selfe that daye, I name it unto yow not in any doubt that yow doe not remember it: But to shewe yow that I never said any thinge that may in favor to my people; but by the Grace of God I will punctually and wholly performe.

My Lords I knowe that they have very much insisted upon greivances; I will not say that[4] they are alltogether free; though it

1 Clarendon claims to have spoken, opposing such 'a captious question,' and suggesting 'instead a straight yes or no for supply, which could then be followed by discussion as to proportion and manner' (Clarendon, *History,* II. 74).

2 See below, App., 5 May, p. 316.

3 '. . . *you took it, so that* . . . faults *nor mine* . . .' (B.L., E.203(1), p. 43).

4 '. . . *but* that *there may be some* (though *I will confidently affirm that there are not by many degrees so many,* as the public voice . . .' (B.L., E.203(1), p. 44).

may bee not soe much as the publique voyce would make them; Yet
I desire yow to know againe and nowe espetially at this tyme; That
out of Parliament I shalbe as readye if not more willinge to heare
any, and to redresse just greivances as in Parliament.

There is one thinge I have heard much spoken of, though not soe
much insisted upon as others, and that is Religion. I have exprest
my selfe therein the last daye and I doubt not but yow remember it;
That certaynely I shalbe as carefull (as I am most concernd) in the
preservation of that puritie of Religion which I thanke God is
established in the Church of England. And I shalbe as carefull out
of Parliament as in Parliament to doe it.

My Lords I shall not trouble yow longe with words it is not my
fashion. What I offerd the last daye to the Howse of Comons, I
thinke my Lords is very well knowne to yow all and howe they
accepted it[1] I thinke alsoe is well knowne unto yow.

My Lords yow knowe at the first I expressed my selfe by my Lo
Keeper that delay was[2] more dangerous then refuseinge. I will not
put this fault on all the whole Howse for I will not judge so un-
charitablye,[3] But it hath beene in some cunninge and illaffectionate
men That hath beene the cause of this misunderstandinge.

I shall onely end as I began giveinge yor lopps thanks for[4] the care
that yow have had of my honor desireinge yow my lords to goe on,
and assist me for the mainteyneing of[5] government, and the libertyes
of my people; That they soe much start at; for my lords noe kinge
in the world shalbe more carefull to maynteyne the propriety of
[*p. 83*] their goods the libertye of their persons and honor of Religion
then I shall be.

And nowe my Lord Keeper doe as I commanded yow.

[*Lord*] Keeper. My Lords and Gentlemen of the Howse of Commons. The Kings Majestye doth dissolve this Parliament. *Finis.*

---

[1] '. . . *which I desire not to remember but wish* that *they* had *rememberd'*
(B.L., E.203(1), p. 45).
[2] '. . . *the worst kinde of deniall* . . .' (B.L., E.203(1), p. 45).
[3] '. . . *of those who for the most part I take to be loyall and well-affected subjects*
but, *that* it hath been *the malicious* cunning *of some few sediciously-affected* men
. . .' (B.L., E.203(1), p. 46).
[4] '. . . *your affection shewn to me at this time,* desiring . . .' (B.L., E.203(1),
p. 46).
[5] '. . . *that regall power, that if truly mine, and as for* the libertie . . .' (B.L.
E.203(1), p. 46).

[H.R.O., M36/1]   **[21 April 1640, House of Commons]**[1]

[*p. 1*]   **21 APRIL**

It was moved that there might be copies of ye records off ye Kings bench.

Saving ye priviledge off this house.

A petition preferred by a particular man not of ye house ought to be signed by him, otherwise not to be read.

He ye same day signed it, *vid.* one Mr. Smart; then it was read.[2]

The King sent that ye house of Commons should attend him in [*Whitehall*] which accordingly they [*p. 2*] did, and ye Speaker was there.

It was said all committees were to forbeare sitting when ye King was to be attended.

2 Bills were read.

1 against common recoveries suffred by infants by their gardians.

2 Against excesse in apparell, an old bill sent from ye Lords. Last parliament. It was said uppon ye 2d reading. It was to be spoken to or els committed.

The manner off a message from ye lower house to the Lords was declared, To knock at ye doore, send up. Then when let in, To goe up and meete, and with a low voyce to deliver it.[3] The party sent to be fittingly attended by some off ye house.

It was moved[4] that there was a new commission to ye Convocation, to authorize them to peruse alter or make *de novo*, such cannons as they should think fit.

A committee of 5[5] was appointed to find o[*ut the*] same and to have a view thereoff, and to rep[*ort*] ye effect thereoff.

[*p. 3*] It was said, That records should not be taken out off officers hands, but copies to be taken thereoff. But the pattents had beene taken.

It was moved, That letters concerning ye ship money should be viewed and perused. But it was said, That to ye Kings Councel booke, they had not sent. So it was declared, That some off ye letters should be sent for to some sheriffs adjoyning.

[Banqueting House]

At ye conferens with ye King, ye Lord Keeper declared, That his Majestyes occasions were pressing and urgent.[6] He had an army on

---

[1] See above, for 20 April, pp. 162–63.
[2] *Cf. C.J.*, ii, p. 8; see also below, Petition, Smart, p. 280.
[3] Hist. MSS Comm., x, New Series, *House of Lords*, p. 4, Standing Order 24.
[4] By Sir Walter Erle.   [5] 15 (*C.J.*, ii, p. 8).
[6] See below, App., L.K. (21 April), p. 303.

foote the charge of yt and all his designes would perish, without a present supply.

Ireland had given 4 subsidies cheerefully every one amounting to 55000^{li} and promised futurely to give.

An objection was concerning ship money. His Majesty never intended to make it a constant revenue and but had imploied it and much more of his owne, in providing ships for his owne Honore to preserve his right of moderator off ye seas, and for our safety. He was resolved this yeare [*p. 4*] not to have sent for it but hearing off grea[*t*] preparations at sea, he was forced to send for i[*t*].

It is for extraordinary preparations.

Yet iff ye parliament would put him in a way to mainteyne his ancient right off ye seas he was content to relinquish it.

His Majesty declared he expected a speedy accompt and would graciously heare and redresse all their greivances, within short time after.

[*H.R.O., M36/1*]   [*?23 April 1640, House of Commons*]

[*p. 4*]   **THE NEXT DAY[1]**

It was pressed by MR. COMPTROLLER. That we might proceede to a present supply, and be confident uppon ye Kings promise to be heard concerning our greivances.

It was no new thing. It had beene done 6.*E*.3. and in other Kings reignes. That a supply preceded.

SR. FR SEYMOR said. It was a case off great difficulty. His duty and love to his King drew him one way. And ye trust ye country reposed in him another way.

It is pressed that out trust in ye King uppon his gracious promise ought to take pr[*ecedence*] and that an aide to him should preceede. It is not only a trust in ye King, but in others, that are off his Councell, or others that may make glosses, so strung to spoile any good thing [*p. 5*] as ye petition off right, hath beene done. My opinion is, That a supply and redresse should goe hand in hand.

SIR RAFE HOPTON said The countryman had a thorne in his foote that he could not run to doe ye King service. Meaning ye greivances. Plucking out that, He would be ready to run to doe his Majesty service.

It was resolved, That we should confer with ye Lords concerning redresse off our greivances concerning innovations in religion, Property off goods and Priviledge of Parliament before any supply.[2]

---

[1] The question of supply was not debated until 23 April (*C.J.*, ii, p. 9). See below, for proceedings on 22 April

[2] For other business of 23 April, see below, p. 201.

[H.R.O., M36/1]   ***[22 April 1640, House of Commons]***

[p. 5]   ***[22 APRIL 1640]***

It was moved that consideracion might be had concerning cannons intended to be made by ye clergy, whereby they would put burdens upon us.

MR. PIM said. No cannons of theirs ought to bind us, unles confirmed by Parliament. He cited a record 51.*E*.3, *Numero* 46, to be That no ordinances should be made by ye Clergy without consent off ye Commons.

[p. 6] 6.*R*.2. The Lords assented to ye repeale off an act made 5.*R*.2, and enacted ye same to be voide, for Heresy, because ye Commons consented not.

Therefore he prayed It might be considered, what power ye convocation had to bind ye Commons.

MR. ST. JOHN off ye same mind. The summons is to us ye Commons *ad tractandum et consentiendum de arduis concernentibus/ regnum et ecclesiam.* The summons to ye convocation is, *ad consentiendum.*

In ye greatest time of their power, their Cannons did not bind ye Commons.

25 *H*.8. Is that they shal not presume to make any cannons, whereto ye King shal not assent by his letters pattents.

But that law makes not such cannons so assented to, binding to ye commons.[1]

[p. 7]   ***[23 APRIL 1640]***[2]

[H.R.O., M36/1]   ***[25 April 1640, House of Commons]***

[p. 7]   **25 APRIL**

Two Judges were sent by ye Lords to let us know, ye Lords desired a conferens with us. All ye house went saving Mr. Speaker.

[Conference]

And in ye painted chamber A table was placed and double formes round it. Without these formes we all stood bare headed. The Lords after we had attended some time, came and sate within ye formes, where we heard ye Lord Keepers speech, bare headed. His Lop also being bare headed all ye ti[*me*] he spake.

It was said by ye Lord Chamberlaine, That their Lops ought to sit, as they did in Parliament, but they did not.

[1] 25 *Hen.* VIII, c. 19, An Act for the Submission of the Clergy to the King's Majesty.   [2] See above, pp. 169–74.

The Lord Keeper[1] spake to this purpose.

That ye King ye day before did them ye Honor to be amongst them in person, and there expressed that he desired a speedy supply, and that delay [*p. 8*] was as bad to him as a deniall. Because danger and his Honor did depend uppon it; and his Honor as he had declared was more deare to him than his life.

In civility and good manners his Majesty is first to be trusted, and ye trust is for no long time uppon ye matter but for an houre.

We may well trust him in part, for we must trust him for ye whole.

And delay may cause that mischeife, that it may be impossible for both houses to repaire it.

Let a supply precede, His Majesty promises a gracious and princely eare to all your greivances.

He protests. He esteemes his glory greatest in a free and rich people.

I am appointed by the Lords to acquaint you with a matter lately come to their knowledge.

That ye war is begun. The Scots having pitched themselves at Dunch, and intend ye invading Northumberland, and have taken part off Sir Wm Brunkards troopes.

Without these great necessities he would not desire any supply should preceede your greivances.

The King hath expressed himselfe that you shal have a gracious answeare concerning mat[*ters*] off religion, He wil prevent Innovation therein and hath charged his Archbishops and bishops to see to ye same. Also concerning propriety he will [*p. 9*] listen graciously to you and concerning priviledge off Parliament.

For ye shipmony, we of his councel know It hath beene no profit to him.

All his aime hath beene ye preservation off us and off ye kingdome. In which he hath spent much mony also off his owne.

And iff you can find him out any other way for ye fortification off ye seas, without which ye kingdome cannot be safe, and his Majesty will joyne with you in any way, and relinquish it.

The Lords have denied to meddle with any subsidy, or to give advise concerning it. It is left to you.

Their Lordships by vote have declared, That a supply uppon this occasion shal preceede their greivances.

This Conferens was desired, That you might know their opinions.

The King saith. An obligation off trust is his greatest ty. He desires a speedy answeare.

[1] See below, App. L.K. (25 April), p. 310.

[*House of Commons*]

Then we returned to ye house, where we expected some 4 who were appointed by ye house to be ye reporters, to have made report hereoff. [*p. 10*] But they sent word by a member off ye house that they were comparing their notes and should not be ready this day.

It was said, That some of them ought to come in person and tell us so.

Then came ye Kings solecitor Mr. Herbert and Mr. Hampden, 2 off them; and said so much.

So time was given them to report til Munday.[1]

It was moved by ye SPEAKER, That Mr. Elsing ye clark off ye lower house, for his better effecting ye service, desired an assistant, one Mr. Rushworth, who by vote was admitted.

But ordered that he should not use his writing off stenography to take mens speeches. But only to take orders truly, and enter reports faithfully.

27 APRIL[2]

[*p. 11*] ### 28 APRIL[3]

[*H.R.O., M36/1*]   [*29 April 1640, House of Commons*]

[*p. 11*]   [*29 APRIL 1640*]

29 April was spent, in debating a report made by a committee concerning Innovations in religion.[4]

1. The removing of ye Communion table in parish churches and chappels in ye University, and placing them altar wise.

Resolved upon ye question to be a head for a conferns with ye Lords.

The Kings chappel not to be medled with.

2. The setting up off Crosses Images or Crucifixes in churches or chappels in ye Universities, and divers places elswhere, and specially in Cathedral churches who ought to give good examples.

To be another head.

3. The refusing to administer ye sacrament without comming up to ye raile before ye Communion table and excommunicating for not doing it.

4. The making and enjoyning Articles at visitations without any authority saving off ye bishop.

[*p. 12*] 5. The molesting suspending and depriving off Godly and conformable ministers, for not yeelding to matters enjoyned without

---

[1] *Cf. C.J.*, ii, p. 12.   [2] See above, pp. 177–80.
[3] See above, p. 180.   [4] Erle reported.

warrant of law. As for instans in not reading ye booke for recreations on Sunday.

6. The printing preaching and determining Popish bookes tenents and questions contrary to ye doctrine off ye Church off England.

7. The enjoyning and preaching bowing to ye Altar; and enquiry of ye not doing theroff.

8. The restraint of conformable ministers from preaching when they please in their charges.

Liberty reserved to adde to these heads.

SR. THO. LITTLETON said. Recusants had too much liberty. A monastery was erected in ye metropolis off ye kingdome. An army off preists swarmed up and downe. And one had taken up his settlement in the University off Oxford.

It was said. He who makes a report may speake as oft as he wil to vindicate ye same.

A committee was appointed [*to*] present ye case for ship mony, as it stood uppon ye records. And it [*is*] to be first spoken to too morrow. Being ye 1st [*p. 13*] head concerning ye property off goods.

[*p. 13*]　　　　　　**30 APRIL**[1]

[***H.R.O., M36/1***]　　　　　　[*1 May 1640, House of Commons*]

[*p. 14*]　　　　　　**1 MAII**

An extract of a Sermon preached by Dr. Beale Master Off St. Johns Colledge in Cambridge, in ye said University on ye 27th of March. 1635. was read, wherein was expressed, That all we had was ye Kings. He might command all wifes, children, estates and all.[2]

And speaking against ye Parliament, who seemed to give with one hand but did take away more with ye other, using ye King as men did Apes, with a bit and a knock.

These things were not yet fully proved.

It was appointed to be examined.

The question was whether he should be sent for. Held fit.

Then it was said He was off ye Convocat[*ion*][3] House.

Then to be sent for by Summons left at hi[*s*] lodging. If he came not. To goe to ye Lor[*ds*] against him. Then grew a great Question [*p. 15*] whether he should be s[*ent*] for as yet, ti[*ll*] further proved.[4] And whether his stud[*y*] and papers should be seised on or seale[*d*].

Resolved not to seise or seale.

The 1st part off sending for, was very doubtfull. The Is and Noes

---

[1] See above, pp. 182–85.

[2] Pym raised the question.　　　　　　[3] MS. damaged.

[4] Rossingham says there were objections to sending for him, 'upon a bare information till wittnesses were producst' (B.L., Add. MS. 11045, fo 115ᵛ).

being dubiou[s]. The Question as put was. As many as would have him forborne to be sent for to say I. And who would have him sent for, to say I.

It was thought a smal matter for ye house to be divided about. Yet for order sake unles all had waiv[ed] one part, It was t[o] be observed and ye house divided.

The Question then was whether ye I.s or N[oes] were to goe forth. The Is did goe out, and uppon numbering 2 for ye Is and 2 for ye Noes being appointed by Mr. Speaker to number, vid. Sir Jo. Wray Sir. Jo. Hales. Mr. Kirton and Mr. Stroud, who did it bare headed. They returned ye noes most.

Mr. Stroud tooke exception [?] Speakers [?][1] [p. 16] put it in ye [affir]mative.

Also that he was nominated an Trier[2] before he had declared. How he was.

It was ordered a summons should be left at his Chamber to attend this house by Thursday next, to answeare a complaint made against him, concerning such a Sermon.

A dis[sent] was put, That ye Is alwaies goe out uppon a bill. Whether uppon this Question, que, but resolved so.

The 1st to be numbered, are ye persons in ye house. Then they out.

The Lords sent by 2 Judges to let us know they desired a present Conferens in ye painted chamber.

Answeare was, they were very busy, but would send a messenger to their Lops off their owne, which about an houre after was done. Mr. Thesaurer well attended. I was there. He knocks at ye Lords doore. Word is carried up. Then goe in. The Lord Keeper with ye se[al] on his arme, comes to ye lower bar, There it is [deliver]ed. Then we went out. Then called [?]. The Lord Keeper then sitting [?][3] [p. 17] in his place, gives ye Lords answeare, That we should presently meete uppon a Conference. Which we did.[4]

[Conference]

Then ye Lord Keeper said. At ye last Conferens; the desire and care off union betwixt both houses, was much endevored by ye lower house, as was expressed.

As their Lops was wel knowing their owne great priviledges, so they were not ignorant of what pertained to us off ye lower house. And that what ye Lords challenged, were not to be attempted uppon.

The King comming to ye upper house, and conceiving ye supply set aside, which he had so much pressed, and hearing that ye treaty

---

[1] MS. damaged at bottom of pp. 15 and 16.
[2] *Elector* corrected to *Trier* in MS.   [3] MS. damaged.
[4] See below, App., L.K. (1 May), p. 314.

was off matters of religion, off property off goods, and priviledge off parliament, wishd us to advise ye Commons off his pressing occasions, and of our opinion herein.

After a solemne debate amongst us, our opinions were, That supply should preceede, so voted by us. Only for our opinions. And uppon conferens so related to you, It was mistaken, That this was conceived a transporting beyond our bounds, [*p. 18*] or that reparation should be demanded for it.

We have not varied or beene transported herein. Nor invaded your ground.

We acknowledge subsidies ought to move first from you. And then to us, and from us back to you and so to be presented by your Speaker.

To conferre or talk off a supply in generall, can be no breach off your liberty.

The *Indempmity des Commons*, 9.*H*.4, at Oxford pressed uppon your Conferens. Is also *des segneurs et Commons*. The King demanded off ye Lords what ye aide should be. 12 off ye Commons were sent for to them.

They were troubled at it.

Hereuppon It was established That ye Lords should [?] commence of busines by themselves, and ye Commons by themselves. And that no report should be to ye King till they were both agreed.

In which is not any word to barre ye Lords off treating with ye Commons.

Our proceedings were according to antient usage. Other reasons I could give you. But ye record may satisfy, So no cause of reparation.

[*p. 19*] 2 Excep[*tions t*]hat were taken notice off 3 things treated off amongst you: Religion, property, priviledge, and therein a breach off your liberties.

We tooke no notice of it, but as it pleased ye King to tell us and we reported it to you uppon ye Conferens, as ye King appointed and It was no good manners in us to aske how ye King knew it.

In this also we justify our proceedings.

In a faire and affectionate manner we desire to stir you up. To a consideracion off yt great danger which time cannot prevent hereafter, you have beene told how much it concernes his majesty in his honor and our safety.

[*H.R.O., M36/1*]   [*2 May 1640, House of Commons*]

[*p. 19*]   **2 MAII**

The King sent a message in writing by Mr. Secretary,[1] to this purpose. He had severall times expressed his pressing occasions, and

[1] Treasurer. *Cf. C.J.*, ii, p. 18. The House went into committee to debate the message.

for a speedy supply, and had received no answeare, which he expected out of hand.

[*Committee*]

Many[1] expressed themselves severall waies, some to [*p. 20*] have supply preceede [*and accept*] the Kings word for redresse off our greivances,

Others[2] to have greivances preceede.

Others[3] to have ship mony and coate and conduct mony overthrowne by act of parliament, then to supply.

Lo. Digby.[4] It was said, That ye question was whether ye King should be considered first in his necessities or we in ours.

It was more necessary to quench our house a fire, Then to stay to sweepe and clense on. Sc[*otland*] was on fire.

They who gave him largely in his subjects affections did him better service then they who gave him off ye purse.

That there was no greater animation to an enemy, then ye discontent off ye nation.

Another said. It was fit to deale cleerely.

If ye aide was required concerning ye Warre against ye Scots. That busines was unknowne to us. If we gave mony generally That was an approbation off yt Warre, of which we understood nothing, nor have heard any thing off. Then it was fit we should know ye reasons and grounds of this necessity. It was a great [*p. 21*] in gagement of [*the*] Kings expence being 100000^{li} a month as we have beene told, and ye subjects lifes drawne into ye defence thereoff.

Mr. Tresorer said. His opinion was a supply should preceede And trust ye King uppon his gracious promise. If we grasped at all, we might take hold of nothing.

Proceeding with moderation, may gaine our ends.

Some said, ship mony being taken away would be a settling off property off goods which being removed, we might be able to give.[5]

Religion was to be preferd, iff it was so desperate as our other necessities.[6]

Mr. Tresorer pressed that ye King expected an answeare. Also said there was no cleere resolution to take away ship mony with equivalent consideracion.

That it had cost ye King 230000^{li} more in shipping, Then ever he had received.

It was resolved, That til Munday an answeare could not be, Then

1 Parry, Herbert, Jones.　2 Strode and Hampden.
3 Perhaps Pym.　4 See below, App., Digby, p. 316.
5 Seymour, North, Godbolt.　6 Perhaps Hotham.

it should, unles ye Kings Councel speaking in defence off ship money prevented it.

[*p. 22*]   **4 MAII**

His Majesty sent a message to ye house in writing by one off his Secretaries, whereby he did recite ye message he sent on Saterday last. And that uppon grace and favor, he made us this offer, That iff we would presently passe an act for 12 subsidies to be paid in 3 yeares, with a proviso not to determine this Session, ship money should cease and be presently laid downe, and relinquished. And that his Majesty expected a present and positive answeare.

[*Committee*]

Sr Benj. Rudierd[1] said. It was not a gift. It would purchace more parliaments.

And in his opinion, our mony could not be laid out to purchace a greater advantage.

Others[2] said. If it was legal, It was a gracious offer: If not legal. There was no cause to purchace it.

Also It was necessary coate and conduct mony should be taken off, which is a great burden and an illegal charge.

It was necessary to determin ye legality. If it did not depend uppon law more acts were unnecessary against it. There being several Judgments in parliament, That no tax tallage or levy shalbe made or [*p. 23*] levied by ye King, but what shalbe set by parliament.

Mr. Holborne said It had beene published by some off ye Judges That ship mony was such a prerogative so incident to ye Crowne, That an act off parliament could not take it away.

Mr. Comptroller said. The King would allow us our owne meanes to suppres it.

Sr Fr. Seymor said. His conscience told him, That iff but 12^d was demanded, whereas 12 subsidies were demanded, He could not consent to give it, before greivances were redressed.

He conceived it dangerous to speake off any subsidies, specially any certain numbers, because ye Lords had voted it and in ye upper house. What hold might be taken of it. He knew not.

His opinion was that there should be an humble remonstrans to his Majesty, That it could not be.

Mr. Serjeant Glanvil, being out off ye chaire as Speaker the house

---

[1] MS. does not indicate that the House was in committee until Glanville's speech (below).

[2] *E.g.*, Cholmley.

being dissolved into a Committee, asked whether he might speake with their leaves, which being allowed. He said That he thought a Judgment in parliament against ye former Judgment for ship money, more necessary than a new act. And that it should be in this manner. [*p. 24*] A Judgment declaratory, That ye former Judgement was illegall, and that it did never bind, nor ever should, and to have it taken away. For my part I alwaie thought it a most illegal thing.

Let us use ye subtilty off ye serpent, as wel as ye innocency off ye Dove, and use that course that may draw ye being and subsistans off parliaments rather then looke to priviledge of parliament, which is nothing with out being.

For redress of monopolies. The best way is to bring an action uppon ye Statut, who hinders it incurs a *premunire*. This is a better way then to bring actions off [?] letters or ye like. We had one tried in ye westerne Circuit, and prevailed.[1]

For military affaires, when ye petition of right was in question, a way was propounded for them, and a bil put in here to reduce them to some certainty and way of levying.[2]

For ports they to be discharged of ship mony as wel as Inland countries. Yet there was more colour to charge them. But both illegall.

Mr. Comptroller signified his Majesty so intended.

He concluded. Mr. Speaker I meane, That 12 subsidies to be paid by 5, 4, 3 yearly, little enough for ye Kings favor to [?] call[3] parliament.

[*p. 25*] Mr. Hampden moved. That besides ship money there were other things pressing uppon us. As matters of religion, great burdens were imposed uppon Countries by eccl[*esiastical*] officers.

Mr. St. John said. It was necessary to make provision against all charges off ye like nature els there might be a Judgment off as ill consequens in some other thing, under pretence that *salus regni periclibatur*.

If any declaracion off necessity [by ye King] should make a charge, as for land soldiers, or iff ye King would make Banks throughout ye Kingdome against ye low water marke to keep out ye sea, alledging it *pro bono publico* and such like.

To have a declaration, That all taxes and levies made by ye King, alledging case off necessity to be voide, unles such necessity be allowed of in parliament.

14*E*.3. when ye French were coming by sea and ye Scots by land, which was great necessity yet ye King moved it in parliament.[4]

---

[1] We have not been able to identify this case.
[2] *C.J.*, i, p. 912.   [3] MS. damaged.
[4] *Rot. Parl.*, ii, pp. 112, 117.

This day was spent in general discourses of greivances and, ye answeare to ye King not agreed on, but to be [*p. 26*] further debated on, on next day.

[H.R.O., M36/1]   [*5 May 1640, House of Commons*]

[*p. 26*]   **5 MAII. TUESDAY**

The Speaker came not to ye house.

The King came to ye upper house. All ye Lords were in their robes.

The Speaker of ye house of Commons was in ye upper house, before we of ye lower house knew it.

Then ye usher off ye black rod, came into ye lower house, and told us his Majesty pleasure was we should presently attend him in ye upper house, which we did.

Then ye King made this speech.[1]

I am sorry off my being at ye house this day, for that purpose which I come.

I did in ye beginning of this parliament declare to you my urgent necessities, and that delay was as bad as a denial. I told you ye same by my Lord Keeper in ye banqueting house. I came to ye upper house and told ye Lords ye like. I thanke their Lops they were considerative of my occasions, and by their votes shewed their redines.

In ye lower house have beene pretences off greivances, in this common wealth, no question there are some, but I think not so many as [*p. 27*] have beene spoken off. Concerning monopolies I shal take care to reforme them.

Concerning religion, I hope by ye grace of God to mainteyne ye purity thereoff according to ye doctrine off ye Church off England.

Concerning property off goods, I intend not to invade it.

I cannot blame all ye lower house, but some only, disaffected persons, and stuffed with ill will.

I hope your Lops will joyne with mee in ye carefull government off ye people.

And now my Lord Keeper you are to speake.

Then his Lop said, My Lords Knts, Citizen[s] and Burgesses, the Kings Majesty doth dissolve this present parliament.

So we all departed, without any returne to ye lower house.

Finis per dissolutionem.

[*p. 27*]   **[6 MAY 1640]**[2]

1 See below, App. (5 May), p. 316.
2 See *CSP*, 1640, pp. 152–56.

[Worc. Coll. MS. 5.20]   *[13 April 1640, House of Commons]*

[fo 1ʳ]

DIURNALL OCCURANCES OR HEADS OF THE DAYLY
PROCEEDINGS OF YE LAST PARLIAMENT WHICH
BEGUN AT WESTMINSTER THE 13 OF APRILL AND
ENDED THE 5TH OF MAY 1640 HOLDING IN ALL BUT
20 DAYES

MUNDAY, THE 13TH OF APRILL

The Kings Majestie with the Lords and Peeres went in their
Parliament roabes to the Upper House, where (both houses being
settled) his Majestie spake as followeth [The King]. . . .[1]

[Worc. Coll. MS. 5.20]   *[15 April 1640, House of Commons]*

[fo 6ʳ]   WEDNESDAY THE 15TH OF APRILL[2]

About two of ye clocke in ye afternoone being the day [and houre]
appointed for the House of Commons to present their Speaker,
both houses being mett in the Upper House of Parliament, and his
Majestie being seated in his Throne, Mr. Sergeant Glanvill was
called,[3] etc. [Mr. Glanvill]. . . *[fo 6ᵛ]*

---

[1] The King's and Lord Keeper's speeches, fos 1ʳ–6ʳ, see above, pp. 115–23,
A Perfect Diurnall gives the king's speech, then continues: 'After which the
Lord Finch, then Lord Keeper, made a very elegant and learned Speech, the
precedeum whereof was an Encomium of his Majestie, a plausible Character of
His government, and a large description of the ungratefull Rebellion of the
Scottish Nation; with an invitation to the Parliament, that upon those press-
ing and urgent occasions they would lay aside all other debates, and passe an
Act for such and so many Subsidies as they in their hearty affection to Him
and the common good should think convenient, and withall that the Bill for
Tonage and Poundage from the first yeer of his Majesties raigne might passe;
and assuring them that his Majesty would afterwards give them time for
considering such Petitions as should be good for the Common-wealth.
    'After this the King caused a Letter from the Lord Louden and other
Scotch Lords, to the French King, directed *An[sic] Roy*, to be read; and then
the Lord Keeper declared his Majesties pleasure touching the choice of a
Speaker against Wednesday following.'
[2] See Hunt. Cal. HM 1554, p. 252, below, p. 229.
[3] '. . . to the Bar, being presented to the House of Commons as their Speaker;
and being come to the Bar, he made a very patheticall Speech, excusing
himselfe from the undertaking of so great an imployment. To which the Lord
Keeper made a very Rhetoricall Reply. After which the King commanded the
Speaker to report the cause of the meeting, as it was made by the Lord Keeper;
and so both Houses departed for that day' (*A Perfect Diurnall*). For speeches
of Glanville and the Lord Keeper see, fos 7ʳ–15ʳ above, pp. 123–34.

TO THE HOUSE OF COMMONS IN PARLIAMENT
(NOW ASSEMBLED)

My Master you that undertake the game,
Looke to it your Countries safetie, and her fame
Are now att stake. Bee carefull how you cutt
And deale, as knowne occasions putt you to it.
The Cards are strangelie shuffled. For your parts
Tis ods you never gett the Ace of Hearts:
Yett the fine finger and some helpes besides
Lie in the packe disperst: Bee these your guides,
That you possesse. To tell you what you want.
Lest the mistake of a poore tricke should daunt
Your spiritts quite, and make you flinge away
Your liberties; nott to be lost by play.
Detest foule Ingling: now Tis in your powers,
Lett none square play passe. The game is yours.

These verses were dropt in the Parliament house.[1]

[*Worc. Coll. MS. 5.20*]   [*16–18 April 1640, House of Commons*]

[*fo 15ʳ*]
THURSDAY, FRIDAY, AND SATERDAY THE 16TH, 17TH
AND 18TH DAYES OF APRILL.[2]

The House of Commons was observed in the generallitie of itt to
bee stirring in the highest way that ever itt was knowne to goe. As
alsoe divers particuler members of itt, *viz.* Sir Francis Seymor, Mr.
Pymme, Sir [*Benjamin*] Rudyer, Mr. Rowse, Mr. Grimston and
others[3] in their speeches each severall day moved stronglie[4] to take
beginning where they had left the last Parliament, they ripped uppe
the greivances both of Church and Commonwealth, propounded the
establishment of Religion in the first place, and to purge out the
Innovations and errors which were crept in, they inveighed against
the undue and unaccostomed [*fo 15ᵛ*] proceedings in the severall
Courts of Justice,[5] and in particular that the Court of Starchamber
contrarie to the primarie Institution thereof which was for punishment onlie of such enormities and crimes as the common lawe could
nott reach unto, was now become a verie Court of Exchequer and

---

[1] See also, B.L., Add. MS. 6411, fo 43ʳ.
[2] See also Hunt. Cal., HM 1554, pp. 252–53.
[3] See the Appendix, below.
[4] *strangely and took* beginning (*A Perfect Diurnall*).
[5] *A Perfect Diurnall* ends its entry for the day here.

revenue for the Kinge, by the Imposition of heavie and deepe fines which were soe insupportable that they tended to the utter ruine and subversion of mens estates and fortunes.

The speeches spoken in the Lower House on these 3 dayes were these, *viz.*

First SIR BENJAMIN RUDYARD spake as followeth.[1] . . .

[*fo 17*ʳ] MR. HARBOTTLE GRIMSTON, ESQ., his speech *eodem die*, April 16.[2] . . .

MR ROWSE, his speech (*eodem die*).[3] . . .

[Seymour, *p. 1*]

SIR FRANCIS SEYMORS SPEECH IN YE PARLIAMENT 1640[4]

Mr. Speaker, his Majestie I beleeve hath as great affection to Parliaments as ever[5] hee had, and now especiallie for subsidies. Butt what time is fitt for the granting of them, is the Question, for if wee should grant[6] subsidies, before wee doe anie thinge else trulie our Judgements may verie well bee questioned by them who sent us hither; for if subsidies should bee granted before greivances redressed,[7] itt would bee taken as confirmation of our greivances.[8]

This greate Counsell (as *Tully* said of the Senate of *Rome*) is the soule of the *Common-wealth*; wherein one may heare and see all the Greevances of the subjects and in the Multitude of such Counsellors is safety.

Amongst whom, the greatest priviledge, is liberty of speech. And therefore, I humbly offer it unto you, to take into consideration, what wrong hath bin done herein, what Judgments hath bin against the *Members* of this House, for speaking nothing, but what concerned the good of the *Commonwealth*. Which said Judgments hath beene against Law and Reason, and without president.

What Law or Reason is there, that a *Parliament*, [*p. 2*] which is the highest of all Courts, should be questioned by inferiour *Courts*, and Judges: as if the *Common pleas* should question the *Kings bench*, or the *Chancery* be questioned by either of them.

---

[1] Rudyerd's speech, fos 15ᵛ–16ʳ, unnumbered, see above, pp. 138–40.

[2] Grimston's speech, fos 28ʳ, 29ᵛ, 16ᵛ (numbering in MS. is erratic); see above, pp. 135–38.

[3] 1½ fos unnumbered; see above, pp. 145–48.

[4] MS., fo 17ʳ dates the speech 17 April. See below, App., Seymour, p. 297.

[5] '. . . had *any of his predecessors*' (B.L., Add. MS. 6411, fo 31ᵛ; Bodl., MS. Eng. Hist. C.199, fo 25ʳ).

[6] . . . *the King* . . . (Hunt. Cal., HM 1554, p. 145; S.R.O., DD/M1, Box 18, 96; Bodl., MS. Eng. Hist. C.199, fo 25ʳ).

[7] . . . *and reduced* . . . (S.R.O., DD/M1, Box 18, 96).

[8] This paragraph is a handwritten preface to the printed speech. The printed portion begins with the following paragraphs. *Cf.* B.L., E.199(35), p. 1.

Perhaps[1] the Authors of it, have nature to pleade for themselves, which indeed teacheth every man to preserve himselfe.

This perhaps, makes them advance[2] that, and those members which otherwise must condemne themselves. And such things have[3] bin done, to maintaine their proceedings, as not only trench upon the liberties of Parliament, but also upon the liberties of the whole[4] *Common-wealth*: wherein I had rather suffer for speaking the truth, then the truth should suffer for want of my speaking.

Where was ever more Piety in a Prince, and more loyalty in Subjects, and yet what Common-wealth ever suffered like[5] this.

His Majesty is the Sunne, which[6] though it ever shines alike in it selfe gloriously; yet by reason of Clouds, many times it doth not so appeare, and if his Majesty, by reason of bad members may not appeare in such splendor, Let us labour to cleere those Clouds: what will it availe us, if the Fountaine be cleere, if the streames that issue there-from be not so also. I will instance in some particulars.

If we looke into the face of Religion, that is [*p. 3*] out-faced, and such as heretofore durst not appeare, come boldly into our houses, as if they had a concealed toleration, I meane the Seminary preists, who though they have lesse power, yet have they not lesse malice, but more, so long as the Pope hath his Agents amongst us. See wee not how they go to *Somerset house*, and to S. *James* with too much countenance:[7] These are the enemies of the church, without the church: I wish we had none with in it: who[8] pull downe churches, and I am sure build none upp againe: Amongst which are our *Non-Residents*, who o're-sway all by worldly preferments, and many livings.

Christ made it the Touch-stone of *Peters* love unto him, to feed his sheepe and lambes; but these men looke at theire own private gaines, not taking pains for their own double honours, which are daily gotten.

What thing is there more against Reason and Nature, then for one man to have above one wife, and for one shepheard to have more then one sheepefold.

---

[1] '. . . *they have matter to plead*' (B.L., Add. MS. 6411, fo 32ʳ; Bodl., MS. Eng. Hist. C.199, fo 25ʳ). For the following paragraphs, *cf.* S.R.O., DD/M1, Box 18, 96, below, pp. 251–53.

[2] *renounce* (B.L., Add. MS. 6411, fo 32ʳ; Bodl., MS. Eng. Hist. C.199, fo 25ʳ).

[3] '. . . *not onlye* beene done, not onely which *touching upon the Priviledges* of Parliaments' (B.L., Add. MS. 6411, fo. 32ʳ).

[4] '. . . *House of Commons and of the* . . .' (Hunt. Cal., HM 1554, p. 146).

[5] *more then* (B.L., Add. MS. 6411, fo 32ᵛ; Bodl., MS. Eng. Hist. C.199, fo 25ᵛ).

[6] '. . . allwaies shines in it selfe alike . . . by reason of *words* may not soe appeare if . . . splendor what will . . .' (B.L., Add. MS. 6411, fo 32ᵛ).

[7] *confidence* (Bodl., MS. Eng. Hist. C.199, fo 25ᵛ).

[8] '. . . though they pull *no* Churches downe' (B.L., Add. MS. 6411, fo 33ʳ; Bodl., MS. Eng. Hist. C.199, fo 25ᵛ).

These are dumbe dogs, that cannot speak a word for God, of whom the people may seeke spirituall food, but can find none.

Others there are that preach, but it is not the Gospell, but themselves, that the *King* hath an unlimited power, and the Subjects noe propriety in their goods.

[*p. 4*] These are bad Divines, and worse, and more ignorant Statesmen; who under the name of Puritans condemne all, who truly professe Religion. There are surely many,[1] who under a forme of godlinesse, cloake impiety; but to teach, that a man can be too holy, is the Doctrine of Divels.[2]

And now, for feare I have bin over-long, I will speake of the Subjects Liberties, wherein I remember, what was confirmed unto us by the word of a King; and God forbid, that I, or any other should imagine, that the King did[3] otherwise, then he granted us.

But some there be, that have betrayed the *King* unto himselfe, and so committed worse treason then those, who betray him to others, who tell him his Prerogative is above all Lawes, and that his subjects are but slaves: whereby the King is neither preserved in Honour, nor the *Commonwealth* in safety.[4]

If all that bee Judges, who by their lawes[5] will (though contrarie to law, experience, and Presidents) binds us, and by their doomes, if wee of this House shall suffer Imprisonment, I knowe nott what in time that may come to, for such power will nott stay there, neither hath itt for they have taken upon them to committ some, and remitt others as they shall thinke fitting.

The abuses done by sheriffes in leavying of Monies[6] are most intolerable.

1. The imploying in most places none butt Rogues to execute their warrants is most dangerous, butt itt is soe as one of them hath said to mee, That none else can bee procured to serve.

If this be tollerated, I know nott butt the law of villenage weere better to bee in force.

In all things I doubt nott of his Majesties Justice and protection.

---

[1] *scarcely any* (Hunt. Cal., HM 1554, p. 147).
[2] End of major variations in S.R.O., DD/M1, Box 18, 96 (below, pp. 251–53).
[3] . . . *intend* . . . (Hunt. Cal., HM 1554, p. 147; B.L., Add. MS. 6411, fo 33ᵛ).
[4] The remainder of the speech is written in by hand. *Cf.* B.L., E.199(35), p. 4.
[5] *places* (Hunt. Cal., HM 1554, p. 147); 'who *have not their places*' (B.L., Add. MS. 6411, fo 33ᵛ; Bodl., MS. Eng. Hist. C.199, fo 26ʳ); 'who *have but their places during life, and will do these things* contrary to' (S.R.O., DD/M1, Box 18, 96).
[6] . . . *ship*money (B.L., Harl. MS. 6801, fo 117ᵛ; Bodl., MS. Eng. Hist. C.199, fo 26ʳ).

[Pym, *p. 1*]

THE FIRST SPEECH OF MASTER PYM, THE LAST PAR-
LIAMENT, CONCERNING LIBERTY OF PARLIAMENT,
GENERALS CONCERNING RELIGION, GENERALS CON-
CERNING CIVILL GOVERNMENT. London, 1641[1]

Hee that takes away weights from the motions, doth as good service as hee that addes wings unto it. These weights are old[2] grievances, whereof there are three heads.

1. First, liberty of Parliament.
2. Generals concerning Religion.
3. Generals concerning civill government.[3]

I shall prove that these grievances are more grievous to the King,
then they are to the Subject.

I shall propose some waies of remedy, just and easie.

[*p. 2*] That Kings can doe no wrong, is their just prerogative; The
distemper of the world is not caused by the celestiall bodies, but by
the inferiour: In like manner of a Kingdome.[4]

Generall grievances concerning Religion, which wee possesse[5] by
the Lawes of God, and of the Land.[6]

Encouragements given to the Popish Religion, I desire no new
Lawes to be made against them, not[7] a rigid execution of those that
are already enacted.

But this we are sure of, that if they once get the superiority, their
Religion is destructive of all others.

Wee must[8] looke upon a Papist as he is in himselfe, but not as he
is in the Church.

The Planets have a quiet motion of theire owne, but they are
interrupted[9] by another.

---

[1] See below, App., Pym (17 April), p. 299.
[2] *our* (Hunt. Cal., HM 1554, p. 157).
[3] . . . *of this kingdome* (Hunt. Cal., HM 1554 p. 157); D'Ewes adds: '*First I
shall propound what and how many these greivances are and whence they proceed*'
(B.L., Harl. MS. 165, fo 25ʳ; see also Bodl., MS. Rawl. A.487, unnumbered;
B.L., Harl. MS. 6801, fo 70ʳ), App., Pym (17 April).
[4] '*The liberties of Parliament infringed. 1. By taking away freedome of speech
from the members thereof. 2. By imprisoning the members during Parliament. 3.
By questioning in inferiour courts parliamentmen for speech and acts done in
Parliament*' (B.L., Harl. MS. 165, fo. 25ʳ; Bodl., MS. Rawl. A.487, unnumbered; B.L., Harl. MS. 6801, fos 70ᵛ–71ʳ).
[5] *professe* (Hunt. Cal., HM 1554, p. 157).
[6] Bodl., MS. Rawl. A.487, unnumbered, adds: *proceed from.*
[7] *nor* (B.L., Harl. MS. 165, fo 25ʳ).
[8] Hunt. Cal., HM 1554, p. 157; B.L., Sloane MS. 1200, fo 22ʳ; B.L., Harl.
MS. 165, fo 25ʳ, insert *not* here and omit it from the following clause.
[9] *rapt* (B.L., Harl. MS. 165, fo 25ʳ; Hunt. Cal., HM 1554, p. 157).

The particular encouragements.

First, cessation of all[1] law, that were not made to raise a Revenue to the King, but to suppresse Idolatry, and to restrain Errors.

A free communication of Councels through the Kingdome.

Papists being admitted to places[2] of trust, and power in the Commonwealth.

There is a Congregation at Rome, who plot how England may be reduced, and here in England we have a *Nuncio*, to put in execution what they resolve of there.

[*p. 3*] *Innovations to prepare us to Poperie.*

1. First, divers Bookes printed, Questions published, and maintained in the Universitie.

2. Secondly, Popish Ceremonies introduced: when the drie bones were to be made a man, they were joyned first in the sinewes, and then they were to be animated.[3]

3. Thirdly, Discouragements upon the professors of Protestant Religion, things of indifferency urged, to make the difference wider[4] amongst as many questions, where there is no ground in Law, upon the Bishops authority, not upon the Kings authority, under the great Seale or Proclamation.

4. Fourthly, Encroachments[5] of authority to Ecclesiasticall Courts.

1. First, To fine and imprison in some cases illegally.

2. Secondly, To affirme[6] their jurisdiction to be derived from the Crowne, and say it is *jure divinio*, and therefore wee are[7] bound to maintain the prerogative of the Crowne.

3. Thirdly, Many ordinances[8] set out, new Articles to examine Churchwardens.

In the Common-Law there is a title of extravagants, and so are these.

[*p. 4*] Fourthly, Generals against civill Government.

1. First, taking of tunnage and poundage, and all[9] other impositions.

2. Secondly, Knighthood.

---

[1] D'Ewes says: '*A suspending of the execution of . . .*' (B.L., Harl. MS. 165, fo 25ʳ); Hunt. Cal., HM 1554, p. 157, omits: all.
[2] *offices* (Bodl., MS. Rawl. A.487, unnumbered; B.L., Harl. MS. 165, fo 25ʳ).
[3] Ezekiel 37.
[4] wyder amongst *us* (Hunt. Cal., HM 1554, p. 158); D'Ewes adds: '. . . wider *and irreconcilable* amongst *us*' (B.L., Harl. MS. 165, fo 25ʳ); D'Ewes begins a new item after *us*; see also, Bodl., MS. Rawl. A.487, unnumbered.
[5] '*Enlargements* of authority by . . .' (B.L., Harl. MS. 165, fo 25ᵛ; Bodl., MS. Rawl. A.487, unnumbered).
[6] *disclaime* (Hunt. Cal., HM 1554, p. 158; B.L., Harl. MS. 165, fo 25ᵛ); *declyne* (Bodl., MS. Rawl. A.487, unnumbered).
[7] Hunt. Cal., HM 1554, p. 158, inserts: *all*.
[8] *ordinaries* (Hunt. Cal., HM 1554, p. 158; B.L., Harl. MS. 165, fo 25ᵛ).
[9] Hunt. Cal., HM 1554, p. 158, and B.L., Harl. MS. 165, fo 25ᵛ, omit: all.

3. Thirdly, Inundation of Monopolies, and commodities not only exported, but consumed at home, as Sope, Drink,[1] Salt, and that which is very comprehensive, the Shipmoney.

4. Fourthly, There is a countenance of judgement for it [shipmoney] against all other judgements, and book Cases.

5. Fifthly, That which somewhat stickes by me that is, the Forrest, and I might easily looke [sic] myselfe in it.

6. Sixthly, the sale and farming of Nusances, being compounded for the assesse[2] to be Nusances, and are licensed as buildings, depopulations, etc.

7. Seventhly, military charges, and compositions[3] raised upon the Subject without ground of Law, conduct monies, pressing Carthorses, etc.

8. Eighthly, Extrajudiciall proceedings, a teeming grievance, the Judges will presume to anticipate their judgements.

9. Ninthly, the authorities of Courts of Justice have countenanced these Monopolies, as the Star-Chamber hath done against the Sheriffes, for not collecting Ship-money.

10. Tenthly, The Lords of the privy Councell have assisted them.

[p. 5] 11. Eleventhly, the prerogative hath been vouched for the maintainance of them.

12. Twelvethly, The Conscience hath been pressed in this point,[4] betwixt the prerogative, and liberty broken.

Manwaring[5] for his offence in this kinde, was as neere the ground as ever I saw any, and I did not thinke he should[6] have leapt into a Bishops Chaire.

Intermissions of Parliament, the King summons them, but we humbly[7] desire the benefit of the law in that point.

As these grievances are to the Subject prejudiciall, so are they to the King much more.

1. First, this not liberty of the Parliament cuts off the sweete communion that ought to be betwixt the head and the members.

2. Secondly, it deprives the King of the present[8] supply, and benefit the King hath by[9] Subsidie.

---

[1] *wyne* (Hunt. Cal., HM 1554, p. 158); after 'salt' D'Ewes adds: *and others* (B.L., Harl. MS. 165, fo 25ᵛ).
[2] *they assist* nusances (Hunt. Cal., HM 1554, p. 159).
[3] *impositions* (Hunt. Cal., HM 1554, p. 159).
[4] '. . . *and all bonds between* the prerogative . . .' (Hunt. Cal., HM 1554, p. 159; B.L., Sloane MS. 1200, fo 23ᵛ; B.L., Harl. MS. 165, fo 25ᵛ).
[5] '*Doctor* Manwaring, *now Bishop of St. Davids*' (Hunt. Cal., HM 1554, p. 159).
[6] '. . . *soe soone* have leaped' (Hunt. Cal., HM 1554, p. 159; B.L., Harl. MS. 165, fo 25ᵛ).
[7] 'we *may onely* desire' (Hunt. Cal., HM 1554, p. 159).
[8] the *cheifest supply* (Hunt. Cal., HM 1554, p. 159).
[9] hath *noe* subsidies (B.L., Harl. MS. 165, fo 26ʳ).

3. Thirdly, it lesseneth his reputation abroad.

4. Fourthly, by the breaches in, and upon Religion he hath lost a great part of his Alliance with Protestant States abroad, lost a great many Subsidies[1] at home, because of the pressing of indifferent things.

5. Fifthly, who will be industrious where he hath no propriety. [p. 6] Sixthly, It breeds many jealousies, wee can remember when it hath bred distempers, and one Summers distemper will consume more wealth than ever this Monopoly brought in.

7. Seaventhly, The Princes that have maintained their Subjects liberty, have been most glorious therein.

What he omitted in each due place, is here inserted.

That not only composition[2] was laid on goods imported and exported out of this Kingdome, but also on goods that were carried from one forraigne Countrey to another, as from Spaine to France, etc. and *vice versa.*

Another way is that for want of a legall way of accounting a great deale of the profit stickes by the way, and comes not to the Kings purse.

The King hath farmed the Wines for thirty thousand pounds, the Farmors make forty thousand pounds,[3] at the sale by retaile, it amounts to two hundred thirty and two thousand pounds.

Remedies.

First, present it to the higher house, they joyning[4] to goe to the King, as in the land of Egypt whilest the darkness was amongst them the Sun did give light, and the people had their visionable faculty, which was only hindred by the interposition of the darknesse.

Dabit Deus his quoque finem.[5]

[*Worc. Coll. MS. 5.20*]   **[*16 April 1640, House of Commons*]**

[*fo 17ʳ*]   **SATERDAY THE 18TH OF APRILL.[6]**

THE ARCHBISHOP OF CANT[*ERBURY*] moving in the Upper House, that they of the Clergie might have respite two dayes

---

[1] *subjects* (Hunt. Cal., HM 1554, p. 160; Bodl., MS. Rawl. A.487, unnumbered; B.L., Harl. MS. 165, fo 26ʳ).

[2] *imposition* (B.L., Harl. MS. 165, fo 26ʳ).

[3] 80,000 (Hunt, Cal., HM 1554, p. 160).

[4] D'Ewes says: '. . . *with the Commons wee may make it known to God*, to the Kinge for otherwise *as in the land* . . . did give *them* noe light and *yet* the people . . . darknesse. *Soe heere though the King bee habituallie disposed with justice to redresse his peoples extreame greivances and sufferings, yet whilst the mists and darknes of Flatterie and misinformation are about him; the poore subjects can never partake of his grace and goodnes*' (B.L., Harl. MS. 165, fo 26ʳ).

[5] Phrase added by hand in MS.

[6] These are proceedings of 16 April. See also Hunt. Cal. HM 1554, p. 253.

in the weeke, for the proceedings in the Convocation House and High Commission Court, was answered by the LORD SAY AND SEALE, That when they had occasion, they might bee absent and that the High Court of Parliament could proceede without the Bishops who satt there onlie as they were Barons.

[*Worc. Coll. MS. 5.20*]   [*20 April 1640, House of Commons*]

[*fo 17ʳ*]   **MUNDAY THE 20TH OF APRILL.**[1]

The debate that day in the House of Commons was, whither the Speaker in the last Parliament (leaving the chaire and refusing to vote the adjournment of the House) was a greivance or noe,[2] itt was resolved to bee one, and that verie evill consequence hath ensued thereupon, the thinge itt self, and the manner of doing itt, being both illegall and unwarrantable.

The House ordered to send a Message to desire the Lords to joyne with them in petitioning to his Majestie that itt might bee soe noe more.

They fell upon the severe suite brought against Sir John Elliott, Walter Longe,[3] and the rest in severall courts, [*fo 17ᵛ*] and especiallie upon the Judgement entred for shippemonie, wherupon they sent some members of the house to comand the officers of the severall courts, *vizt.* Starchamber, Exchequer Chamber, the 2 courts of Plees, and the Pipe to bringe into the House the proceedings and the Rolles of each severall court, which accordinglie was done,[4] onlie the Lord Cheif Justice of the Kings Bench in a mannerlie way, refused to send in the Records of that Court, saying they were nott to bee trusted out of the Court with anie butt himself, being Plees of the Crowne, butt said if itt pleased them to send anie members of their House whom they might trust, they should have Copies and Transcripts thereof to their full content.[5]

[*Worc. Coll. MS. 5.20*]   [*21 April 1640, House of Commons*]

[*fo 17ᵛ*]   **TUESDAY APRIL 21**[6]

This day the House of Commons received[7] a Messenger from his Majestie that they and the Lords should give him a meeting in the

---

[1] See also Hunt. Cal. H.M. 1554, p. 253–54.
[2] Debate occurred 18 and 20 April.
[3] *A Perfect Diurnall* omits: Walter Longe.
[4] *A Perfect Diurnall* ends its entry for the day here.
[5] *C.J.*, ii, p. 7.
[6] See also below, p. 230–31.
[7] . . . *read* a *message* (*A Perfect Diurnall*).

Banquetting House where att their coming the Lord Keeper made a speech in behalf of his Majestie.[1] The heads wherof were as followeth.[2] . . .

[*Worc. Coll. MS. 5.20*]   **[*22 April 1640, House of Commons*]**

[*fo 19ᵛ*]   **WEDNESDAY APRILL 22[3]**

The next morning the House tooke this [*the king's request*] into debate, being a Case of soe high a nature, as must unavoidable devide the whole House and trie the severall strengthes therein. The Councellors of State putt itt home and desired to have an order entred, that itt might receive a determination the same day butt that was deferred and a worthy member (Mr. Waller)[4] of the House said: that they were first to consider what they had to give, for as the Case stood they had neither goods nor liberties, this was seconded by divers and everie man declared his willingnesse to give yea an ample and annuall supply in a Parliamentarie way, butt nott before their greivances were heard and redressed.[5]

[*Worc. Coll. MS. 5.20*]   **[?*23 April 1640, House of Commons*]**

[*fo 19ᵛ*]   **[?*THURSDAY 23 APRIL*][6]**

The two reasons which stucke most in the sence of the House were these: first. That the Kinge in his owne nature was undoubtedlie the best of kings, butt hee had some about him who had nott failed to divert his gracious Intentions, labouring undoubtedlie by secrett insinuations and suggestions to turne all the good Intendements of the House of Commons into poyson,[7] that they had formerlie given much and brought nothinge home, that if his Majestie had called them for soe speedy and instant giving hee might have beene pleased to have done itt sooner.[8]

---

[1] '. . . again pressing them that the cause of assembling that Parliament was for his reducing unto obedience the rebellious Scots' (*A Perfect Diurnall*).

[2] His speech, fos 17ᵛ–19ʳ; see above, pp. 164–67.

[3] See Hunt. Cal. HM 1554, pp. 255–6.

[4] In margin in MS. The speech may have been given 23 April. See below, App., Waller, p. 307. *A Perfect Diurnall* does not name the member.

[5] *A Perfect Diurnall* continues: 'In fine, The house concluded and voted, that if his Majesty would be graciously pleased to redresse these inconveniences: 1. Innovasions in Religion. 2. The invading the properties of their goods. 3. The infringing of the liberties of the persons of his Subjects, He shall then finde their willingnesse and chearfulnesse to give him supplies.'

[6] See Hunt. Cal. HM 1554, pp. 256–57.

[7] For example, Sir Francis Seymour's speech.

[8] Grimston makes the point 27 April.

H

The second reason (and of more waight) was this, That if they should now give as is desired, and the shippemonie nott been taken off they should nott discharge the Trust, that was imposed[1] in them, and the leavies of the one and the other meeting att one instant would bee undoubtedlie incompatible[2] itt being found by wofull experience [*fo 20^r*] that the greatest motive to ratifie the Judgement of shippemonie for the Kinge was one bare President, that formerlie such an aid was in leavying, a Parliament then sitting. This (is held a weake pretence for such a matter) was presented to the House to bee taken into consideration, for one of the greatest greivances ever imposed upon the subjects.[3] The House concluded and voted, That if his Majestie would bee graciouslie pleased to redresse these inconveniencies:

1. First Innovations in Religion
2. The Invading the proprieties of their goods
3. The infringing of the liberties of the persons of his subjects: Hee shall then finde their willingnesse and cheefulnesse to give him supplies.

Itt was further concluded to send to desire the lords to joyne with them in presenting their greivances to his Majestie by way of petition; (being the mildest and sweatest way) that hee would bee graciouslie pleased to graunt their just desires; if the Lords should refuse to joyne with them; then the Resolution, was to goe by way of Remonstrance or Protestation; as the House should thinke fitt. This was ill taken by those about the chaire att the first, butt they quicklie sawe their owne weaknesse, there being (att the least) on the other side foure voices against their one;[4] Secondlie itt would indeed have beene their Masterpiece if itt had beene possible to have devided the two houses. Lastlie they feared that in handling the Heads of these greivances the House would undoubtedlie fall on personall criminations.

[*fo 20^v*] The right honorable GEORGE LORD DIGBYE his speech, Wednesday April 22.[5] [*fo 30^r*][6] Hee cannot bee a good Councellor whose end is to please himselfe and will bee forward to goe a safe way for himselfe and a dangerous way for his Majestie but hee that goes a dangerous way for himselfe and a safe way for his Majestie hee itt is that loves his Majestie. The dangerous way of expressing my faithfull affections I have chosen, and I pray God bless and preserve his Majestie, whatsoever becomes of mee.

Wee are required to give present answer concerning supplies to

[1] Grimston's speech.   [2] Peard.   [3] Glyn.
[4] There is no record of an actual division of the House.
[5] MS. (fo. 20^v): 'Then insert Mr. Wallers and the Lord Digbys speeches with these titles. . . .' For Digby's speech, see below, App., Digby, p. 316. It may have been given 2 May.   [6] Foliation of the MS is irregular.

his Majestie to ingage himself in a warre, and that in a civill warre, for soe I must call itt, seeing wee are of the same religion, under the same king.

First wee are not permitted to redresse or heare of redress to cure our greivances.

Secondlie wee are nott permitted soe much as to represent to his Majestie the generall dissaffection of his subjects to this warre.

Thirdlie wee are not permitted to say wee thinke they are the same persons and nominate them, which are the originall cause of our greivances[1] and soe much that wee thinke the cutting of these incendiarie persons and firebrands of State will bee a safe, easie, and honorable cure.

Wee are nott permitted to say that warre makes the breach greater and the remedie desperate.

Wee are not permitted to say that the best justice is to fill pitts that are made to intrappe others with the bodie of them that digged them.

[fo 30ᵛ] Lett us first satisfie[2] his Majestie that wee feare the sparkes of the Scottish fire may bee catching heere att home if wee remaine unsatisfied.

Lett us then cover our owne houses with clothes wett in his Majesties grace, and unanimouslie with care indeavour to quench the Scottish fire and supplie his Majesties occasions, for if wee give supplie without redresse of our manifold greivances, wee shew our feares and nott our affections.

[*Worc. Coll. MS. 5.20*]   [*23 April 1640, House of Commons*]

[fo 20ᵛ]   **THURSDAY APRILL THE 23**[3]

The House of Commons were still in debate concerning the former matters.

[*Worc. Coll. MS. 5.20*]   [*24, 25 April 1640, House of Commons*]

[fo 20ᵛ]   **FRIDAY APRILL 24 AND SATERDAY 25.**

After longe debate in the House of Commons about greivances in Religion and other materiall inconveniences itt was resolved as

[1] Hunt. Cal., HM 1554, p. 177, adds: '*and those grievances of the Scottish nation.*' B.L., Harl. MS. 7162, fo 213ʳ, reads: 'We are not permitted to say wee thinke they are the same persons originally who have caused both our greivances and theirs. Wee are not permitted to thinke that the cutting of[*f*] of those persons will be. . . .'

[2] *cirtifie* (B.L., Harl. MS. 7162, fo 213ʳ).

[3] Most of the proceedings reported for 22 April (above, Worc. Coll. MS. fo 19ᵛ, p. 221), probably occurred 23 April. *A Perfect Diurnall* gives no entry for 23 April.

followeth. That the Select Committees shall conferre with the Upper House of these 3 generalls.[1]

1. First concerning matters of Innovation in Religion and therein, or to that end they are to consider of the present Commission now graunted to the Convocation touching making and altering of canons and other matters in the Church.

2dly. The complaints of Innovations brought in by the Byshops and Clergie.

3dly. The molesting and suppressing of manie worthy and conformable ministers because they would nott obey the byshops in their unwarrantable comands.

4thly. The receiving of Popish Tenents and printing of Popish bookes and maintaining of Popish doctrines in eminent disputations.

5thly. The restraining of conformable ministers from [*fo 21ʳ*] preaching in their owne charges.

The second generall to bee considered of is: the Proprietie of the subjects estates and therin are these greivances.

1. Patents and Monopolies.

2. Shippemonie.

3. The inlarging of the forrests beyond their due bounds.

4. Militarie charges and billetting of souldiers, etc.

5. The denying of the Execution of Justice in the Courts of Justice within Westminster Hall.

6. The frequent punishment and imprisonment of such as would nott condiscend to unlawfull Taxes and Monopolies.

The third generall is the breach of the priviledges of Parliament and the necessitie of frequent Parliaments.

[*Worc. Coll. MS. 5.20*]   [*27 April 1640, House of Commons*]

[*fo 21ʳ*]   **MUNDAY APRILL 27**[2]

The Kings sollicitor MR. HERBERT this morning made a report from the Lords [committee] to the House of Commons, the most materiall heads wherof[3] are these following: *viz.*[4] . . .

[*fo 22ʳ*] SIR BENJAMIN RUDYARD[5] said that necessitie had

[1] These proceedings occurred on 24 April. On 25 April the Commons attended a conference where they heard about the king's speech to the Lords and the Lords' resolutions concerning the supply.

[2] See also below, pp. 231–32.

[3] '. . . was to ingage the House to a present supply, That the Scots had pitcht their Tents at Dundee, etc. That the Lords would never be guilty of distrusting so good and pious a King' (*A Perfect Diurnall*).

[4] fos 21ʳ–22ʳ; for the beginning of the speech to fo 21ᵛ 'tents at Dunce, etc.' see above, p. 176; then: 'And that his Majestie upon our assisting him would lend . . .' below, pp. 231–32.

[5] Hunt. Cal., HM 1554, p. 258, dates the speech 29 April.

forced the Kinge to these things and that necessitie was the worst Councellour the Kinge could have;[1] therefore humblie besought the House to take itt into consideration how to remove soe ill a Councellour from about him. Hee said att another time.[2] That hee did acknowledge the splinter of the last Parliament stucke in their sides, butt his advice was that with great caution and tendernesse they should bee readie to plucke out the same gentlie and by degrees least the wound should fester and gangreene.

[*Worc. Coll. MS. 5.20*]   [*28 April 1640, House of Commons*]

[*fo 22ʳ*]   **TUESDAY APRILL 28**

The House of Commons continued their debate about Religion, and concerning the extrajudiciall proceedings of the High Commission Court and the unlawfullnesse of administering the oath *ex officio*.

Concerning which Sr John Elliott spake this following speech. [*fo 22ᵛ*] SIR JOHN ELLIOTT his speech in the House of Commons, April 28, 1640.[3]

Mr. Speaker, I assure my selfe wee are heere mett together both to discover and reforme (as much as in us lies) all[4] abuses of this Church and Comon wealth manie and great ones have beene spoken against found[5] contrarie to all law and some established by new Lawes.

The wolfe having putt on the lions skin and rapine presumes to passe undiscovered under the roabe of Justice: Butt I shall not neede to light a candle to search out that which alreadie the sunne hath made manifest. That, That I shall speake [of] hath nott yett beene spoken against, butt if I shall speake that which seemes to bee against law, I shall[6] crave pardon of this House, since if itt bee law itt is *summum Jus* [or *rather summa Juristia*]; Law without Conscience. That, that I shall speake against is the oath *ex officio*; as itt is acknowledged by themselves that administer this oath, that itt is unjustlie done to tender itt to anie man, unlesse there bee a publicke fame or particuler presentment of Articles[7] testified

---

[1] *A Perfect Diurnall* ends its entry for the day here.
[2] 16 April.
[3] John Eliot (St. Germans), son of the famous Sir John Eliot. See below, App., Eliot, pp. 313–34. The speech may have been given 29 April.
[4] Hunt. Cal., HM 1554, p. 173, omits: all.
[5] *some* (Hunt. Cal., HM 1554, p. 173; *CSP 1640*, p. 36).
[6] . . . *humbly* . . . (Hunt. Cal., HM 1554, p. 173; *CSP 1640*, p. 37); . . . *honourable* House (B.L., Add. MS. 6411, fo 63ʳ).
[7] 'articles or *accusations* against him *who is to have the oath*' (B.L., Sloane MS. 1200, fo 33ʳ).

against him. I make noe Question butt the practice of this confest, this Injustice will bee found common[1] amongst them, and I hope itt shall bee severelie censured, since unjust proceedings upon unjust grounds are double Injustices; I shall therefore leave that as a cleere Case and examine the first[2] grounds.

First fame (they say) is a just cause for them to take Cognizance of a matter to proceed against itt.

[*fo 23ʳ*] Fame wee knowe may arise upon verie small and groundlesse suspitions, by secrett whisperings, creeping att the first butt itt quicklie getts wings and as the Poett saith; *Crescit eundo*.[3] This is the manner of all fame and if this bee fame, their Court shall never want worke, as longe as a Promooter hath an ill tongue, or a knave can slander an honest man. Therefore I thinke fame noe good ground to proceede upon; if fame bee just, what should[4] men say. Some man will justifie itt, if noe man will testifie itt, then itt is false. There shall noe accusation stande butt[5] under the mouth of two or three wittnesses. Wittnesses of Presentment are a just ground of proceeding in all Courts, and upon all causes. Butt neither wittnesse nor Presentment can bee a just ground of the oath *ex officio*. For if the partie accused bee examined noe further then is testified, then the oath *ex officio* is superfluous. If hee bee examined further or upon other matter then is testified, then a man is made to betray himselfe which is unjust.

Mr. Speaker Such is the mercie of our Common lawes, that murtherers and poysoners are nott examined upon the wracke, but the Civill law uppon everie occasion[6] wracks the Conscience.

Mr. Speaker these are the lime twigges that catcht the poore Martyrs in Queene Maries dayes, and in our dayes I beleeve itt will appeare some good men are fallne into this snare. If the foundations fall,[7] what shall the righteous doe. If the infirmities of good men shall ruine them, who shall stand? I desire that evill men may suffer. I desire the law may punish, nott make, offenders, I desire that our words and actions, may bee subject to the lawes I would have thoughtes free.

---

[1] *very frequent* (B.L., Sloane MS. 1200, fo 33ᵛ).
[2] *best* (Hunt. Cal., HM 1554, p. 173; B.L., Add. MS. 6411, fo 63ᵛ).
[3] '. . . *it increaseth in the carriage*. Therefore I *hold* fame no *good ground*' (B.L., Sloane MS. 1200, fo 33ᵛ, thus condensing the text).
[4] 'what *most* men say, *certainely* some *men* will testifie' (Hunt. Cal., HM 1554, pp. 173–74; B.L., Add. MS. 6411, fo 64ʳ, follows, but omits: certainely; *CSP 1640*, p. 37, follows, but gives *speak* instead of 'say.'
[5] B.L., Add. MS. 6411, fo 64ʳ, omits: butt.
[6] *accusation* (Hunt. Cal., HM 1554, p. 174).
[7] *faile* (Hunt. Cal., HM 1554, p. 174).

[Worc. Coll. MS. 5.20]   *[29 April 1640, House of Commons]*

[fo 23ᵛ]   **WEDNESDAY APRILL 29**[1]

The Lords should have sent some Message to the House of Commons according to appointment,[2] butt after longe expectation and none coming; when the Kings Councell came into the House, the House of Commons fell upon religion.[3]

[Worc. Coll. MS. 5.20]   *[30 April 1640, House of Commons]*

[fo 23ᵛ]   **THURSDAY APRILL 30**[4]

They fell this day upon shippe monie and impeachment of Trade. The Heads whereof are nott yett fullie prepared, whereupon they desired a Conference with the Lords, the next day[5] being Friday which was accordinglie accomplished.

Itt is generallie doubted that they will shortlie rise without doing anie thinge, yea I heard from a good hand that the Kinge hath beene stronglie importuned to dissolve this Parliament butt as yett denies itt.

[Worc. Coll. MS. 5.20]   *[1 May 1640, House of Commons]*

[fo 23ᵛ]   **FRIDAY MAY THE FIRST**

There was a Conference betweene both Houses att which Mr. Pymme delivered[6] this insuing speech [to the Lords] in behalf of the House of Commons.

MR. PYMME his speech.[7] . . .

[Worc. Coll. MS. 5.20]   *[2 May 1640, House of Commons]*

[fo 25ʳ]   **SATERDAY MAY 2**

The House fell in debate of divers greivances particuler and generall over the whole kingedome; Sir John Wray made this following speech declaring the greivances of the Countie of Lincolne.

---

[1] See Hunt. Cal. HM 1554, pp. 258–9.
[2] Perhaps as a result of the conference 28 April. *A Perfect Diurnall*: 'The Lords not sending to the Commons according to appointment; they fell in debate about Religion.'
[3] The Heads concerning religion for the conference were reported.
[4] See Hunt. Cal. HM 1554, p. 259.
[5] *A Perfect Diurnall* ends its entry for the day here.
[6] '. . . a very Patheticall Speech' (*A Perfect Diurnall*).
[7] fos 23ᵛ–25ʳ, see above, pp. 182–84.

SIR JOHN WRAYES speech.[1] Mr. Speaker, Itt is granted by law, that a Justice of peace may present[2] a nusance or other misdemeanour that offers itt selfe to his viewe.[3] Then I hope (Mr. Speaker) itt will bee lawfull for mee as a member of this House and knight of the shire for the Countie of Lincolne, to tender unto this House, such greivances as to my knowledge have beene latelie obtayned[4] uppon our Countie and they are these: First,

1. Concerning our goods, wherin wee have noe proprietie if they may bee converted to anie other use by the demand of shippemonie.[5]

2. 2dly wee stand nott ensured of our *Terra firma*, for the fennedrayners have entred our lands, and nott onlie made wast of them, butt alsoe have disseised us of part of our soyle and freehold.[6]

3. Thirdlie, Concerning our Armes; I meane them of our Traine bands, they are taken from us butt I knowe nott by what warrant, soe that our goods, and lands (if wee have anie) together with our lives are lost for the present, and wee left without defence to [*fo 25ᵛ*] the Romish invasion if anie such should arise.

These thinges to some may seeme butt Molehills, butt trulie weighed they are sandie[7] Mountaines, and worthy to bee taken into consideration, and to receive redresse from this House.

[*Worc. Coll. MS. 5.20*]   [*4 May 1640, House of Commons*]

[*fo 25ᵛ*]   **MUNDAY MAY 4**[8]

The House were in a great and solemne debate to have these greivances following to bee redressed before the supply were given to his Majestie and they desired the Lords to joyne with them in presenting these Heads of greivances to his Majestie which the Lords denied except them heerafter named.[9]

Greivances voted and discussed in the House of Commons, comprehended under these 3 generall heads.[10] . . .

[*fo 26ʳ*] All which being voted by the House, itt was thought fitt a Conference should bee held [*fo 26ᵛ*] with the Lords to joyne with the House of Commons in proposing a way for the redresse of these

---

[1] See below, App., Wray, p. 306.
[2] *reforme* (B.L., Add. MS. 6411, fo 34ᵛ).
[3] '. . . *and that it should find redress then*' (B.L., Add. MS. 6411, fo 34ᵛ).
[4] have been *obtruded* (Hunt. Cal., HM 1554, p. 169).
[5] . . . *without lawe* (Hunt. Cal., HM 1554, p. 169).
[6] See S.P. 16/450/90; S.P. 16/450/97, letters fearing complaints against fendrainers. Wray presented a petition concerning them in November 1640 (Notestein, *D'Ewes*, p. 19).
[7] *found* (Hunt. Cal., HM 1554, p. 169).
[8] See Hunt. Cal. HM 1554, pp. 259–62.
[9] This is a confused account of the proceedings of 24 April.
[10] fos 25ᵛ–26ʳ, see *C.J.*, ii, p. 11.

greivances and that a speciall committee should bee named to prepare those things with due proofes for the presenting of them to the
Lords.

Which was done accordinglie the most part [of the Lords] dissented from the votes of the House of Commons.

The names of the Lords who voted with the House of Commons
are these:[1] Southampton, Bedford, Essex, Hartford, Bullinbrooke,
Nottingham, Bath, Ruttland, Clare, Lincolne, Warwicke, Say,
Savile, Dunsmore, Paulett, Lovelace, Stanhopp, Mountague,
Mandevile, North, Pagett, Wharton, Howard, Brooke, Roberts.

Other greivances were proposed to the House butt nott voted,
which were these.[2] . . .

[*Worc. Coll. MS. 5.20*]   [*5 May 1640, House of Commons*]

[*fo 27ʳ*]   **TUESDAY THE 5TH OF MAY**

His Majestie determining to dissolve the Parliament that day
came unto the Lords House (the House of Commons being present)
where hee spake this following speech.

His Majesties speech at the dissolving of the Parliament. May 5
1640.[3] . . .

**A JOURNALL OF SUCH PASSAGES OF MOMENT AS
HAPPENED IN PARLIAMENT 16 *CAROLI* 1640[4]**

[*Hunt. Cal. HM 1554*]   [*15 April 1640, House of Commons*]

[*p 252*]   **WEDNESDAY THE FIFTEENTH OF APRILL**

Sergeant Glanvill[5] was presented and chosen Speaker for the
House of Commons. The severall heads hee recommended to be
taken into consideration were these: 1. Religion; 2. Monarchicall
government; 3. Mercy; 4. Justice; 5. Resolution; 6. Union and
closed upp all with this *Si sumus inseparabiles, sumus insuperabiles.*

---

1 Francis Russell, 4th earl of Bedford; Robert Devereux, 3rd earl of Essex;
Oliver St. John, 1st earl of Bolingbroke; Charles Howard, 2nd earl of Nottingham; Henry Bourchier, 5th earl of Bath; Theophilus Howard, 4th earl of
Lincoln; Charles, Baron Paulet; John, 2nd Baron Lovelace; William, 5th Baron
Paget; John, 2nd Baron Robartes. Probably the Lords who dissented from the
resolutions of 24 April; see also S.P. 16/451/39, the Lords who voted 'in the
question . . . against the King.' The list in S.P. 16/451/39 adds Deinecourt
and substitutes Willoughby of Parham for Stanhope.
2 fo 26ᵛ, see *C.J.*, ii, p. 12.   3 fos 27ʳ–27ᵛ, see above, pp. 197–98.
4 Title supplied from Yale Law Library, Glanville MS., p. 1.
5 See below, App., Glanville (15 April), p. 294.
н*

The Lo: Keeper[1] in his speech runs over all the forementioned heads and as the Speaker had done, insisted longest upon the last, which was best,[2] union and craved leave to conclude with a borrowed saying but a good[3] one, *Si collidamur frangimur.*

[*Hunt. Cal. HM 1554*]   [*16-18 April 1640, House of Commons*]

[*pp. 252–3*] THURSDAY 16, FRIDAY 17, SATERDAY 18 APRILL.[4] . . .

[*Hunt. Cal. HM 1554*]   [*20 April 1640, House of Commons*]

[*pp. 253–4*]   MONDAY THE 20TH APRILL[5]

[*Hunt. Cal., HM 1554*]   [*21 April 1640, House of Commons*]

[*p. 254*]   TEWSDAY [*21*] OF APRILL

The same day they received a message from his Majestie That they and the Lords should give him a meeting that after noone in the banquetting howse where at their comeing the Lord Keeper[6] made a speach declareing the Kings goodnes in calling a parliament soe much and soe long desired, That parliaments were budds of reconciliacion[7] where Kings understood the grevances of their subjects and redressed them, and subjects gave unto their soveraignes Ayde and supply etc. further intimating that the shipmoney being now in leavying his majesties desire was that it might bee paid for the present, and if they would devise any other way howe hee might be supplyed for the mainetenance of his honor and the safetie of the kingdome hee would willingly declare the enforcement thereof which hee never intended should be drawne into such a way as to be made an Annuall Revenue. And by degrees hee proceeded to tell us what great charge his majestie was at with these forces of horse and foote amounting to 100000*li*[8] a moneth at the least That the Scotts were ready to invade the kingdome and his Majesty destitute of monies and soe [*p. 255*] desired that his Majestie might have a present and speedy supply and that they should take it into con-

---

[1] See below, App., L.K., (15 April), p. 294.
[2] Glanville MS., p. 1, omits: best.
[3] *true* (Glanville MS., p. 1).
[4] pp. 252–53, see above Worc. Coll. MS. fos 15–15ᵛ, 17, pp. 212–13, 219.
[5] pp. 253–54, see above Worc. Coll. MS. fos 17–17ᵛ, p. 220.
[6] See below, App., L.K. (21 April), p. 303.
[7] Harvard MS., fo 25, *Cf.* Rudyerd, above, p. 139.
[8] 160,000*li* (Glanville MS., p. 2).

sideration in the first place how to accomodate the same, for that it would admitt of noe delay in respect of the instant dainger of subverting and overthroweing the whole designe, wherein there was expended allready at least 300,000^{li} That they might withall security and confidence repose trust in his majesties word and promisse to have freedome and leave to goe on in their just grevances and not onely to present them to him; but to receive such full satisfaction in redresse thereof as should give every good subject great cause to rejoyce. That this trust would prove an indissolubility betweene his Majestie and them and would never be forgotten, his Majestie scorning in matter of trust to be faileing in any part of his royall promisse. Still pressing that hee might be trusted first, which hee said would give unto him as much content as the guift itselfe. The speach ended his Majestie in fewe words[1] told them That hee expected their speaker should very speediely give him an accompt of theire proceedings therein.

[**Hunt. Cal., HM 1554**]   [**22 April 1640, House of Commons**]

[*pp.* 255–7]   **WEDNESDAY 22 APRILL.**[2] . . .

[**Hunt. Cal., HM 1554**]   [**27 April 1640, House of Commons**]

[*p257*]   **MONDAY 27 APRILL**

MR. HARBERT,[3] the Kings sollicitor that morning made a report from the Lords to the House of Commons, The most materiall heads whereof weere these followeing: That his Majestie made unto them soe many gratious expressions that the harts of the whole Howse weere thereby inclyned, That hee had intimated unto them That hee should take a delay for a denyall [*p. 258*] and that the least retardation would utterly frustrate his designe. Hee told them that they had the word of a King and a gent, for redresse of their grevances and that his honor was as deere unto him as his life.

That seeing there must be a trust and that wee must trust him in the future, Then as well in civilitie as good manners that trust ought to be in him in the first place, which if wee should doe, then hee[4] would lend a gratious and princely eare to our grevances and grant as much as wee could in justice aske and for establishment of Religion, hee will gratiously listen to that also. Hee further reported

---

[1] Glanville MS., p. 2, omits: in fewe words.
[2] pp. 255–57, see above, Worc. Coll. MS., fos 19^v–20. p.221.
[3] See below, App., Herbert, p. 310.
[4] Worc. Coll. MS. 5.20, fo 21^v, begins to follow this version here.

that the Lords thereupon[1] declared, they would never be guilty of distrusting soe good and pious a King, And the obligation hee had given was the greatest tye they could desire and thereupon had voated that the ayde should be first taken into consideration and then they would willingly and cheerefully joyne with the House of Commons in all the rest.

[*Hunt. Cal., HM 1554*]   [*29 April, 1640, House of Commons*]

[*pp. 258-9*]   WEDNESDAY 29 APRILL.[2] . . .

[*Hunt. Cal., HM 1554*]   [*30 April 1640, House of Commons*]

[*pp. 259-62*]   THURSDAY 30 APRILL.[3] . . .

[1] '. . . (*except some fewe hereafter mentioned*) . . .' (Worc. Coll. MS. 5.20, fo 22r).
[2] pp. 258-59, see above, Worc. Coll. fos 22r-23v, pp. 225-27.
[3] pp. 259-62, see above, Worc. Coll. fos 20v-21, 23, pp. 223-24, 227.

TEXTS: LORDS AND COMMONS

[*B.L., Harl. MS. 4931*]   [*13 April 1640, Lords and Commons*]

PARLIAMENTARY PROCEEDINGS, APRIL 13, 1640

[*fo 47ʳ*]   APR[*IL*] 13

Ye King rode in his parliamentary pompe, and yn at Parliament made a speach, showing his need of money, bec[*ause*] against ye Scotts, and mentioned my Lord of Lowden's lettre, which after ye King, my Lord Keep read.[1]

[*B.L., Harl. MS. 4931*]   [*14 April 1640, House of Commons*]

[*fo 47ʳ*]   APR[*IL*] 14

The Parliament adjourned.

[*B.L., Harl. MS. 4931*]   [*16 April 1640, House of Commons*]

[*fo 47ʳ*]   APR[*IL 16*][2]

LOWER HOUSE

MR. GRIMSTONE[3] of Essex's speach, wherin he principally taxed the injustice of ye judges, and also run over all the abuses in Church and Commonwealth.

My Lord Lowdens letter read, and many aggravations of it.

UPPER HOUSE

Matters of formality.

[*B.L., Harl. MS. 4931*]   [*16 April 1640, House of Commons*]

[*fo 47ʳ*]   APR[*IL*] 16

LOWER HOUSE

SR FRANCIS SEAMER[4] speach, shewing ye corruption of ye cleargy, ye non-resedens, neither preach, nor suffer ye people to goe else where; yt we know not of what religion we are of. Yt Puritans

---

[1] See below, App. (13 April), p. 293.
[2] MS.: *15*; the Speaker was presented 15 April.
[3] See below, App., Grimston, p. 296.
[4] See below, App., Seymour, p. 297.

(ye only true subjects of ye land, and servants of God) are now accounted rebells, etc.

SR BENJAMIN RYDYER[1] liked well yt what y spoke but pleaded yt they would goe with a moderation.

SR WM MASHAM,[2] motioned yt ye countees might have freedome in yr elections of Burgesses, and Lords or Justices not intermeddle in it.

SR ROBT HARLOWES[3] speach.

MR GLANVILL[4] Speaker, sayd yt ye K can wrong no man if he rules not by lawes, its the officers fault.

UPPER HOUSE

THE ARCHBP[5] desired an adjourning of ye House till Saturday, bec[ause] y shold be imployed in ye Convocation on ye next day, which was friday. My LORD SAY answeared, yt its not fitt ye whole house shold waite upon ym, and yt y could enact this without ye bishops; yn A. BP. answeared, That y desired yt not as of right, but of courtesy. My LORD KEEP yn joyned with ym bec[ause] of his illness, yt he was not able to supply the service of ye house. Others then assented to him. At last my LORD BROOKE sayd, Let it be yn entred, yt ye House is adjourned not bec[ause] ye Bishops cannot be here, but bec[ause] my Lord Keep is not well; and yt passed.

[*B.L., Harl. MS. 4931*]   [*17 April 1640, Lords and Commons*]

[*fo 47ʳ*]   APR[IL] 17

LOWER HOUSE

MR. PIM[6] layed open all ye grievances etc. of Church and Commonwealth, in a speech of nere two hours long; ye best feared it wold scarse have taken bec[ause] he was so plaine, but at ye end of it all cried out, A good motion.

This day ye petitions read of Midd[l]esex, Suffolke, Northamptonshire, which petitions [?]stunned ye royalists more yn any thing, to see county joyne together against ye new, and illegall courses; of which petitions some before hand sayd, yt they wr ye Scottish Coven[an]t wanting only hands.

MR. PIM[7] ran on thse 3 heads, The breach of ye priviledges of ye house, Grievances in Commonwealth, Innovations in religion. He

---

[1] See below, App., Rudyerd, p. 296.
[2] M.P. for Colchester.   [3] Harley.
[4] Probably his speech of 15 April (below, App. (15 April), p. 294).
[5] Laud.   [6] See below, App., Pym, p. 299.
[7] The speech noted above.

spoke of ye corruptions of Judges, Star-Chamber, Councell table, the King.

MR. VASSALL cried to have all ye patentees out of ye howse.

Another said, yt hanging was too good for ym.

SR NICHOLAS CRISPE[1] spake, and y bid silence, till hee had right to be [?heard].

UPPER HOUSE

The house adjourned.

The Bishops this day went to ye Convocation and [the Archbishop] made a grave speech, and told ym yt he was glad of yt day, for hee had ye Kings broad seale to confirme what [the]y yr should enact.

[B.L., Harl. MS. 4931]   **[18 April 1640, Lords and Commons]**

[fo 47^r]   **APRIL 18**

LOWER HOUSE

The petitions read of Essex, Hartfordshire, Northampton towne and Norwich. The House handles ye matter of the priviledges, and who broke ye priviledges of ye House in the last parliament, and what men suffered in it.

UPPER HOUSE

Bishop Mannering is questioned, who ye last parliament was made uncapable of ecclesiastical preferment, and yet presently after was made a Bp.

[B.L., Harl. MS. 4931]   **[20 April 1640, Lords and Commons]**

[fo 47^v]   **APRIL 20**

LOWER HOUSE

Matters ecclesiastical treated on.[2]

Also whether yt ye Speaker of ye House hath power to pronounce ye Kings breaking up of ye parliament, unles yt ye House doth consent to it.

UPPER HOUSE

Their questioning still of Mannering, and yr being like to confound him.

A question, whether ye Bps make a distinct state in ye kingdome, ye affirme, ye House deny, ye house say yr is The King, The Barons,

---

[1] M.P. for Winchelsea.   [2] Debate of 21 April.

The Commons; ye bps yn wold make 4 states, or exclude the King.

[B.L., Harl. MS. 4931]   **[21 April 1640, Lords and Commons]**

[fo 47ᵛ]   APR[IL] 21

LOWER HOUSE

The businesse of Shippmoney, which formerly only mentioned, now seriously treated of.

The patent for ye Convocation, from ye King, is questioned by ye Parliament.

MR. PIM[1] sayd, yt the Convocations assent is nothing without ye Parliaments consent; ye House commands ye Patent to be brought to ym, yt so they may examine it.

UPPER HOUSE

BP HALL of Exeter spoke against one of ye Lords, (if I mistake not it was my Ld Say) who was appointed one of ye Committees in a businesse, ye BP said, yt ye Lord savoured of A Scottish Covenanter, for which speach ye Bp was made openly before all ye House to goe downe to ye Barre, who yr said, If I have offended I cry pardon; they all cried out, No Ifs, whereupon hee begged pardon positively.

[B.L., Harl. MS. 4931]   **[22 April 1640, Lords and Commons]**

[fo 47ᵛ]   APR[IL] 22

LOWER HOUSE

The Countie petitions examined.

A Committee chosen for ye examining of Mr. Smarts businesse of Durham, and y sett about it.[2]

The House required ye day after to give in yr answeare [to morrow] to ye K, what y will do for him.[3]

UPPER HOUSE

MR. DELL ye Archbishop of Yorkes[4] secretary speaking somewhat more yn came to his share was like to have beene turned out of ye house. This was in ye Lower house.

This day ye King convents ye lower house to propound his mind to them about moneyes.[5]

Adjourned in ye Afternoone.

[1] Debate of 22 April.   [2] See below, Petition, Smart, p. 280.
[3] C.J., ii, p. 9.   [4] Canterbury.
[5] The Lord Keeper spoke to both Lords and Commons at the Banqueting House, 21 April (see below, App. (21 April), p. 303).

[B.L., Harl. MS. 4931]   **[23 April 1640, Lords and Commons]**

[fo 47ᵛ]   APRIL 23

LOWER HOUSE

This day ye House gave in yr answeare to ye King about monies, *sc.* yt yr could be no moneyes given without yr w[e]r[e] first a reformation granted of grievances; and also yt still the liberties of ye House, and Kingdome w[e]r[e] cleared, y knew not whether ye had any th[ing] to give or noe, *sc.* y doubted of y propriety of yr goods.[1] This day A Fast agreed on for Saturday sennett Dr. Holseworth, and Mr. Marshall to preach, and Dr. Brownrigg ye day after at ye sacrament, and Sr Tho Barington and Sr Wm Masham Churchwardens at it.[2] And a generall fast in Whitsun weeke. Windebanke named one Shepeheard[3] to preach one of ye sermons at ye Fast, others denied, for some said, yt one Sheepheard ye last Parliament had said, yt y enacted many lawes against Papists, but not a jot of one against Puritans.

Mr. Pim getts ye reputation to bee as wise as Solom[on].[4]

UPPER HOUSE

The Upper House, and lower house joyne together in one committee for ye redressing ye grievances of ye kingdome.[5]

[B.L., Harl. MS. 4931]   **[24 April 1640, Lords and Commons]**

[fo 47ᵛ]   APRIL 24

LOWER HOUSE

Its voted in the Lower, whether first subsidies, and yn a reformation, and ye King was extremely cut 400 voices against him, and but 30 for him.[6]

UPPER HOUSE

Feare of breaking up ye Parliament, for ye king sends to ye lower house for money saying yt yt is ye thing yt [?] he stands most in need of [fo 48ʳ] yt he can stay noe longer; yn he propounds it to ye

---

[1] No formal answer was given to the king (*C.J.*, ii, p. 9).
[2] Stephen Marshall, leading preacher for the Long Parliament; Ralph Brownrig, bishop of Exeter, 1641; Sir Thomas Barrington (Essex).
[3] We have been unable to identify Shepeheard.
[4] Perhaps a reference to his speech at the conference 28 April (below, Harl. MS. 4931, fos 48–48ᵛ, p. 239).
[5] No conference was held.
[6] *C.J.* gives no evidence of this. For the figures to be accurate virtually all M.P.s would have to have been present.

upper house, whether yt the Parliament shold first give ye K subsidies, and stand to his courtesy for a reformation, or whether to stand upon it first to have reformation and yn subsidies; after ye voting of it, it is carried for ye King by above 20 voices.

[B.L., Harl. MS. 4931]   **[25 April 1640, Lords and Commons]**

[fo 48ʳ]   **APR[IL] 25**

LOWER HOUSE

The House concludes yt ye act of ye last day of ye former [parliament][1] was a breach of priviledge, concerning ye breaking up the parliament in such a manner.[2]

UPPER HOUSE

The King againe send the Lord Keeper to ye Lower House, telling ym, what ye upper house had yielded to, sc. to give moneyes, for ye warr (as was said was by ye Scotts allready begun). A certaine English [officer] lost a troope (as some report) which was thought to be taken by a Scott; herupon ye lower house is called to a conference with ye upper house, in which conference my Lord Keeper spake all.[3]

[B.L., Harl. MS. 4931]   **[27 April 1640, Lords and Commons]**

[fo 48ʳ]   **APRIL 27**

LOWER HOUSE

The Lower House chooseth a committee to treate with ye upper house to know by what right they shold give subsidies, sc. ye grant of ym, without ye consent of ye lower House, y affirming yt what was done by ym [the Lords] was but a personall act, but what was don by ymselves sc. ye lower house, yt was a publique act, and reputed ye act of ye kingdome.

This day was presented to ye House all ye popish pictures, which had beene brought hither to be sold out of popish places, as Italy etc, and also the bible yt is printed with ye severall acts of the story in ye new testament, and related yt hundreds of every kind of those were here to be sold. This presented by Mr. Estwicke.[4]

---

[1] MS.: priviledge.
[2] Debate of 20 April.
[3] The Lord Keeper spoke for the House of Lords, not for the king (see below, App., L.K. (25 April), p. 310).
[4] There is no record of a Mr. Estwicke in the Parliament. The business may be that in orders for committees, 29 April (C.J., ii, p. 15).

The lower house sayd yt all supplies of money shold begin with ye lower house.

The house began to have thought of given the King money with a declaration yt it was not against ye Scotts, etc. but MR. PIM said yt y need to be carefull in yt point, bec[*ause*] yt if it w[*e*]r[*e*] given who shold bind to the keeping of ye conditions of ye gift.[1]

UPPER HOUSE

The House begins to proceed to censure Mannering, but ye K sent word[2] yt y shold desist, or not censure him so farr as to make him uncapable of his Bishoprick.

The ARCHBISHOP affirmed, yt if ye Parliament did deprive a man of his bishopricke yt it was in the kings power to remitt yt censure; some said yt he pleaded his owne case.

My LORD SAY spoke nobly for ye kingdome, but he had many adversaries; he answeared ye Lord Keep, ye Archbishop etc, but none was found a match for him but the Deputy of Ireland.[3]

[B.L., Harl. MS. 4931]   **[28 April 1640, Lords and Commons]**

[*fo 48ʳ*]   **APR[IL] 28**

UPPER HOUSE

The Lower House choose a man to make a speech to ye Upper House in ye painted chamber, concerning the priviledges of ye Howse, and yt no supplyes could be given unless yt y w[*e*]r[*e*] first consented to by ye lower house, yt ye lower house had to determine first about ye priviledges of ye House, The propriety of goods, and the power of reformation. To make this speech was first put upon Mr. St. John, and he refused it bec[*ause*] it was ye first time yt he was of yt house; y yn put it to Mr. Pim, and a halfe an houres [*fo 48ᵛ*] warning he made ye speach, brought in all ye particulars yt w[*e*]r[*e*] by ye House given him, in a side in folio, make ye preface, and a conclusion, all this to be don speechwise in so Honourable assembly, he did it well to admiration. Secretary Windebanke gave him many thanks for it, and said yt the House could not sufficiently reward him for what he had done, unles yt y did enter it in record ye act yt he had done.[4]

---

[1] Perhaps the debate of Jones and Pym, 23 April.
[2] 28 April.
[3] See debates of 24 and 29 April.
[4] *C.J.*, ii, p. 15, and below, App., Pym (28 April), p. 312. Rossingham says the motion of thanks came from 'both the Secretaries' (B.L., Add. MS. 11045, fo 114ʳ).

LOWER HOUSE

The Lower House setts upon grievances.

LITTLETON (a privy counsellour) said, ye papists did much increase in the land, and yt yr w[e]r[e] many nunneryes and monasteries privily among us, and shewed how yt many thousands followed masses daily. VANE (ye controller of ye Ks house) seconded him; but this did not take in the House, for this by ym was laid as a mere plot to see if y could divide the House, to make some of ym to fall one way, and some another; and Littletons [?]ye motion (though it did not take) made some of ye Ks side to say, yt y w[e]r[e] falne upon the Queene.

[*B.M., Harl. MS. 4931*]   [*29 April 1640, Lords and Commons*]

[*fo 48ᵛ*]   APR[*IL*] 29

UPPER HOUSE

The House sitts close till 1 a clocke, when was voted, whether yt ye Upper House had wronged ye lower house or no in yr priviledges, as y by Mr. Pim ye day before charged on the Upper House;[1] by voting it was carried yt by such a charge ye Lower House had wronged the Upper House, and y yms[*elves*] could justify what y had done; this like to make a jarre in ye parliament betweene the Houses; ye Upper House must stand upon yr Honour, the lower house must stand upon Right on yr side; and this like to breake ye parliament; in the upper house but few cordiall for ye commonweale, y yt doe speake speake so cautelously as doth not become a free commonweale. On ye Ks side are 26 Bishops, 30 lords of ye Councell, close save [?], 18 Lords wherof many Popish, absent, who make some of ye Kings counsell yr proxyes; besides many other Lords who professe (in ye up[*per*] House) yt y come to doe those thi[*ngs*] yt are against yr conscience, as Carlisle etc.[2] They in ye Ypper House fully fitted for slavery.

LOWER HOUSE

The Lower House examine about ye suspending ministers about ye booke of ye sabbath, and about Altars and Grievances.

LITTLETON makes a speech for ye K and tells what urgent occasions ye K had for money, yt he could not stay a day longer without a supply; to which answeared

SR FRANCIS SEAMER,[3] yt in a good councell yn had ye K yt

---

[1] See below, App., Pym (28 April), p. 312.
[2] Jas. Hay, 2nd earl of Carlisle. The bishop of Carlisle was not present.
[3] Perhaps on 23 April.

had brought him to these extremities by yr councell; and SR
HARBOTTLE GRIMSTONS[1] answeare was this, Then ye King
might have sent for us sooner.

[B.L., Harl. MS. 4931]   *[30 April 1640, Lords and Commons]*

[fo 48ᵛ]   **APR[IL] 30**

UPPER HOUSE

The Upper House still stands to its Justification of its priviledges,
and of what y had don. The House yields not to ye motion of having
May ye 2d a Fast for ye Parliament which before the Lower House
had appointed, and ye up[per] h[ou]se holding off, saying yt y had
other matters to thinke of.

LOWER HOUSE

The House prepares to ripen grievances to present the full state
of thi[ngs] in ye Kingdome to ye K. The House treates about shippmoney. Ye K sent to ye House to desire yt before y determined any
th[ing] concerning shipp-money, yt his councell might pleade for
him yr about it; y said, yt yt was against ye priviledges of the house;
yet at last y to gratify ye K did promise to heare his councell
pleading and this was to be done May 4th. The House to save yr
priviledges, w[he]n y yielded in this to the K; y protest against it,
yt so it might not be a president for future time; and to save ye
case [?], y resolve, yt w[he]n ye Ks councell shold pleade, yt for yt
time y will turne ye whole House into a grand Committee, which
differrs from ye House in this in yt yn ye House commands ye
Speaker out of his chaire, [and choose one of yr owne] and also it yn
lawfull for any to reply upon any occasion as oft as he will.

[B.L., Harl. MS. 4931]   *[1 May 1640, Lords and Commons]*

[fo 48ᵛ]   **MAY 1**

UPPER HOUSE

The Upper House conferrs with ye Lower in ye painted chamber,
where my Lord Keeper[2] speakes only, and tells ym, yt ye Upper
house did not vote subsidies as intending yt ye lower House w[e]r[e]
tied to what y did, or yt yr voting of subsidies wold make it legall
without ye consent of ye Lower House, but y did it only to show yr
forwardnes to gratify ye K. As for moneyes he said, at another time

1 Perhaps on 27 April.
2 See below, App., L.K. (1 May), p. 314.

yr grievances might first be remedied, and yn subsidies given, but at this time most fitt subsidies first.

LOWER HOUSE

The Lower House upon Grievances, MR. PIM makes a speech telling them how yt some cleargy men in yr sermons did intrench on ye liberties of ye House; and speakes against ym, as Dr. Beale for one, which he was able to prove; yn it was voted whither to send for him or no, it was carried yt he shold be sent for, and yt by private letter, subscribed by ye Speaker (bec[*ause*] he was ye Ks chaplaine, and y wold not justly injure ye K) he yn sent for to answeare against next thursday to allegations.

[B.L., Harl. MS. 4931]   [*2 May 1640, Lords and Commons*]

[*fo 49ʳ*]   MAY 2

UPPER HOUSE

This day yr shold have beene a Fast for ye 2 Houses of Parliament, it was granted by ye lower house for this day, but ye Upper House never did yield.. Yrfore y sate in Parliament, and ye Lower House sate all day close, whereupon some of ye Upper House said, yt although a Fast wr not granted, yet ye lower house was resolved to fast (bec[*ause*] they sate so long)[1] and yt y wold on ye day following (being ye Lords day, and Dr. Brownrigg shold have preached at ye sacrament, which also was putt off) y wold pray, and yt on Munday y wold give ye King his answeare.

The DEPUTY said, yt he wondred ye Parliament wold stand about moneyes, seeing yt Ireland had declared yms[*elves*] for ye K too, and ye Ks urgent occasions, And yt if y did not yeild presently yt ye K was resolved to breake up ye parliament. The EARLE OF BRISTOLL answeares, That yn ye K wold have but a disjoynted Kingdome; Ye DEPUTY answeares,[2] you find fault with his Majesties government he answeares againe, words are as y ar interpreted [?]

The K sends a message to the House about a supply, which message you have in a transcript.

LOWER HOUSE

The K sends to ye House to grant him moneyes without any delay, and yt he wold have 12 subsidies. Ye House sitts close all ye day debating what to doe. *The King had desired yt his Councell might pleade for him before ye House about ye shipmoney.*

[1] See below, B.L. Harl. MS., 4931, fo 49 (Commons), p. 242.
[2] Perhaps the debate of 30 April.

But K offerred yt if ye House wold give him 12 subsidies for his [present] necessity yt yn he wold take off ye shipp-money.

[B.L., Harl. MS. 4931]   **[4 May 1640, Lords and Commons]**

[fo 49ʳ]   **MAY 4**

UPPER HOUSE

The K sends a 2d message to the House, more particular yn the former, a transcript of which is in etc.[1]

LOWER HOUSE

The House became dubious not knowing what to doe about ye giving subsidies, loth y wr to yield and yet loth to have ye House dissolved, but y wr discovered by some among yms[elve]s: to be so farr yielding, yt y wr not willing to putt it to vote, fearing least yt it might be carried for ye K.

The Ks councell shold have this day pleaded about ye shipp-money, but yt designe was altered upon ye present urgent occasion of money.

[Committee]

The Speaker makes a speech to ye House to desire ym for a supply to the K, in which speech he spoke most bitterly against ye shipp-money, That it was a senseless judgment yt was given by ye judges and yt all yr arguments might easily have beene answeared. Let not yr judgment stand upon record, yt after ages shold see ye folly of or times etc, with which speech he so moved ye House, yt if ye Ks supply had beene voted, he had carried it.

[B.L., Harl. MS. 4931]   **[5 May 1640, Lords and Commons]**

[fo 49ʳ]   **MAY 5**

UPPER HOUSE

The K commands ye Speaker not to goe into ye Lower House this day, fearing (perhapps) lest yt y shold urge him to preferre any petition to ye upper house, but calls in ye house into that painted chamber,[2] and speakes this to ym,[3] I called this great assembly to gett moneyes for my great occasions and as for ye upper house those

---

[1] The message went to the House of Commons.

[2] Lords' House. Rossingham and Montereul mention a protestation against shipmoney which was to have been presented to the Commons (*CSP 1640*, p. 153; P.R.O. 31/3/72, fo 140ʳ); see also Clarendon, *History*, II. 76.

[3] See below, App. (5 May), p. 316.

I find willing to comply with me, and some also of ye lower house, but ye greater numbers of ym are against it, and y are factious too, complaining of many grievances, yt y must be first redressed, as if grievances could not be redressed but by a Parliament. Yrfore (sayth he) Lord Keeper proceed. Ye KEEPER yn sayth, In his Majesties name I dissolve this Parliament. All of you to your severall places.

LOWER HOUSE

The House consulted what to doe, and what answeare to give. It was feared yt y wold have yielded to have given 6 subsidies, but before it came to voting ye K breakes up ye House, as being unwilling to have yt dishonour, yt ye parliament shold vote against him. W[he]n ye Lord Keep had broke it up, every one of ym gott ym out of the painted chamber, and rode home divers yt day.[1] *Finis.*

[*S.P. 16/451/16*]   [*13-16 April 1640, Lords and Commons*]
[*ROSSINGHAM TO CONWAY*]
London, 21 Aprill 1640.

My Lo of Lowdine contynues still in the tower close prisoner. His lettre hitherto haveing been red only in the Parliament, being for a while layd aside till the House be well settled and the subjects grievances prepared to present to the King when the bill of subsidies come to be allowed of.

13TH [*APRIL*]

The King went in state to the Parliament and in his speech[2] declared the calling of the Parliament was for present supplies to reduce the Scotts to obedience and not to delay it.

14TH [*APRIL*]

My Lo Cottington, Secretary Windebanke, and Mr. Attorney examined my Lo of Lowdaine at the Tower touching the lettre who as it is said confessed it but that it was writt before ye pacification at Barwicke.

15TH [*APRIL*]

The House of Commons presented Sargeant Glanvile[3] for there Speaker to ye King.

---

[1] There is no record of debate 5 May (*C.J.*, ii, p. 19).
[2] See below, App. (13 April), p. 293.
[3] See below, App. (15 April), p. 299.

16TH [APRIL]

The Scottish lettre was red upon which Mr. Grimston[1] of Lincolns Inn made the first speach moving the House to settle things at home and then abroad.

(2d Sir Benjamin Rudeard[2] advised the House to proceed with all humility to supply the King with moneys and to heed of the splint-[er]s of a broken Parliament for they will sticke in the flesh but withall shewed a necessity to reform things amisse in Church and Common wealth, then Sir Francis Seymor[3] in particular against ship money and innovations.

In the Upper House my Lord Say, Lord Brooke and Lo Savile would not condescend to adjourne that house 2 daies, in regard of my Lord of Canterburys request to sit for the Convocation busines for a day, but adjourned in regard my Lo Keeper was not well.

17TH [APRIL]

Mr. Pymme[4] made a speach almost 2 howers long particularizing all the generall grievances of the Church and State without medling with any mans person, also mentioned the counsell table and starr chamber together with the pattents of soape, salt, stearch, and tobacco, etc.

18TH [APRIL]

Warrants sent to all the courts at Westminster to bring in the judges oppinions recorded for ship money and the writt, judgments, and records, also the proceedings in the King Bench and against parliament men after the last Parliament was done.

19TH [APRIL]

My Lo Deputy came to courte but sicke and weake and my Lo Keeper is very ill.

20 [APRIL]

The whole day spent in stating the question for the King touching grievances against the priviledges of the Parliament, and Dr. Mannering being made an Ep[iscopus] after he was dismissed by the Parliament is one thing instanced on. Mr. Jones of Lincolns Inn sits in the chaire for priviledges and Mr. Grimston in the chaire for the grand committee in generall.

---

1 See below, App., Grimston, p. 296.
2 See below, App., Rudyerd, p. 296.
3 See below, App., Seymour, p. 297.
4 See below, App., Pym, p. 299.

I

We verily hope the Parliament will give the King content and that his gracious Majestie will (when he sees how he hath bin misinformed by those that have procured patents who pretended to his Majesty a common good but proved a common grievance) gave way to the Parliaments to question such persons especially that of wines where it will appeare 100000^{li} a yeare is paid more then what comes to the King out of the subjects purses.

21 [APRIL]

The Lower House sent to the Upper House to joyne with them in petition for a fast to which they bend afterward referring to his Majestie for a day. All the ship money records were brought into the House of Commons and viewed in part. Declaration made by most of the House against all such recoveryes as have bin acknowledged by infants to be voyd and a bill in Parliament for that purpose is preferred. Both Houses attend the King this afternoone at Whitehall who caused my L Keeper[1] to declare to them that his army was marching and no delayes of supplyes must be made in a gracious mild, and meek expression.

[S.P. 16/451/57]   [22-25 April 1640, Lords and Commons]

[ROSSINGHAM TO CONWAY]

I shall add this to my last new newes dated the 21th Aprill. The House questioned a commission graunted to my Lo of Canterbury to make new cannons, etc. warrants for the bringing it to a committee.

[22 APRIL]

Mr Dell. my Lo of Canterburyes secretary, because hee misrepeated what Mr Pymme had said, had beene brought to ye barre but for Mr. Hampden his friend.

The same day a peticion was read against Doctor Cousins and warrants is sent to fetch him for saying the King had nothing to doe with ecclesiasticall matters.[2]

23⁰ APRIL

The House satt till 3 of ye clocke debating the question whether to give subsidies before a redresse of greevances concluded that the example was dangerous to posterity. The King and the Lords[3] had a conference about it at eight of the clocke at night and was in person the next day at the Upper House, being

[1] See below, App., L.K., p. 303.
[2] See below, Petition, Smart, p. 280.
[3] The Privy Council (below, S.P. 16/450/113, p. 290).

[*24 APRIL*]

24⁰ Aprill where my Lo Deputy made a speech and voted through the House whether to fall in hand to give ayde to the Kinge or to reforme things amisse but the major voyces for present ayde.[1]

25 APRIL[2]

It was feared a dissolucion but my Lo Keep[3] at a conference of both howses declared the warr was begun, for some of S. Will. Brunkards troope was taken by the Scotts and now delay was worse then denyall.

This day the Howse of Commons is to give an answer to the Kinge. The clergy have given six subsidies.

But it is conceaved the House of Commons will present to his Majestie a schedule of greevances under theise three heads.[4]

1. Innovacion in Religion; 2. greevances in the Commonwealth per ship moneys and monopolies; 3. offences against the priviledges of the Parliament instanced in Doctor Manwarings being made a Bishopp and the imprisonment of Parliament men.

27 APRIL[5]

Debated that it was a trenching on the priviledges of the Howse to chalke them a way to give subsidies first and then to redresse greevances, the honor and thanks belonges to them for subsidies and not to the Upper House. Referred to a Committee.

[1] *Cf.* S.P. 16/451/10, and below.
[2] Wrongly dated 27 April in S.P. 16/450/94 and S.P. 16/451/10; *CSP 1640*, pp. 39–40, is correct.
[3] See below, App., L.K. (25 April), p. 310.
[4] See below, App., Grievances, p. 308.
[5] See above, 25 April, p. 247, n. 2.

III. SPEECHES

[*Bodl., MS. Clarendon 18, 1376*]   [*16 April 1640, Rudyerd*]

[*fo 147ʳ*] [*SIR BENJAMIN RUDYERD'S SPEECH IN THE HOUSE OF COMMONS*][1]

Mr. Speaker by Gods blessing and the Kings favor a greate doore and effectuall is opened unto us of doeing a greate deale of good, if wee doe not shutt it against oursealves. That wee are heere togither in this house is an evident demonstracon that the kinges heart stands right towards us, for which wee doe owe him a thankefull and bounti-full retribucon.

Parliaments of late times have been disasterous and unfortunate, insoemuch as the very name of parliament hath bene a reproach, a byword, a hissing it now lyes in our hands, by Gods assistance and it ought to be our cheife endeavor to restore parliaments to their wonted luster.

There are some heere in this house whoe were present and many whoe doe well remember when the first parliament was broken that ever was broken in England.[2] Wee know from what side it came and for the most part the same [?]demons hath prevailed ever since full of subtelty full of malignity but now they have taken uppon them such a boldnes such an arrogance, as they stand in competicon with us whoe are the better subjects and some beleive they have carried it. Their emulacon I shall like, and doe hope but their presumption is not to be borne, for certeinly the best religion makes the best sub-jects. I wish them noe harme, for I wish their convercon and noe harsh way to it. Let us sett upp more and better lights to lighten their darknes burneing shineing lights, not lukewarm glowwoorme lights That the people in all places of the kingdome may be dilligently taught carefully instructed, in soundenes of doctrine by gods example in their pastors [*fo 147ᵛ*] taught and instructed too to heare prayers, how to use prayers for whoe soer first made the quarrell betweene prayeing and preaching never meant well to religion beeing both soe necessary dutyes not defraudeing one another but I know not how it comes aboute, that in our religion only a man may be too religious. The best way to suppress all other religion is to uphold our owne to the height. Light dispells darkenes without noyse and bustle, But I never yet knew any man beaten into an oppinion. I have

---

[1] Endorsement (fo 150ʳ), 'Sir B.R. Sp. in Par. 1640.' See also below, App., Rudyerd, p. 296.
[2] Rudyerd had been an M.P. since 1621.

knowne many freighted into dissimulacon. Animosity and feircenes becomes noe religion. Although heretofore wee have had experiences that by their cunning workeing of distempers in this House, and by their powerfull working upon those distempers out of the house, they have contributed as much to the breakeing of parliaments as any thinge else whatsoever. Yet I am persuaded they will not be soe active in this because of their common interest with us as subjects as Englishmen there beeing now such a generall necessity of having a whole, a happy parliament. How soon it wilbe wisdom in us to beware of infusions to keepe steady to our tempers.

The maine causes of the infelicitye and distraccions of these times have bene the frequent breakeing of parliaments. Beleive it (Mr Speaker) the splinters of a broken parliament doe make the most daungerous wounds in ye body politique which haveing soe long festered must be pulled out with a skillfull gentle hand els they may rather ven then cure the wounds they have made but noe neede not despaire [fo 148ʳ] of a cure for in the 14th yeere of Ed. the 3rd that king had great sumes of money granted him in parliament by way of subsidy for an expedicion in France; he went over entred into a warr, but the illmanaging of his treasure at home by his officers, and the withdrawing of some payments by the people, for not perform- ance of condicions inforced him to accept of a truce when he was in the full hope of gayninge a great victory. This could not but worke strongly upon the grave hearted prince. He retourned presently in the 15th yeere he summoned a parliament wherein were nothing but jealousies, contestacions, and distemper soe that the parliament ended without fruite. In the 17th yeere he called another parliament for noe other end but only to make an attonement betweene him and his people which intencion wrought the successe for by the prudence and patience of the king by the wisdome and humblenes of both howses all breaches were closed up and such a perfect union made, as there never fell out any differences betweene him and his people, during the whole tyme of his longe life after. Why may not wee be as wise [?]round. I presume wee shall. A parliament is the bed of recon- ciliacion betweene a king and his people mutually best for boath, soe that it will be proper and fitt for us to lay aside all acerbity and exasperacion to demeane ourselves with calmenese sweetenes dutifullnes.

Although the prerogative have gone very high, yet, if we can but bringe ourselves to an equanimity to an indifferency of judgment wee shall finde that all kings doe as naturally love power, as all peopple doe affect liberty. Then it is noe noe [sic] marvaile [fo 148ᵛ] That princes doe harken to them who look to improve power, then that Parliaments have too much yeelded to some who have pressed to extend their liberty. Whereas indeed both prerogative and liberty are best preserved when they are executed within theyr bounds. The law saith that a king of England can doe noe wrong. As for instruments if the matters doe start and expose the men, if the things they have misdone be condemned and reformed the men without any more adoe will quickly be despised, grow as uselesse as they are worthlesse wither and weare away to the nothing they deserve. It is true that in some tymes examples are more necessary then lawes, especially when lawes growe infirme for want of exercise because examples make a deeper impression strike a greater terror. But at this tyme wee should very unhansomely celebrate the reintegracion and union wee desire and expect with inscruitable sovereignty and extremities.

The levying of money to releive the kings necessities hath alsoe bread a great disturbance, and it will doe soe for the penury and scarcity of the crowne will keepe a perpetuall interferring betweene the king and the people untill it be supplyed. The power of a king and the power of necessity both joyned in one hand. Mr Speaker will not longe be disapoynted But I doe hope before this parliament bee finally concluded we shall establish such a constant revenewe to his majestie as shall enable him to live plentifully, royally at home set at high formidable estimacion upon him abroade. And that without taking away any thinge from them, [*fo 149ʳ*] but such things onely as will fall away of themselves. This nothing but parliaments canne doe. As for subsist[*ance*] I could never heare that poore narrowe projecting word applyed to the king without scorne and indignacion.

Lett us sett our thoughts and desyres but six months backe when wee had noe hope of any parliament at all, Remember what then wee would have given, what wee would have done then to have had a parliament, And we cannot but doe well now. It doth not consist with the wisdome and settlednes of this assembly to value more a parliament wee had not, then the parliament we have. To thinke better of an imaginary parliament than of a reall one.

I have observed that whilest parliaments are sitting they carry themselves soe high, soe sharpe as if parliaments should sitt alwayes, which indeed doth still shorten their sitting. And when parliaments are ended, there are others who carry buisines in such a strayne as if parliaments should never sitt againe. Soe that commonly a parliament comes halfe broken into this house as soone as it sitts wherefore it concernes us, dextrously and tenderly to sett and hold the peece together, least wee breake it out right and our selves with it.

Mr Speaker it soe farre from being strange as it can hardly be otherwise but that in soe long a vaccacion betweene parliaments many disorders must needs grow in upon us as deviation in religion, violacion of lawes, invasion upon liberties. But the works and labour is how to reduce them, how to sett them right againe. The manner of doeing of it ought to be the principall in our consideracion for the matters carry in them stirring [?]movement tempting provocacions for that very reason, Mr Speaker. It behooves us to be the more weary the more composed least wee be transported beyond our ende. I confesse I doe now feele myselfe in a strength. Shall wee onely looke forward as wee call it. Altogether omitt and neglect God in his religion, the King in his honor; the common wealth in her gasping extremity. That stands not with the integrity of this house, with the trust reposed in us by our Country, Shall wee encounter these enormityes, with the full force of a parliamentary strictnes, rigor and exactnes. In doeing thus wee may turne the medicine into a worse disease, and so undoe all, even roote out the race of parliaments for ever. Men and brethren what shall wee doe. Truely Mr Speaker, If I should speak for my life, as I doe for more I should humbly beseach this house that wee may all of us strive to make this a breeding, teeming parliament, that it may be the mother of many more, and not cast our selves upon the hazard of desperate dismall events. As long as wee have parliaments, wee shall know where to find our selves, when they are gone, wee are lost.

[*S.R.O., DD/M1, Box 18, 96*]   [*16 April 1640, Seymour*][1]
[*unnumbered*]

SIR FRANCIS SEAMOURS SPEECH IN THE PARLIAMENT HOUSE[2]

Perhapps the[*y*] have custome, fashion, and nature to pleade for themselves; which ought not to be so; but that every man is interested and concerned properly and perfectly to looke to performe his affection, abillity, duty, and office himselfe; happily some thinke it is no advantage to him; indeede it is the best and greatest advantage of all, to bee free men in justice, light, truth, and tyme; why should we deferre one minute of our tyme, or pitch uppon any example or fashion, but what is agreable to truth and justice; knoweing all our aydes and helpes are dirived from the father of lights and life [?] and increase, where their is no variablenes, shadowe, or turning, but creates, renewes, and performes comfort, and benifitts hourely and dayly to the all the world whoe respects not persons, but without exception; But indeede this fashion is multiplied, and hath bene done in such thinges, which have not onely intrenched upon the priviledges of Parliaments, but to the liberty, propriety, and

---

[1] For the first part of the speech, see above, p. 213.
[2] See below, App., Seymour, p. 297.

prosperity of the whole common wealth; wherin I had rather suffer for speaking the truth, then truth should suffer for wante of my speakeing; where was ever more piety, wisedome, and goodnes in a prince and loyalty and affection in subjects; And yet what common wealth ever suffered more then this; his Majestie is ye sun which though it ever shines alike in itselfe gloriously, yet by reason of clouds, may not so appeare; If his Majestie by reason of bad members may not appeare in such splendor, what will it avayle us if the fountayne be cleere, that the streames that issueth from thence, be not purified and cleane alsoe.

[2nd p.]I will instance in some particulers.

If wee looke in the ground and action and subsequent condicion of religion that is persecuted, outfaced, and discountenanced; nowe indeede their is such painted sepulch[r]es in the action of Christs religion and formalytes; as if they were authorized and allowed a dispensation and tolleration for their deceiptes and sines; I meane the seminary preists and others, whoe are the fighters and contemners of the practitione[r]s of religion. Whoe though they have lesse in the lord God, yett they have no lesse anger and malice, but more. Indeede so longe as theise varnisht sepulcrhes have their agents amongst us; I feare the Kingdome and church of christendome suffers unknowed and in credible; see we not howe they goe to Somersett house, and to St Jeames and about the common wealth; whoe are two much countenanced, and maynteyned. Theise are enimes in the Church, out of the Church. I wishe wee had none within, whoe pull churches, truth and the executions of justice downe. I ame sure build none upp, amongst which are all our conformities and conformers to the dayly practizes of of dishonest liveing. Whoe have the forme of godlynes, humility and truth but denie the power of them. Truely all truth and good workes for the most parte are overcome with wordly preferments and subtilties of humane corruption and tradition, in our dayly practises and executinges; But it was this that made the worthies of God and Peters love, the feeding of his sheepe; It should be our hourely actions and moderation the reducing, converting, of people and executing good lawes, for a double honor dayly gott to God and our soules, when men proceede universally aright, and pitch their indeavours every where and with all their hearts and affections, faculties, and abillities uppon the Almighty and every member of the world; and doe generally and continually move to the Almighty to converte the lambes ye blynde, the deaffe, and those that are heardned in their sines; and those that are fighters agaynst the commandements of obedience to righteousnesse; that is the mercy we ought to celebrate to particuler persons as well as generall people; wee knowe not which he will have mercy and which he will hardneth, but I am sure it is most safe and advantagious to us, when we doe aright to all, when we have a regarde to all the commandements, and all the members for the reduceing and converting of the most abject and despised; for the judgment and mercy of God is one, and the judgment and mercy of the world is another; we people in the world are miserable, pore, and blynde, he mercyfull, light, and rich what avaylement is it to us if all the world be pittifull and tender unto us; If God hardneth and shutteth up his hid treasures, of his grace and eternall light and truth from us.

[*3rd p.*] Therefore lett us all heartyly pray with all manner of prayers and supplications, that we may be delievered from the darknes and bondage of sathan; that this whole nation and others may be converted to the faith in truth and that the inward man may be framed and renewed to the obedience and truth and godly conversation, to the perpetuity and advancement of his glory and our eternall salvation, what more against nature, reason, and religion, then for one man to have justice and righteousnes above another; theise that doe other waies are double dogges and cannot abide to doe the will of the Almighty God in all thinges, and the afflicted, presecuted members of his wee all knowe in the world, and all that is therein is but a confused chaos and a masse of corruption, and a ruinated building without of his continuall influence and inspiration of his grace, light, strenght, mercy, and power; oh the unsearchable wisedome and incomprehensible mercy that frames order and dispose all thinges created in heaven and in earth for the conscionation, negotiation, participation, and distribution; that every newe sinecure, office, and member of every particuler person has for ornament, benifit, and use, from his boundles and unfathomed mercy; Their be some, that hold that the King hath an unlimitted power, and the subjects hath no propriety in their goods, and liberty of their persons. Theise are bad people in Church and Common wealth; and ignorant and foolishe as atheists and heathen; and others whoe under the name of Puritanes condemne all, who truely professe religion; yet their are some under the name of Godlynes clooke impiety; but to teach that a man can be too godly and too honest is a doctrine of divells.[1] . . .

---

[1] For the remainder of the speech see above, p. 215.

[B.L., Harl. MS. 6801]   **[17 April 1640, Pym]**

MR. PYMMS SPEECH IN THE HOWSE OF COMMONS,
[fo 58ʳ]   ANNᵒ 1640[1]

Hee will doe a good worke for the King who the sooner to expedite his designes will sett rules and paternes for effecting thereof.

When God made the world, hee did it by a paterne, which himselfe had conceived; Moyses[2] according to the paterne hee sawe in the Mount.

I thinke it therefore best to represent before you a modell of the greevances under which wee specially groane which may bee reduced to three heads. First greevances against the priviledges and liberties of Parliament. Secondly innovations in matters of religion. [fo 58ᵛ] Thirdly greevances against the free propriety of our goods, which greevances I will propound and shew that the permission of these is as prejudiciall to his Majestie as to the Comon wealth. Likewise I will shew what way they may bee remedied.

Greevances against the priviledges of Parliament.

Parliaments are those which purge us from all errors and prevent others[3] to come. If the understanding part bee hurt, the mynd cannot performe its function. A Parliament is the soule of the comon wealth which is the reason that by the lawes and antient customes thereof our persons and estates are free from arrests and [fo 59ʳ] imprisonments during Parliaments, that wee should not bee distracted. The other two greevances are in shew the greatest, but this seemes to bee of the greatest consequence, the breaches that have beene made are:

1. That the Speaker the last Parliament, the last day of it did refuse to putt the question, being comaunded soe to doe by the Howse of Commons and without their consent did upon a verball commaund from his Majestie adjourne the Howse. This is the source of all the other breaches.

2. That the Parliament was then dissolved before our greevances had redresse or before wee could make our wills, dying [fo 59ᵛ] men have the priviledge to bee heard before condemned is not denyed to private persons.

3. The severall imprisonments of divers gentlemen for speakeing freely in Parliament.

4. That inferiour courts should bee in force to punish Acts done in this High Court, whereby divers members of this Howse were so kept

---

[1] See below, App., Pym (17 April), p. 299. *Cf.* Rushworth, iii, pp. 1131–36.

[2] . . . *did* (Petyt MS. 538/11, fo 238ʳ). Exodus 34.

[3] . . . *for tyme* . . . (Petyt MS. 538/11, fo 238ᵛ).

in prison, that some of them dyed in prison,[1] others not released untill
the writts came out for this Parliament. It is to bee observed that in
this and the other greevances though the King bee no partie for his
highnes prerogative is to doe noe wronge, yet most of theise distempers of State arise and doe invade the subjects by meanes of
misinformacion as the celestiall bodies of [*fo 60ʳ*] themselves send
forth nothinge but wholsomnes[2] soe by the distemper in terrestiall
bodies much hurt ariseth.

Greevances in matters of religion.

1. That Religion[3] is possession whereof the lawes of the land have
placed us, and preserved it for us, that the first greevance is the
great incouragement which is given to them of the Popish Religion
by an universall suspention of the execution of all lawes that are
against them. I desire to have no newe lawes made against them,
God bee thanked wee have enough of good old lawes, neither doe I
desire a strict execution of them but such a practice of them that the
Religion which can brooke no corrivall. [*fo 60ᵛ*] may not bee the
destruction of ours by being too concurrent with it. I doe believe
that there bee divers great persons of that religion which naturally
and of themselves thinke noe hurt to us, but as the planetts, beside
their naturall motion have a rapt motion by the *primo mobile*, soe
have theise by the Pope whereby they are after diverted. Wee may
remember Hen. 3 of Fraunce, who was taken away not soe much
that he utterly forbadd or hindred the protestants, but for bearing
with them.

2. There is a free commerce and trading with them,[4] men openly
without rebuke resenting [*sic*] to Jesuiticall counsells and [*fo 61ʳ*]
meetings where they make and establish Acts amongst themselves.

3. Papists are admitted to places of trust and power in the Church
and Comon wealth (Note that heere hee craved pardon for naming
the Church, for hee meant onely the Comon wealth.)

4. There is an intention of a *Nuncio* from the Pope, who is to bee
resident heere to give secrett intelligence to Rome how wee inclyne
heere and what will bee thought[5] best to seduce us.

5. There are divers innovations amongst ourselves to make us more
capable of a translation to which purpose Bookes and disputations
are and have beene in the universities and elsewhere by Papists
tenents are mainteyned.

6. The introducing of popish [*fo 61ᵛ*] ceremonyes as Altars, bowing
towards the East, pictures, crosses, crucifixes, and the like, which of

---

[1] *E.g.*, Eliot.   [2] . . . *to man* . . . (Petyt MS. 538/11, fo 239ʳ).
[3] . . . *in the* possession (Petyt MS. 538/11, fo 239ʳ).
[4] '. . . *and public communication*, men openly . . .' (Petyt MS. 538/11, fo
239ᵛ).
[5] '. . . *fitted to wynne us*' (Petyt MS. 538/11, fo 239ᵛ).

themselves considered are as soe many dry bones,[1] which being putt together make not a man.

7. The discouraging of all Godly men who professe Religion as though men could bee too religious.

8. Some things opposed by Ecclesiasticall Men without any ground [in lawe][2] by any cannon or Article established, and without any comaund from the King either, under his great seale or by Proclamation as reading the booke for recreation on the Sabbath Day which was a device of their owne heads.

9. Incroachments upon the Kings [fo 62ʳ] authority by Ecclesiasticall Courts as the high commission, which takes upon them to fyne and imprison for all things before them, which are punishments belonging only to temporall jurisdictions, and it hath beene resolved in the tyme of King James that the statute of 1 El. cap. 1 gives them no such power,[3] Moreover the power which they clayme they derive not from the King, nor from any lawe or statute, but they will have it imediately from heaven, divers particuler Ordinaries, Chancellors, and Archdeacons take upon them to make and ordayne constitutions, within the particular lymitts all those things are true to the knowledge [fo 62ᵛ] of most that are heere.

As for greevances which belong to our goods and are in civill matters, the heads thereof are too many, I will bee as moderate as I can in the pressing[4] of them, alwayes observing the fidelity I owe to the Howse. [1.] The takeing of Tonnage and Poundage and divers other imposicions without any ground[5] in Lawe soe to doe is a great greevance. There are divers antient customes due to the Kinge, but they are certaine what they are and are due by prescription, theise customes being too narrowe for his service, The King of England often in [fo 63ʳ] tymes of extreame danger and necessitie did make imposicions by necessity not by president. After this they were granted for yeares to them, and afterwards by this Howse were granted for lives, but never were taken by the Kings owne act without a Parliament, for doing which there is noe president unlesse in a yeare or two in the later end of Queene Elizabeth. And for that pretended Judgement in the case of [currants],[6] the Barons, though they agreed all for the King, yet they differed in the grounds and

---

[1] '. . . but being layd togither make the man' (Petyt MS. 538/11, fo 240ʳ). Ezekiel 37: 6–7.

[2] Petyt MS. 538/11, fo 240ʳ, omits: in law.

[3] State Trials, ii, 131–59, does not confirm this. Petyt MS. 538/11, fo 240ʳ, omits the remainder of the paragraph.

[4] expressing (Petyt MS. 538/11, fo 240ʳ).

[5] . . . or lawe (Petyt MS. 538/11, fo 240ʳ).

[6] Curtis in MS; Bate's Case, 1606; '. . . in 3 Jac in the case . . .' (Petyt MS. 538/11, fo 240ᵛ).

reasons of their Judgement which was theise, beinge[1] [blank]
comodities and matters of pleasure rather then of necessity, the
King might lay [fo 63ᵛ] an Imposition uppon them; after this Judgement the same question came in debate into this Howse, and this
judgement was conceived a barr,[2] but God defend that ever Court
and a Judgement thereon should conclude the whole Realme for by
that meanes a custome taken away may bee equall too, and some
tymes exceed the value of the comoditites, but the great greevance is
that what his Majestie takes this way as custome or imposition shall
not bee thought to bee taken as necessarily wherewith the sea ought
to bee guarded but meerely out of prerogative.
2. Knighthood the originall whereof was that persons fitt for chivalry
might bee [fo 64ʳ] improved but this was stretched for another end
as for money and extended not only to undertenants but to lessees
and merchants who first were to appeare and then to pleade and in
case of refusall, distresses infinite were taken untill the fynes were
paid which were imposed not by Courts but by commissioners
assigned for that purpose and this being a contynuing offence, they
are by the same rule as lyable nowe to fynes as ever.
3. Monopolies and inundation of them whereby a burthen is laid
[not] upon forraine, but upon native comodities as soape, salt, drinke,
etc. The particulers thereof are fitt for the [fo 64ᵛ] committee of
greevances.
4. Shippmoney, although there bee a judgement for it, yet I dare bee
bold to say, it is against all former precedents and lawes and not one
Judgement that ever mainteyned it, nor one lawe booke for it. This
is a greevance that all are greeved att having no lymitts for tyme or
proportion.
5. The inlarging of the bounds of forrests, though our ancestors were
heeretofore questioned for the same thinges, yet upon the satisfaction
of all the objections that were or could bee made,[3] yet now the same
thinges are turned uppon us, I tax not that noble person that was
imployed [fo 65ʳ] in that busines, for hee did nothing but as informed
by the judges.
6. The sale of publique nusances many great nusances have beene
complayned against but when there hath beene money and com-
posicions made, then they are noe nuzances, as building and
depopulation, etc.
7. Millitary charges and imposicions upon counties by letters onely
from the counsell table, whereby coates and conduct money for
souldiers are to bee paid att the countryes charge and horses provided

---

[1] being *exoticke* commodities (Petyt MS. 538/11, fo 240ᵛ).
[2] Foster, ii, p. 82.
[3] '... *they had them saved to them* ...' (Petyt MS. 538/11, fo 241ʳ).

alsoe, without ground of lawes, many thinges in this kinde being done by deputie lieutenants of their owne accord.

8. Extrajudiciall judgements and [*fo 65ᵛ*] opinions of the judges without any[1] course shewed before them whereby they have anticipated their judgements which is not[2] legall and publique and circumvented one of the parties of just remedies in that no writt of error lyes but only upon the judiciall proceedings.

9. The court of Star chamber advancing or countenancinge of monopolies, which should bee in succession of this great counsell of the kingdome and the Star chamber is nowe become a court of revenue, Informations there being putt in against sherriffes for not makeing returne of moneys upon the writts of shippmoney.[3]

10. The Privy counsellors should bee lights of the Realme. [*fo 66ʳ*] Surely in them is the greatest trust, and they by *Magna Charta* are to doe Justice: as it was urged by one of this House the last Parliament,[4] but nowe if theise counsellors should soe farr descend belowe themselves as to countenance, nay to plott projects and monopolies, what shall wee thinke of this, surely it is much beneath their dignitie, this is a great greevance, but yet I must goe higher. I knowe the King hath a transcendent power whereby Proclamations hee may prevent and provide against suddaine accidents, but that this power should bee applied to countenance monopolies, the projectors beinge not content with their private [*fo 66ᵛ*] graunts without a proclamacion as without president, yet I must goe higher then this.

12. The truth of God is the bone of the conscience and should tye every one, and yet this hath beene in pulpitts applied and alsoe in Bookes and disputations to extoll a power unlymitted in the King, that hee may doe what hee pleaseth. This greevance was complayned of the last Parliament in the case of Dr Manwaring whoe for mainteyning that opinion in a sermon that a subject had noe propriety in his goods but that all was att the Kings pleasure made his submission upon his knees in this place and was [5] belowe that then I thought he [*fo 67ʳ*] would not soe soone beene made a bishopp. [*1.*] There is one great greevance more which is the fountaine of all theise and that is the intermission of Parliaments, whereas by two statuts not repealed nor expired, a Parliament ought to bee once a yeare.[6] Theise

[1]. . . *case* before them (Petyt MS. 538/11, fo 241ᵛ).
[2] Petyt MS. 538/11, fo 241ᵛ, omits: not.
[3] Petyt MS. 538/11, fo 241ᵛ, adds: '*It was not used that men and tun.* [?] *should bee discussed here.*'
[4] Perhaps Sir Humphrey May in connection with Rolle's case (*Commons Debates, 1629*, p. 187; also p. 197). Pym's diary for 1624 cites such a remark from Strafford in that Parliament (quoted in Foster, 'Monopolies', p. 79, note). *Cf.* B.L., E.78(12), p. 17.
[5] 'was *soe lowe* that . . .' (Petyt MS. 538/11, fo 242ʳ).
[6] Petyt MS. 538/11, fo 242ᵛ, adds: *videst* 4 *E*. 3, 14; 36 *E* 3, 10.

greevances are as prejudiciall to his Majestie as to the comon wealth, for by this meanes the union [and] love which should bee kept and communicated betwixt the King and his subjects is interrupted. They cannot make knowne their peticions, nor the King his wants to have supplies where the intercourse betwixt the head and the members is hindred, the body prospers not.

[*fo 67ᵛ*] 2. There is a hindrance of subsedies which are a cleer revenue and not lyable to any charge in lands and such like.

3. If Parliaments had beene more frequent, the King had more supplies from his freinds abroad, and I beleive, if Parliaments might have had their free current, the Palatinate had not beene nowe in the possession of Spaine.

4. By our great greevances in Religion the Kings partie abroade much weakened, and that great part of his ayde abroade doe forsake us for that they thinke wee are forsakeing or religion.

5. Many of the Kings subjects for that they cannot bee quiett [*fo 68ʳ*] in thinges indifferent and knowe not where an end shall bee of them have departed this land with their goods, estates, and posterity.

6. By the preferment of men ill deserving and neglecting others, the vulgar sort of our nation is much weakened and discouraged.

7. The not observing of our lawes but countenancing of monopolies and such like imbredd jealousies in the mynds of many and may prepare a way of distemper though thankes bee to God as yet there have beene none. Our religion having preserved us, but if any thing but well should happen one summers distemper if such should happen would breed great change and more then all unlawfull courses would recompense.

[*fo 68ᵛ*] 8. Wee knowe how unfortunate Hen. 3 [*of France*] and other Princes have beene by the occasion of such breakeing theire lawes. I pray God that we never see such tymes.

9. Wee are not content to multiplye impositions uppon merchants goods which are exported and imported into this kingdome, but nowe there is a growing mischeife in plotting for an imposition upon such goods as never see England, but are conveyed from Fraunce to Spaine or the like by English merchants, and such illegall thinges are ever badly accompted for the King, whereas legall thinges will bee soone discovered if not well accompted, [*fo 69ʳ*] besides in monopolies and such like the third part comes not to his Majestie as to instance in that of wines.

The King hath thirty thousand pounds *per annum* upon them, whereby the wines in the gaines by the patent comes to eighty thousand pounds att the first and being drawn comes to two hundred and thirty thousand pounds and the same proportion holds in all other monopolies, whereby it appeares how much the subject is damnified and how little the King gaines.

[*Dublin, Trinity College MS. 623*]   [*17 April 1640, Pym*]

[*A NOTE*[1] *ABOUT PYM'S STATEMENT CONCERNING*
[*fo 28^r*]   *THE WINE PATENT*][2]

Hee saith the Kinge hath 30000^{li} *per annum* rent for the wyne pattents, 40^s per tonne is exacted for the Vintners to defraye the charge of the Pattentt, 45000 tonne is imported yearely which produceth 90000^{li}, by this it appeares their gaine towards their charge is 60000^{li}.

Hee saith the wyne is advaunced in the Vintners sale 2^d per quart which comes to (saith hee) 8^{li} per tonne. This is a mistake, hee followes it with two conclusions, one 360, but what that meanes I knowe not, and then saieth the kingdome looseth above the Kings rent 330000^{li} *per Annum*.

Sure this is some mistake, for (as I take it) we account 236 gallons to a tonne which makes 944 quarts which att 2^d per quart comes to 7^{li} 17^s 4^d per tonne, which beinge 45000 tonnes, as much comes to 355500^{li} *per annum* but here is to be remembered that sacks and all wynes of that kind pay 2^d per quart more then formerlye but all French wynes but a penye in the quart, this penye for the French wyne is to bee abated out of ye 355500^{li} *per annum*. Everye man in the comonwealth that drinkes wyne beares his share in this.

The Pattentees gaine by the Vintners (if the proporcion hould 40^s per tonne which is 90000^{li} *per annum*, they paye 30000^{li} to his Majestie soe here is 60000^{li} towards their charges.

This I thought good to sett downe that this worthie man might peruse againe that part concerninge the wynes, for it is not fitt soe honest worthie and religious a speech, should have the least blast upon it by coppies cominge abroad unperfect.

[*Bodl., MS. Clarendon 18*]   [*18 April 1640, Hyde*]

MY SPEECH IN APRILL 1640 AGAINST THE MARSHALLS
[*fo 155^r*]   COURTE IN PARLYAMENT[3]

Mr Speaker, Those worthy gentlemen who have so happily discharged their dutyes to ther country in presentinge the greate

---

[1] See below, App., Pym, p. 299. This loose sheet found among the pages of Pym's speech of 17 April appears to be in a different hand from that of the speech itself.
[2] See above, p. 156.   [3] See below, App., Hyde, p. 302.

grievances under which we groane have yet left one grievance un-
mencioned, unnamed, uninferred, a grievance (Mr Speaker) if wee
looke upon the present pressures and waye the [?]conclusyons that
must necessarily follow those pr[e]ambles, not inferiour to any that
hath beene named. I wish it had bene remembred by some man who
might with more lustre and advantage have presented it to the
house. Tis my Ld. marshalls courte, the courte of honour. A glorious
title (Mr Speaker) who would not looke heare for a sanctuary, a
place of privyledge and protection to the nobility and gentry of this
kingdome. I would it were so (Mr Sp[eake]r). I believe tis not. Oh,
Mr Speaker, to have a courte in one night grow up to that vast and
unlimited power,[1] to dispose of libertyes by imprysoninge our
persons and of our estates by fynes and damages, arbitrarily and
without law. If I ow my Taylor mony (Mr Speaker) if his hunger, his
wante of bread, dryve him to much importunity, I can heare quitt
shores with him and pay his bills with his owne ill manners.[2] How
fatall a jest that proved to him who called a swann a goose, many
heare have heard, the poore man (whose [?]favor I never sued) lyes
now imprysoned, ruined and undone under that sentence, though
thence a marchant of good quality.[3] I am not so ignorant (Mr
Speaker) to thinke my Ld marshalls office a newe office or my Ld
marshalls courte a new courte. I know they are both very auncient
and possibly of greate use to, but this courte, with these processes
and proceedinges I am bold to say is very new, and I hope that as the
youngest man heare can remember its beginnings, so the oldest shall
see the determinacion. Tis now in the hande and under the govern-
ance of a greate and honorable person,[4] who no doubt when he shall
be informed of the greate grievances the common wealth suffred by
it will joyne with us in the reformation. But if this place shall come
into the hands of an insolent and [?] person as what place may not,
even in the rainge of the most gracious prince I must be bold to say
he shall have a greater power of our parsons [sic] and our fortunes
then any courte in Westminster Hall. An appendent to this courte is
the pageantry of it, the heralds: who have now gotten shares and
porcions out of all our estates, and those to be payd before debts or
leggacies. There have not bene a grievance mencioned, Mr Speaker,
that lasts longer then life, in the grave ther used to be all peace, but

---

[1] There was a new patent 1 August 1623; records begin in 1633. (G. D.
Squibb, The High Court of Chivalry (Oxford, 1959), pp. 46, 56; also pp. 48–62,
passim); also Notestein, D'Ewes, p. 375.
[2] Cf. Clarendon, Life, i, p. 79; perhaps the case of Gardiner v. Gilbert (1640)
(Squibb, p. 64n.); see also Rushworth, iii, p. 1055.
[3] Clarendon, Life, i, p. 78, gives the story in greater detail; Dover (earl) v.
Fox (1638) (Squibb, p. 64 and n.).
[4] Thomas Howard, second earl of Arundel, was Earl Marshal.

heare is a tax outlived and an imposicion upon our carcasses. Some, Mr Speaker, of the knights of this house when they entered into that order thought though they might happily be engaged to lyve at a higher rater, yet they might [*fo 155ᵛ*] dy as good cheape as other men. They cannot, Mr Speaker. [*It*] will cost them 5ˡⁱ¹ more at court, and Yet a gentleman cannot dy for nothinge nether. I hope I have sayd nothinge but what becomes me and Yet halfe this spoken a yeere since would have undone a better man then I am. I my selfe know a gentleman of the law, a worthy and a learned gentleman, for telling his clyent, a lady who had newly buryed her husbande and was called on by these gentlemen, that he knew no law by which these fees were dew, was summoned into this courte and because he refused to set it under his hande, that they were dew by law, and bounde over *de die in diem* and for ought I know is not yet discharged.² I shall move, Mr Speaker, that a committee of a few may be appointed to view those pattents and commissions that thereupon this house may take such order for the reformacion of so greate a grievance as in these instances and justice shall be fitt.³

[*Bodl., MS. Tanner 321*]   [?*20 April 1640, Holland*]

MY FIRST AND ONLY SPEECH AT THE COMITTEE OF GRIEVANCES IN THIS SHORT PARLIAMENT IN THE [*fo 3ᵛ*]   YEERE 1639 THE FIRST DAY IT SATT⁴

Mr Glinn, I conceive this a comittee to receive and examine the generall grevances of this kingdome and soe proper for this work in my hand, being a petition of greivances from the weavors, hosyers, and wolecomers within the Citty of Norwich⁵ and County of Norfolk, for which I serve. Trades, if I mistake not, that well deserves the favour countenance and reliefe of this Honorable Comittee, since they are such as deal especially in one of the cheife and staple comodityes of this kingdome such as setts many thousand hands on

---

¹ 'ten pounds more. . . . The Heralds had procured such an Order from the Earl Marshal, to force all Persons to pay at their Funerals such several Sums, according to their several Degrees' (Clarendon, *Life*, i, p. 80).

² 'Mr. Say, a *lawyer* but advising a widow not to pay *those fees*, etc. questioned by Mr. Philpot Somerset herald, etc.' (Notestein, *D'Ewes*, p. 376n.).

³ No action was taken, but see *C.J.*, ii, p. 16; also Hyde's report from the Long Parliament's committee (Notestein, *D'Ewes*, p. 376 and note).

⁴ Perhaps the committee appointed 20 April (*C.J.*, ii, p. 7). The speech seems to be addressed to Glyn, perhaps as chairman. Glyn is not listed as a committee member (H.L.R.O., Main Papers, 20 April 1640). The speech is not mentioned in other accounts. It appears in a book of speeches of Sir John Holland, knight of the shire for Norfolk. Most of the speeches date from the Long Parliament.

⁵ See also below, Petition, Norwich, p. 279.

work in the Citty of Norwich and County of Norfolk. Ther greatest greivance derives from the pattent of soap, a great and generall greivance if I mistake not to the whole kingdome, both by enhansment wherby of the price and the late sophistication in the composition of the soap itself by which these poore trades are much impoverished and discouraged, the wares and comodityes disparaged and the whole kingdome in them diserved. My humble motion I desire is, that it will please this honorable committee that the petition may be received and red and that they will further please to take into consideration the consequences of these trades, the grevances, the mischiefes, and the remedyes.

[Hunt. Cal., HM 1554]   **[21 April 1640, Lord Keeper]**

[THE LORD KEEPER'S SPEECH AT THE
[p. 165]   BANQUETING HOUSE]

[*Tuesday the 21st*][1] of Aprill The Lord Keeper declared at Whitehall as followeth:

That this army stands the King in 100000^{li} a moneth and without a speedy supply that charg wilbe lost.

That after the dispatch of this they shall have free scope and libertie to shewe their grevances and shall find a gratious heareing, that his Majestie never intended to make a benifitt in requireing of shipmoney but for the good and preservation of the kingdome.

That his Majestie was resolved that no shipmoney should have bene required this yeare, but that necessitie requires it.

First that neighboring princes are preparing great fleets att sea, and therefore his Majestie strengthens himselfe, that hee may preserve his dominion of the seas and be moderator there without which the kingdome is lost.

Secondly the insolencies of the Algiers who have provided a fleet of 60 saile and have taken divers of the Kings shipps, the *Rebecca* by name worth at least 200000^{li}.

That if the Parliament devise any other way of supply to the value of the shipmoney his Majestie will gratiously accept it.

That his Majestie requires the Lords to further him in his busines.

That his Majestie hath allready given the moytie of tunnage and poundage for the setting forth of his army.

[1] MS.: *Monday the 20th*. See also below, App., L.K. (21 April), p. 303.

[*H.L.R.O., Draft Journal*] [*24 April 1640, Charles I*]

[*THE KING'S SPEECH IN THE UPPER HOUSE*][1]

[*p. 32*]

His Majestie presented himselfe unto the Lls Spirituall and Temporall in the high court of Parlement, and being without his Roabes, sitting in his chaire of state, the Lords being not in their Roabes, his Majestie coming unexpected, his Majestie spake to them to this effect, *viz.*

My Lords, the necessity of calling this Parlement makes me to come this day [hither] contrary to expectation; you maye remember what the Lo Keep said concerning the occation of this meeting the first and second dayes, but chiefly on the day of Conference of both houses at Whitehall. The House of Commons did seeme to take into consideracon my weightie affaires, but they have in a manner concluded the Contrary; and instead of preferring my occasions in the first place, they have held consultacion of Innovacion of Religion. Propertie of Goods and Priviledges of Parlement, and soe have putt the carte before the horse. If it were a tyme [*p. 33*] to dispute, I should not much stand upon it, but my necessities are soe urgent that there can be no delay. If the House of Commons will trust me, I will make good what I have promised by my Lo Keep. As for Religion, my harte and *actions* [conscience] shall goe together [with the Religion now established in the Church of England]. For the ship-money, God is my wittnes I never converted any of it to my owne profitt, but to the ende of preserving the dominion of the seas, *which I hope no English harte but will consent to* [nor never intended it], As for Property of Goods it is a thinge I never but intended; and it is my desire to be kinge of a free and a rich people and if no property in goods, no rich people. I tould the Commons that if they would speedily supply my occasions for the present, I would give them further tyme at winter to present and debate all their just grievances *The tyme I must be trusted with, now whether I or they must be trusted is the Question.* If they will not trust me first, all my busines [*p. 34*] this summer will be lost; and before the yeare goeth about I must [be] trust *them* [-ed at last]. For in the winter I must call them to give me a greater supply. If the House of Commons will not joyne to preferre my occasions before their' greevances, I conjure your Lordships to consider your owne honors and myne and the pre-posterous course of the House of Commons and desire that your Lops will not joyne with them, but leave them to themselves. I desire you to be carefull in this pointe, else *there maye be such a*

---

[1] See below, App., Charles I (24 April), p. 308.

breach [if the supply come not in tyme] I will not saye what [mis-cheife] maye and must follow.

[H.L.R.O., Braye MS. 2]   **[25 April 1640, Lord Keeper]**

THE HEADS OF WHAT I WAS COMMAUNDED BY THE LORDS TO SPEAKE TO THE HOUSE OF COMMONS AT THE CONFERENCE, 25⁰ APRIL 1640[1]

[fo 65ʳ]

1. His Majestys comming to the house yesterday and the effect of what he sayd.

He put us in mynd of what had bene sayd to both houses, both heere in the Ls house and in the banquetting house.

That he would make it all good.

That the necessity of affaires can beare no delay.

In regard of the affaires themselves and their danger—Distempers of Scotland. Putting themselves into protection, etc. Scottish tents allready sett up. Lettre from Berrick. At Duns and they threaten invasion of Northumberl[*and*].[2]

His Majestys honor in forreyn parts which concern him to uphold as much as his life.

That in all civility and good manners as well as necessity the trust is fitt to be put upon him in the first place.

Notwithstanding his Majesty exprest he must also trust them. They shall but trust him first in part he must in conclusion trust them in all.

1. K cannot now transfer the trust, for both houses cannot recover if tyme now lost. 2. But a supply for the present. 3. Delay as good as deniall. 4. K would else let them go on in any way they pleased.

And a whole trust for all execution. And he will not break it.

That for the 3 grievances, Religion, Property, and libertie of Parliament, he will graciously harken to them and relieve them, and give them what can in reason be desired.

K of a free and rich people, etc.

And as much as tyme will permitt now. The rest at winter.

For religion, his hart and conscience stood with religion of church of England and he would lyve and dye in it. He would be as forward to prevent innovations as any and see that his Archbishops and Bps should take order accordingly.

For shipmoney, so they will give him meanes to preserv the seas in

---

[1] Endorsement, fo 66ᵛ. See also below, App., L.K. (25 April), p. 310. These notes, in the Lord Keeper's hand, do not show clearly the order in which the content should be arranged.

[2] *Cf. CSP 1640*, pp. 22, 50.

any way, etc. He hath made no benefitt but bene out of proxe many thousands.

Our voting.

Conclusion. Our desire they would goe on with that first as that which wee in our opinions hold most necessary. This don we shalbe ready to joyne, etc. Not move subsidies from us, but declyne it. Duty give advice.

[*Neilson MS. 2688*]   [*?29 April 1640, ?Eliot*]

[*A NOTE ABOUT THE OATH EX OFFICIO*][1]

[*p. 1042*]

There is a point of form in proceedings which may deserve reformacion ye rather because itt is contrary to ye laws and customs of this land and state, which though they do nott rule those proceedings yett may they be advised with for better direction and yt is ye oath *ex officio* whereby men are inforced to accuse themselves and yt which is more are sworne unto blanques and nott to accusacions and charges declared. By ye laws of England no man is bound to accuse himself. In ye highest cases of treason torture is used for discovery and nott for evidence in capitall matters. No delinquents answer upon oath is required, no nott permitted. In criminall matters, nott capitall handled in ye Starr Chamber and in causes of conscience in ye Chancery for ye most part grounded upon trust and secrecy ye oath of ye party is required. Butt honor where there is an accusacion and an accusor which we call Bills of Complaint from which ye complaint cannott varry and out of ye compass of which ye defendant may nott be examined) exhibited unto ye court and by process notified to ye defendant. Butt to examine a man upon oath out of ye insinuacion of fame or out of accusacion, secret and undeclared things itt have some countenance from ye civill law, yett itt is so opposite or demean to ye tenor and courte of ye common law as itt may well receive [?] limitacions, reformacion.

[*H.L.R.O., Braye MS. 2*]   [*1 May 1640, Lord Keeper*]

1o MAII 1640. SPEECH TO THE HOUSE OF COMMONS IN
[*fo 70ʳ*]   THE PAINTED CHAMBER[2]

My Lords have commaunded mee to lett you know, That the desire and care on your parts at the last conference represented unto

---

[1] These notes appear in the margin of a speech about the oath *ex officio*, attributed on this copy to Glyn. See below, App., [?]Eliot, [?] 29 April), p. 313.

[2] Endorsement, fo 74ᵛ. See also below, App., L.K. (1 May), p. 314.

them, for preserving a good union and correspondence betweene their Lops and you is by them entertained with all respect, and requyted with all good affection, as that which is the best way to bring both our consultations and resolutions to an happie issue, to give his Majesty a dutifull account of our zeale and forwardnes in those great and weighty affaires for which wee were assembled, and to further those united proceedings, that may tend to the happines of this kingdome and the contentment of both houses.

Their Lops well know the great priviledges belonging to both houses of Parliament, of which they and you are alyke participant, and they are not ignorant of those that are distinctly proper to each house. What belongs to you of the House of Commons, they never had thought to impeach or diminish in the least kynd.

And what they may justly challenge to themselves they presume you will not attempt upon; since you cannot doubt but they wilbe as tender of their honor in [the] preservation and upholding of their owne as they are and shalbe carefull not to invade or violate any of yours.

This their Lops have commaund[ed] mee to tell you, will best and most cleerely appeare by the course hath bene held in their owne house, and by their proceedings with you.

Their[1] Lops, as in duty and affection to his Majesties crowne and government they are bound, tooke into serious consideration, the great and weighty motives of [fo 70ᵛ] his Majesties calling us together at this tyme.

The great evills and calamities, that hang over our heads and the apparant danger this kingdome is lyke to run into, if by speedy and fitting supply his Majesty be not enabled to prevent it.

These with the reasons enforcing how insupportable delay and protraction was, and how impossible [it is] for both houses to recover the losse of tyme in a matter of so pressing and urgent consequence,[2] were by his Majesties commaund delivered to their Lops and you, both in the Lords House and in the Banquetting House at Whitehall, his Majesty being present.

His Majesty both those tymes, exprest his gracious and princely desire to doe all (that from a just and gracious King might be expected) whereby this Parliament might have a happy[3] and blessed conclusion and bring joy and consolation to his Majesty and all his subjects.

He told you, that all your just grievances should be graciously heard and relieved.

---

[1] B.L., E.203(1), p. 27, begins here.
[2] *necessity* (B.L., E.203(1), p. 28).
[3] happy conclusion (remainder of sentence omitted (B.L., E.203(1), p. 28)).

That[1] he would therein lett you be at no losse of tyme but for the present before you parted, you should have without abridging, as much as the season and great affaires in hand would possibly permitt, and what you could not now perfect, you should have tyme towards winter to goe through with.

Their Lops were witnesses that his Majesty gave his royall word herein, and for their parts lodg'd in their harts as much trust and confidence of his Majesties royall performance, as ever subjects did. Not long after his Majestie,[2] [*fo 71ʳ*] was pleased to honor the Lords House with his presence againe.

To renew the remembrance of all what had before bene delivered to both houses, both for the necessity of the supply desired, with the impossibility of admitting delay and the clearenes of his Majesties intentions and resolutions to give all just satisfaction to what with reason could be desired of him.

His Majesty then tooke notice to their Lops of somewhat that had bene voted in your house, concerning Religion, Propertie of goods and Libertie of Parliament, whereby his Majesty conceaved the matter of his supply sett asyde, which he had so often and with such weight of reason desired might have precedence.

And after very gracious assurances to their Lops, of his Majesties constant affection and zeale for true religion and [for] preventing all innovations therein, of his so often iterated promise[3] to give a gracious eare and just reliefe to all your just greivances, and in particular expressing his royall intentions in that of shipmoney, which he found [so] much stood upon, he was pleased to desire their Lops (as persons in rank and degree neerest to him, in honor as much or more concern'd then others, and in the safety and prosperity of this kingdome, at least equally interested with the rest[4] of his subjects) That in a case of this great and important weight, they would by their counsell and perswasion enclyne you of the House of Comons to give his Majesty a speedy answer and resolution in the matter of supply. Their Lops tooke his Majestyes desire into serious and dutifull consideration, and after great and solemn debate, they resolved.

That theyr opinion was that the matter of his Majesties supply should have precedence and be resolved of [*fo 71ᵛ*] before any other matter whatsoever.

And did think fitt there should be a conference desired with you of the House of Comons to dispose you thereunto. And this was all

---

[1] Paragraph omitted (B.L., E.203(1), p. 28).
[2] Several lines written and crossed out in MS.
[3] '*reiterating* his often promise*s for relieving* all *their* just grievances *with* his royal intentions in that *particular* of ship money . . .' (B.L., E.203(1), p. 30).
[4] with *others* (B.L., E.203(1), p. 30).

they then voted or concluded; with which at the conference their Lops acquaynted you.

This as it was just and honorable for them to doe so it[1] neither extended the boundes and limitts of their owne priviledges, nor narrow'd or streightened any of yours. And yet at the last conference (which their Lops are apt and willing to believe proceeded rather from some mistaking then any intention to lessen theirs or enlarge your own priviledges) It was urged in your name That the voting of this was a breach of your priviledge; and that therein their Lops had bene transported beyond the grounds which they had sett to them-selves. Because in the former conference their Lops had admitted, that matter of supply ought to begin in the House of Comons as naturally belonging to that House and wherein their Lops would not meddle, no not so much as to give advice.

And yet by voting what they did had not only medled with matter of supply, but as farre as in their Lops lay had concluded both the matter and order of proceeding. [For which you demaunded repara-tion from their lordships], wherein I am comaunded by their Lops to lett you know that they have neither varied nor bene transported from their owne groundes, or voted any thing contrary to your rights and priviledges or to that admitting of them at that conference which is pretended.

For their Lops did and doe admitt, that the Bill of Subsidies ought to[2] have his inception and beginning in your house, That when it comes up to their Lops and is by them agreed unto, it must be returned backe to you and be by your Speaker presented.

And therefore as they disclayme any thought or intention [*fo 72ʳ*] of such beginning in their house, so they did at their debate and at their conference with you, disclayme to meddle with the matter of subsidy or supply, that is by naming the tyme or number or any such circumstances incident to the bill which ought to begin with you, or therein to give you any the least advice. But to conferre and talke with you about supplyes in generall or to give theyre advice therein,[3] they doe not nor ever did hold derogatory to yours or exceeding the priviledges of their owne house.

For as you frequently impart your grievances to them, so it is all the reason in the world they should communicate their feares and foresight of dangers unto you.

Their Lops being a body that moves in an orbe neerer to the royall

---

[1] '. . . so it *was no breach of any* privilege of *the House of Commons'* (B.L., E.203(1), p. 31; remainder of paragraph and following paragraph omitted).
[2] Remainder of paragraph and that following condensed (B.L., E.203(1), pp. 31–32).
[3] '. . . *that being no whit* derogatory to the priviledges of *the* House *of Com-mons'* (B.L., E.203(1), p. 32; following paragraph omitted).

throne then you doe, and thereby the lykelyer to communicate in the Councells and secrets of state,[1] and for their persons and fortunes [at least as] *more* considerable in poynt of danger.

Their[2] Lops are not unacquainted with that establishment in Parliament, which was by you at the conference styled the Indempnity of the Commons, but is indeede the Indempnity of Lords and Commons and so styled in the record it selfe.[3]

For by that record made at Glouc. 9 *H.* 4 it appeares there was conference between the Lords and Comons about the state of the realm and the defence of it. After which the King demaunding of the Lords what ayde was fitt to be granted they sayd a tenth and a half [of citties and boroughs] and a fifteenth and a half of others and a subsidy of tonnage and poundage for 2 yeares.

Upon which the King sent to the Comons to send up to him [*fo* 72ᵛ] and the Lords 12 of their company; to whome when they came, it was by the Kings commaund declared, what had bene by the King demaunded of the Lords and the Lords answer thereunto, which the King willed them to report to their compagnions, that they might with better speede conforme themselves to the intention of the Lords.

This indeede the Commons were troubled at, as being in great derogation of their liberties.

Whereupon to prevent for the future any thing that might turn to the prejudice of their liberty, or against the libertie of the Lords, It was established, That it should allways be lawfull for the Lords to [?]comun among themselves in the Kings absence of the estate of the realm and the remedies needefull, and so for the Comons among themselves. Provided allways that neither Lords nor Comons report to the King any thing granted by the Comons and assented to by the Lords, nor the communications of it, before the Lords and Comons be agreed, and then as the manner is by the Speaker of the House of Comons.

This is the substance of that establishment, which only hath relation to the manner of presenting subsidies and aydes to the King, and giving him knowledge of them.

And as it hath not one word that barres the Lords or Comons from conferring about them, so it plainly declares that Lords or Comons

---

[1] '. . . and *having just cause therein to impart their fears and foresight* of dangers *to the House of Commons*' (B.L., E.203(1), p. 32; preceding part of paragraph condensed).

[2] B.L., E.203(1), p. 32, substitutes '*That such proceedings of their lordships, as they were grounded upon just and weighty reason, so they were agreeable to ancient usage and custome, and were fully justified by that establishment.* . . .'

[3] Several lines written and crossed out in MS. B.L., E.203(1), p. 33, omits details about 9 *Hen.* IV and continues with speech as in MS., fo 73ʳ.

in their severall houses may [equally] treate among themselves of the
dangers the kingdome is in and of the way to remedy them.

And this my Lords have well weighed, and are satisfied, verifyes
their proceedings to have bene according to auncient usage and
custome, as they are grounded upon just and weighty reasons.

[Many other reasons their Lops have to justify their proceedings in
this particular, but they conceyve this record alone mencioned by
yourselves will herein give you abundant satisfaction and plainly
show that the house of Commons had no cause to demaund reparation herein from theyr lordships.]

[*fo 73ʳ*] A second thing was objected, wherein their Lops have
bene sayd to have broken another[1] great priviledge of the House of
Comons established by that ordnance which I have mencioned
before.

Which is that theyre Lops have taken notice of some proceedings
in the House of Comons concerning three particulars: Religion,
Propriety of goods, and priviledge of Parliament.

To which their Lops have commaunded mee to give [you] this just
and honorable answer.[2]

His Majesty told their Lops you had resolved something concerning those three heads, and by that way of proceeding preferred the
greivances before the matter of supply.

How his Majesty knew you had so resolved, belongs not to their
Lops to enquyre into.[3] [*fo 73ᵛ*] [Their Lops not medling with any
thing that others sayd to the King, but what his Majestie sayd to
their lordships] *which way to right yourselves is the question* [And for
their lordships to heare what] his Majestie [declared] to them and
[for them thereupon to report the same to the House of Commons]
theire Lops are so farre from holding it any diminution or violation of
your priviledges, that on the contrary in duty to his Majesty they
could doe no other, and the communicating it to you in that manner
they thinke merritts rather your opinion and beliefe of their affections [to you] and desire of good correspondence with you, then any
other misconstruction whatsoever. [And that which you called the
Indemnity of the Commons hath no words in it that can be construed
to make that any breach of your priviledges.] And therefore their
Lops having thus cleered and justified their own proceedings, and
freed themselves from any imputation of invading your liberties,
They cannot but return to their first groundes and resolutions which
were in all faire and affectionate manner, to stirre up in you the just

[1] B.L., E.203(1), p. 33, resumes but condenses this and three following
paragraphs.
[2] Two paragraphs written and struck out in MS.
[3] MS. revised here.

consideration of those great and imminent dangers that threaten this kingdome at this tyme [and] how dangerous and irrecoverable delay is and [withall to dispose you to][1] take into your first and best thoughts the matter of his Majesties supply, and give him a speedy answer therein. This their Lops are confident wilbe the meanes to preserve and continue a good union and understanding betweene their Lops and you, to make this a happie parliament, and to avert the publick calamaties that menace the ruine and overthrow of this famous and renowned monarchy.[2]

[1] MS. revised here.
[2] Paragraph written and struck out in MS.

BILLS

[*H.L.R.O., Main Papers*]   [*23 April 1640, Cloth Bill*]

THE BREIFE OF THE BILL FOR DRESSED CLOATHES[1]

That his Majestys subjects may have the benefitt of the manufacture of woolls, and for the encrease of the trade of shipping of cloathes. Bee it enacted that the maior, constables, and fellowshipp of the Merchants of the Staple of England, and the freemen thereof, and that all other merchants of this realme, may as well transport dyed and coulored cloathes, as also all kersies cottons, etc, and all draperies made of wooll or mixt with wooll into all the partes beyonde the seas, without restraint or impeachment of any other company of merchants, or any other. Notwithstanding any statute or charter to the contrary.

And if any company of merchants or others of them shall arrest or staye such cloathes or draperie, the partie greived shall recover treble damages in what country or place hee please.

Provided that this act shall not extend to dissolve or anihilate certeyne lettres patents of the late Q. *Eliz.* dated 17 *Junii anno Regni sui*, whereby certeyne merchants of Exeter and their successors bee incorporated for merchants adventurers of that Citty.

[*H.L.R.O., Main Papers*]   [*2 May 1640, Clergy Bill*]

AN ACT FOR THE EASE OF THE CLERGIE FROM [SOME] LAY EMPLOYMENTS[2]

For the more quiett and vertuous increase and mainteynance of divine ser[*vices*] the preaching and teaching the word of God with godly and good examp[*les*] giving the better discharge of the duty of the Spirituall and ecclesiasti[*cal*] persons, the increase of devotion and the good opinion of the lay [?]fee towards the Spirituall and ecclesiasticall persons, May itt please your most excellent Majestie that itt may bee inacted by your most sacred Majestie with the assent of the Lords Spirituall and Temporall and the Commons in

---

[1] Endorsed: '17 Mar. 1629. The breef for venting of dyed cloathes. 1640.' First reading 16 April; second reading and commitment, 23 April; committee sheet also, H.L.R.O., Main Papers, 23 April 1640.

[2] Endorsement faint and damaged: '[?] An Act for the Ease of the Clergie from some lay employments, *1⁰ vice lecta, 2ᵈᵒ Maii* [?].' See *C.J.*, ii, p. 18; also *C.J.*, ii, p. 16.

this present Parliament assembled And bee it inacted by the authoritie of the same That every spirituall and Ecclesiastical person of what degree or qualitie soever he be other then such as bee and hereafter shallbe of your Majesties privy councell shallbee adjudged a disabled person in the law to all intents and purposes to exercise any temporall or lay office commission or authority whatsoever in any of your Majesties courts of justice within this kingdome of England and dominions of Wales, (other then in the High court of Parliament) Any lawe statute or ordinance to the contrary hereof made in anywise nott withstanding.

PETITIONS

[*S.P. 16/450/25*]   [*17 April 1640, Northampton*]

THE HUMBLE PETICION OF THE FREEHOLDERS OF THE COUNTY OF NORTHAMPTON TO THE HONORABLE HOUSE OF COMMONS OF THE INTENDED PARLIAMENT[1]

SHEWETH: That whereas of late we have bine unusually and unsupportably charged, troubled and greived in our consciences, persons and estates by innovacion in religion, exaccions in Spirituall courts, molestacions off our most godly and learned ministers, shipp monie, monopolies, undue imposicions, armie monie, waggon monie, horse monie, conducte monie, and inlardging the forrest, beyond the auncient bounds and other such for not yeildinge to which things or some of them diverse of us have bine molested distrayned and imprisoned. Wee have intrusted John Crewe, Esq. and Sir Gilbert Pickeringe, kt and Barronett chosen Kts for our said county to present these our greivances humbly desiring that you will be pleased deeply to take them into yr tender consideracion and that these may for the present be redressed and that it may be soe ordered that we may have a Parliament once a yeare as by lawe we ought *4to Edw 3o Stat* [1]4, 36 *Edw 3 Stat*. 10 for preventinge the like inconveniences in time to come.

[*B.L., Harl. MS. 4931*]   [*18 April 1640, Essex*]

[*fo 41ʳ*]

TO THE RIGHT HONOURABLE THE HOUSE OF COMMONS NOW ASSEMBLED IN PARLIAMENT.

THE HUMBLE PETITION OF YE FREEHOLDERS OF YE COUNTY OF ESSEX[2]

SHEWETH: That ye petitioners having of late yeares beene unwontedly overcharged and insupportably burdened in their consciences, Estates, and Freedomes.

By innovations in matters of Religion, both in doctrine and discipline; By molesting and depriving of godly and learned Ministers, [By tolerating and countenancing of ye profanation of the Lords

---

[1] Endorsed: 'Freeholders petition of Northt. to ye knights of ye shire. Rec'd Ap. 4. 1640.'
[2] A copy, not the original petition.

Holy day;] By [wronging] *raging against and abusing* to new inventions about ye blessed sacrament. By chargeable various and vaine alterations in and about Churches; By greate expenses, losse, and molestation through unnecessary, and unreasonable attendance and unjust vexation, insolency, and extortions by Ecclesiasticall Courts and Officers; All which do evidently tend to ye Hazarding of mens Soules, ye Encreasing of errours, and heresies, ye decreasing of mens Estates, ye Cherishing and Augmenting of Schisms among ourselves, and Disaffection one to another and ye greate Endangering of ye peace of ye Commonwealth.

And by Impositions and great paiments upon Merchants goods and necessary commodities both native and forraine.

And also by Inhaunsing and making worse both our Countrey, and Beyond-sea commodities through Monopolies and Restraints whereby also a free trade is hindered and allmost wholly ruined to ye undoing of many, and ye heavy grievance of all.

And furder by Inforresting ye greatest part of our County, whereby for the present wee are charged with sore paiments, and for ye future [our lands like to be much incombered] *ye title to our lands is made doubtfull;* the legality of which proceeding wee humbly pray may be fairely and according to law and justice againe examined.

And lastly by ye paiment of shipp-money, which is a burden unknowne to our fathers, insupportably grievous to ourselves, and exceedingly prejudiciall to *ourselves* ye Liberties and Immunities of his Majestyes subjects. All which are so intolerable, that unles ther be a timely redresse, wee must unavoidable, and heavily suffer and ye whole County (if not the Kingdome) soone runne to ruine. And therefore (wee being constrained) *heretofor* have taken humble boldness to informe this most Honourable assembly by this our humble Petition, with the delivery whereof wee have intrusted the two Knights who *serv* by and for our County,[1] with such furder just and true information as this greate and weighty matter doth and shall require.

Humbly praying that you wold please to take ye premises deeply to heart and to endeavour a full and perfect redresse therein in this present Parliament; and for prevention of ye saime, or ye like grievances in time to come, to provide that a Parliament may be held at least once every yeare, as of right it ought to be done by the lawes, and statutes of this Realme.

And we shall humbly pray etc

[1] Sir Thomas Barrington and Sir Harbottle Grimston.

[B.L., Harl. MS. 4931]   **[18 April 1640, Hertfordshire]**

[fo 42ʳ]

TO YE *RIGHT* HONOURABLE YE HOUSE OF COMMONS NOW SHORTLY TO BE ASSEMBLED IN PARLIAMENT THE HUMBLE PETITION OF YE FREEHOLDERS AND FREEMEN OF YE COUNTY AND BURROUGH TOWNES OF HARTFORDSHIRE[1]

SHEWETH: That your Petitioners having of late yeares beene unusually overcharged and insupportably burdened in their Consciences, Persons, Estates, and Freedomes

First by Innovations in matters of religion by some violent and indiscreete cleargy men, who in many Towns of this County under pretense of authority have boldly violated and audaciously attempted many things contrary to ye Canons of ye Church, ye Rubrick, and Book of Common Prayer, ye Proclamations of our religious Kings and Princes, and our most gracious Soveraigne King Charles and to ye acts of Parliament established, and in our Bibles imprinted. They daring to deny even ye holy sacrament, even for a yeare together, to hundreds in our Congregations, and *where they have found opposition* to reject great numbers which wee well know to be conformable persons and to give no offence in ther live[s] to ye Congregation. And where they have found opposition by ther Parishioners herein, ye course hath beene to cite great nombers of ye poorer sort of people to ye Ecclesiasticall Courts (wherein themselves are for ye most part ye Judges) which Courts are oftener held more frequented, and more chargeable to our country then our Assemblies for ye preservation of ye peace of our Realme his Majesties crowne and dignity, ye Sessions, and Assizes, thereby so to molest and impoverish poore people by such unjust vexations, exactions and excommunications for small causes, as that such poore people, who (God knowes) are ye greatest number of our shire, are not able to withstand them, but are enforced to submitt, fly their dwellings, or remaine excommunicated, ye numbers whereof in this county are very many; they having by these meanes also exhausted more money in one yeare out of some townes, then his Majesty hath in any yeare yet required for shipp-money, or hath in our remembrances beene paid for subsidies, or fifteenths, whereof not one penny gott into his Majesties coffers; whereby ye most happy unity and uniformity of our Church is not only violated and much broken, but his Majesties peace and quiett of ye Common wealth in some townes hath beene much endangered.

---

[1] A copy, not the original petition. In margin 'Hartford, March 12, 1639.'

K

Secondly by ye manifest abuses of feodaries and Escheators pretending tenures for his Majesty where none are, and so to exact greate summes of money from ye meaner sort of commons without any benefitt also to his Majesty.

Thirdly ye manifest abuses, and incroachments of Purveyors, the particulars whereof we shalbe ready at large to manifest.

Fourthly by monopolies, restraints, and impositions, whereby free trade is interrupted, and allmost all commodities their Countreymen buy so inhaunsed and abased as tendes to ye utter undoing of many and to ye heavy and insupportable grievance of all sorts of people.

Lastly by ye paiment of Shipp-money, ye legality whereof wee most humbly pray may be reexamined. All which are so intolerable, as by reason of ye cheapnesse of corne, wooll, and other our countrey commodities, we shall not be able to relieve ye poore, maintaine our families and children, uphold our houses, pay our rents and other taxations and to grant unto his Majesty such subsidies as ye high court of Parliament shall thinke fitt, which we shall chearfully, and liberally give for ye maintenance of our religion established, ye defense of his Majestyes person, his realmes, and dominions. We having also besides these many other grievances, and being so constrained we have taken humble boldness thereof to informe this most Honourable Assembly by this our humble Petition, with ye delivery whereof we have intrusted [*fo 42ᵛ*] our knights and burgesses chosen for this present parliament;[1] praying that you wold all with your best assistance endeavour the blessed peace, and unity of these his Majestyes Kingdomes, and that you wold be pleased to take ye premisses deapely to heart, and to advance by your allowance this our most humble petition to our most Gracious Soveraigne, and to ye upper house of Parliament and to andeavour for us a full and fast redresse hearin, in this present Parliament and for prevention of ye same and ye like grievances in time to come to provide that Parliaments may be more frequently holden according to ye lawes and statutes of this realme. And we shall pray, etc.

[1] Sir Wm. Lytton and Arthur Capel (knights of the shire); Chas. Cecil, Viscount Cranborne and Sir Thomas Fanshawe (Hertford Borough).

[H.L.R.O., Main Papers]   *[18 April 1640, Norwich]*

TO THE RIGHT HONORABLE THE HOWSE OF COMMONS IN THIS PRESENT PARLIAMENT ASSEMBLED THE HUMBLE PETITION OF THE MAIOR; SHREIFFES, ALDERMEN AND CITIZENS OF THE CITTY OF NORWICH.[1]

Humbly Sheweth That whereas within these twelve yeares last past there have beene five remooves of Bishopes by death and otherwise in the diocese of Norwich These are humblye to informe this honorable assembly that at the two last visitations of the Lord Bishope of Ely[2] that nowe is, beinge then Bishoppe of Norwich, and this last of the present Lord Bishoppe of Norwich,[3] there have beene such an exceedinge number of Articles more then in former times, that they have not only bin excessive chargible to every particular parish more then in times past, but alsoe the number beinge so greate and the qualitie and inquirie made into many of them so diffringe from the Articles of former Bishoppes that it soe perplexeth the consciences of the Church wardens and other sidemen that they cannot possible keepe the oath that they are inforced to take and the people in generall are much agreived at the varietie and vast number of severall articles being neere two hundred which hath made many very honest and able men to sell their estates, and transplant themselves into parte beyond the seas in consideration wherof wee humblye intreate this honorable assemblie that they would be pleased to take this greivous complainte into your honorable consideracion and take such course that not onlye the greate extraordinarie charge at visitations may be reduced to the former moderate rate for there verdictes as it was thirtie yeares agoe and our consciences freede from so many needles and unprofitable Articles, as are nowe pressed uppon us.

1 Endorsed, 'The Commons of Norwich, their Petition. Petition of Norwich referred to a subcommittee.'
2 Matthew Wren.
3 Richard Montagu, author of *Appello Caesarem* (1625), and target of complaints in Parliament, 1625, 1626, 1628.

[H.L.R.O., Main Papers]   *[22 April 1640, Peter Smart]*

TO THE HONORABLE THE KNIGHTS CITTIZENS AND BURGESSES OF THE COMMONS HOWSE OF PARLIA-MENT

THE HUMBLE PETICION OF PETER SMART A POORE DISTRESSED PRISONER IN THE KINGS BENCHE[1]

Humblie sheweth: That after ye death of Bishopp James, Bishopp Neale comeinge to ye sea of Durham the deane and prebendaries of that Cathedrall Church cast ye communion table out of ye same and erected an high alter att ye east end of ye quire, of marble stones with a carved screene most gloriouslie painted and guilded which cost about 200*li* and bought for 40*s* one cope found in a search for masse preists whereon was imbroidered ye image of ye Trinitie and another cope which cost them about tenn groats which had been a longe time used for a fooles coate in May games and sports by ye youth of Durham both which copes they used att the administracion of ye holy communion att their new alter to which themselves both did and forced others to use most unreasonable frequent bowinge, Doctor Cosins[2] officiatinge thereat with his face towards ye east and back towards ye people, and did likewise take away morninge praier to which about 200 persons usuallie resorted used for the space of about 60 yeares in ye cathedrall church of Durham (as in all other cathedrall and collegiat churches in England) to be read att six of ye clock plainelie and destinctlie in a peculier place appointed for that purpose by commissioners under ye greate seale of England 25º September [?]1 *Eliz.*[3] and instead thereof altered the same into singinge with instruments without readinge any chapters or psalmes [?] And did likewise sett upp 53 glorious images and picktures on the Bishops throne and about ye quire in ye said church and burnt 200 wax candles in one candlemass night in ye honor of our Ladie and brought in sondrie other superstitious and unwarrantable innova-cions into that church to ye observacion whereof they forced divers and publiquely brawled in ye time of divine service in ye church with others whoe would not observe ye same. Callinge them lasie sowes and durtie whores teareinge some gentlewomans apparell callinge others pagans and thrusting them out of the church who refused to

---

[1] Endorsed: 'Smart, Peter. Read *22do* Apr., *16to Car. R.* Peter Smart.' Brought in but not signed, consequently not read, 21 April (*C.J.*, ii, p. 8); Read and committed, 22 April; see also, *C.J.*, ii, pp. 8–9, 14. *Cf.* his printed petition submitted to the Long Parliament (B.L., 698.h.20(22)). See *D.N.B.*

[2] John Cosin, prebend at Durham under Neile; Dean of Durham, 1640. See *D.N.B.*

[3] Probably the Queen's Injunctions of 1559.

obey them therein some of them preachinge in a cope and sittinge to heare service in a cope and others of them [*vizt.*] Dr Cosins preachinge in ye said cathedrall church upon the parable of ye tares that ye reformers of ye Church when they tooke away the masse took away or mard all religion and ye whole service of God and that it was a deformacion indeede though they called it a reformacion and publiquely mainteined that ye kings majestie is not supreame head of ye church in England nor could be soe called, for that hee had no more power to meddle in ecclesiasticall matters then the fellowe that rubbed his horses heeles for which he was indited A*o* 1629 att ye assizes att Durham aforesaid and found guiltie thereupon by ye oathes of 3 men of worth which inditement yett remaines untraversed,

Your petitioner beinge a senior prebendarie residentiar of that Church and one of his Majesteys high commissioners for causes ecclesiasticall within ye province of Yorke and in judgement and practise punctually conformable to ye doctrine and ceremonies established in ye Church of England opposed ye same innovacions and doctrines accordinge to his dutie place and callinge, but not prevaileinge therein, hee in July 1628 accordinge to the third injunccion preached in the said church against the same for which sermon hee was presentlie convented before the high commission houlden att Durham and before any articles exhibited against him suspended and his liveing sequestered And after his answer upon oath to the articles and six monethes detencion in ye said high commission (where he was proceeded against with all rigour and extremitie accordinge to ye expresse command (as some of the high commissioners in open court said) of some Bishopps from London) He was served with a warrant under ye high commission seale for ye province of Canterbury and hand of William L. Bishopp of London, Samuell lo Bishopp of Norwich, Dr Cesar, Dr Lamb to appeare before ye high commission houlden in London and there forced againe to take the oath *ex officio* and to attend above a quarter of a yeare for Articles which were pretended to bee matters of high nature against him and was afterwards remanded without any articles to Yorke where in August 1630 they proceeded to sentence *ex parte* havinge denied your petitioner a commission to examine witnesses on his behalfe where he was excommunicated degraded, fined 700*li* and imprisoned for opposinge and preachinge against the said doctrines and superstitious innovations; notwithstanding that Dr Cosins and Mr Frances [?]Burgan were indited in August 1629 att Durham assizes upon severall bills and found guiltie thereof which remaines likewise untraversed. This legall conviccion notwithstandinge the said Dr Cosins since is made one of his Majesteys chapleins in ordinary and admitted to his degree of doctor and made master of Peterhouse in Cambridge and now vice chancellor of that universitie and all proceedings upon ye former inditements against him stopped.

That your petitioner peticioned and preferred articles into ye High Commission att London against the said deane and prebendaries for ye said doctrines and innovacions preferring to give sufficient securitie to prove all ye said articles; But the said peticion and articles were utterlie rejected by the said court who said they wouldnot suffer such worthie men to bee questioned.

That your petitioner was two severall times imprisoned att Yorke before their said sentence for which injurious imprisonment he commenced his accion att law against some of ye said high Commissioners and obteyned judgement thereupon and 600^{li} damages yett cannot have any fruit thereof

That your petitioner hath been kept in prison upon the said sentence in great penurie and want almost tenn yeares and lost both his dignitie parsonage and whole estate whereby hee his wife and children are utterlie ruined in theire persons posteritie and fortunes.

That your petitioner is now and hath been about 12 monthes close prisoner and his Majesteys most gratious reference in his behalfe unto ye now Lo Bishopp of Durham revoked upon pretence [?] that he was latelie in Glascoo in Scotland preaching and instigating ye Scotts against episcoapall government, whereas he was never there in his life nor in Scotland this 24 yeares nor had directlie nor indirectlie anye intelligence with the Scotts.

In tender commiseracion whereof your petitioner most humblie beseecheth your serious consideracion both of his miserable distressed condicion and greate oppressions. As also of ye said innovacions and offences of ye said Dr Cosins and ye other prebendaries of Durham with theire abettors who presented and censured your petitioner. And to take such course both for your poore petitioners releefe and release as also for reformacion of ye said doctrines innovacions and proceedings and prevention of ye like hereafter as to your greate wisdomes shall seeme meete. And for that your petitioner is much decaied in his health by reason of his late restraint and verie poore hee humblie beseecheth you presentlie to give order for his release from his close imprisonment. And that he may have present execucion upon the said judgement for ye said 600^{li} whereby he shalbe enabled to prosecute and prove this his most just complaint against these his adversaries.

And your petitioner and all his shall dailie praie, etc.

Peter Smart, Prisoner in the Kings Bench

[H.L.R.O., Main Papers]   *[22 April 1640, Archibald Niccoll]*

TO THE RIGHT REVEREND AND THE RIGHT HONOR-ABLE THE LORDS SPIRITUALL AND TEMPORALL IN THE HIGH COURT OF PARLIAMENT ASSEMBLED.

THE HUMBLE PETICION OF ARCHIBALD NICCOLL IN THE BEHALFE OF HIMSELFE AND HIS PARTNERS BEING THIRTENE IN NOMBER.[1]

Humblie sheweth: That whereas your suppliants having exhibited their humble peticion unto your honors the last session touching 3277^{li} appearing to be injustly due unto them as well by severall orders from the Lords of the councell as also upon record in the Court of Admiraltie your lordshipps were honorably pleased to recomend the examynation of their just complaynts unto the lords committees who having taken the same into their serious consideracions found that after a definitive sentence in the Court of Admiralty for 4577^{li} 18^{s} the lords of the councell Did by warrant command Sir Henry Martin Judge of the foresaid court to tax the charge and [?]proceed for the petitioners which he accordingly did it ammounting to the foresaid sume of 4577^{li} and did accordingly deliver your suppliants goods inventored in full satisfaccion thereof. Notwithstanding Sir John Hippsley came afterwards with a warrant from the Lords of the councell and tooke away all the goods leaving onely soe much thereof as was worth 2000^{li} whereof the petitioners were ordered to pay a third part to their marryners And your said suppliants being still damnifyed 3277^{li} the lords committees saw noe cause why the petitioner should loose their moneys but referred it to the honorable house where they should have the residue either of Sir John Heppisley or of the lord Threasurer if he have delivered the moneys unto him in his accompt as by the said peticion and a report under the right honorable the earle of Warwicks hand (made with the consent of the rest of the Lords committees) and remayning with the clerk of the parliament appeares. But by reason the Parliament dissolving shortly after the petitioners to their utter undoing remayne yett unsatisfied.

Whose most humble suite is That your lordships (who next under god and his majestie are the fountaines of justice and upon whome their whole hopes relyes) will in commisseracon of their greate oppression longe since and extreame poverty occasioned thereby be honorably pleased to settle some speedy and constant course whereby they may be paid the said some of 3277^{li} appearing to be justly due

---

[1] Endorsed '22 Apr. 1640. Archibald Nicoll.' Motion, 30 April; earl of Dorset to present case to the king, 2 May; see also *L.J.*, iv, p. 78.

unto them without which they shall loose all and end their dayes most miserably in prison being with many of their freinds engaged in severall somes of money taken upp to followe this longe tedious and chargeable suite.

And they with their poore wyves and many small children (now in greate distresse and misery) shall ever pray for all your honors. Archibald Niccoll.

[*H.L.R.O., Main Papers*]   [*24 April 1640, Oxford Constables*]

TO THE RIGHT HONORABLE THE KNIGHTS BURG-HESSES AND CITTIZENS OF THE HOUSE OF COMMONS.

THE HUMBLE PETICION OF RICHARD APPLETREE ONE OF THE HIGH CONSTABLES OF WOOTTON HUNDRED, JOSEPH COLEMAN ONE OF THE HIGH CONSTABLES OF THE HUNDRED OF BANBURY AND DIVERS OTHER PETTY CONSTABLES WITHIN THE COUNTY OF *OXON* NOWE PRISONERS IN THE CASTLE OF *OXON*.[1]

Humbly shewe that your peticioners have receaved severall warrants from Rodolph Warcupp High Sheriff for the County of *Oxon.* for the leveying collecting gathering and distreyning (in case of non payment) of the shipp money in theire severall divisions within the foresayd county of *Oxon,* that in obedience to the most parte of the said High sheriffs warrants they have collected and gathered the said shipp money and returned the same to the said High Sheriff togeather with the names of such as refused to pay whereuppon issued a third warrant from the said High sheriff directed to your peticioners personally to distrayne and the distresses to sell away rendring the surplusage to the owners: your petitioners desired the said High sheriff to secure them from accions to be brought in case they should distreyne which he refused to doe and your petitioners denyed the execucon of the sayd warrants for the which they alsoe denying to be bound to appear at the councell table stand committed by the sayd High sheriff.

Humbly crave theire inlardgement and referr the consideracon hereof to your honors. And they shall praye etc. Thos Etrey, sollicitor for the Prisoners.

---

[1] Endorsed: 'Recd *Veneris* 24to April 1640. Constables of the county of *Oxon.* their peticon.' Presented'24 April (*C.J.*, ii, p. 10); see also P.R.O., P.C. 2/10/431–32, 462, 463, and *CSP 1640*, pp. 253, 370–71.

[H.L.R.O., Main Papers]   *[28 April 1640, Henry Presse]*

TO THE RIGHT HONORABLE THE LORDES SPIRITUALL
AND TEMPORALL IN THE UPPER HOUSE OF PARLIA-
MENT ASSEMBLED. THE HUMBLE PETITION OF
HENRY PRESSE GENT.[1]

Most humblie shewing. That your petitioner is howshold servant
to the right honorable the lord Pagitt (whose letters of priviledge
under his lordships hand and seale are extant.)

That your petitioner was latelie arrested in the Towne of Weymouth and Melcombe Regis in the Countie of Dorsett by Joseph
Mander and Justinian Bagg sergeants at mace of the said Towne by
virtue of a warrant from George Churchey Maior of the Towne of
Weymouth aforesaid at the suite of Joseph Perkins of Dorchester in
the said countie of Dorset Merchant; And notwithstanding the said
letters of priviledge (being at the arrest shewed to the said maior and
serjeants and the said [?]plaintiff) they did refuse to release or sett
your petitioner at libertie; alleadging that the said lettres of priviledge was a pretended proteccon and the said maior tooke a bond
of 100[li] from the [?]plaintiff to have him harmles touching the
detayning of your petitioner.

Your petitioner (having suffered much damage by his imprisonment and restraint besides his disparagement and the breach of the
priviledges of this high court); Doth humblie leave the premisses to
the honorable consideracon of this great assemblie And to vouchsafe
to take such order with the said maior sergeants and [?]plaintiff for
the petitioners release maintayning the priviledges of parliament as
in your great wisdomes shalbe thought meete.

And your petitioner as in dutie bound shall ever praie etc.

[H.L.R.O., Main Papers]   *[30 April 1640, Walter Oke]*

TO THE HONORABLE THE KNIGHTS CITTIZENS AND
BURGESSES ASSEMBLED IN THE HOUSE OF COMMONS
IN PARLIAMENT. THE HUMBLE PETICION OF WALTER
OKE, CITTIZEN OF LONDON.[2]

Sheweth: That in the yeare 1637 Sr Edward Bromfeild Kt being
then Lord Maior of London, your peticioner and one Wm. Newet

---

[1] Endorsed: '28 April 1640. Henry Presse petition.' Note: '*Lecta 28º* Aprile
1640. Ord[*ered*] the maior, 2 sergeants and the plaintiff to be sent for.' Draft
order, H.L.R.O., Main Papers, 28 April 1640; see *L.J.*, iv, p. 71.

[2] Endorsed: 'Walter, Citizen of London.' Note: '*Lecta* 30 April 1640. Walter
Oke his petition. To be moved in when the House falls into the debate of the
shippmoney.' See *C.J.*, ii, p. 16. The petition was considered in the Long
Parliament (Notestein, *D'Ewes*, p. 218).

dec[*eased*] were appointed collectors of shipmony for part of Cord-wayner Ward. Who having paid in severall sommes which they had received. Afterwards on Monday the 18th of September in the yeare aforesaid the said Sr. Edward made a warrant for the conventing of one Robert Gibbon of that Ward to shew cause why he would not pay the shipp money demanded of him, the said Newet being then present after the said Gibbon was dismissed Sr. Edward charged the said Newet with negligence and carelessesnes in collecting the shippmony and told the said Newet that unlesse he would promise to pay in 50^{li} of his colleccion more then was received within 3 daies next ensuing he would send him to Newgate which the said Newet (who with your peticioner had lately paid in the money by them received) refused to doe and thereupon was committed to prison. Whereof the said Newets wife having notice being then great with child ready to laye downe went with a freind to Sr Edward to desire her husbands enlargement in regard of her pute[*tive*] condicion and for that she had no body to follow her husbands shopp and trade which the said Sr Edward denying, she then desired him in regard her husband was a sick weake melancolique man that he might not be alone but that his partner Collector your petitioner might be likewise committed for company; the said Sr Edward told her that was but a reasonable request And thereupon the same day sent for your peticioner by his officer and told him his partner collector was gon to Newgate and he would send him thither for company and then did send your peticioner to Newgate where he and the said Newet remained prisoners 6 daies to their great losse and hinderance in their estates and trades; During which imprisonment the deputy and common councellmen of the ward aforesaid tenderly commiserating the case of your peticioner and his partner in their families and trades repaired to the said Sr Edward Bromfeild and acquainted him therewith and prayed their enlargement to whom Sr Edward replyed they did not relish the busines to speake on your petitioners and his partners behalfe and further said they should not be released unlesse they would pay 60^{li} of the colleccion more then they received and that he would keepe them in prison to spurre on others.

Which unjust imprisonment and greivances done unto your peticioner by the said Sr Edward and his officers being injuries of a high nature contrary to the Lawes and Statutes of this kingdome and the ancient liberties of the subjects thereof, Your petitioner humbly prayeth this honorable assembly to take into your grave and judicious consideracions and to be pleased to affoard the peticioner such remedy and releife therein for his damage and losse sustained and for the suppressing of the like daring insolencies in time to come and for establishing of the rights and liberties of the petitioner and all other subjects as this honorable assembly shall in their great judgements and wisdomes think fitt.

And your petitioner and all other loyall subjects shall praye, etc. Walter Oke

[*H.L.R.O., Main Papers*]   [*1 May 1640, Peter Vanlore*]

TO THE HONORABLE ASSEMBLY OF THE COMMONS HOUSE IN PARLIAMENT THE HUMBLE PETICION OF SR PEETER VANLORE, KNT AND BARRONETT AGAINST JOHN LITTLETON, DOCTOUR IN DIVINITY[1]

Sheweth that your petitioner having preferred his peticion to this honorable assemblie against Mr Doctor Littleton concerninge the viccarage of Tylehurst and some proceedment in the Common Pleas [?]court whereby the ordinary course of justice is hindered in a *quare impedit*.

In respect the case is of great importance for the publike and that your petitioner and his clarks perticuler interests are much concerned.

Hee humbly prayes that councel may bee assigned him and in some speedy day appoynted for discusment thereof and that such other prothonatories [?]secondaries of the common Pleas as have the records and rules in this case may bee moved to attend at such time as other waighty affaires will permitt.

[*H.L.R.O., Main Papers*]   [*1 May 1640, Tynge and Poole*]

TO THE HONORABLE THE COMMONS IN THE HIGH COURT OF PARLIAMENT ASSEMBLED. THE HUMBLE PETICION OF JOHN TYNGE AND THOMAS POOLE OF FYFEILD IN THE COUNTY OF ESSEX.[2]

Sheweth that your poore peticioners being constables of Fyfeild aforesaid *anno do* 1637 were the three and twentieth day of January in the same yeare sent for by a messenger to appeare before the lords of his Majesteys most honorable privie counsell as touching the shipping busines for not makeing a rate for the same in the said Parishe which your peticioners had of them selves no warrant to doe

---

[1] Note: 'Mr [?] Hidson; Mr Herne; Mr Chute; Mr Hale; Mr Newdegate.' Presented 1 May 1640 (*C.J.*, ii, p. 17). Only Mr Hale is identifiable as an M.P.

[2] Endorsed: 'Read 1º May 1640. Rcd. John Tynge and Thos. Pooles Petition.' See *C.J.*, ii, p. 17.

whereto wee did appeare and there the clarke of the counsell shewed unto us the Lords order which was that wee should enter into bond of 100^{li} a man to make a rate for the shipp money and to carry it to the high shreife and to doe and performe whatsoever the said shreife should further require of us laying all excuses aside or to the like effecte which wee your peticioners refuseing to doe were by the said Lords committed prisoners to the fleete the 31 of the said month of January and there did remayne five weekes and three dayes closse prisoners kept asunder locked up in fouall chambers remote debarred from all accesse of wife, frends pen inke and paper and all others but such as the warden of the fleete should thinke fytt And also there did remaine more for ye space of three weekes and fower dayes having the libertie of the prison.

And that your poore peticioners could not bee discharged out of prison untill they had entered into bond with suerties in a greate summe to answere to his Majesteys attorneys informacon in ye starr chamber touching the said shipp service which bond your peticioners did enter into with suerties and have answered to the said informacion being examined upon interrogatories, but as yett there hath byne no further proceeding against us. And that the charge of the imprisonment the messengers and lawyers fees and other expenses touching the same amounts to the sume of 45^{li} and upwards besides the damage they sustained in beeing detayned from their wives children and caleings which [?]mon[i]es your peticioners are still out of purse and for want of the same and other damage they sustayned are greatly impoverished.

They therefore most humbly pray that they may have their bond delivered in which they entered into unto his said Majesteys attorney generall and may have such further releife as this grave and honorable assembly shall thinke fytt. And your poor peticioners as in duty bound will dayly pray for his Majestie and all his loyall and true harted subjects. Thomas Poole John Tynge.

[H.L.R.O., Main Papers]   *[2 May 1640, Edward Bishop]*

TO THE HONORABLE THE HOUSE OF COMMONS IN THE HIGH COURT OF PARLIAMENT. THE HUMBLE PETICION OF SIR EDWARD BISHOPP, KNT AND BARONETT[1]

Sheweth. That by virtue of his Majestyes writt directed to the sheriff of Sussex for eleccion of Burgesses for the borrough of

---

[1] Endorsed: 'Sir Edward Bishop peticion received 2 May and referred to a select committee.' Note: 'No date.' See *C.J.*, ii, p. 18; Committee and order, H.L.R.O., Main Papers, 2 May 1640.

Bramber in the said countie for this present Parliament, the right honorable the Lord Cranfeild and Sr Thomas Bowyer, Barronett were elected and returned burgesses for the said Towne.

And the petitioner understanding that the said Lord Cranfeild intended to refuse the said eleccion writt his letter to the said borrough desiring them to elect the petitioner in case of such refusall Whereupon all the inhabitants (without further labour or meanes by the petitioner) returned answeare to the petitioner under all their hands that if the said lord Cranfeild refused, they would upon a new writt elect the petitioner.

And the said lord Cranfeild after refusing the said eleccion and a new writt being to issue Sr John Suckling knt by undue meanes obtained the said writt into his hands and with some powerfull letters obteyned in his favour for eleccion, repaired to the said Towne and of his owne authoritie without the sheriff drew the said burgesses together, who with one consent did declare that they meant to elect the petitioner (then absent) to bee burgesse for the said towne.

Whereupon the said Sr John used threatening speeches to the better sort and offered money and rewards to the meaner sort but not then prevailing to obtaine their consents departed towards London leaving the writt in the hands of one Mr Cranfeild to labour his eleccion before the delivery of the said writt who complying with one Mr Damport Minister of the said Towne did deliver into his hands 20^{li} to bee distributed amongst such of the said towne as would give their voyces for the eleccion of the said Sir John Suckling.

For which rewards the poorer sort of the said towne by the working and perswasion of the said Mr Damport were drawne to elect the said Sr John Suckling And the better sort of the said Burggesses being terrified with the said threatenyngs and fearing to bee undone as they were threatened by the said Sir John Suckling and others (if they did not elect him) did depart without giving any voices at all.

Most humblie desireth this high and honorable court to take the said abuses into consideracion and to punish the same and rectifie the said eleccion in such sort as to your wisdomes shall seeme meet. And your petitioner shall pray etc.

COUNCIL AND MESSAGE TO THE COMMONS

[*S.P. 16/450/113*]   [*23 April 1640, ?Windebanke*]

[*COUNCIL*] [?] 23 APRIL 1640[1]

For the joyning with the Llss the best wilbe to exhort them to supply the King.

If they do not supply a lost K in honor in the face of Christendome, he that will not relieve him in that instance where I [?] I cannot believe he will ever do him good.

To prevent the joyning with the Llss, if it cannot be the K must prevent it.

The Llss to be putt to it whether they will joyne with the Commons before the supplies be agreed upon.

They was not to be joined with if they desert the K.

The Llss to demand a conference with them and so to prevent them before the conference.

The K to go to the Upper House and to lett them know yt the House of Commons are slow and so to desire a conference.[2]

[*S.P. 16/452/9*]   [*2 May 1640, Charles I*]

[*MESSAGE TO THE HOUSE OF COMMONS*][3]

That his Majesty hath divers times, and by sondry wayes acquainted [this] *the* House of *Commons* with the urgent necessity of supply, and with the greate danger inevitably to fall upon the whole state, upon his owne honor, and the honor of this nation if more time shalbe lost therein. That neverthelesse *his Majesty understandeth there hath bene so much neglect of these his representations and commandements, that hitherto there hath bene very little discourse or treaty*

---

[1] The date is written over. These notes, which are on the back of a letter of 18 April and not mentioned in *CSP 1640*, pp. 49–50, are probably in Windebanke's hand. The meeting is probably that to which Rossingham refers: 'Thursday after 3 o'clock, when the House of Commons was risen, and when it was made known at Court how the House had voted to prefer the redress of their grievances before the supply to his Majesty, tne King sent for his Lords and sat in council after sunset' (B.L., Add. MS. 11045, fo 112ᵛ). Rossetti describes the king's agitation when he heard about the Commons' vote (P.R.O. 31/9/18, fos 184ʳ–86ʳ).

[2] Montereul notes that Strafford's opinion was that the king should go to the House of Lords the next day before the Commons had sent a message and attempt to obtain the Lords' support for the priority of supply (P.R.O. 31/3/72, fo 133ʳ).

[3] Endorsed: '2 May 1640: His Majestyes Message to the Lower House, This day Saturday.'

among them to that effect. *Nor hath* his Majesty hitherto [hath] receaved no *any kind of* answer at all, *which he cannot but take as a greate neglect of duety in them and ressent it, as that which peradventure is without* [any] *president of such behavior from subjectes to their King, and not suitable to that ancient revenue and duety formerly paid by the House of Commons to the Crowne in cases of this nature.*

And therefore considering, this as heeretofore; his Majesty hath tolde them, a delay of his supply is as destructive as a deniall, his Majesty doth againe desire them to [give him a] *take more* present [answer concerning] *consideration* his supply, *with other debate laid asyde,—forthwith to resolve by vote to give him an account of what they purpose to doe herein.* His Majesty still resolved on his part to make good whatsoever he hath promised by himself or the Lo Keeper.

APPENDIX

EDITORIAL NOTE

LISTS OF SPEECHES

These lists serve as a guide to the locations, whether in manuscript collections or in print, of speeches of the Short Parliament. The lists are arranged chronologically by the dates on which the speech was probably given. The accompanying explanatory paragraphs treat problems of text and content associated with the speeches. Where no particular explanation seems necessary, such paragraphs are omitted. When there is a close relationship between material, such as with the king's speech of 24 April, the Lord Keeper's statement at the conference on 25 April, and Mr. Herbert's report of that conference, the lists and notes for each item should be consulted. Separation of such closely related material is difficult, and its distribution is at times arbitrary.

Footnotes throughout the volume make references to the lists. Versions of the speeches, and of the resolutions of the Commons about grievances, printed here are indicated by an asterisk and placed at the top of each list. Reports in the Lords' and Commons' *Journals* and seventeenth-century printed copies are cited next, followed by other manuscript copies. Modern printed copies conclude the list. If a speech appears in more than one version, letters in bold inside brackets are used to identify each of the versions after the first. Pagination and foliation are given where they appear in the original, but they are not marked on all manuscripts.

LIST OF BILLS

The bills are listed according to the chamber wherein they were first read and the date on which the reading occurred. The titles are given as they appear in the Lords' or Commons' *Journals*. With each bill are references to the appropriate places in the *Journals* and diaries.

LIST OF PRECEDENTS

The precedents cited in the text are listed in chronological order in four groups: proceedings in Parliament; proceedings in Convocation; statutes; cases. With each are references to the *Rolls of Parliament* or a comparable source and to the appropriate places in the diaries.

LISTS OF SPEECHES

KING CHARLES I and JOHN, BARON FINCH OF FORD-WICH, Lord Keeper, 13 April 1640, at the opening of the Parliament, House of Lords

*H.L.R.O., Braye MS. 16, fos 3^r–4^r [A].
*Montagu, pp. 1–1b [B].
*Lee Warner 1/2(441x1), p. 1.
*Finch-Hatton MS. 50, pp. 1–4, continued by Harvard MS. Eng. 982, fos 5^r–9^r.
C.J., ii, pp. 4–5.
L.J., iv, pp. 46–48.
His Majesties Declaration to all his Loving Subjects of the Causes which moved him to Dissolve the Late Parliament, printed by Robert Barker and the Assignees of John Bill, 1640, [B.L., E.203(1)], pp. 4–10.
Nalson, i, pp. 306–11.
Rushworth, iii, pp. 1114–20.
Bodl., MS. Ashmole 800, fos 83^r–95^r.
Bodl., MS. Carte 119, fos 56^r–66^v.
Bodl., MS. Clarendon 18, fos 110^r–16^v.
Bodl., MS. Clarendon 18, fos 131^r–36^v.
Bodl., MS. Eng. Hist. C.199, fos 8^r–13^r.
Bodl., MS. Rawl. A.346, fos 218^r–23^r.
Bodl., MS. Rawl. D.356, fos 187^r–97^r.
B.L., Add. MS. 6411, fos 2^r–10^r.
B.L., Add. MS. 26640, fos 1^r–9^v.
B.L. Harl. MS. 6801, fos 2^r–8^r.
B.L., Loan MS. 29/172 (Portland Papers).
Cambridge, St. Johns College, S.37, fos 29^r–30^r.
Cambridge, Trinity College, R.5.12, fos 245^r–49^r.
H.L.R.O., Braye MS. 88, pp. 1–8.
Hunt. Cal., HA, Parl. Papers, Box 2.
Hunt. Cal., HM 1554, pp. 109–22.
Inner Temple, Petyt MS. 538/11, fos 217^r–24^v.
National Library of Scotland, Neilson MS. 2688, fos 687^r–701^r.
National Library of Scotland, Neilson MS. 2688, fos 1153^r–68^r.
Worc. Coll. MS. 5.20, fos 1^r–6^r.
Yale, Beinecke Library, Osborn Collection, Box 27, 15, fos 404^r–409^v.
Yale, Beinecke Library, Osborn Collection, Box 41, 5.

Yale, Beinecke Library, Osborn Collection, Box 45, 19, item 104.
Yale, Beinecke Library, Osborn Collection, Stanford (Braye) MS. 95, fos 90^v–115^r (2 copies).
Yale, Beinecke Library, Osborn Collection, Stanford (Braye) MS. 95, fos 119^r–26^v.
Yale, Beinecke Library, Osborn Collection, Tracts, Box 2, 35.

An address from the Crown was a customary part of the opening of Parliament. On 13 April 1640, King Charles made a brief statement. Then Lord Keeper Finch explained his Majesty's reasons for calling the Parliament and his expectations for its proceedings. A standard version of the speeches was probably available. It may have come from notes made at the time by John Browne, clerk of the Parliament. There are several other accounts such as the brief one in Lord Montagu's diary, but most of these are improbable sources for a full text. The absence of major variations among the extant copies of the speech makes it most likely that the Crown itself provided a text. Reported to the House of Commons by Speaker John Glanville on 17 April and summarized in *His Majesties Declaration . . . of the Causes which moved him to Dissolve . . . Parliament*, the speech was widely enough circulated so that without a standard text many versions could have developed.

The content of the speech was important. Its requests, promises, and information played a part in the debates and controversies of the Parliament. It ought to be compared and contrasted with other official speeches of the Parliament, especially that of the Lord Keeper of 21 April.

SERGEANT JOHN GLANVILLE, Speaker, and JOHN, BARON FINCH OF FORDWICH, Lord Keeper, 15 April 1640, at the presentation of the Speaker, House of Lords

*H.L.R.O., Braye MS. 16, fos 5^r–7^r [A].
*Montagu, p. 1c [B].
*Lee Warner 1/2(441x1), p. 1.
*Harvard MS. Eng. 982, fos 9^v–20^r.
L.J., iv, pp. 50–54.
The Lord Keeper His Speech . . . Concerning His Majesties Reigne with the Bishops, Judges, and Peeres . . . with the Kings Majesties Speech, or Charge to the Speaker, 1641, printed and are to be sold by Richard Cotton, [B.L., E.199(43)] [C].
Nalson, i, pp. 312–18.
Rushworth, iii, pp. 1121–27.

*The Speech of Sergeant Glanvill in the Upper House of Parliament
for Peace and Unitie . . .*, London, 1641, [B.L., E.198(32)] [**D**].
Bodl., MS. Carte 119, fos 67^r–88^r.
Bodl., MS. Clarendon 18, fos 116^v–28^r.
Bodl., MS. Clarendon 18, fos 139^r–45^v.
Bodl., MS. Eng. Hist. C.199, fos 14^r–19^v.
Bodl., MS. Rawl. A. 346, fos 257^r–69^r.
B.L., Add. MS. 6411, fos 12^v–27^r.
B.L., Add. MS. 26640, fos 10^r–24^v.
B.L., Harl. MS. 6801, fos 38^r–57^r.
B.L., Sloane MS. 1200, fos 4^v–12^v.
Cambridge, Trinity College, R.5.12, fos 252^r–69^r.
Folger Shakespeare Library, X.d.23 (Finch's copy).
H.L.R.O., Braye MS. 88, pp. 8–20.
Hunt, Cal., AH, Parl. Papers, Box 2.
Hunt. Cal., HM 1554, pp. 122–40.
Inner Temple, Petyt MS. 538/11, fos 225^r–36^r.
National Library of Scotland, Neilson MS. 2688, fos 667^r–77^r.
National Library of Scotland, Neilson MS. 2688, fos 1081^r–1115^r.
S.R.O., DD/M1, Box 18, 96.
S.P. 16/450/94.
Worc. Coll. MS. 5.20, fos 7^r–15^r.
Yale, Beinecke Library, Osborn Collection, Box 27, 15, fos 410^r–16^v.
Yale, Beinecke Library, Osborn Collection, Box 41, 5.
Yale, Beinecke Library, Osborn Collection, Box 45, 19, item 54.
Yale, Beinecke Library, Osborn Collection, Stanford (Braye) MS.
95, fos 135^r–49^r.
Yale, Beinecke Library, Osborn Collection, Tracts, Box 2, 35.

At his presentation to the king, the Speaker of the House of
Commons made two speeches, the first a traditional protestation of
his disability to perform the job and the second a statement of his
hopes for the Parliament. The Lord Keeper responded to both on
the king's behalf. As with the speeches of 13 April, John Browne
took notes during the proceedings. An official text, from his notes
or directly from the Crown, was probably the basis of most contemporary copies. Two variations appeared in print in 1641. *The Lord
Keeper His Speech* . . . (B.L., E.199(43)) omits the first part of the
speech and differs in several other respects from the printed text.
The Speech of Sergeant Glanvill . . . (B.L., E.198(32)) shows signs of
editorial revision to eliminate phrases which reflected favorably
upon the monarchy. Despite the existence of these printed versions,
the speeches of 15 April seem to have had more limited circulation

than those of 13 April. Their specific function may explain the difference. By custom these speeches were not so directly connected with the issues which would be considered in the Parliament as were those of the opening day. Nevertheless mingled with their expressions of hope for cooperation are some comments about current questions.

HARBOTTLE GRIMSTON (Colchester), 16 April 1640, House of Commons

*Harvard MS. Eng. 982, fos 21^v–24^r.

Master Grimston His Worthy and learned Speech Spoken in the High Court of Parliament concerning Troubles Abroad and Greevances at Home, London, 1641, printed for W.H., [B.L., E.199(25)].

Nalson, i, pp. 319–21.

Rushworth, iii, pp. 1128–29.

Bodl., MS. Eng. Hist. C.199, fos 29^r–31^r.

Bodl., MS. Rawl. A.103, fos 19^r–22^r.

Bodl., MS. Rawl. A.346, fos 163^r–64^r.

B.L., Add. MS. 6411, fos 35^v–39^r.

B.L., Eg. MS. 2651, fos 93^r–94^r.

B.L., Harl. MS. 6801, fos 32^r–37^v.

B.L., Harl. MS. 7162, fos 229^r–34^r.

B.L., Sloane MS. 1200, fos 13^r–16^r.

Dublin, Trinity College, MS. 623.

Hunt. Cal., HM 1554,pp. 149–53.

Inner Temple, Petyt MS. 538/11, fos 249^r–51^v.

National Library of Scotland, Neilson MS. 2688, pp. 1117–23.

S.R.O., DD/M1, Box 18, 97.

Worc. Coll. MS. 5.20, fos 28^r–29^r, 16^v.

Yale, Beinecke Library, Osborn Collection, Box 27, 15, fos 395^r–96^v.

Yale, Beinecke Library, Osborn Collection, Box 41, 5.

Yale, Beinecke Library, Osborn Collection, Tracts, Box 2, 45^a.

Yale, Center for Parliamentary History, Misc. Speeches, Herriard Collection (photostat, Misc. Box 5).

SIR BENJAMIN RUDYERD (Wilton), 16 April 1640, House of Commons

*Harvard MS. Eng. 982, fos 24^r–26^r.

*Bodl., MS. Clarendon 18, fos 147^r–49^r [A].

Nalson, i, pp. 321–22.

Rushworth, iii, pp. 1129–31.

A Speech delivered in Parliament by Sir Benjamin Rudyerd,
printed 1641, [B.L., E.198(28)]
Bodl., MS. Clarendon 18, fos 152ʳ–54ᵛ.
Bodl., MS. Eng. Hist. C.199, fos 50ʳ–51ʳ.
Bodl., MS. Rawl. A.103, fos 23ʳ–25ʳ.
Bodl., MS. Rawl, A.346, fos 161ʳ–62ʳ.
B.L., Add. MS. 6411, fos 60ᵛ–61ʳ.
B.L., Harl. MS. 6801, fos 118ʳ–22ᵛ.
B.L., Sloane MS. 1200, fos 17ʳ–18ᵛ.
Dublin, Trinity College, MS. 623.
Hunt. Cal., HM 1554, pp. 193–96.
Inner Temple, Petyt MS. 538/11, fos 252–53ᵛ.
S.R.O., DD/M1, Box 18, 96.
S.P. 16/450/94.
Worc. Coll. MS. 5.20, fos 15ᵛ, 16ʳ, unnumbered.
Yale, Center for Parliamentary History, Misc. Speeches, Herriard
Collection (photostat, Misc. Box 5).
Manning, J. A., *Memoirs of Sir Benjamin Rudyerd, Knt.*, (London,
1841), pp. 148–51.

Rudyerd responded to Grimston, whose complaints about grievances had opened debate on 16 April, the first day of regular
business. Although Bishop Warner reported that Rudyerd had
'moved for subsidies' (above, Lee Warner, p. 2, p. 107), the writer
of the Worc. Coll. and Glanville diurnal named him among those
who wished 'to take beginning where they had left the last Parliament' (above, Worc. Coll. MS. to 15ʳ (16–18 April) p. 212). Most
copies of Rudyerd's speech, whether printed or manuscript, are very
similar. One, that in the Clarendon Papers (Bodl., MS. Clarendon
18, fos 147ʳ–49ʳ), is longer and more embellished than the others.
Clarendon offers no explanation of the MS. which is not in his hand.

SIR FRANCIS SEYMOUR (Wiltshire), 16 April 1640, House of Commons

*Harvard MS. Eng. 982, fos 26ʳ–29ʳ [**A**].
*Worc. Coll. MS. 5.20, 4 printed pages, title page lacking, *An
Honourable Speech Spoken in the High Court of Parliament;*
another copy, B.L., E.199(35), *Sir Francis Seymour His Honorable and Worthy Speech Spoken in the High Court of Parliament,
shewing What dangers do insue by Want of Priviledge of Parliament,* 1641, printed for W. H.
*S.R.O., DD/M1, Box 18, 96 [**B**].
Bodl., MS. Eng. Hist. C.199, fos 25ʳ–26ʳ.

Bodl., MS. Rawl. A.346, fos 235^r–36^r.
B.L., Add. MS. 6411, fos 31^v–34^r.
B.L., Harl. MS. 6801, fos 112^r–17^v.
B.L., Harl. MS. 7162, fos 350^r–55^v.
B.L., Sloane MS. 1200, fos 19^v–21^v.
Dublin, Trinity College, MS. 623.
Folger Shakespeare Library, V.a.192, fos 54^r–57^r.
Hunt. Cal., HM 1554, pp. 145–48.
Inner Temple, Petyt MS. 538/11, fos 246^v–48^v.
Kent Archives Office, U951–010/2.
National Library of Scotland, Neilson MS. 2687, pp. 121–26.
Yale, Beinecke Library, Osborn Collection, Box 27, 15, fos 401^r–402^v.
Yale, Beinecke Library, Osborn Collection, Box 41, 5.
Yale, Beinecke Library, Osborn Collection, Tracts, Box 2, 45^e.
Yale, Center for Parliamentary History, Misc. Speeches, Herriard Collection (photostat, Misc. Box 5).

Although Seymour's speech is sometimes dated 17 April, its content fits logically in the place to which the Finch-Hatton/Harvard diarist has assigned it. As it appears in that diary, the speech is slightly longer and more embellished than it is in most manuscript copies or in the printed edition of 1641. An even longer version can be found in the Mildmay Papers at the Somerset Record Office. Although the version printed in 1641 is essentially that of the most common manuscript copies, it lacks the opening and closing paragraphs of the manuscript. It consequently omits both the specific claim that redress of grievances should precede supply and the most strongly worded of Seymour's attacks on the procedure of judges and sheriffs. The omissions could easily be the result of a desire to be cautious or of doubts about the course of events. Despite its printing and fairly widespread circulation, the speech is not included in Rushworth's *Collections*. The reasons for its absence are not known.

FRANCIS ROUS (Truro), 17 April 1640, House of Commons

*Harvard MS. Eng. 982, fos 31^v–34^r.
Bodl., MS. Ashmole 800, fos 100^v–105^r.
Bodl., MS. Eng. Hist. C.199, fos 48^r–49^v.
Bodl., MS. Rawl. A.346, fos 165^r–66^r.
B.L., Add. MS. 6411, fos 39^v–41^v.
B.L., Harl. MS. 6801, fos 102^r–107^v.
B.L., Harl. MS. 7162, fos 345^r–49^r.

B.L., Sloane MS. 1200, fos 24^v–26^v.

B.L., Sloane MS. 1200, fos 35^r–35^v (marked as Pym's second speech).

B.L., Sloane MS. 1430, fos 61^r–62^r.

CSP 1640, pp. 37–39. (S.P. 16/450/94, 1. A second copy, with some but not too many differences, and neither printed nor noted in the *CSP* appears with the first in S.P. 16/450/94. See below.)

Cambridge University Library, MS. Add. 335, fo 40^r.

Hunt. Cal., HM 1554, pp. 161–64.

Inner Temple, Petyt MS. 538/11, fos 244^r–46^r.

National Library of Scotland, Neilson MS. 2688, pp. 1073–79.

S.R.O., DD/M1, Box 18, 98.

S.P. 16/450/94, 2 (possibly Laud's copy).

Worc. Coll. MS. 5.20.

Yale, Beinecke Library, Osborn Collection, Box 27, 15, fos 397^r–98^v.

Yale, Beinecke Library, Osborn Collection, Box 45, 19, item 103.

Yale, Center for Parliamentary History, Misc. Speeches, Herriard Collection (photostat, Misc. Box 5).

JOHN PYM (Tavistock), 17 April 1640, House of Commons

*Harvard MS. Eng. 982, fo 34^r–Finch-Hatton MS. 50, p. 43[**A**].

*Worc. Coll. MS. 5.20, 6 printed pages, *The First Speech of Master Pym the Last Parliament*, (London, 1641); another copy, B.L., E.105(3).

*B.L., Harl. MS. 6801, fos 58^r–69^r [**B**].

The Kingdomes Manifestation ... Delivered in a speech by John Pym, (London, 1643), printed just after Pym's death, B.L., E.78(12); another copy, titled *A Remonstrance or a Declaration Presented to the Honorable House of Commons*, (London, 1643), B.L., 1486.s.47 [**C**].

Rushworth, iii, pp. 1131–36 [**B**].

Rushworth, iv, pp. 21–24 [**C**].

Somers, *Tracts*, iv, pp. 390–404 [**C**].

A Speech Delivered in Parliament by a worthy member thereof, (London, 1641), B.L., E.198(35); another edition (1642), B.L., 100.d.27 [**C**].

Bodl., MS. Ashmole 800, fos 105^v–108^v.

Bodl., MS. Eng. Hist. C.199, fos 20^r–24^v [**B**].

Bodl., MS. Eng. Hist. C.199, fos 27^r–28^v.

Bodl., MS. Rawl. A. 346, fos 149^r–50^r.

Bodl., MS. Rawl. A.487.

B.L., Add. MS. 6411, fos 27^v–31^r.
B.L., Add. MS. 11045, fos 111^v–112^r.
B.L., Add. MS. 25275, fos 48^r–66^r [C] (incomplete, MS. damaged).
B.L., Add. MS. 33469, fos 46^r–47^r.
B.L., Harl. MS. 165, fos 25^r–26^r (corrected by D'Ewes, see above, pp. 216.)
B.L., Harl. MS. 6801, fos 70^r–77^v.
B.L., Harl. MS. 6801, fos 80^r–83^r.
B.L., Harl. MS. 7162, fos 339^r–43^v.
B.L., Sloane MS. 1200, fos 21^v–24^v.
B.L., Sloane MS. 1200, fos 37^r–37^v.
Dublin, Trinity College, MS. 623 [C].
Folger Shakespeare Library, V.a.192, fos 3^r–6^r.
Folger Shakespeare Library, V.a.192, fos 23^r–33^r [B].
Hunt. Cal., HM 1554, pp. 157–60.
Inner Temple, Petyt MS. 538/11, fos 238^r–43^v [B].
National Library of Scotland, Neilson MS. 2687, pp. 165–78 [A].
S.R.O., DD/Mi, Box 18, 96.
S.P. 16/450/108.
Yale, Beinecke Library, Osborn Collection, Box 27, 15, fos 399^r–400^v.
Yale, Beinecke Library, Osborn Collection, Box 45, 19, item 65.
Yale, Beinecke Library, Osborn Collection, Tracts, Box 2, 45^f.
Yale, Center for Parliamentary History, Misc. Speeches, Herriard Collection (photostat, Misc. Box 5) [B].

For almost two hours on 17 April, John Pym recited grievances from which he believed Englishmen were suffering. Many of these had been mentioned by previous speakers, petitions from the country, or complaints of earlier Parliaments. Others would be voiced again by subsequent speakers. Pym brought the grievances together and placed them within the three general categories that had also been used in the past. His speech quickly came to be regarded as the fundamental statement of the ills of the Commonwealth. At times contemporaries confused it with the committee's report about grievances on 24 April. Although the two were not identical, the report was sufficiently similar to explain the confusion and to illustrate their close relationship. The structure of Pym's speech and the comprehensive nature of its content provided a basis and direction for action by the Commons.

The speech was widely circulated. There are four major versions; arbitrarily selected examples of three of these are printed here. The outline which appears in Worc. Coll. MS. 5.20 (above, pp. 216–19) as it was printed in 1641, may have come from Pym himself. If not, it probably was the work of one who heard the speech. It could be notes taken in the House, a revision of such notes, or a summary composed soon after the occasion. In contrast the long version [C], printed in the same year, seems to have been revised and edited specifically for publication. The length of this version, its relative remoteness from actual proceedings in the House, and its availability in collections such as Rushworth's and Somers' have led to its omission here except for specific passages which are cited in notes. The second and third versions included here seem to have circulated in manuscript rather than in print. Both B.L., Harl. MS. 6801, fos 58^r–69^r, and Harvard MS. Eng. 982, fo. 34^r–Finch-hatton MS. 50, p. 43, but especially the latter, preserve the style of oral delivery. With the exception of a reference to lack of time and confusion in memory leading him to condense his conclusion, this is lacking in the longest version. Pym's reference to positions in the Church obtained by papists and his subsequent request for pardon because his tongue had slipped appear in both the manuscript versions but not in the long printed one. Also included in the Finch-Hatton/Harvard though omitted in the longest version is Pym's preface to his complaint about enlarging the bounds of the forests—that he had almost lost himself in the forest and forgot what he had to say. The entire final section of the speech is reorganized in the longest version. The point about wines which comes last in the manuscripts is worked in at a logical place in the text. Complaints about grievances are supported with precedents and lists of ways in which the subject is thereby burdened. This version seems calculated to present as persuasively as possible the case for redress of grievances. The initial justification of giving priority to grievances is far more extensive than that which appears in the manuscript versions. It emphasizes that such procedure was in the king's interest as well as that of the subject. The long printed version also makes a careful apology for discussing such difficult topics. Some statements in the speech appear to have been modified. Where the Finch-Hatton says (p. 40), concerning shipmoney. 'if any here shall endeavor to defend it, hee must know that his reputation and conscience lye at stake in the defence,' the printed version says (B.L., E.78(12), p. 13), 'he thought no man would venture his reputation or conscience in the defence of that judgement, being so contrary to the grounds of the law, to the practice of former times, and so inconsistent in itself.' Although not so extensively revised and polished as the long printed version, these two manuscript versions seem to have been rewritten, perhaps from the outline or from other rough notes. Some examples and explanations support the citations of grievances. Both follow the outline in their central points, but vary in emphasis and illustrative detail.

Harl. MS. 6801, for example, gives much attention to tonnage and poundage.

Whatever additions and revisions may have been made by Pym or others following delivery, the speech itself with its broad scope and skilful arguments must have been carefully prepared. Like many successful speeches, it seems to have evoked response from its audience.[1] The grievances mentioned were wrongs which parliamentmen felt and for which they could join in demanding redress. With the protest he delivered to the Lords on 28 April about the violation of the liberties of the Commons, the speech of 17 April helped establish Pym as a leader of the Lower House, a role which he would assume more clearly in the Long Parliament.

EDWARD HYDE (Wootton Bassett), 18 April 1640, House of Commons

*Finch-Hatton MS. 50, p. 44.
*Bodl., MS. Clarendon 18, fos 155^r–55^v [A].
Clarendon, *Life*, i, pp. 78–80.

Edward Hyde began his parliamentary career with this speech complaining about the court of honour. He does not mention it in his *History of the Rebellion*, but both the Commons' *Journal* and the Finch-Hatton/Harvard diary note the speech. The version in the diary is more concise but not otherwise different from that in Hyde's own papers. That in his *Life* gives more details of the cases about the swan called a goose and the insolent tailor. Hyde's use of quotations from the speech in his *Life* points to the existence of yet another manuscript version. The text from which he quotes is not that of Bodl., MS. Clarendon 18. Hyde's interest in the court of honour was demonstrated again in the Long Parliament where he urged the appointment of an investigating committee and later reported from that committee, including in his report some of the same points which he had made in the speech of 18 April. Although his attack on the court was in accord with arguments against other grievances, the Commons seem not to have taken action upon his remarks during the Short Parliament. The matter was not referred to committee and was not listed among the grievances reported back to the House on 24 April. In recounting the speech in his *Life*, Hyde declared, 'This Representation was very acceptable to the House, both in Respect of the Matter, which was odious enough; and in Regard of the Person that usurped that monstrous Jurisdiction, who was in no Degree

---

[1] See Goodwin Berquist's analysis, 'Revolution through Persuasion: John Pym's Appeal to the Moderates in 1640,' *The Quarterly Journal of Speech*, xlix (1963).

grateful to them; upon whom He that made the Motion, had not made the least Reflection. The Modesty of that Time not permitting the Mention of great Men, with any Reproach, until their Offences were first examined, and proved; and this being the first Part He had acted upon that Stage, brought him much Applause; and He was ever afterwards heard with great Benignity' (i, p. 80).

JOHN, BARON FINCH OF FORDWICH, Lord Keeper, 21 April 1640, Banqueting House, Whitehall

*H.L.R.O., Braye MS. 16, fos 17ʳ–18ʳ [A].
*Montagu, p. 2b [B].
*Lee Warner 1/2(441x1), p. 3.
*Finch-Hatton MS. 50, pp. 50–52 [C].
*H.R.O., M36/1, pp. 3–4 [D].
*Hunt. Cal., HM 1554, pp. 254–55 [E].
*Hunt. Cal., HM 1554, p. 165.
L.J., iv, pp. 62–63 [F].
His Majesties Declaration ... of the Causes ... to Dissolve ...,
     1640, [B.L., E.203(1)], pp. 11–16 [G].
Nalson, i, pp. 342–46.
Rushworth, iii, pp. 1137–39 [H].
Bodl., MS. Eng. Hist. C.199, fo 26ᵛ.
Bodl., MS. Eng. Hist. C.199, fos 37ʳ–39ʳ [G].
Bodl., MS. Rawl. A.346, fos 157ʳ–58ᵛ [C].
Bodl., MS. Rawl. D. 356, pp. 198–201 [C].
B.L., Add. MS. 6411, fos 42ʳ–42ᵛ.
B.L., Add. MS. 6411, fos 43ᵛ–46ᵛ [C].
B.L., Add. MS. 11045, fo 111ʳ [H].
H.L.R.O., Braye MS. 88, pp. 21–25 [F].
Hunt. Cal., HA, Parl. Papers, Box 2, p. 181 [C].
Hunt. Cal., HM 1554, pp. 181–86 [G].
Worc. Coll. MS. 5.20, fos 17ᵛ–19ʳ [C].
Yale, Beinecke Library, Osborn Collection, Stanford (Braye) MS.
     95, fos 151ʳ–58ʳ [F].
Yale, Beinecke Library, Osborn Collection, Stanford (Braye) MS.
     95, fos 166ʳ–72ʳ [F].

When the king summoned the Lords and Commons to the Banqueting House at Whitehall on 21 April, Lord Keeper Finch addressed them on his Majesty's behalf. The theme of the speech was the king's urgent need for supply. Points made in the statement to both houses at the opening of Parliament on 13 April were repeated and underlined with a few details added. Finch made some brief and general comments about shipmoney, which had not been mentioned on 13 April. A full explanation of the king's finances and plans was not given, nor was advice asked from Parliament. The speech was widely reported; many accounts survive today among manuscript collections. These accounts differ more in extent, content, organization, and wording than do reports of many of the parliamentary speeches of the time.

Finch himself reported the speech to the House of Lords on 22 April. He excused himself to the Lords for having only 'short heads' rather than a written copy. No official written version of the speech seems to have existed. Repeating points made a week earlier at the opening of Parliament probably meant for Finch that he did not have to write out the speech. Nevertheless the account in the Lords' *Journal* is not just short heads, but a rather lengthy and somewhat repetitious disquisition about the king's intentions with regard to finance and the kingdom. This report could have been based on either the short heads, of which a number of manuscript copies are extant or the somewhat longer notes taken by the clerk, John Browne, during the statement to the House. With effort the clerk's notes could have been converted and extended from an outline to the report in the printed *Journal*.

Neither in Browne's scribbled book nor elsewhere is there evidence that notes were taken during the actual speech at the Banqueting House. Copies of the 'short heads' to which Finch referred were probably available soon afterward. Many of the differing versions of the speech can be reduced to these heads. The Finch-Hatton compilation gives one such version, Rushworth another, the latter possibly being a combination of two reports of the speech. From the beginning through the section on tonnage and poundage which comes at the end of most versions, Rushworth gives an account which roughly follows the heads. After that point he repeats information and adds details, some of which appear in other versions of the speech but which had not been included earlier in Rushworth's.

The House of Commons probably heard a report on 22 April. The *Journal* implies that a report was made although it records neither any report nor an explanation of its absence. The lack of an official written speech, scruples about including royal messages in the *Journal*, or clerical lapses may be responsible for the *Journal*'s silence.

In addition to the versions apparently based on the heads, a few more independent accounts of the speech survive. Robert Bernard included the main points in his diary. Lord Montagu, who could not remember the details, notes (p. 2b) that the speech was long, and 'like many to come out in printe.' It all 'tended to quicken supply.'

In the Glanville MS. is a clearly organized summary, which might have been written at home in the evening. The principal theme of the king's needs is expressed effectively although references to the grants of the Irish Parliament, the loss of the ship *Rebecca*, and the accounts of Sir William Russell which appear in other versions are omitted. The king's contribution of £300,000 from his own funds, mentioned in the speech of 13 April, is cited here but not elsewhere. Another independent account of the speech appears in the newsletters of Captain Rossingham (B.L., Add. MS. 11045, fo. 111^r). Although some of the common details are absent from his account, he placed greater emphasis upon the king's willingness to make concessions in return for immediate supply and termed the speech 'a gracious, mild, and meek expression' (S.P. 16/451/16, above). Montereul, the French ambassador, described the tone of the Lord Keeper's remarks in a similar fashion (P.R.O. 31/3/72, fo 121^r). Rossingham also gave more information about the uses of tonnage and poundage and about the actions of the Irish Parliament, both of which he had reported in an earlier letter. In the absence of a standard text, the exact contents of the speech must remain in doubt. Both the versions developed from the 'short heads' and those written from memory or other sources could have been shaped by the previous exposure of many of the writers to the subject matter.

The speech failed to impress its audience. Although its generalizations, admonitions, and repetition may have had a clear purpose such as lessening Finch's burdens or increasing the impact of the content on the hearers and thereby hastening supply, its nature may have resulted from singlemindedness, impatience, and inadequate thought about tactics. Boredom and, in some quarters, disappointment at the lack of additional information seem to have been the response. The Lower House, where a bill of subsidies had to begin, deferred consideration of the statement until 23 April. Then, instead of granting supply, the members debated whether supply or grievances should come first. They concluded with a decision to prepare their grievances for presentation to the Lords so that the two houses could petition the king for relief. Finding that the speech had not solved his problem, Charles appealed to the Lords 24 April. The address of 21 April became one part of the series of royal efforts to stir the Short Parliament to action.

SIR JOHN WRAY (Lincolnshire), ?23 April 1640, House of Commons

*Finch-Hatton MS. 50, p. 56 [A] (brief note only).
*Worc. Coll. MS. 5.20, fos 25^r–25^v.

Bodl., MS. Eng. Hist. C.199, fos 35^r–35^v.
Bodl., MS. Rawl. A.346, fo 147^r.
B.L., Add. MS. 6411, fos 34^v–35^r.
B.L., Harl. MS. 7162, fos 99^r–100^r.
B.L., Sloane MS. 1200, fos 18^v–19^r.
Hunt. Cal., HM 1554, p. 169.
Inner Temple, Petyt MS. 538/11, fos 237^v–38^r.
National Library of Scotland, Neilson MS. 2688, pp. 1071–72.
Yale, Center for Parliamentary History, Misc. Speeches, Herriard
Collection (photostat, Misc. Box 5).

Sir John Wray, knight for Lincolnshire, voiced a particular concern of his countrymen in his complaint about fendrainers. Others of his points were more general grievances among the Englishmen of the time. The form and content of these complaints seem appropriate for the presentation of a petition but do not fit the debates of 20 April, the date usually given for Wray's remarks. No petition from Lincolnshire is recorded, but it may have been among the petitions from the country brought into the Commons on 17–18 April. Another possible date for the speech is 23 April, when the Finch-Hatton/Harvard diarist notes that Wray spoke on behalf of property.

EDMUND WALLER (Amersham), ?23 April 1640, House of Commons

An Honorable and Learned Speech made by Mr. Waller in Parliament, 1641, printed for Richard Smithers, [B.L., E.199(42)].
   Handwritten note, 'this speech was spoken the last Parliament before this.' (Only final portion, that dealing with religion.)
Nalson, i, pp. 326–29.
Rushworth, iii, pp. 1140–43.
A Worthy Speech Made in the House of Commons This Present Parliament, 1641, (London, 1641), printed for John Nicholson, Worc. Coll. MS. 5.20, 6 printed pages; another copy, B.L., E.198(11), identifies Waller as the speaker.
Bodl., MS. Add. C.132, fos 20^r–22^r.
Bodl., MS. Eng. Hist. C.199, fos 31^r–35^r.
B.L., Add. MS. 6411, fos 65^r–73^r.
B.L., Harl. MS. 6801, fos 90^r–101^v.
B.L., Harl. MS. 7162, fos 324^r–35^v.
Cambridge University Library, Add. MS. 7569, pp. 87–90.
Dublin, Trinity College, MS. 867, fos 244^r–55^r.
Folger Shakespeare Library, V.a.192, fos 15^r–22^r.

Hunt. Cal., HM 1554, pp. 203–11.
National Library of Scotland, Neilson MS. 2688, pp. 1044–59.
Yale, Beinecke Library, Osborn Collection, Box 45, 19, item 94.
Yale, Center for Parliamentary History, Misc. Speeches, Herriard
Collection (photostat, Misc. Box 5).

Edmund Waller may never have delivered this speech to the House of Commons. Although the Worcester College diarist and Rushworth both state that the speech was given 22 April in response to the Lord Keeper's address at the Banqueting House the day before, neither the Finch-Hatton/Harvard MS. nor any of the other principal sources mentions the speech. The statements in Rushworth and Worcester College seem mistaken, at least in regard to the date, since the House deferred debate on the royal address until 23 April.

Waller, the poet, has been accused of seeking fame and favour. He may have prepared and circulated the speech in manuscript to impress contemporaries. It is a polished work with Latin expressions and extensive classical, Christian, and historical allusions, which seem more appropriate for written than for oral delivery. It is possible, however, that the speech was originally composed for use in the House and then not given.

The content includes themes which appear in other speeches but there is no reason to think that the speech is borrowed or adapted from someone else and distributed under Waller's name. Professor Jack G. Gilbert of Louisiana State University, who is preparing an edition of Waller's speeches and who has saved us from several errors in connection with Waller, confirms that the style is his.

An additional problem concerning the speech is represented by the two editions which were printed in 1641. B.L., E.198(11) deals with both supply and religion while B.L., E.199(42) includes only the remarks about religion, which had appeared as the final portion of the longer speech. The full titles of these editions reflect their content: (B.L., E.198(11)) *A Worthy Speech Made in the house of Commons this present Parliament 1641. 1. That Parliaments are the onely way for advancing the Kings affaires. 2. That the restoring of the property of goods and freedome of the Subject is a chiefe means to maintaine Religion and obedience to his Majestie;* (B.L., E.199(42)) *An Honorable and Learned Speech made by Mr Waller in Parliament against the Prelates Innovations, False doctrine and discipline, reproving the perswation of some clergie-men to his majestie of inconveniencies, who themselves, instead of tilling the ground, are become sowers of tares, with a motion for the fundamental and vital liberties of this nation, which it was wont to have.* Professor Gilbert has pointed out that Waller's views at that time make it unlikely that he authorized these editions. The speech, not given in Parliament in 1640, seems to have been martialled to serve the political needs and controversies of 1641. It belongs to that period rather than to the era of the Short Parliament and is not included here.

KING CHARLES I, 24 April 1640, House of Lords

*H.L.R.O., Braye MS. 16, fos 20ᵛ–21ʳ
*Lee Warner 1/2(441xi), p. 3.
*H.L.R.O., Draft Journal, pp. 32–34.
L.J., iv, pp. 66–67.
His Majesties Declaration . . . of the Causes . . . to Dissolve . . .,
    1640, [B.L., E.203(1)], pp. 17–20.
B.L., Add. 11045, fo 112ᵛ.
H.L.R.O., Braye MS. 88, pp. 25–26.

When Charles I went to the Upper House on 24 April and asked the Lords to urge the Lower House to vote subsidies before considering grievances, he took a step which critically affected the history of the Short Parliament. John Browne's notes (Braye MS. 16) are probably the basis of most of the copies of the speech. The texts in the Draft Journal and Braye MS. 88 were derived independently from Braye MS. 16. Although the speech in the Journal was taken from D.J. and not Braye MS. 88, the latter is not only a smoother text but also one which follows Browne's scribbled book more closely. A version which may also have come from Browne's but with more editorial alteration is printed in the Declaration explaining the dissolution of the Parliament. Some of its variations are given in the notes. Despite the importance of the speech, few other copies have survived.

GRIEVANCES (24 April unless otherwise marked).

*Lee Warner 1/2(441xi), p. 5 (28 April).
*Finch-Hatton MS. 50, p. 59.
*Finch-Hatton MS. 50, pp. 67–68 (29 April).
*H.R.O., M36/1, p. 11 (29 April).
*Worc. Coll. MS. 5.20, fos 20ᵛ–21ʳ.
C.J., ii, p. 11.
C.J., ii, p. 16 (29 April).
Nalson, i, p. 332.
A Perfect Diurnall (listed twice).
Rushworth, iii, pp. 1147–48 (religion 29 April; rest 24 April).
Bodl., MS. Add. C.132, fo 80ʳ.

Bodl., MS. Ashmole 800, fos 99^r–100^r.
Bodl., MS. Eng. Hist. C.199, fos 36^r–36^v.
B.L., Add. MS. 6411, fos 73^v–75^r.
B.L., Add. MS. 11045, fos 112^r–112^v.
B.L., Add. MS. 11045, fo. 114^v (29 April).
B.L., Harl. MS. 7162, fos 21^r–23^v.
B.L., Sloane MS. 1200, fos 3^r–4^r.
B.L., Sloane MS. 1200, fo 36^r.
Folger Shakespeare Library, V.a.192, fos 44^r–45^r.
Hunt. Cal., HM 1554, pp. 189–90.
Hunt. Cal., HM 1554, pp. 259–60.
Hunt. Cal., HM 1554, pp. 261–62.
Inner Temple, Petyt MS. 538/11, fos 236^v–37^r.
National Library of Scotland, Neilson MS. 2688, pp. 1124–25.
S.P. 16/450/94.
S.P. 16/451/30.
Worc. Coll. MS. 5.20, fos 25^v–26^r.
Yale, Beinecke Library, Osborn Collection, Box 27, 15, fo 389^r.
Yale, Law Library, Glanville MS., p. 5.
Townshend, Henry, *Diary*, ed. J. W. Willis Bund, Worcestershire
Historical Society, 1920, I, pp. 1–3.

Among collections of seventeenth-century manuscripts are many copies of the Heads of Grievances voted by the House of Commons 24 April 1640. These are variously titled and phrased. They also differ somewhat in their content. In the initial step toward what the Commons hoped could be a petition from both Houses to the king, the Lower House heard grievances reported from committee. Not all the points the committee presented received consideration that day. Those under the third head, parliamentary liberties, were not discussed, and the question of the trained bands was deferred until another day for additional debate. The Commons seem to have followed the procedure which Pym on 17 April had urged them to adopt, to proceed first with matters on which members could agree, debate about controversial questions later, and add to the grievances when decisions were reached. The procedure was a sensible one. The king himself had indicated that he did not intend the session to be long. Too much discussion before grievances were presented to the Lords might mean that time would run out before anything was accomplished. As it was, the king's demands for supply and the disputes with the Lords about privileges prevented the Lower House from completing its work. The heads concerning religion were reported to the House on 29 April, but neither those concerning property nor those about Parliament reached that stage. When

L

Parliament was dissolved, no petition had been prepared. None of the grievances had even been presented to the Lords. This meant that there was no definitive statement of the grievances. The versions which circulated varied from those including only grievances actually resolved by the House as fit for a conference to those labelled 'heads of grievances' but which in actuality embodied points from Pym's speech of 17 April. The thirty-five grievances to which Montereul refers in his account of the proceedings of 24 April are probably taken from Pym's speech. Many fewer were actually dealt with by the House (P.R.O. 31/3/72, fo 121^r).

JOHN, BARON FINCH OF FORDWICH, Lord Keeper, 25 April 1640, conference

*H.L.R.O., Braye MS. 16, fos 32^r–32^v, heads.
*Finch-Hatton MS. 50, pp. 60–62 [A].
*H.R.O., M36/1, pp. 7–9 [B].
*H.L.R.O., Braye MS. 2, fos 65^r–66^v [C] (his notes).
L.J., iv, p. 68 (heads).
His Majesties Declaration ... of the Causes ... to Dissolve ..., 1640, [B.L., E.203(1)], pp. 22–23 [D].
B.L., Add. MS. 11045, fo 113^r.
S.P. 16/451/66.
Yale, Beinecke Library, Osborn Collection, Stanford (Braye) MS. 95, fos 89^r–89^v.

When the Lord Keeper reported the king's speech and the Lords' resolutions of the preceding day to the House of Commons at the conference on 25 April, he seems to have spoken from notes or heads as he had done on 21 April, rather than from a complete text. These notes have survived in Braye MS. 2. Browne may have used them when extending the heads in his scribbled book to those which appear in the Journal, but his working draft in Braye MS. 95, fos 89^r–89^v, shows greater dependence on his own previous list of heads. Herbert's report to the House of Commons which follows the heads very closely is another source for accounts of the conference (see below).

EDWARD HERBERT (Reading), 27 April 1640, House of Commons. Report from conference

*Hunt. Cal., HM 1554, pp. 257–58.
C.J., ii, p. 13.
Nalson, i, pp. 333–35.

Rushworth, iii, pp. 1144–46.
Bodl., MS. Eng. Hist. C.199, fos 46^r–47^v.
B.L., Add. MS. 6411, fos 47^r–50^v.
B.L., Harl. MS. 6801, fos 19^r–27^v.
B.L., Harl. MS. 6801, fos 84^r–89^v.
B.L., Sloane MS. 1200, fos 27^r–29^v.
Finch-Hatton MS. 50, pp. 62–64.
Hunt. Cal., HM 1554, pp. 197–200.
National Library of Scotland, Neilson MS. 2688, pp. 1129–35.
Worc. Coll. MS. 5.20, fos 21^r–22^r.
Yale, Beinecke Library, Osborn Collection, Box 27, 15, fos 393^r–94^r.
Yale, Beinecke Library, Osborn Collection, Tracts, Box 2, 45^b.
Yale, Center for Parliamentary History, Misc. Speeches, Herriard Collection (photostat, Misc. Box 5).

On 27 April, Mr Solicitor Herbert delivered the report of the conference of 25 April to the House of Commons. This was an official report made on behalf of the Commons' committee which had been charged with that responsibility. Although the whole House was apparently present at the conference, the reporters took their responsibility seriously. They did not report immediately after the conference on Saturday, but asked permission to wait until Monday so they could prepare their notes. There is no evidence that they obtained for these purposes an official text of the speech. (A complete text may not have existed.) The report which Herbert delivered probably itself became the standard version; it was entered in the Commons' *Journal*. The copies which have survived in manuscript and print show only minor variations. The Finch-Hatton/Harvard MS. provides a summary in the proceedings of 25 April (it is listed above among copies of the Lord Keeper's speech that day) in addition to a report on 27 April. The summary does not differ significantly from the Lord Keeper's notes of which it seems to be an elaboration or from the report of which it is a condensation. The Glanville MS. uses the first portion of the Finch-Hatton summary but adds its own conclusion. Rossingham's account likewise has individual characteristics. In his letters he emphasized both a royal intention to give up shipmoney in return for an adequate supply and the limited time for which supply would make the king independent of Parliament.

Reaction to the report in the House of Commons showed less confidence in the king's intentions. The Commons moved to respond with protest to the speech and resolutions which were reported to them on 27 April. More conferences followed.

JOHN PYM (Tavistock), 28 April 1640, conference

*H.L.R.O., Braye MS. 16, fo 35^r [A] (report to House of Lords).
*Finch-Hatton MS. 50, pp. 69–70.
C.J., ii, p. 15 [B].
L.J., iv, pp. 72–73.
Bodl., MS. Carte 80, fos 30^r–30^v.
Bodl., MS. Eng. Hist. C.199, fos 40^v–42^r.
Bodl., MS. Rawl. A.346, fos 151^r–52^r.
B.L., Add. MS. 6411, fos 57^r–60^r.
B.L., Add. MS. 11045, fo. 114^r [C].
B.L., Harl. MS. 6801, fos 28^r–31^v.
B.L., Sloane MS. 1200, fos 31^r–32^v.
H.L.R.O., Braye MS. 2, fos 67^r–68^v.
H.L.R.O., Braye MS. 88.
Hunt. Cal., HA, Parl. Papers, Box 2, p. 213.
Hunt. Cal., HM 1554, pp. 213–15.
Inner Temple, Petyt MS. 538/11, fos 255^v–57^r.
National Library of Scotland, Neilson MS. 2688, pp. 1136–40.
S.R.O., DD/M1, Box 18, 96.
Worc. Coll. MS. 5.20, fos 23^v–25^r.
Yale, Beinecke Library, Osborn Collection, Box 41, 5.
Yale, Beinecke Library, Osborn Collection, Stanford (Braye) MS.
   Miscellaneous, I, 29 [D] (report to the House of Lords).
Yale, Center for Parliamentary History, Misc. Speeches, Herriard
   Collection (photostat, Misc. Box 5).

John Pym was the spokesman of the Lower House at the conference of 28 April when the Commons protested that the Lords had
violated their privileges by taking the action which had led to the
conference of 25 April. The speech which Pym delivered had been
prepared in writing by a committee of the Commons. Probably as a
result, there are few variations among the surviving copies. Browne
took notes when the Lord Keeper reported the conference to the
Lords, and from them drew up a longer version (Yale, Braye MS.
Misc. I, 29). Nevertheless the speech appears in the Lords' *Journal*
essentially as it does elsewhere. Neither Bernard nor Glanville offers
independent accounts on this occasion. The Commons' *Journal*
itself seems to provide the only significant supplement to the standard version of the speech. It is apparently the committee's written
report to the House which was entered in the Commons' *Journal* on
28 April. This report is concise. It contains the same points but lacks
the embellishment of Pym's statement at the conference. Even the
reference to the Indemnity of the Commons is omitted in the report

although the Commons' claim that privileges were violated is clearly maintained. The report which appears in the *Journal* could have been sufficient basis for a speech, but Pym's habits of preparation, the similarity of the longer versions of the speech, and the absence of copies of the report which appears in the *Journal* all indicate that he had written an expanded text from the report for use at the conference.

The House demonstrated its satisfaction with Pym's performance by offering him a vote of thanks. Although less famous than the speech of 17 April, the address of 28 April contributed to Pym's renown as a parliamentarian. At the same time the speech continued the debate with the Lords about the privileges of the House of Commons. The Lords answered at another conference on 1 May.

?JOHN ELIOT (St. Germans), or WILLIAM ELLIOT [Haselmere], ?29 April 1640, House of Commons

*Worc. Coll. MS. 5.20, fos 22ᵛ–23ʳ.

Bodl., MS. Eng. Hist. C.199, fos 40ʳ–40ᵛ.

B.L., Add. MS. 6411, fos 63ʳ–64ᵛ.

B.L., Harl. MS. 6801, fos 108ʳ–10ᵛ.

B.L., Harl. MS. 7162, fos 318ʳ–22ᵛ ('Peard's').

B.L., Sloane MS. 1200, fos 33ʳ–34ʳ.

CSP 1640, pp. 36–37 (S.P. 16/450/94).

Dublin, Trinity College, MS. 623.

Hunt. Cal., HM 1554, pp. 173–74.

Inner Temple, Petyt MS. 538/11, fos 254ʳ–55ʳ.

National Library of Scotland, Neilson MS. 2688, pp. 1041–44 ('Glyn's'; includes marginal notes).

Yale, Beinecke Library, Osborn Collection, Box 27, 15, fos 391ʳ–391ᵛ.

Yale, Center for Parliamentary History. Misc. Speeches, Herriard Collection (photostat, Misc. Box 5) ('Glyn's').

The speech usually attributed to Eliot, probably John, son of the famous Sir John of the 1620s, at times has been assigned to Glyn or Peard. If the speech was Peard's, it is not one of those noted in the diaries. Peard might have made the speech in the committee for courts of justice from which he reported on 25 April. Proceedings in committee are not well documented. Glyn also could have had occasion to make the speech. He sat on the committee to prepare the grievances for a conference with the Lords, and he too was associated with questions of justice. Less is known about the activities of the

two Eliots during the Parliament. The information is not adequate
to establish definite authorship.

The date of the speech is also uncertain. Worc. Coll. MS. 5.20 says
28 April, but if the statements in the speech itself are to be taken
literally, it occurred some time prior to that of John Pym on 17
April. The speaker noted that although a number of complaints had
been made, 'that which I shall speake hath not yet been spoken.'
Some of the petitions from the country brought in at the beginning
of the session complained about ecclesiastical courts, but none of
those surviving specifically cited the oath. On 17 April Pym listed it
among the grievances in religion. It is possible that the speaker may
have missed or discounted Pym's remarks on the subject, for in the
course of almost two hours, Pym discussed many topics. The
questions of justice which the oath *ex officio* raises are not too different from those which Mr Hyde put on 18 April with regard to the
court of honour. Hyde's remarks could either have prompted or
have been prompted by those about the oath. Some evidence suggests
even later dates. The oath was mentioned as a cause of injustice in
the petition of Peter Smart which was presented on 22 April. The
speech might have occurred during proceedings connected with the
petition. Consideration of the Commons' heads of grievances concerning religion are another possible occasion. The oath was not
among the grievances reported on 24 or 29 April. Its absence might
have provoked the speech, particularly on 29 April when the religious
heads were discussed in more detail. The speech has been assigned
to that date here, but the date cannot be verified from existing
evidence. It seems surprising that if the speech was made during the
Short Parliament, it was not better reported. The possibility that
the speech belonged to another Parliament was explored without
success. The content is compatible with proceedings in the spring of
1640. Until proven to belong elsewhere, the speech must be considered as part of the business of this Parliament.

JOHN, BARON FINCH OF FORDWICH, Lord Keeper, 1 May 1640, conference

*H.L.R.O., Braye MS. 16, fo 44ᵛ [A].
*Harvard MS. Eng. 982, fos 74ʳ–74ᵛ [B].
*H.R.O., M36/1, pp. 17–19 [C].
*B.L., Harl. MS. 4931, fo 48ᵛ [D].
*H.L.R.O., Braye MS. 2, fos 70ʳ–73ᵛ.
L.J., iv, pp. 75–77.
His Majesties Declaration . . . of the Causes . . . to Dissolve . . .,
    1640, [B.L., E.203(1)], pp. 29–35.

Nalson, i, pp. 337–40.
Rushworth, iii, pp. 1149–53.
Bodl., MS. Eng. Hist. C.199, fos 42^r–45^v.
Bodl., MS. Rawl. A.346, fos 153^r–56^v.
B.L., Add. MS. 6411, fos 51^r–56^v.
B.L., Add. MS. 11045, fo 115^v [**E**].
H.L.R.O., Braye MS. 88 [**A**].

The conference held 1 May was called by the Lords so that they might respond to the protest the Commons made at the conference of 28 April. The Upper House asked the same committee which had prepared the heads for the conference of 25 April to do so again, and, as he had then, the Lord Keeper delivered the address to the Commons. On this occasion, he may have had a written text. There is one in his hand in Braye MS. 2, fos 70^r–73^v. In some places the wording is crossed out and corrections inserted, but for the most part the text is fairly written. It is endorsed '1° May 1640, Speech to the House of Commons in the Painted Chamber.' It is this version rather than one based on Browne's notes of the heads, which appears in the Lords' *Journal*, Rushworth, and in a number of manuscript copies. No report appears in the Commons' *Journal* although the clerk left a space for it to be entered. The Commons' reporters had not reported on the day of the conference but had requested that the House grant them time, until the next day to prepare their report. Immediately following the report, the next day, Secretary Vane announced that he had a message from the king. The message asked for an answer that day to his Majesty's pleas for supply. During the remainder of the Parliament debate in the Lower House focussed on the question of supply or grievances. The royal message and the ensuing debate undoubtedly diverted interest from the Lord Keeper's statement at the conference. Nevertheless some accounts were written. The *Declaration* about the causes of dissolution includes a revised version of the speech which asserts the legitimacy of the Lords' action without resorting to some of the explanations and arguments of the Braye MS. The lengthy discussion of the Indemnity of 9 *Hen*. IV is omitted, but the Lords' claim that their proceedings were 'fully justified by that establishment' is stated in even stronger terms than in the standard version. In contrast the summary of the conference which appears among the proceedings of 1 May in the Finch-Hatton/Harvard MS. hardly does justice to the arguments which the Lords had offered in self-defence. Bernard's diary provides a more balanced and precise report. It follows the version in Braye MS. 2 closely enough to suggest that either Bernard was taking good notes or he had a copy of the speech itself.

GEORGE, LORD DIGBY (Dorset), ?2 May 1640, House of Commons

*Harvard MS. Eng. 982, fo 78ᵛ [A].
*H.R.O., M36/1, pp. 20–21 [B].
*Worc. Coll. MS. 5.20, fos 30ʳ–30ᵛ.
Bodl., MS. Eng. Hist. C.199, fo 51ᵛ.
B.L., Add. MS. 6411, fos 61ᵛ–62ᵛ.
B.L., Harl. MS. 6801, fos 78ʳ–79ᵛ.
B.L., Harl. MS. 7162, fos 212ʳ–13ᵛ.
B.L., Sloane MS. 1200, fos 16ʳ–16ᵛ.
Hunt, Cal., HM 1554, pp. 177–78.
Inner Temple, Petyt MS. 538/11, fos 257ᵛ–58ʳ.
National Library of Scotland, Neilson MS. 2688, pp. 1059–61.
Yale, Center for Parliamentary History, Misc. Speeches, Herriard
    Collection (photostat, Misc. Box 5).

Although sometimes labelled the earl of Bristol's, this speech was that of George, Lord Digby, later second earl of Bristol, who sat in the House of Commons during the Short Parliament, and not his father, John who was attracting attention at the same time for debates with the earl of Strafford in the Upper House. Various dates appear on separates of the speech. Both Bernard's notes, which are much closer to the separate version than is the report in the Finch-Hatton/Harvard diary, and the Finch-Hatton/Harvard MS. place the speech among the proceedings of 2 May.

KING CHARLES I, 5 May 1640, House of Lords (to both Houses)

*Montagu, p. 3d [A].
*Lee Warner 1/2 (441x1), p. 5.
*Finch-Hatton MS. 50, pp. 81–83.
*H.R.O., M36/1, pp. 26–27 [B].
*B.L., Harl. MS. 4931, fo 49ʳ [C].
L.J., iv, p. 81.
His Majesties Declaration . . . of the Causes . . . to Dissolve . . .,
    1640, B.L., E.203(1), pp. 42–47 [D].
Nalson, i, p. 342 [D].
A Perfect Diurnall.
Rushworth, iii, pp. 1154–55.
Bodl., MS. Clarendon 18, fos 160ʳ–60ᵛ.
Bodl., MS. Eng. Hist. C.199, fos 52ʳ–52ᵛ.
Bodl., MS. Rawl. A. 346, fos 239ʳ–40ʳ.

Bodl., MS. Rawl. D.356, pp. 203–204.
B.L., Add. MS. 6411, fos 75ᵛ–77ʳ.
B.L., Eg. MS. 2651, fos 95ʳ–95ᵛ.
B.L., Harl. MS. 165, fos 26ʳ–26ᵛ (D'Ewes' copy).
B.L., Harl. MS. 6801, fos 129ʳ–32ʳ.
MSS of the Duke of Buccleuch and Queensberry, Montagu Papers, XIII, 75.
National Library of Scotland, Neilson MS. 2687, pp. 129–31.
S.R.O., DD/M1, Box 18, 99.
S.P. 16/450/94.
S.P. 16/452/29.
Worc. Coll. MS. 5.20, fos 27ʳ–27ᵛ.
Yale, Beinecke Library, Osborn Collection, Box 41, 5.
Yale, Beinecke Library, Osborn Collection, Stanford (Braye) MS. Miscellaneous, II, 80 (in Browne's hand).

King Charles himself made the principal speech on 5 May when he ordered the Parliament dissolved. A version of this speech was printed soon after in *His Majesties Declaration . . . of the Causes . . . to Dissolve.* . . . This version shows signs of careful editing to strengthen the king's attack on the uncooperative members of the Lower House from the version which appears in most copies, including the Lords' *Journal*, Finch-Hatton/Harvard, and Rushworth. The similarity of these suggests the existence of a standard text prior to the issuance of the *Declaration*. No notes of the speech are included in Browne's scribbled book. It is possible that the copy in his hand in Braye, Miscellaneous II (at Yale) was written while the king spoke. The copy, which shows some corrections, is more complete than Browne's rough notes of other speeches. It is similar, though not identical, to the version in the Draft Journal. An early official copy could have been the basis for both.

With the exception of Bernard's, most of the independent accounts of the king's speech are brief. Bernard reports the main points and even notes that the king made assurances that he would reform monopolies as well as protect religion and property. Neither the version in the *Declaration* nor the other mentions anything about monopolies. Nevertheless Bernard's notes are not sufficiently detailed or precise to contribute much to a study of differences between the two versions. Montagu is even less helpful. He simply says in his diary that the king 'made a short speech, get what it was.' His papers show that he apparently did acquire a copy. Rossingham's report, like Montagu's, was brief. He referred to the speech in connection with the Council's subsequent demands that the clerk hand in petitions of grievances. On the basis of the speech Rossingham thought that the petitions were to be handed in so that the king could carry out his sincere intention of reform. For many people, however, the content of the speech was of little interest. It was not what the king said, but what his Majesty did that was most important. On 5 May he had dissolved the Parliament.

LIST OF BILLS

HOUSE OF LORDS

'For the better venting of dyed and dressed cloths, etc.' *1º* Read,
16 April (*L.J.*, iv, p. 56; Braye, fo 10ᵛ, Montagu Papers, p. 1d,
Lee Warner, p. 2 above, pp. 60, 98, 107; *2º* Read, committed, 23
April (*L.J.*, iv, p. 65; Braye, fo 20, above, p. 69; also Bills, above,
p. 273; above, pp. 69, 98, 107, 273.

'For the Confirmation of several letters patents . . . made to . . .
the . . . Queen . . . [*her jointure*].' *1º* Read, *2º* Read, committed, 20
April (*L.J.*, iv, p. 59; Braye, fo 14, Montagu Papers, p. 2, Lee
Warner, p. 2, above, pp. 63, 99, 108); reported, 23 April (*L.J.*, iv,
p. 65; Braye, fo 19ᵛ above, p. 69); *3º* Read and passed, 2 May (*L.J.*,
iv, p. 78; above, Braye, fo 45ᵛ, p. 93.

'For the Maintenance of Hospitals *et Maisons de Dieu*, etc.' *1º*
Read, *2º* Read, committed, 21 April (*L.J.*, iv, p. 60; above,
Braye fo 15 Montagu Papers, 2b, Lee Warner, p. 2 (21 April)
pp. 64, 99, 108); see also *L.J.*, iv, p. 65.

'To make the Arms of the Kingdom more serviceable, etc.' *1º*
Read, 28 April (*L.J.*, iv, p. 71; above, Braye fo 34, p. 38).

'For better preserving of corn, etc.' *1º* Read, 28 April (*L.J.*, iv,
p. 71; above, Braye fo 34, p. 83).

HOUSE OF COMMONS

'Concerning Apparel,' *1º* Read, 15 April (*C.J.*, ii, p. 3; *cf.* above,
Harvard MS. fo 9, p. 123); *2º* Read, committed, 21 April (*C.J.*, ii,
p. 8).

'To avoid the abuse of Common Recoveries to be suffered by
infants.' *1º* Read, 16 April (*C.J.*, ii, p. 3; *cf.* above, Harvard MS.
fo 20ᵛ, p. 134); *2º* Read, committed, 21 April (*C.J.*, ii, p. 8),

'To prevent inconveniences happening by occupancy.' *1º* Read,
23 April (*C.J.*, ii, p. 9); *2º* Read, committed, 24 April (*C.J.*, ii,
p. 10).

'For the Naturalizing of James Boene, Merchant, etc.' *1º* Read,
25 April (*C.J.*, ii, p. 12).

'Touching Needlemakers and Steelwiredrawers.' *1º* Read, 27
April (*C.J.*, ii, p. 13); *2º* Read, committed, 1 May (*C.J.*, ii, p. 17).

'For Reformation of Divers Abuses in Ecclesiastical Courts.' *1º*
Read, 27 April (*C.J.*, ii, p. 13); *2º* Read, committed, 1 May (*C.J.*,
ii, p. 17).

'Against the exportation of wools. . . .' I^o Read, 28 April (C.J., ii, p. 14).

'For the better ordering of the office of the Clerk of the Market, etc.' I^o Read, 28 April (C.J., ii, p. 14).

'For the more due election of Knights, Citizens and Burgesses to serve in Parliament.' I^o Read, 28 April (C.J., ii, p. 14); also 'For Reformation of Abuses in the Election of Knights, Citizens, and Burgesses.' I^o Read, referred with preceding to Committee of Privileges, 29 April (C.J., ii, p. 16).

'Concerning the hearing the word of God preached.' I^o Read, 29 April (C.J., ii, p. 16).

'Concerning the disposing of Money received for commutation of Penance.' I^o Read, 29 April (C.J., ii, p. 16); 2° Read, committed, 2 May (C.J., ii, p. 18).

'Concerning the granting of administrations.' I^o Read, 29 April (C.J., ii, p. 16); 2° Read, committed, 1 May (C.J., ii, p. 17).

'Concerning the disposing of goods unadministered.' I^o Read, 29 April (C.J., ii, p. 16); 2° Read, committed, 2 May (C.J., ii, p. 18).

'For the exemption of the four shires . . . from the jurisdiction of the Lord President of Wales.' I^o Read, 30 April (C.J., ii, p. 16).

'That certain clergymen shall not be Justices of the peace.' I^o Read, 30 April (C.J., ii, p. 16); also 'For the ease of the clergy from some lay employments.' I^o Read, 2 May (C.J., ii, p. 18; above, p. 273).

'Concerning the Confirming . . . of the copyhold estates of his Majesties Tenants of the manors of Colne, Ichtenhill, etc.' I^o Read, 30 April (C.J., ii, p. 16).

'For avoiding causeless suits and for ease in just suits at the common law.' I^o Read, 2 May (C.J., ii, p. 18).

'Concerning Non-Residents, pluralities of benefices, and taking of Farms by Spiritual Men.' I^o Read, 2 May (C.J., ii, p. 18).

[Bill for the Reformation of Religion], apparently not introduced; see notes concerning, S.P. 16/450/122.

LIST OF PRECEDENTS

PROCEEDINGS IN PARLIAMENT

6 *Edw.* III (*Rot. Parl.*, ii, pp. 66–67: Braye 16, fo 27^v; Finch-Hatton MS., p. 56; H.R.O., p. 4; Lee Warner, p. 3, above, pp. 77, 171, 200, 110.

14 *Edw.* III (*Rot. Parl.*, ii, pp. 112–17): Harvard MS., fo 25; H.R.O., p. 25, Speeches, Rudyerd, fo 148, above, pp. 139, 209, 249.

15 *Edw.* III (*Rot. Parl.*, i, pp. 126–34): Harvard MS., fo 25, Speeches, Rudyerd, fo 148, above, 139, 249.

17 *Edw.* III (*Rot. Parl.*, i, pp. 135–45): Harvard MS., fo 25, Speeches, Rudyerd, fo 148, above, pp. 139, 249.

50 *Edw.* III (*Rot. Parl.*, ii, p. 322): Finch-Hatton MS., p. 66, p. 179.

51 *Edw.* III (*Rot. Parl.*, ii, p. 368): Finch-Hatton MS., p. 53; H.R.O., p. 5, above, pp. 168, 201.

1 *Ric.* II (*Rot. Parl.*, iii, p. 5): Braye 16, fo 27^v; Finch-Hatton MS., p. 66; Lee Warner, p. 3, above, pp. 77, 179, 110.

2 *Ric.* II (*Rot. Parl.*, iii, pp. 55–56): Braye 16, fo 44, (30 April) above, p. 92, n. 1.

4 *Ric.* II (*Rot. Parl.*, iii, p. 89): Braye 16, fo 27^v; Finch-Hatton MS., p. 66; Lee Warner, p. 3, above, pp. 77, 179, 110.

6 *Ric.* II (*Rot. Parl.*, iii, p. 141): Finch-Hatton MS., p. 53; H.R.O., p. 6, above, pp. 168, 201.

9 *Hen.* IV (*Rot. Parl.*, iii, p. 611: Braye 16, fos 22^v, 27^v, 38^v, 42^v, 44, 44^v; Finch-Hatton MS., pp. 66, 70; H.R.O., p. 18; Braye 2, fo 72, above, pp. 72, 77, 87, 90, 92, 179, 184, 206, 270.

13 *Hen.* IV (*Rot. Parl.*, iii, pp. 662–63): Finch-Hatton MS., p. 81, above, p. 196.

2 *Hen.* V (*Rot. Parl.*, iv, p. 16 or 35): Braye 16, fos 27^v; Lee Warner, p. 3, above, pp. 77, 110.

39 *Hen.* VI (*Rot. Parl.*, vi, pp. 375–67); Harvard MS., fo 79^v, above, p. 192.

8 *Eliz.* (Neale, *Eliz. Parl.*, i, p. 141): Harvard MS., fos 75^v–76, above, p. 188.

35 *Eliz.* (D'Ewes, *Parliaments of Eliz.*, pp. 480–89): Finch-Hatton MS., p. 66, above, p. 179.

7 *Jac.* (Foster, ii, pp. 85–86): Finch-Hatton MS., p. 47, above, p. 161.

12 *Jac.* (*C.J.*, i, pp. 496, 499): Braye 16, fos 23^v, 26^v; Lee Warner, p. 3, above, pp. 73, 76, 110.

21 & 22 *Jac.* (*L.J.*, iii, pp. 250, 275): Braye 16, fo 24; Finch-Hatton MS., p. 58, above, pp. 74, 173.

4 *Car.* (*Commons Debates, 1629*, pp. 103–106, 239–44): Harvard MS., fo 35; Finch-Hatton MS., pp. 46, 48; Worc. Coll. fo 17, above, pp. 149, 160–1, 163, 220.

PROCEEDINGS IN CONVOCATION

2 *Jac.* (Wilkins, *Magna Concilia*, iv, pp. 378–79): Finch-Hatton MS., pp. 59–60, above, pp. 175–6.

STATUTES

Magna Carta (17 *John*): Harvard MS. fo 22, Finch-Hatton MS., p. 40, Harl. MS., 6801 fo 66^r, above, pp. 135, 154, 258.

Charter of the Forest (2 *Hen.* III): Finch-Hatton MS., p. 40, (17 April), above, p. 153, n. 3.

4 *Edw.* III, *c.* 14: Finch-Hatton MS., p. 41, Harl. MS., 6801, fo 67^r; S.P. 16/450/25, above, pp. 155, 258 n., 275.

28 *Edw.* III, *c.* 1: Finch-Hatton MS., p. 40 (17 April), above, p. 153, n. 3.

36 *Edw.* III, *c.* 10: Finch-Hatton MS., p. 41; Harl MS., 6801, fo 67^r; S.P. 16/450/25, above, pp. 155, 258 n., 275.

4 *Hen.* VIII, *c.* 8: Braye 16, fo 27^v, above, p. 77.

25 *Hen.* VIII, *c.* 19: H.R.O., p. 6, Lee Warner, p. 2 (17 April), above, pp. 201, 107.

1 *Eliz.*, *c.* 1: Harl. MS., 6801, fo 62, above, p. 256.

21 & 22 *Jac.*, *c.* 23: Finch-Hatton MS., p. 58, above, p. 173.

Petition of Right (3 *Car.*, *c.* 1): Braye 16, fos 23^v, 25; Harvard MS., fo 22^v; H.R.O., p. 24; Lee Warner, p. 3 (24 April), above, pp. 73, 75, 136, 209, 110.

CASES

Bate (impositions) (*State Trials*, ii, 371–94): Finch-Hatton MS., pp. 39, 50; Harl. MS., 6801, fo 63, above, pp. 152, 164, 256.

Dover (earl) *v.* Fox (Squibb, *High Court of Chivalry*, p. 64n.): Bodl. Clar. 18, fo 155, above, p. 261.

Duke of Buckingham (*L.J.*, iii, pp. 570, 576–77: Finch-Hatton MS., p. 45, above, p. 159.

Duke of Lancaster (*Rot. Parl.*, ii, pp. 323ff.): Finch-Hatton MS., p. 45, above, p. 159.

Duke of Suffolk (*Rot. Parl.*, v, pp. 176–83): Finch-Hatton MS., p. 45, above, p. 159.

Eliot *et al.* (*State Trials*, iii, 293–310): Harvard MS., fos 26ᵛ–27, 35ᵛ; Finch-Hatton MS., pp. 45, 49; Worc. Coll., Seymour p. 1, Harl. MS., 6801, fo 59ᵛ, above, pp. 141, 150, 159, 164, 213, 254–5.

Floyd (*C.J.*, i, pp. 600–602, 610, 619, 621): Braye 16, fo 37, above, p. 86.

Francis Bacon (*L.J.*, iii, pp. 53–55): Finch-Hatton MS., p. 45, above, p. 159.

Gardiner *v.* Gilbert (Squibb, *High Court of Chivalry*, p. 64n.): Finch-Hatton MS., p. 44; Bodl. Clar. 18, fo 155, above, pp. 158, 261.

Hampden (shipmoney) (*State Trials*, iii, 825–1316): Finch-Hatton MS., pp. 39, 49; Harvard MS., fo 81ᵛ; Worc. Coll., Pym, p. 4; Harl MS., 6801, fo 64ᵛ, above, pp. 152, 164, 195, 218, 257.

Manwaring (*L.J.*, iii, pp. 855–56): Braye 16, fos 12ᵛ, 15ᵛ; Montagu Papers, p. 2; Finch-Hatton MS., p. 41; Worc. Coll., Pym, p. 5; Harl. MS., 6801, fo 66ᵛ; Harl MS., 4931, fo 47, above, pp. 63, 65, 91–98, 155, 218, 258, 235

Saltpetre (12 Coke *Rep.* 12–13): Finch-Hatton MS., p. 81, above, p. 196.

Soap (Starchamber) (Rushworth, ii, pp. 189–90, 252–53): Finch-Hatton MS., p. 40, above, p. 154.

Strode (see 4 *Hen.* VIII, *c.* 8).

GENERAL INDEX

CHRONOLOGICAL INDEX*

* [See above, pp. 49–52, Brief Calendar of the Parliament.]